PITTSBURG

D0460912

REFERENCE

U·X·L ENCYCLOPEDIA OF
NATIVE
AMERICAN
TRIBES

U·X·L ENCYCLOPEDIA OF
NATIVE AMERICAN TRIBES

VOLUME

1

Northeast
Southeast

WITHDRAWN

Sharon Malinowski, Anna Sheets
& Linda Schmittroth, *Editors*

CONTRA COSTA COUNTY LIBRARY

AN IMPRINT OF THE GALE GROUP

DETROIT · SAN FRANCISCO · LONDON
BOSTON · WOODBRIDGE, CT

3 1901 02884 2104

U•X•L Encyclopedia of Native American Tribes

Sharon Malinowski, Anna Sheets, and Linda Schmittroth, *Editors*

Staff

Sonia Benson, *U•X•L Senior Editor*
Carol DeKane Nagel, *U•X•L Managing Editor*
Thomas L. Romig, *U•X•L Publisher*
Jeffrey Lehman, *Editor*
Melissa Walsh Doig, *Editor*
Dorothy Maki, *Manufacturing Manager*
Evi Seoud, *Assistant Production Manager*
Rita Wimberley, *Senior Buyer*
Cynthia Baldwin, *Product Design Manager*
Barbara Yarrow, *Graphic Services Director*
Michelle DiMercurio, *Senior Art Director*
Keasha Jack-Lyles, *Permissions Associate*
LM Design, *Typesetter*

Library of Congress Cataloging-in-Publication Data

U•X•L Encyclopedia of Native American Tribes / Sharon Malinowski, Anna Sheets, and Linda Schmittroth, editors

p. cm.

Includes bibliographical references.

Contents: v. 1. The Northeast and Southeast – v. 2. The Great Basin and Southwest – v. 3. The Arctic, Subarctic, Great Plains, and Plateau – v. 4. California and the Pacific Northwest.

ISBN 0-7876-2838-7 (set).

ISBN 0-7876-2839-5 (volume 1)   ISBN 0-7876-2841-7 (volume 3)

ISBN 0-7876-2840-9 (volume 2)   ISBN 0-7876-2842-5 (volume 4)

1. Indians of North America – Encyclopedias, Juvenile. [1. Indians of North America – Encyclopedias.] I. Malinowski, Sharon. II. Sheets, Anna J. (Anna Jean), 1970– . III. Schmittroth, Linda. IV. Title: Encyclopedia of Native American tribes.

E76.2.U85 1999

970'.003—dc21

98-54353
CIP
AC

This publication is a creative work copyrighted by U•X•L and fully protected by all applicable copyright laws, as well as by misappropriation, trade secret, unfair competition, and other applicable laws. The authors and editors of this work have added value to the underlying factual material herein through one or more of the following: unique and original selection, coordination, expression, arrangement, and classification of the information. All rights to this publication will be vigorously defended.

Copyright © 1999
U•X•L, An Imprint of the Gale Group
DETROIT•SAN FRANCISCO•LONDON•BOSTON•WOODBRIDGE, CT

Contents

VOLUME 1

VOLUME 2

The Great Basin

Southwest

VOLUME 3

VOLUME 4

Tribes Alphabetically

*First numeral signifies volume number. The numeral after the colon signifies page number. For example, **3:871** means Volume 3, page 871.*

Reader's Guide

Long before the Vikings, Spaniards, and Portuguese made landfall on North American shores, the continent already had a rich history of human settlement. The *U•X•L Encyclopedia of Native American Tribes* opens up for students the array of tribal ways in the United States and Canada past and present. Included in these volumes, readers will find the stories of:

- the well-known nineteenth century Lakota hunting the buffalo on the Great Plains

- the contemporary Inuit of the Arctic, who have recently won their battle for Nunavut, a vast, self-governing territory in Canada

- the Seminole in Florida, drawing tourists with their alligator wrestling shows

- the Haida of the Pacific Northwest, whose totem poles have become a familiar adornment of the landscape

- the Anasazi in the Southwest, who were building spectacular cities long before Europeans arrived

- the Mohawk men in the Northeast who made such a name for themselves as ironworkers on skyscrapers and bridges that they have long been in demand for such projects as the World Trade Center and the Golden Gate Bridge

- the Yahi of California, who became extinct when their last member Ishi died in 1916.

The *U•X•L Encyclopedia of Native American Tribes* presents eighty tribes, confederacies, and Native American groups. Among the tribes included are large and well-known nations, smaller communities with their own fascinating stories, and prehistoric peoples. The tribes are grouped in the ten major geographical/cultural areas of North America in which tribes shared environmental and cultural connections. The ten sections, each beginning with an introductory essay on the geographical area and the shared history and culture within it, are arranged in the volumes as follows:

- Volume 1: Northeast and Southeast

- Volume 2: The Great Basin and Southwest

- Volume 3: Arctic, Subarctic, Great Plains, and Plateau

- Volume 4: California and Pacific Northwest

The *U•X•L Encyclopedia of Native American Tribes* provides the history of each of the tribes featured and a fascinating look at their ways of life: how families lived in centuries past and today, what people ate and wore, what their homes were like, how they worshiped, celebrated, governed themselves, and much more. A student can learn in depth about one tribe or compare aspects of many tribes. Each detailed entry is presented in consistent rubrics that allow for easy access and comparison, as follows:

- History

- Religion

- Language

- Government

- Economy

- Daily Life

- Arts

- Customs

- Current Tribal Issues

- Notable People

Each entry begins with vital data on the tribe: name, location, population, language family, origins and group affiliations. A locator map follows, showing the traditional homelands and contemporary communities of the group; regional and migration maps throughout aid in locating the many groups and at different times in history. Brief timelines in each entry chronicle important dates of the tribe's history, while an overall timeline at the beginning of all the volumes outlines key events in history pertinent to all Native Americans. Other sidebars present recipes, oral literature or stories, population statistics, language keys, and background material on the tribe. Black-and-white photographs and illustrations, further reading sections, a thorough subject index, and a glossary are special features that make the volumes easy, fun, and informative to use.

A note on terminology

Throughout the *U•X•L Encyclopedia of Native American Tribes* various terms are used for Native North Americans, such as *Indian, American Indian, Native,* and *aboriginal.* The Native peoples of the Americas have the unfortunate distinction of having been given the wrong name by the Europeans who first arrived on the continent, mistakenly thinking they had arrived in India. The search for a single name, however, has never been entirely successful. The best way to characterize Native North Americans is by recognizing their specific tribal or community identities. In compiling this book, every effort has been made to keep Native tribal and community identities distinct, but by necessity, inclusive terminology is often used. We do not wish to offend anyone, but rather than favor one term for Native North American people, the editors have used a variety of terminology, trying always to use the most appropriate term in the particular context.

Europeans also had a hand in giving names to tribes, often misunderstanding their languages and the relations between different Native communities. Most tribes have their own names for themselves, and many have succeeded in gaining public acceptance of traditional names. The Inuit, for example, objected to the name Eskimo, which means "eaters of raw meat," and in time their name for themselves was accepted. In the interest of clarity the editors of this book have used the currently accepted terms, while acknowledging the traditional ones or the outmoded ones at the beginning of each entry.

The term *tribe* itself is not accepted by all Native groups. The people living in North America before the Europeans arrived had many different ways of organizing themselves politically and relating to other groups around them—from complex confederacies and powerful unified nations to isolated villages with little need for political structure. Groups divided, absorbed each other, intermarried, allied, and dissolved. The epidemics and wars that came with non-Native expansion into North America created a demographic catastrophe to many Native groups and greatly affected tribal affiliations. Although in modern times there are actual rules about what comprises a tribe (federal requirements for recognition of tribes are specific, complicated, and often difficult to fulfill), the hundreds of groups living in the Americas in early times did not have any one way of categorizing themselves. Some Native American peoples today find the word *tribe* misleading. In a study of Indian peoples, it can also be an elusive defining term. But in facing the challenges of maintaining traditions and heritage in modern times, tribal or community identity is acutely important to many Native Americans. Tremendous efforts have been undertaken to preserve native languages, oral traditions, religions, ceremonies, and traditional arts and economies— the things that, put together, make a tribe a cultural and political unit.

Advisors and contributors

For the invaluable contributions, suggestions, and advice on the *U•X•L Encyclopedia of Native American Tribes,* special thanks are due to: Edward D. Castillo, (Cahuilla-Luiseño), Director, Native American Studies Program, Sonoma State University, California; Ned Blackhawk; Elizabeth Hanson, Ph.D., Research Associate to the Dean, The College of Charleston, South Carolina; Daniel Boxberger, Department of Anthropology, Western Washington University; John H. Moore, Ph.D., Anthropology Department, University of Florida, Gainesville; Amanda Beresford McCarthy; George Cornell, Ph.D., Associate Professor, History and American Studies, Michigan State University; Brian Wescott, Athabascan/Yup'ik; Gordon L. Pullar, Director, Department of Alaska Native and Rural Development, College of Rural Alaska,UAF; and Barbara Bigelow.

Comments and suggestions

In this first edition of the *U•X•L Encyclopedia of Native American Tribes* we have presented in-depth information on eighty of the hundreds of tribes of North America. While every attempt was made to include a wide representation of groups, many historically important and interesting tribes are not covered in these volumes. We welcome your suggestions for tribes to be featured in future editions, as well as any other comments you may have on this set. Please write: Editors, *U•X•L Encyclopedia of Native American Tribes,* U•X•L, 27500 Drake Road, Farmington Hills, Michigan 48331–3535; call toll-free 1-800-347-4253; or fax: 313-699-8066; or send e-mail via http://www.galegroup.com.

Words to Know

A

Aboriginal: native, or relating to the first or earliest group living in a particular area.

Activism: taking action for or against a controversial issue; political and social activists may organize or take part in protest demonstrations, rallies, petitioning the government, sit-ins, civil disobedience, and many other forms of activities that draw attention to an issue and/or challenge the authorities to make a change.

Adobe: (pronounced *uh-DOE-bee*) a brick or other building material made from sun-dried mud, a mixture of clay, sand, and sometimes ashes, rocks, or straw.

Alaska Native Claims Settlement Act (ANCSA): an act of Congress passed in 1971 that gave Alaska Natives 44 million acres of land and $962.5 million. In exchange, Alaska Natives gave up all claim to other lands in Alaska. The ANCSA also resulted in the formation of 12 regional corporations in Alaska in charge of Native communities' economic development and land use.

Allotment: the practice of dividing and distributing something into individual lots. In 1887 the U.S. Congress passed the Dawes Act, or the General Allotment Act, which divided Indian reservations into privately owned parcels (pieces) of land. Under allotment, tribes could no longer own their lands in common (as a group) in the traditional way. Instead, the head of a family received a lot, generally 160 acres. Land not allotted was sold to non-Natives.

American Indian Movement (AIM): an activist movement founded in 1966 to aggressively press for Indian rights. The movement was formed to improve federal, state, and local social services to Native Americans in urban neighborhoods. AIM sought the reorganization of the Bureau of Indian Affairs to make it more responsive to Native

American needs and fought for the return of Indian lands illegally taken from them.

Anthropology: the study of human beings in terms of their populations, cultures, social relations, ethnic characteristics, customs, and adaptation to their environment.

Archaeology: the study of the remains of past human life, such as fossil relics, artifacts, and monuments, in order to understand earlier human cultures.

Arctic: relating to the area surrounding the North Pole.

Assimilate: to absorb, or to be absorbed, into the dominant society (those in power, or in the majority). U.S. assimilation policies were directed at causing Native Americans to become like European-Americans in terms of jobs and economics, religion, customs, language, education, family life, and dress.

B

Band: a small, loosely organized social group composed of several families. In Canada, the word *band* originally referred to a social unit of nomadic (those who moved from place to place) hunting peoples, but now refers to a community of Indians registered with the government.

Boarding school: a live-in school.

Breechcloth: a garment with front and back flaps that hang from the waist. *Breechcloths* were one of the most common articles of clothing worn by many Native American men and sometimes women in pre-European/American settlement times.

Bureau of Indian Affairs (BIA): the U.S. government agency that oversees tribal lands, education, and other aspects of Indian life.

C

Census: a count of the population.

Ceremony: a special act or set of acts (such as a wedding or a funeral) performed by members of a group on important occasions, usually organized according to the group's traditions and beliefs.

Clan: a group of related house groups and families that trace back to a common ancestor or a common symbol or totem, usually an animal such as the bear or the turtle. The *clan* forms the basic social and political unit for many Indian societies.

Colonialism: a state or nation's control over a foreign territory.

Colonize: to establish a group of people from a mother country or state in a foreign territory; the colonists set up a community that remains tied to the mother country.

Confederacy: a group of people, states, or nations joined together for mutual support or for a special purpose.

Convert: (as verb) to cause a person or group to change their beliefs or practices. A *convert* (noun) is a person who has been *converted* to a new belief or practice.

Coup: (pronounced *COO*) a feat of bravery, especially the touching of an enemy's body during battle without causing or receiving injury. To *count coup* is to count the number of such feats of bravery.

Cradleboard: a board or frame on which an infant was bound or wrapped by some Native American peoples. It was used as a portable carrier or for carrying an infant on the back.

Creation stories: sacred myths or stories that explain how the Earth and its beings were created.

Culture: the set of beliefs, social habits, and ways of surviving in the environment that are held by a particular social group.

D

Dentalium: (pronounced *den-TAIL-ee-um*; from the Latin word for tooth). Dentalia (plural) are the tooth-like shells that some tribes used as money. The shells were rubbed smooth and strung like beads on strands of animal skin.

Depletion: decreasing the amount of something; *depletion* of resources such as animals or minerals through overuse reduces essential elements from the environment.

Dialect: (pronounced *DY-uh-lect*) a local variety of a particular language, with unique differences in words, grammar, and pronunciation.

E

Economy: the way a group obtains, produces, and distributes the goods it needs; the overall system by which it supports itself and accumulates its wealth.

Ecosystem: the overall way that a community and its surrounding environment function together in nature.

Epidemic: the rapid spread of a disease so that many people in an area have it at the same time.

Ethnic group: a group of people who are classed according to certain aspects of their common background, usually by tribal, racial, national, cultural, and language origins.

Extended family: a family group that includes close relatives such as mother, father, and children, plus grandparents, aunts and uncles, and cousins.

F

Federally recognized tribes: tribes with which the U.S. government maintains official relations as established by treaty, executive order, or act of Congress.

First Nations: one of Canada's terms for its Indian nations.

Five Civilized Tribes: a name given to the Cherokee, Choctaw, Chickasaw, Creek, and Seminole during the mid-1800s. The tribes were given this name by non-Natives because they had democratic constitutional governments, a high literacy rate (many people who could read and write), and ran effective schools.

Formal education: structured learning that takes place in a school or college under the supervision of trained teachers.

G

Ghost Dance: a revitalization (renewal or rebirth) movement that arose in the 1870s after many tribes moved to reservations and were being encouraged to give up their traditional beliefs. Many Native Americans hoped that, if they performed it earnestly, the Ghost Dance would bring back traditional Native lifestyles and values, and that the buffalo and Indian ancestors would return to the Earth as in the days before the white settlers.

Great Basin: an elevated region in the western United States in which all water drains toward the center. The *Great Basin* covers part of Nevada, California, Colorado, Utah, Oregon, and Wyoming.

Guardian spirit: a sacred power, usually embodied in an animal such as a hawk, deer, or turtle, that reveals itself to an individual, offering help throughout the person's lifetime in important matters such as hunting or healing the sick.

H

Haudenosaunee: (pronounced *hoo-dee-noh-SHAW-nee*) the name of the people often called Iroquois or Five Nations. It means "People of the Longhouse."

Head flattening: a practice in which a baby was placed in a cradle, and a padded board was tied to its forehead to mold the head into a desired shape. Sometimes the effect of flattening the back of the head was achieved by binding the infant tightly to a cradleboard.

I

Immunity: resistance to disease; the ability to be exposed to a disease with less chance of getting it, and less severe effects if infected.

Indian Territory: an area in present-day Kansas and Oklahoma where the U.S. government once planned to move all Indians, and, eventually, to allow them to run their own province or state. In 1880 nearly one-third of all U.S. Indians lived there, but with the formation of the state of Oklahoma in 1906, the promise of an Indian state dissolved.

Indigenous: (pronounced *in-DIJ-uh-nus*) native, or first, in a specific area. Native Americans are often referred to as *indigenous* peoples of North America.

Intermarriage: marriage between people of different groups, as between a Native American and a non-Native, or between people from two different tribes.

K

Kachina: (pronounced *kuh-CHEE-nuh*) a group of spirits celebrated by the Pueblo Indians; the word also refers to dolls made in the image of *kachina* spirits.

Kiva: (pronounced *KEE-va*) among the Pueblo, a circular (sometimes rectangular) underground room used for religious ceremonies.

L

Lacrosse: a game of Native American origin in which players use a long stick with a webbed pouch at the end for catching and throwing a ball.

Language family: a group of languages that are different from one another but are related. These languages share similar words, sounds, or word structures. The languages are alike either because they have borrowed words from each other or because they originally came from the same parent language.

Legend: a story or folktale that tells about people or events in the past.

Life expectancy: the average number of years a person may expect to live.

Linguistics: the study of human speech and language.

Literacy: the state of being able to read and write.

Longhouse: a large, long building in which several families live together; usually found among Northwest Coast and Iroquois peoples.

Long Walk of the Navajo: the enforced 300-mile walk of the Navajo people in 1864, when they were being removed from their homelands to the Bosque Redondo Reservation in New Mexico.

M

Matrilineal: tracing family relations through the mother; in a *matrilineal* society, names and inheritances are passed down through the mother's side of the family.

Medicine bundle: a pouch in which were kept sacred objects believed to have powers that would protect and aid an individual, a clan or family, or a community.

Midewiwin Society: the Medicine Lodge Religion, whose main purpose was to prolong life. The society taught morality, proper conduct, and a knowledge of plants and herbs for healing.

Migration: movement from one place to another. The *migrations* of Native peoples were often done by the group, with whole nations moving from one area to another.

Mission: an organized effort by a religious group to spread its beliefs to other parts of the world; *mission* refers either to the project of spreading a belief system or to the building(s)—such as a church—in which this takes place.

Mission school: a school established by missionaries to teach people religious beliefs, as well as other subjects.

Myth: a story passed down through generations, often involving supernatural beings. *Myths* often express religious beliefs or the values of a people. They may attempt to explain how the Earth and its beings were created, or why things are as they are. They are not always meant to be taken as factual.

N

Natural resources: the sources of supplies provided by the environment for survival and enrichment, such as animals to be hunted, land for farming, minerals, and timber.

Neophyte: (pronounced *NEE-oh-fite*) beginner; often used to mean a new convert to a religion.

Nomadic: traveling and relocating often, usually in search of food and other resources or a better climate.

Nunavut: a new territory in Canada as of April 1, 1999, with the status of a province and an Inuit majority. It is a huge area, covering most of Canada north of the treeline. *Nunavut* means "Our Land" in Inuk-itut (the Inuit language).

O

Oral literature: oral traditions that are written down after enjoying a long life in spoken form among a people.

Oral traditions: history, mythology, folklore, and other foundations of a culture that have been passed by spoken word, often in the form of stories, from generation to generation within a culture group.

P

Parent language: a language that is the common source of two or more languages that came into being at a later time.

Per capita income: *per capita* is a Latin phrase that means "for each person." Per capita income is the average personal income per person.

Petroglyph: a carving or engraving on rock; a common form of ancient art.

Peyote: (pronounced *pay-OH-tee*) a substance obtained from cactus that some Indian groups use as part of their religious practice. After eating the substance, which stimulates the nervous system, a person may go into a trance state and see visions. The Peyote Religion features the use of this substance.

Pictograph: a simple picture representing a historical event.

Policy: the overall plan or course of action issued by the government, establishing how it will handle certain situations or people and what its goals are.

Post-European contact: relating to the time and state of Native Americans and their lands after the Europeans arrived. Depending on the part of the country in which they lived, Native groups experienced contact at differing times in the history of white expansion into the West.

Potlatch: a feast or ceremony, commonly held among Northwest Coast groups; also called a "giveaway." During a *potlatch,* goods are given to guests to show the host's generosity and wealth. Potlatches are used to celebrate major life events such as birth, death, or marriage.

Powwow: a celebration at which the main activity is traditional singing and dancing. In modern times, the singers and dancers at powwows come from many different tribes.

Province: a district or division of a country (like a state in the United States).

R

Raiding: entering into another tribe or community's territory, usually by stealth or force, and stealing their livestock and supplies.

Rancheria: a small Indian reservation, usually in California.

Ratify: to approve or confirm. In the United States, the U.S. Senate *ratified* treaties with the Indians.

Red Power: a term used to describe the Native American activism movement of the 1960s, in which people from many tribes came together to protest the injustices of American policies toward Native Americans.

Removal Act: an act passed by the U.S. Congress in 1830 that directed all Indians to be moved to Indian Territory, west of the Mississippi River.

Removal Period: the time, mostly between 1830 and 1860, when most Indians of the eastern United States were forced to leave their homelands and relocate west of the Mississippi River.

Reservation: land set aside by the U.S. government for the use of a group or groups of Indians.

Reserve: in Canada, lands set aside for specific Indian bands. *Reserve* means in Canada approximately what *reservation* means in the United States.

Revitalization: the feeling or movement in which something seems to come back to life after having been quiet or inactive for a period of time.

Ritual: a formal act that is performed in basically the same way each time; rituals are often performed as part of a ceremony.

Rural: having to do with the country; opposite of urban.

S

Sachem: the chief of a confederation of tribes.

Shaman: (can be pronounced either *SHAY-mun* or *SHAH-mun*) a priest or medicine person in many Native American groups who understands and works with supernatural matters. *Shamans* traditionally performed in rituals and were expected to cure the sick, see the future, and obtain supernatural help with hunting and other economic activities.

Smallpox: a very contagious disease that spread across North America and killed many thousands of Indians. Survivors had skin that was badly scarred.

Subsistence economy: an economic system in which people provide themselves with the things they need for survival and their way of life rather than working for money or making a surplus of goods for trade.

Sun Dance: a renewal and purification (cleansing) ceremony performed by many Plains Indians such as the Sioux and Cheyenne. A striking aspect of the ceremony was the personal sacrifice made by some men. They undertook self-torture in order to gain a vision that might provide spiritual insight and knowledge beneficial to the community.

Sweat lodge: an airtight hut containing hot stones that were sprinkled with water to make them steam. A person remained inside until he or she was perspiring. The person then usually rushed out and plunged into a cold stream. This treatment was used before a ceremony or for the healing of physical or spiritual ailments. *Sweat lodge* is also the name of a sacred Native American ceremony involving the building of the lodge and the pouring of water on the stones, usually by a medicine person, accompanied by praying and singing. The ceremony has many purposes, including spiritual cleansing and healing.

T

Taboo: a forbidden thing or action. Many Indians believe that the sacred order of the world must be maintained if one is to avoid illness or other misfortunes. This is accomplished, in part, by observing a large assortment of taboos.

Termination: the policy of the U.S. government during the 1950s and 1960s to end the relationships set up by treaties with Indian nations.

Toloache: a substance obtained from a plant called jimsonweed. When consumed, the drug causes a person to go into a trance and see visions. It is used in some religious ceremonies.

Totem: an object that serves as an emblem or represents a family or clan, usually in the form of an animal, bird, fish, plant, or other natural object. A *totem pole* is a pillar built in front of the homes of Natives in the Northwest. It is painted and carved with a series of totems that show the family background and either mythical or historical events.

Trail of Tears: a series of forced marches of Native Americans of the Southeast in the 1830s, causing the deaths of thousands. The marches were the result of the U.S. government's removal policy, which ordered Native Americans to be moved to Indian Territory (now Oklahoma).

Treaty: an agreement between two parties or two nations, signed by both, usually defining the benefits to both parties that will result from one side giving up title to a territory of land.

Tribe: a group of Natives who share a name, language, culture, and ancestors; in Canada, called a band.

Tribelet: a community within an organization of communities in which one main settlement was surrounded by a few minor outlying settlements.

Trickster: a common culture hero in Indian myth and legend. *Tricksters* generally have supernatural powers that can be used to do good or harm, and stories about them take into account the different forces of the universe, such as good and evil or night and day. The Trickster takes different forms among various groups; for example, Coyote in the Southwest; Ikhtomi Spider in the High Plains, and Jay or Wolverine in Canada.

Trust: a relationship between two parties (or groups) in which one is responsible for acting in the other's best interests. The U.S. government has a *trust* relationship with tribal nations. Many tribes do not own their lands outright; according to treaty, the government owns the land "in trust" and tribes are given the use of it.

U

Unemployment rate: the percentage of the population that is looking for work but unable to find any. (People who have quit looking for work are not included in *unemployment* rates.)

Urban: having to do with cities and towns; the opposite of rural.

V

Values: the ideals that a community of people shares.

Vision quest: a sacred ceremony in which a person (often a teenage boy) goes off alone and fasts, living without food or water for a period of days. During that time, he hopes to learn about his spiritual side and to have a vision of a guardian spirit who will give him help and strength throughout his life.

W

Wampum: small cylinder-shaped beads cut from shells. Long strings of *wampum* were used for many different purposes. Indians believed that the exchange of wampum and other goods established a friendship, not just a profit-making relationship.

Wampum belt: a broad woven belt of wampum used to record history, treaties among the tribes, or treaties with colonists or governments.

Weir: a barricade used to funnel fish toward people who wait to catch them.

Timeline

25,000–11,000 B.C.E. Groups of hunters cross from Asia to Alaska on the Bering Sea Land Bridge, which was formed when lands now under the waters of the Bering Strait were exposed for periods of time, according to scientists.

1400 B.C.E. People who live along the lower Mississippi River are building large burial mounds and living in planned communities.

1 C.E. Small, permanent villages of the Hohokam tradition emerge in the Southwest.

400 Anasazi communities emerge in the Four Corners region of the Southwest. Anasazi eventually design communities in large multiroomed apartment buildings, some with more than 1,200 rooms. The Anasazi are farmers and skilled potters.

900 The Mississippian mound-building groups form complex political and social systems, and participate in long-distance trade and an elaborate and widespread religion.

1000–1350 The Iroquois Confederacy is formed among the Mohawk, Oneida, Onondaga, Cayuga, and Seneca nations. The Five Nations of the Haudenosaunee are from this time governed by chiefs from the 49 families who were present at the origin of the confederation.

Anasazi ruins at Pueblo del Arroyo, Chaco Canyon, New Mexico.

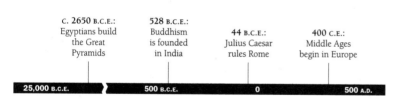

C. 2650 B.C.E.:
Egyptians build
the Great
Pyramids

528 B.C.E.:
Buddhism
is founded
in India

44 B.C.E.:
Julius Caesar
rules Rome

400 C.E.:
Middle Ages
begin in Europe

| 25,000 B.C.E. | 500 B.C.E. | 0 | 500 A.D. |

1040: Pueblos (towns) are flourishing in New Mexico's Chaco Canyon. The pueblos are connected by an extensive road system that stretches many miles across the desert.

1350 Moundville, in present-day Alabama, one of the largest ceremonial centers of the Mound Builders, thrives. With 20 great mounds and a village, it is probably the center of a chiefdom that includes several other related communities.

1494: Christopher Columbus begins the enslavement of American Indians, capturing over 500 Taino of San Salvador and sending them to Spain to be sold.

1503 French explorer Jacques Cartier begins trading with Native Americans along the East Coast.

1539–43 Spanish explorers Hernando de Soto and Francisco Coronado traverse the Southeast and Southwest, bringing with them disease epidemics that kill thousands of Native Americans.

1609 The fur trade begins when British explorer Henry Hudson, sailing for the Netherlands, opens trade in New Netherland (present-day New York) with several Northeast tribes.

1634–37 An army of Puritans, Pilgrims, Mohican, and Narragansett attacks and sets fire to the Pequot fort, killing as many as 700 Pequot men, women, and children.

1648–51 The Iroquois, having exhausted the fur supply in their area, attack other tribes in order to get a new supply. The Beaver Wars begin, and many Northeast tribes are forced to move west toward the Great Lakes area.

1660 The Ojibway, pushed west by settlers and Iroquois expansion, invade Sioux territory in Minnesota. After fighting the Ojibway, many Sioux groups move to the Great Plains.

1760–63 The Delaware Prophet tells Native Americans in the Northeast that they must drive Europeans out of North America and return to the customs of their ancestors. His message influences the Ottawa leader Pontiac, who uses it to unite many tribes against the British.

The attack on the Pequot fort in 1637.

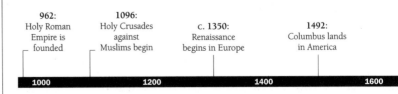

962:
Holy Roman
Empire is
founded

1096:
Holy Crusades
against
Muslims begin

c. 1350:
Renaissance
begins in Europe

1492:
Columbus lands
in America

| 1000 | 1200 | 1400 | 1600 |

1763 England issues the Proclamation of 1763, which assigns all lands west of the Appalachian Mountains to Native Americans, while colonists are allowed to settle all land to the east. The document respects the aboriginal land rights of Native Americans. It is not popular with colonists who want to move onto Indian lands and becomes one of the conflicts between England and the colonies leading to the American Revolution.

Franciscan priest with an Indian child at a Spanish mission, California.

1769 The Spanish build their first mission in California. There will be 23 Spanish missions in California, which are used to convert Native Californians to Christianity, but also reduces them to slave labor.

c. 1770 Horses, brought to the continent by the Spanish in the sixteenth century, spread onto the Great Plains and lead to the development of a new High Plains Culture.

1778 The treaty-making period begins, when the first of 370 treaties between Indian nations and the U.S. government is signed. The treaty-making period ends in 1871.

1786 The first federal Indian reservations are established.

1789 The Spanish establish a post at Nootka Sound on Vancouver Island, the first permanent European establishment in the territory of the Pacific Northwest Coast tribes.

1805–06 Explorers Meriwether Lewis and William Clark, led by Sacajawea, travel through the Plateau area, encountering the Cayuse, Nez Perce, Walla Walla, Wishram, and Yakima.

Sacajawea points out the way to Lewis and Clark.

1830 The removal period begins when the U.S. Congress passes the Indian Removal Act. Over the course of the next 30 years many tribes from the Northeast and Southeast are removed to Indian Territory in present-day Oklahoma and Kansas, often forcibly and at great expense in human lives.

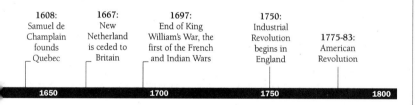

1608:
Samuel de Champlain founds Quebec

1667:
New Netherland is ceded to Britain

1697:
End of King William's War, the first of the French and Indian Wars

1750:
Industrial Revolution begins in England

1775-83:
American Revolution

1650   1700   1750   1800

1851 Early reservations are created in California to protect the Native population from the violence of U.S. citizens. These reservations are inadequate and serve only a small portion of the Native Californians, while others endure continued violence and hardship.

1870 The First Ghost Dance Movement begins when Wodzibwob, a Paiute, learns in a vision that a great earthquake will swallow the Earth, and that all Indians will be spared or resurrected within three days of the disaster. Thus, their world will return to its state before the Europeans had arrived.

1870–90 The Peyote Religion spreads through the Great Plains. Peyote (obtained from a cactus plant) brings on a dreamlike feeling that followers believe moves them closer to the spirit world. Tribes develop their own ceremonies, songs, and symbolism, and vow to be trustworthy, honorable, and community-oriented and to follow the Peyote Road.

1876 The Indian Act in Canada establishes an Indian reserve system, in which reserves were governed by voluntary elected band councils. The Act does not recognize Canadian Indians' right to self-government. With the passage of the act, Canadian peoples in Canada are divided into three groups: status Indian, treaty Indian, and non-status Indian. The categories affect the benefits and rights Indians are given by the government.

1880s The buffalo on the Great Plains are slaughtered until there are almost none left. Without adequate supplies of buffalo for food, the Plains Indians cannot survive. Many move to reservations.

1884 Potlatches are banned by the Canadian government. The elaborate gift-giving ceremonies have long been a vital part of Pacific Northwest Indian culture.

1887 The Dawes Act, or the General Allotment Act, is passed by Congress. The act calls for the allotment (or parceling out) of tribal lands. Tribes are no longer to own their lands in common in the traditional way. Instead, the land is to be assigned to

Preparing for a potlatch ceremony in the Pacific Northwest.

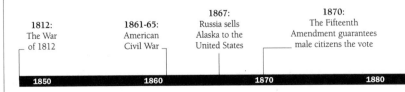

1812:
The War
of 1812

1861-65:
American
Civil War

1867:
Russia sells
Alaska to the
United States

1870:
The Fifteenth
Amendment guarantees
male citizens the vote

1850   1860   1870   1880

individuals. The head of a family receives 160 acres, and other family members get smaller pieces of land. Many Native Americans, unable to make a living from their land, end up having to sell their parcels. All Indian lands that are not allotted are sold to settlers. Millions of acres of Indian lands are lost.

1889 The Oklahoma Land Runs open Indian Territory to non-Natives. (Indian Territory had been set aside solely for Indian use.) At noon on April 22, an estimated 50,000 people line up at the boundaries of Indian Territory. They claim two million acres of land. By nightfall, tent cities, banks, and stores are doing business there.

1890 The second Ghost Dance movement is initiated by Wovoka, a Paiute. It includes many Paiute traditions. In some versions, the dance is performed in order to help bring back to Earth many dead ancestors and exterminated game. Ghost Dance practitioners hope the rituals in the movement will restore Indians to their former state, before the arrival of the non-Native settlers.

1912 The Alaska Native Brotherhood is formed to promote civil rights issues, such as the right to vote, access to public education, and civil rights in public places. The organization also fights court battles to win land rights.

1920 The Canadian government amends the Indian Act to allow for compulsory, or forced, enfranchisement, the process by which Indians have to give up their tribal loyalties to become Canadian citizens. Only 250 Indians had voluntarily become enfranchised between 1857 and 1920.

1924 All Indians are granted U.S. citizenship. This act does not take away rights that Native Americans had by treaty or the Constitution.

1928 Lewis Meriam is hired to investigate the status of Indian economies, health, and education, and the federal adminis-

The day school at the Sac and Fox Agency in Indian Territory, between 1876 and 1896.

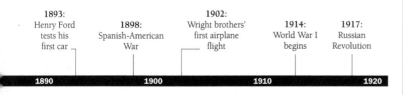

1893:
Henry Ford
tests his
first car

1898:
Spanish-American
War

1902:
Wright brothers'
first airplane
flight

1914:
World War I
begins

1917:
Russian
Revolution

| 1890 | 1900 | 1910 | 1920 |

tration of Indian affairs. His report describes the terrible conditions under which Indians are forced to live, listing problems with health care, education, poverty, malnutrition, and land ownership.

1934 U.S. Congress passes the Indian Reorganization Act (IRA), which ends allotment policies and restores some land to Native Americans. The IRA encourages tribes to govern themselves and set up tribal economic corporations, but with the government overseeing their decisions. The IRA also provides more funding to the reservations.

1946 The Indian Lands Commission (ICC) is created to decide land claims filed by Indian nations. Many tribes expect the ICC to return lost lands, but the ICC chooses to award money instead, and at the value of the land at the time it was lost.

1951 A new Indian Act in Canada reduces the power of the Indian Affairs Office, makes it easier for Indians to gain the right to vote, and helps Indian children enter public schools. It also removes the ban on potlatch and Sun Dance ceremonies.

1952 In an all out effort to make Native Americans "blend in" or assimilate with the rest of society, the U.S. government begins a policy of moving Indians from reservations to cities. The government hopes that Native Americans will find jobs in the city and adopt an "American" lifestyle. Then the government will be able to "terminate" the tribes and eliminate the reservations.

1954–62 The U.S. Congress carries out its policy of "termination." At the same time laws are passed giving states and local governments control over tribal members, taking away the tribes' authority to govern themselves. Under the policy of termination, Indians lose their special privileges and are treated as any other U.S. citizens. The tribes that are terminated face extreme poverty and the threat of loss of their

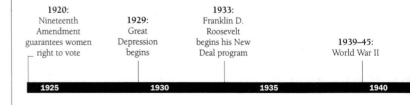

1920:
Nineteenth
Amendment
guarantees women
right to vote

1929:
Great
Depression
begins

1933:
Franklin D.
Roosevelt
begins his New
Deal program

1939–45:
World War II

1925   1930   1935   1940

community and traditions. By 1961 the government begins rethinking this policy because of the damage it is causing.

1955 The Indian Health Service (IHS) assumes responsibility for Native American health care. The IHS operates hospitals, health centers, health stations, clinics, and community service centers.

1960 The queen of England approves a law giving status Indians the right to vote in Canada.

1965 Under the new U. S. government policy, the Self-Determination policy, federal aid to reservations is given directly to Indian tribes and not funneled through the Bureau of Indian Affairs.

1968 The American Indian Movement (AIM) is founded in Minneapolis, Minnesota, by Dennis Banks (Ojibway) and Russell Means (Lakota). AIM is formed to improve federal, state, and local social services to urban neighborhoods and to prevent harassment of Indians by the local police.

1969 Eighty-nine Native Americans land on Alcatraz Island, a former penitentiary in San Francisco Bay in California. The group, calling itself "Indians of All Tribes," claims possession of the island under an 1868 treaty that gave Indians the right to unused federal property on Indian land. Indians of All Tribes occupies the island for 19 months while negotiating with federal officials. They do not win their claim to the island but draw public attention to their cause.

1971 The Alaska Native Claims Settlement Act (ANCSA) is signed into law. With the act, Alaska Natives give up any claim to nine-tenths of Alaska. In return, they are given $962 million and clear title to 44 million acres of land.

1972 Five hundred Indians arrive in Washington, D.C., on a march called the Trail of Broken Treaties to protest the government's policies toward Native Americans. The protestors occupy the Bureau of Indian Affairs building for a week,

The Menominee tribe was terminated by the U.S. government but after much protest, won back federal recognition.

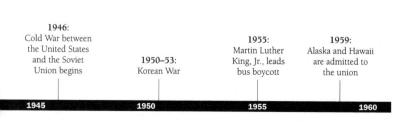

1946:
Cold War between the United States and the Soviet Union begins

1950–53:
Korean War

1955:
Martin Luther King, Jr., leads bus boycott

1959:
Alaska and Hawaii are admitted to the union

1945   1950   1955   1960

The armed takeover of Wounded Knee in 1973.

causing considerable damage. They present the government with a list of reforms, but the administration rejects their demands.

1973 After a dispute over Oglala Sioux (Lakota) tribal chair Robert Wilson and his strong-arm tactics at Pine Ridge Reservation, AIM leaders are called in. Wilson's supporters and local authorities arm themselves against protestors, who are also armed, and a ten-week siege begins in which hundreds of federal marshals and Federal Bureau of Investigation (FBI) agents surround the Indian protestors. Two Native American men are shot and killed.

1974 After strong protests and "fish-ins" bring attention to the restrictions on Native American fishing rights in the Pacific Northwest, the U.S. Supreme Court restores Native fishing rights in the case *Department of Game of Washington v. Puyallup Tribe et al.*

1978 U.S. Congress passes legislation providing support for additional tribal colleges, schools of higher education designed to help Native American students achieve academic success and eventually transfer to four-year colleges and universities. Tribal colleges also work with tribal elders and cultural leaders to record languages, oral traditions, and arts in an effort to preserve cultural traditions.

1978 The American Religious Freedom Act is signed. Its stated purpose is to "protect and preserve for American Indians their inherent right of freedom to believe, express, and exercise their traditional religions."

1978 The Bureau of Indian Affairs publishes regulations for the new Federal Acknowledgment Program. This program is responsible for producing a set of "procedures for establishing that an American Indian group exists as an Indian tribe." Many tribes will later discover that these requirements are complicated and difficult to establish.

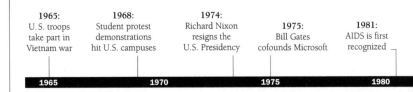

1965:
U.S. troops take part in Vietnam war

1968:
Student protest demonstrations hit U.S. campuses

1974:
Richard Nixon resigns the U.S. Presidency

1975:
Bill Gates cofounds Microsoft

1981:
AIDS is first recognized

| 1965 | 1970 | 1975 | 1980 |

1982 Canada constitutionally recognizes aboriginal peoples in its new Constitution and Charter of Rights and Freedoms. The Constitution officially divides Canada's aboriginal nations into three designations: the Indian, the Inuit, and the Métis peoples. Native groups feel that the new Constitution does not adequately protect their rights, nor does it give them the right to govern themselves.

Chinook Winds Casino, Oregon, 1997.

1988 The Federal Indian Gambling Regulatory Act of 1988 allows any tribe recognized by the U.S. government to engage in gambling activities. With proceeds from gaming casinos, some tribes pay for health care, support of the elderly and sick, housing, and other improvements, while other tribes buy back homelands, establish scholarship funds, and create new jobs.

1989 U.S. Congress approves a bill to establish a National Museum of the American Indian under the administration of the Smithsonian Institution in Washington, D.C. (As of 1999, the Museum has not been built.)

1990 Two important acts are passed by U.S. Congress. The Native American Languages Act is designed to preserve, protect, and promote the practice and development of Indian languages. The Graves Protection and Repatriation Act provides for the protection of American Indian grave sites and the repatriation (return) of Indian remains and cultural artifacts to tribes.

1992 Canadians vote against a new Constitution (the Charlottetown Accord) that contains provisions for aboriginal self-government.

1999 A new territory called Nunavut enters the federation of Canada. Nunavut is comprised of vast areas taken from the Northwest Territories and is populated by an Inuit majority. The largest Native land claim in Canadian history, Nunavut is one-fifth of the landmass of Canada, or the size of the combined states of Alaska and Texas. Meaning "Our Land" in the Inukitut (Inuit) language, Nunavut will be primarily governed by the Inuit.

After many years of struggle, the Inuit celebrate the establishment of a new Canadian territory, Nunavut, or "Our Land," in 1999.

1983:
The Internet is born

1989:
The Berlin Wall is destroyed

1993:
Apartheid is outlawed in South Africa

1999:
NATO forces bomb Serbian military sites

1985   1990   1995   2000

*Historic Locations of
U.S. Native Groups*

Dakota

Sauk

Fox

Menominee

Kickapoo

Winnebago

Potawatomi

Peoria

Illinois

Cahokia

Kaskaskia

Miami

Erie

Adena

Hopewell

Shawnee

Mississippian

Osage

Iowa

Oto

(Kansa)

Missouri

kawa

Waco

akoni

ta

Quapaw

Caddo

Hasinai

Kichai

Tunica

Natchez

Houma

Biloxi

Coushatta

Chitimacha

Chickasaw

Choctaw

Creek

Hitchiti

Alabama

Mobile

Apalachee

Apalachicola

Yazoo

Yamasee

Timucua

Miccosukee

Calusa

Seminole

Guale

Edisto

Cusabo

Santee

Pedee

Cheraw

Catawba

Yuchi

Etowah

Koasati

Cherokee

Lumbee

Saponi

Tutelo

Waccamaw

Pamlico

Meherrin

Coharie

Nansemond

Rappahannock

Chickahominy

Powhatan

Pamunkey

Mattaponi

Monacan

Piscataway

Paugussett

Brothertown

Susquehanna

Schaghticoke

Unami

Seneca

Cayuga

Oneida

Tuscarora

Iroquois

Onondaga

Mohawk

Manhattan

Munsee

Mahican

Wappinger

Narraganset

Pequot

Podunk

Montauk

Shinnecock

Wampanoag

Nipmuk

Massachuset

Stockbridge

Delaware

Nanticoke

Mohegan

Abenaki

Penobscot

Pennacook

Atlantic
Ocean

Gulf
of
Mexico

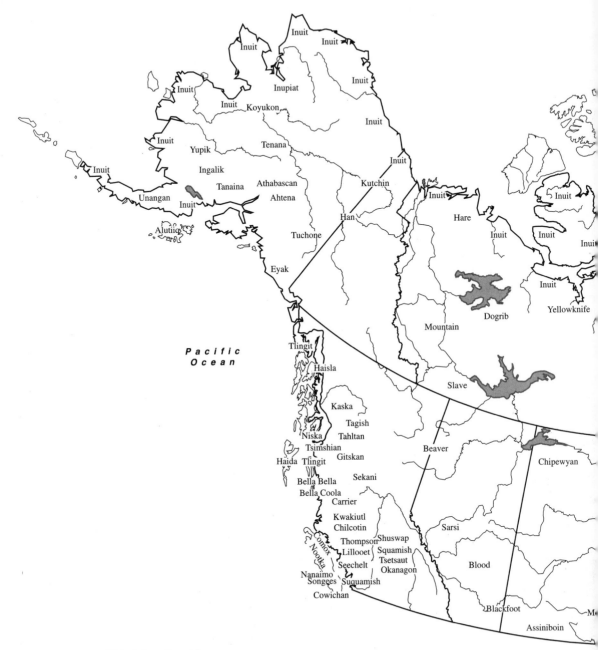

Pacific
Ocean

Historic Locations of
Canadian Native Groups

Inuit
Inuit
Inuit
Inupiat
Inuit
Inuit
Koyukon
Inuit
Inuit
Tenana
Inuit
Yupik
Inuit
Ingalik
Athabascan
Kutchin
Inuit
Tanaina
Ahtena
Inuit
Hare
Inuit
Inuit
Unangan
Inuit
Han
Inuit
Inuit
Aluttiq
Tuchone
Mountain
Dogrib
Yellowknife
Eyak

Tlingit
Slave
Haisla
Kaska
Tagish
Niska
Tahltan
Beaver
Chipewyan
Tsimshian
Haida Tlingit
Gitskan
Bella Bella
Sekani
Bella Coola
Carrier
Sarsi
Kwakiutl
Chilcotin
Comox
Thompson Shuswap
Nootka
Lillooet Squamish
Blood
Seechelt Tsetsaut
Nanaimo
Okanagon
Songees Suquamish
Cowichan
Blackfoot
M
Assiniboin

Inuit

Inuit

Inuit

Inuit

Inuit

Inuit

Inuit

Inuit

Inuit

Inuit

Inuit

Inuit

Inuit

Inuit

Beothuk

Inuit

Intuit

Naskapi

Innu

Cree

Montagnais

Maliseet

Ojibwa

Micmac

Passamaquoddy

Algonkin

Ottawa

Nippissing

Huron

Tobacco

Wenrohronon

Nuetra

Wyandotte

Northeast

Northeast

The American Indian cultures of northeastern North America, also known as the Woodland Indians, inhabited a region that was very rich in natural resources. This large region that includes territory from the Atlantic coast to the Great Lakes was characterized by extensive forests and numerous river systems and bodies of water. The environment supported a wide variety of mammals and fish that provided a valuable source of food for Native peoples. The forests contained large numbers of white-tailed deer, moose, and elk. In some areas of the Northeast woodland bison and caribou also served as primary food sources. In addition, large numbers of bears and beaver as well as smaller mammals and migrating waterfowl provided ready foodstuffs for Native peoples. The rivers and lakes of the region literally teemed with fish and clams.

Although farming was limited in the extreme northern reaches of the area, agriculture was, for the most part, quite productive. A variety of naturally occurring foodstuffs were also available. Wild rice was common to the region and was an important food because it could be stored for long periods of time. The resources that were a part of the ecology of the region helped sustain large populations of Native groups such as the Iroquois, Ojibway, Delaware, Wampanoag (see entries), Ottawa, Huron, and many others over an extensive territory in the period before Europeans arrived.

Tribal autonomy

The large number of tribes that inhabited the Northeast were very diverse in cultural patterns although they shared a very similar environment. The tribes had differences in languages, housing forms, ceremonial life, and kinship patterns as well as in other areas. Each of the tribal groups should be examined independently to understand the specifics of tribal life.

The one thing all of these tribal groups shared was the great emphasis they placed on tribal autonomy—the ability to govern their own affairs. Some of the tribes of the Northeast did confederate (join together in an alliance) over time for mutual purposes, such as the six tribes that formed the Iroquois confederacy, but the vast majority of the Northeast groups maintained a high degree of independence. The primary allegiance was to family and then to related families living within the village. There was little centralized government, and tribes were not easily persuaded to join others for unified political action.

Religion

The Native peoples of the Northeast, like other indigenous peoples, were very religious. Spiritual perceptions dictated their life patterns to a great extent. All of the Northeast tribal groups prayed and fasted before they hunted or gathered plants for food. They marked the changes of the seasons and the harvest with elaborate ceremonials that sought the favor of the spirits of the Earth and sky. Devoted in their beliefs, they acknowledged life as a gift to the people from the creator. Rituals and ceremonies were held to ensure the well-being of the community and the continuity of life.

An illustration of life in the Great Lakes region, with two kinds of dwelling, the conical buffalo skin lodge and the oblong birch bark lodge.

Life was celebrated by Native peoples of the Northeast. They had adequate food stuffs to provide for good health, the tools they needed to farm and hunt, and traditions that promoted social well-being. They made nets and spears to fish with, and they trapped animals with snares and dead-falls. They used fire as a tool to clear the lands for agriculture or to make openings for foraging mammals. With an intimate knowledge of local medicinal plants, they were able to treat a range of illnesses. They had a history of storytelling to make sense of their surroundings and to educate their children. Music and performance were vital parts of their ceremonial life and also an informal means of social expression.

Life for the Native peoples of the Northeast was hard work, though. The people toiled at farming without beasts of burden—with no horses or oxen to aid them. There does not seem to be an extensive history of wars of conquest during the period before European contact, but there were struggles between newcomers to the area and original tribes that sometimes caused entire tribes to have to move to another area. But at the time of contact, the clans in the respective villages prospered, and trade and intercourse between them appears to have been relatively peaceful. This would change dramatically with the arrival to the region of representatives of European nations.

Post-contact period

EARLY CONTACT BRINGS CATASTROPHIC EPIDEMICS The world began to change rapidly for Native peoples in the Northeast in the post-contact period. As Europeans began to explore and to forge relations with Northeastern Indian tribes, diseases were unleashed that were new to the region: smallpox, measles and mumps, scarlet fever and others. With no immunological protection (natural resistance) from the new diseases, Native peoples began to die in large numbers. The phenomenon of introducing a disease into a population that has no immunological protection is called a virgin soil epidemic (VSE). It is not uncommon to lose 85 to 90 percent of a population over a century during the course of a virgin soil epidemic and also to experience a decreasing birth rate at the same time.

The consequences of these VSEs for Native peoples of the region were catastrophic. Native communities lost hunters, shamans, and other specialists from their ranks. Traditional plant remedies had little impact on the new diseases, which came one after the other. The people struggled to understand what was happening. Many fled the unknown maladies, thereby spreading them to neighboring tribes. The new diseases were clearly responsible for devastating Native populations and paving the way for colonial experiments in the Northeast. Most of the Native peoples that inhabited these lands had simply died, leaving their cleared lands and ancestral homes to a small portion of their prior population. These survivors now had to contend with an expanding European population that was interested in the spiritual and physical rewards to be found in the "New World."

Trade with the Europeans

Although we generally remember the early British colonists in the Northeast as refugees from religious persecution back in England, there were strong economic motivations for the colonization of the region as well. Most of the successful early English colonies were founded by joint stock companies. These companies clearly expected a return on their investments in the New World. Land was a much sought-after commodity since it was difficult to obtain within the rigid class structure and inheritance systems of Europe. To complicate matters, European nations established rival colonial empires in the New World. Wars of conquest between these powers soon came to involve the region's Native peoples, when English, Dutch, and French colonies began to compete with each other for Indian allies and Indian trade.

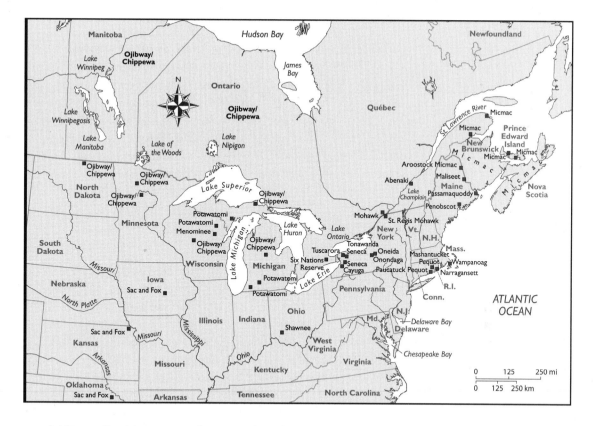

Additionally, Native peoples introduced commodities that quickly became very important in the world economy. As an example, trading and cultivating tobacco was one way in which the Jamestown Colony (the first permanent English colony, settled in 1607 in southeast Virginia) came to prosper. Tobacco was native to the Americas but soon became popular and profitable around the world. The fur trade also became an important part of European and Northeastern Indian relations. Native hunters provided the furs to colonial traders in return for their goods, beginning cycles of trade that would last into the nineteenth century.

The new trade relations were responsible for introducing Native peoples to an entirely new array of manufactured goods. Of course, Native peoples were happy to trade furs for metal pots, knives, and blankets. The problem though, was in establishing the worth of the goods in the market. In other words, how many furs is a blanket worth? Native traders did not initially have access to that information, while European traders purchased the blanket and knew what the furs would bring on the European market. The situation—ripe for exploiting Indian hunters and their families—

A map of contemporary Native American communities in the Northeast region.

was the very root of deteriorating relations between Indians and their new neighbors.

The introduction of alcohol into these trade relations compounded the already complex situation. Alcohol was a new commodity to Indians of the Northeast. They had not had hundreds of years to develop social behaviors around the consumption of alcohol as Europeans had done, and initially Native peoples tended to overindulge. It became a standard practice of European traders to use alcohol to loosen up their Indian clients. Of course, this practice led to increased hostilities between the groups.

What clearly evolved over time was a Native dependency on European trade goods. Native hunters began to spend a great deal of time trapping furs for the trade rather than engaging in more traditional ways of providing for themselves. The profits of these trade relations tended to strengthen colonial governments and outposts. Once these centers of growing economic activity became strong enough, they sought—and sometimes demanded—more Indian land.

The trade between Northeastern Indian tribes and colonial governments also promoted inter-tribal rivalries. For example, after the Dutch were eliminated from trade in the Northeast, most of the tribes of the region split their trade allegiances between the British and the French. Both of these European nations profited from the trade and worked to keep their Indian allies faithful. Northeastern Indians were often sought as allies in military campaigns and this created bitter inter-tribal conflicts in the region. In trade and military interactions with the Europeans, however, Northeastern Indian tribes were very active in adapting to situations that evolved. The tribes attempted to make decisions that would prolong their way of life and guarantee a continuing quality of life to their relations and children.

Indian treaties

Treaties are agreements between two parties, signed by both, usually defining the benefits to both parties that will result from one side giving up title to a territory. It seems evident that the treaties negotiated between European nations and Native groups were introduced by Europeans attempting to build colonial empires and therefore wanting more land. Treaties that ceded Indian lands to European nations or colonial governments were legal documents, and as such were recognized in courts. Unfortunately, those same courts generally did not recognize the rights of Indians, only the fact that Indians had deeded lands to European powers. Signing treaties with Indians provided legal protection of land claims for colonial governments while providing little or no protection to Indian signatories (signers). Clearly, one intention of the treaties was to provide a legally defensible claim to Indian lands. Although Indians entered into these agreements and signed them, there are many questions about their legality, such as whether or not the individuals who signed the treaties had the power to do so.

The net outcome of the treaty process was that giving up tribal lands decreased the range and scope of natural resources that tribes had access to. Access to natural resources was the basis of life for Native peoples in the Northeast. As colonial governments became stronger, Indian tribes in the region came under increased pressures.

The history of the Northeastern tribes' encounter with Europeans is clearly one of sickness, diminishing resources, and eventually, hostility. These same cycles were played out decade after decade in the colonial period as different powers arose. As a result of the French and Indian Wars (1754–63), France lost all colonial interests in North America. Shortly thereafter, the newly formed American federal government declared independence from Great Britain and fought the American Revolutionary War (1775–83). After 1783 the U.S. federal government simply built upon British precedents in Indian affairs. Under the provisions of the Federal Proclamation of 1783, only an authorized representative of the federal government could enter into a treaty for or acquire Indian lands. This was an almost direct restatement of the British Royal Proclamation of 1763. Both of these acts were intended to create a virtual monopoly (exclusive rights) in the acquisition and resale of Indian lands. The sale of Indian lands, acquired via treaty, had proven to be an important source of funds to run governments and pay for military services. Under the burden of these policies, Indian tribes of the region continued to adapt to changing national politics and goals as they sought to maintain their cultural identity and a degree of control over their future.

One of the major problems for tribal groups in the post-revolutionary period was that they were suddenly faced with initiating political relations with a government that had not existed a few years earlier. American policies toward Indians were extremely high-handed and focused on one purpose: to facilitate the orderly transfer of Indian lands to American interests. Northeastern tribal groups were faced with very difficult decisions as they worked to maintain tribal sovereignty (self-government) and lands. Treaty after treaty diminished the Indian land base.

The Northeastern tribal groups during this period of time had little choice but to change and accommodate, the only way to preserve some semblance of tribal autonomy and community. The U.S. Congress had decided that they had plenary (absolute) power over Indian affairs and they were not reluctant to use that power. Those tribes that were fortunate enough to maintain reservations (what was not ceded as a part of a treaty was reserved; hence the common usage of the term "reservation" in Indian affairs) worked very hard to maintain their resource base and adapt to local economies. During the nineteenth century, Northeastern Indians found work in agriculture, the timber industries, ship building, commercial fishing, and mines. They did whatever was necessary to survive. It was a difficult period of time, but Native peoples clung to their heritage and what they believed was their birthright: the land. Many of the tribes lost their reservation base during the nineteenth century. Some of the tribes were affected by the passage of the Indian Removal Act (1830) and segments of their communities were moved to Indian Territory (later to become Oklahoma).

Assimilation

In the nineteenth century, Indians tended to be viewed as standing in the way of progress. Conventional wisdom held that Indian lands were better used by farmers who would make the land profitable. Additionally, Indians were viewed by mainstream society as being inferior and in need of being taught the correct way to live. The federal government, during this period of time, embarked on a large-scale program of assimilation—that is, they wanted Indians to become like the majority of other citizens and give up their ancestral ways. The federal government funded schools that had, as their sole purpose, the assimilation of Indian children. Missionaries and churches were also funded to help remake the Indian. These efforts proved to be an extreme hardship for Native children and parents. The schools were usually boarding schools; parents and children were separated for long periods of time. Many of the children became sick in these institutions. Corporal (physical) punishment was used regularly. These schools, with their very harsh environments, were often the only educational avenues open to Indian children.

The changes witnessed by the Native peoples of the Northeast in their own territory were stark and long-lasting. The ecology of the region has been irreversibly changed. The rise of industrialization changed the patterns of work and family life. Traditional ways of life were supplanted by new occupations; formal education came to replace traditional systems that valued other forms of knowledge.

Throughout all of these changes, tribal governments have persisted and continued to assert their natural rights as indigenous peoples. Throughout the nineteenth and into the twentieth century, tribal governments have continued to advocate for their tribal rights.

Over time, many Americans have come to realize the folly of past conceptions of Indians and the outright prejudice of Indian policies that ruthlessly stripped them of their lands and resources. Many people have also come to see the hypocrisy in attempting to destroy Native cultures while proclaiming democratic principles. This awareness helped foster Indian reform and the idea of self-determination: Indians deciding what their future should be and working to actualize it. The struggle has been long and arduous for Native peoples of the Northeast. After all, they were the first to be colonized and in some cases the first to resist the yoke of colonial oppression.

The struggle to preserve a heritage

The efforts of Northeastern Indian tribes in working to preserve their tribal lands and unique heritage is an incredible story. It spans more than four centuries and is an amazing testament to the human spirit and cultural survival. Great changes have taken place, and yet tribal governments have persisted and overcome many obstacles. The history of the Northeast Indians is a story of how a weakened group of indigenous peoples fought to maintain ancestral lands and natural rights and triumphed in the end. Unfortunately, not all endings are happy. Some of the tribal groups perished as a result of the onslaught of the new American culture and economy. Those tribes that have survived are truly remarkable in their ability to change and find a middle ground between two cultures.

Many questions need to be asked as one learns about the Northeastern tribes. What could have been done differently? Is it ever all right to force another culture to abandon age-old traditions and ways of understanding the world? Is one world view truly superior to another? Is there anything we can learn from these experiences that might aid us in the future? Can we work in the future to re-establish an ecological balance similar to what Native peoples fostered at one point in time? Answering these questions and others will not change the past for Native peoples, but it might change the future for untold generations.

George Cornell, Ph.D.
Associate Professor, History and American Studies,
Michigan State University, East Lansing
Director, Native American Institute

FURTHER READING

Ballantine, Betty, and Ian Ballantine, eds. *The Native Americans: An Illustrated History.* Atlanta: Turner Publishing, 1993.

Champagne, Duane, ed. *The Native North American Almanac.* Detroit: Gale, 1994.

Hyde, George E. *Indians of the Woodlands: From Prehistoric Times to 1725.* Norman: University of Oklahoma Press, 1962.

Josephy, Alvin M., Jr. *500 Nations: An Illustrated History of North American Indians.* New York: Knopf, 1994.

Terrell, John Upton. *American Indian Almanac.* New York, World Publishing, 1971.

Abenaki

Name

The name Abenaki (pronounced *ah–buh–NAH–key*) means "people of the dawnlands." The Abenaki people called themselves *Alnanbal,* meaning "men." Abenaki (also called "Wabanaki" or "Abnaki") was a confederacy of many Algonquian-speaking tribes that existed from the mid-1600s to about 1800.

Location

The group known as Abenaki was actually a union of many tribes. They were divided into eastern and western branches. The eastern Abenaki resided in Maine, east of the White Mountains of New Hampshire, and in the Canadian provinces of New Brunswick and Nova Scotia. The traditional territory of the western Abenaki groups included most of Vermont and New Hampshire, as well as the northern part of Massachusetts. In the late 1990s there were five Abenaki reservations in Maine and more at several sites in Canada. Other groups of Abenaki people who do not have reservations are spread across northern New England and throughout Quebec and New Brunswick, Canada.

Population

In 1524, there were about 40,000 Abenaki (10,000 western Abenaki and 30,0000 eastern Abenaki). In a census (count of the population) conducted in 1990 by the U.S. Bureau of the Census, 1,549 people identified themselves as Abenaki. In 1991, Canadian Abenaki numbered 945.

Language family

Algonquian.

Origins and group affiliations

Some historians believe that the ancestors of the tribes making up the Abenaki confederacy first arrived in North America about 3,000 years ago. The eastern Abenaki, the larger of the two branches, included the Penobscot, the Passamaquoddy, Maliseet, Androscoggin, Kennebec, Ossipee, and Pigwacket tribes. The western Abenaki tribes included the Sokoki, Cowasuck, and Missiquoi.

ABENAKI

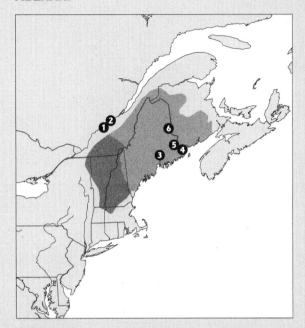

Dark shaded area: Traditional lands of western Abenaki in present-day Vermont, New Hampshire, and Massachusetts

Light shaded area: Traditional lands of eastern Abenaki in present-day Maine, New Hampshire, New Brunswick, and Nova Scotia

For thousands of years the Abenaki people lived tranquil lives, hunting and fishing in the forests, ocean, lakes, and rivers of present-day Maine. Then Europeans came, and from the 1600s through the 1800s the lives of Abenaki groups were terribly affected by war, starvation, and disease. Some tribal groups were forced to abandon their villages in New England and regroup in Canada during times of armed conflict. While the Indians were away from their New England territory, white settlers took over the land. The Canadian Abenaki managed to maintain peace and retain many of their customs and traditions. The Abenaki who remained in their homelands in the United States also tried to live quietly and avoid trouble with European settlers, but they were not always able to do so.

Mythical city lures Europeans

Around the early 1500s people in Europe heard rumors of a wealthy Native city called "Norumbega," which was said to be located in northern Maine. Although Norumbega never existed, tales about the mythical city lured explorers to the area. One of the earliest was a French expedition led by Italian explorer Giovanni da Verrazano in 1524. Though suspicious of the foreigners, many of the Abenaki tribes began to engage in fur trade with Europeans, especially the French and the English. In return they received knives, iron axes, fishhooks, brass for making arrowheads, and cloth.

In 1604 French explorer Samuel de Champlain visited many Abenaki villages while on a mission to trade furs and establish a French fort on the St. Croix River (in territory that is now part of the state of Maine). The English tried to establish a colony on Abenaki land in 1607, but, partly because of hostile encounters with the tribes, the settlement lasted less than a year.

Abenaki relations with the French

For the next 50 years the English and the French fought several wars for control of the Abenaki homeland, regardless of the fact that it belonged to the Native peoples of the area. All this tension led the Abenaki tribes to fight among themselves, and their competition for trade with the French only compounded problems. The French traded mostly with the Penobscot, who became the most powerful of the Abenaki tribes.

The Abenaki had no true friends among the European nations, but their relationship with the French was much better than with the English colonists. The French won over the Natives by providing them with guns and promising them protection from their longtime enemies, the Iroquois (see entry), who conducted raids on Abenaki villages throughout the 1600s.

The English and the Iroquois

The English were unsuccessful in their attempts to befriend the Abenaki. Between 1616 and 1619 deadly epidemics (uncontrolled outbreaks of disease) swept through Native territories, killing many Abenaki. The French convinced the Indians that the English were solely responsible for the devastation of the tribe. The English chose to seek the friendship and support of the Iroquois tribe instead.

THE ABENAKI CONFEDERACY AND THE GREAT COUNCIL FIRE

The Abenaki (also known as Wabanaki) Confederacy was composed of a group of Algonquian–speaking tribes who banded together in the mid–1600s for common defense against the tribes of the Iroquois confederacy. The Iroquois had overtrapped furs in their own homelands and began attacking nearby tribes to gain new hunting territories. The hostilities were further fueled by the Iroquois people's alliance with the English. At the time England and France were bitter enemies. Both countries sought to stake their claim of New World lands and dominate the unsettled territory. The Abenaki were pro-French.

Conflicts between the tribes of the Abenaki Confederacy and the Iroquois Confederacy were settled through a peace pact called the Great Council of Fire, which was made in 1749. Despite the differences between Abenaki and Iroquois tribes, the Great Council endured for more than 25 years. When the American Revolution began in 1775, some Abenaki groups supported the American colonists in their fight for independence from Britain. However, other Abenaki and Iroquois tribes, including the Passamaquoddy (Abenaki), sided with the British and withdrew from the Great Council of Fire. By 1800 the Abenaki Confederacy ceased to exist.

During the 1660s a civil war took place in England. Many people fled from there to the New World and began to settle on Abenaki lands. After a time of peace, King Philip's War erupted in 1675, when a group of southern New England tribes led by the brilliant Wampanoag (see entry) leader Metacomet or King Philip, attacked English settlements on the Indians' homelands. By the time this tragic war was over, the colonists had nearly exterminated the Wampanoag, Nipmuck, and Narragansett (see entry) tribes. King Philip's death in July 1676 ended Native military action in southern New England. The Abenaki resented the growing alliance between the English and the Iroquois (longtime enemies of the Abenaki) and feared the large number of English settlers who had begun to come and take over their land, but most Abenaki groups remained neutral (they did not take sides) throughout the conflict.

The French and Indian Wars begin

Between 1689 and 1763 Native Americans of the Northeast became caught up in a struggle between England and France over who would dominate North America. These conflicts are referred to collectively as the French and Indian Wars, which consisted of occasional outbreaks of hostility followed by periods of quiet. The final struggle in the United States between the English and French (which spread to Europe as the Seven Years's War) is commonly known as the French and Indian War (1756–63).

King William's War

King William's War (1689–97) was the first of the French and Indian Wars. Most Abenaki groups, with the exception of the Penobscot, joined French troops in attacking English towns in eastern New York, New Hampshire, and Maine. The English responded with raids of their own. Soon many Abenaki retreated to northern New England and Canada, where their French allies were based. England and France signed a peace treaty in 1697, but the Abenaki continued to fight, upset

that more and more English colonists were taking over their territory. Worn out from fighting by 1699, the Abenaki signed an agreement to stay neutral in any future conflicts between England and France.

Queen Anne's War

The peace between the English and the French did not last long. Queen Anne's War broke out in 1702, as hostilities once again reached a fever pitch. Although many Abenaki stuck to the terms of their neutrality agreement, others joined the French in attacks on several English towns in present-day Maine.

The most famous raid of the war took place in February 1704 in Deerfield, Massachusetts. A large force of Abenaki and French carried out a sneak attack on the English at daybreak, killing more than 50 people, capturing more than 100, and burning a good part of the town to the ground. The Abenaki then withdrew back up the frozen Connecticut River, out of reach of the English, taking their captives with them. Even though they were successful, the greatly outnumbered Abenaki warriors suffered losses they could not afford. Weakened, the Abenaki were forced to trade more and more of their land to the French in exchange for safety in Canada. The pursuing English often encountered empty Abenaki villages as they marched northward.

Dummer's War

In the treaty that ended Queen Anne's War in 1713, the French gave the territory of Acadia (in present-day Nova Scotia) to England. Acadia was largely made up of Abenaki land. The Abenaki felt angry and betrayed at the French giveaway, and many French people who lived in Acadia agreed with them.

Supported by several French priests, the Abenaki decided to defend their land, and in 1722 Dummer's War broke out. The great Abenaki warrior Grey Lock gained fame for his raids on the English, who were never able to capture him. The conflict was bloody, and the Abenaki eventually met with defeat in 1727.

King George's War

Native peoples in the Northeast experienced relative peace from 1727 to 1744. Years of fighting and outbreaks of smallpox epidemics had greatly lessened their population. Furthermore, the Abenaki people's intermingling with other tribes through ongoing association and intermarriage was changing the identity, culture, and lifestyle of these once fiercely independent groups. Peace ended for the tribes with the outbreak of King George's War in 1744. Some Abenaki tribes once again joined the French in attacking the English because they wanted to stop the English settlers who were pushing their way up the Connecticut River Valley. The Indian raids, which ended in 1748, succeeded in temporarily forcing the settlers to retreat southward.

In 1749 the Penobscot, one of the largest Abenaki tribes, left the confederacy in the hopes of making a separate peace with England and France. The tribe's plan to remain neutral (not take sides) in wars between European nations lasted only until the outbreak of the final battle between the two European nations over land in the Northeast. England drew the Penobscot into battle by offering them very high prices for the scalps they could collect from the enemies of the British.

Wars end but not troubles

The last battle of the French and Indian Wars began in 1755. A year later the Seven Years' War broke out in Europe, and the French, English, and Indians in North America became tangled up in the war as well. When the conflicts were over, all French rule in the northeastern part of the North American continent would come to an end.

The final battle, commonly called the French and Indian War (1755–63), began well for the combined Abenaki and French forces but in time turned in favor of the English. In 1759 the Abenaki were dealt a serious blow when English Major Robert Rogers—nicknamed Wobi Madaondo ("White Devil") by the Abenaki—led a group of soldiers against the Abenaki village of St. Francis, Quebec, and burned the village to the ground. The English ended up defeating the French army and taking full possession of Quebec and all of Canada. With the loss of their French allies, the Abenaki were forced to deal with their longtime enemies—the English—alone. Meanwhile, English colonists began to swarm into Abenaki territory in New England in great numbers.

American Revolution splits Abenaki

After more than 70 years of war, starvation, and disease, the Abenaki were greatly reduced in population and power. But they had not seen the end of hardship. They were forced to endure further warfare and bloodshed when they were drawn into the American Revolution in 1776.

The various Abenaki bands did not agree on which side to support in the revolution. Many of the St. Francis (Quebec) Abenaki supported the British, while a majority of the Penobscot, Passamaquoddy, Maliseet, and Micmac (see entry) bands of Abenaki fought with the freedom-seeking colonists under the command of General George Washington. The colonists promised the Abenaki land in exchange for their support. For the most part, though, those promises would be broken.

Abenaki migrate north

When the United States was formed in 1783, the Abenaki contribution to the victory was quickly forgotten as white-owned lumber companies took over Abenaki lands for their own profit. Abenaki lands were further divided when the United States and Canada drew boundary lines through them. The Indians' dealings with various state governments were largely unsuccessful. For example, on five separate occasions during the 1800s, the Abenaki were denied land by the state of Vermont.

At the beginning of the nineteenth century some Abenaki continued to migrate north into Canada, a process that had been going on for a hundred years. The population of St. Francis, Quebec, swelled as Abenaki moved there to escape from the ever-growing number of American settlers. In 1805 the British government set aside land near St. Francis to accommodate the flood of Abenaki settlers.

IMPORTANT DATES

1524: Abenaki encounter the expedition of Giovanni da Verrazano.

1689–1763: Abenaki are caught up in wars between European nations.

1805: The British government sets aside land near St. Francis, Quebec, to accommodate the flood of Abenaki moving there from the United States.

1980: President Jimmy Carter signs a bill granting the Passamaquoddy and Penobscot $81 million to make up for the loss of their homelands.

1982: Vermont Abenaki apply for recognition by the U.S. government. Ten years later the Supreme Court rules against them.

U.S. Abenaki try to fit in

The Abenaki who stayed in the United States tried to survive by adopting the whites' ways and speaking English. Abenaki ways were lost as white loggers destroyed their hunting, fishing, and trapping grounds. No longer able to support themselves by traditional means, many Abenaki began making and selling baskets and other crafts to survive. In time, though, the Abenaki tribes began a long fight with state and federal governments to preserve their lands and culture. Among themselves, they continued to practice their ancient rituals and customs.

In New England, the Passamaquoddy and the Penobscot survived in their original homeland largely because white settler pressure was less severe in the north. But they barely maintained themselves on small parcels of their old land. In 1786 they refused to sign a treaty with Massachusetts, but in 1794 they ceded the state more than a million acres. By 1820 the Abenaki owned only a few thousand acres and by 1850 they were confined to two separate villages. Some, in fact, were forced out of villages in Vermont by white settlers and fled to relatives in Canada.

Abenaki in the twentieth century

In 1929 a period of severe economic slowdown occurred in the United States. The Great Depression, as it was called, put millions of Americans out of work. But the late 1920s and the 1930s were relatively good years for the Abenaki in the States. They benefitted from programs initiated by President Franklin D. Roosevelt (1882-1945), who called the Native American the "forgotten man." Roosevelt's programs provided food and jobs for people like the Abenaki who were suffering hardships. Throughout Roosevelt's administration, government policies regarding Native Americans changed, and emphasis was placed on maintaining and preserving ancient Indian culture.

But this forward-thinking trend was soon reversed. Some Abenaki became part of a sizeable group of Native Americans who fought in World War II (1939–45). After the war Native soldiers were greatly disappointed to return home and find that the U.S. government's policy had returned to one of assimilation (incorporating or blending Indians into mainstream white society).

Abenaki win rights

In the 1950s American Abenaki voiced their dissatisfaction with federal and state government policies that had taken away most of their land, stripped them of their fishing rights, and virtually destroyed their economy. Then in the 1960s—with the civil rights

ABENAKI TRIBES: THE PENOBSCOT, PASSAMAQUODDY, AND MALISEET

The Penobscot and the Passamaquoddy were the largest of the tribes that made up the Abenaki Confederacy. They were the only ones who managed to remain on their homelands throughout the tremendous upheavals faced by all the Abenaki peoples. In the 1400s, about 10,000 Penobscot lived on the Atlantic Coast. When the United States was established in 1776, the lands of the Penobscot became part of the state of Massachusetts. The state quickly whittled away much of the Penobscot homeland. Later the state of Maine was carved out of Massachusetts, and more land and the right to self-government were taken away from the Penobscot. Most of the people left the reservation in disgust. Today, there are about 2,500 Penobscot. Penobscot territory is made up of a 149,000-acre reservation, which includes 146 islands in Maine's Penobscot River. The village of Old Town is the main population center.

The Passamaquoddy and Maliseet together numbered about 1,000 in the early seventeenth century. The Passamaquoddy lived along the coast of Maine and in New Brunswick, Canada. As of the late 1990s there were about 2,500 Passamaquoddy. They have two reservations: one in Maine at Pleasant Point on the Passamaquoddy Bay and another, Indian Township, located 50 miles inland.

Historians often link the Passamaquoddy with the Maliseet, a nearby tribe who spoke the same language. The Maliseet inhabited a large area north and west of the land of the Passamaquoddy, in Maine, New Brunswick, and Quebec, Canada. Most of the Maliseet fled to Canada after the wars of the seventeenth and eighteenth century. By the 1990s most of the 885 Maliseet people resided in New Brunswick or Quebec, although there was one reservation for the tribe in Houlton, Maine, and other small groups of Maliseet were scattered throughout the United States.

movement (the fight for equal rights for people of all races) in full swing—the Abenaki, along with other Native groups, began to demand a full restoration of their rights as a tribe. They engaged in acts of civil disobedience (making their point by publicly disobeying certain laws) and used other forms of protest as part of a movement to reassert the power of Native peoples.

The efforts of the Abenaki paid off in 1980, when the U.S. government awarded the Passamaquoddy and Penobscot $81 million to make up for the loss of their homelands so many years before. Most of the money was put into a fund that permitted the tribes to buy 300,000 acres of their former land.

Canadian Abenaki in modern times

Meanwhile, the Canadian Abenaki took steps to keep their culture alive in the twentieth century by starting a cultural center, establishing a corporation to provide job opportunities and shops for Native products, and opening a tribal museum.

ABENAKI WORDS

The biggest difficulty in understanding the Abenaki language is that there is not always a literal translation for a given word. For example, Gordon Day's *Abenaki Dictionary* lists the word for clock as *babizookwazik,* which is translated as "that thing that ticks." Because Native Americans and Western Europeans had a very different concept of what time is and how it is measured, such a word could take on a confusing and complicated meaning.

Some other Abenaki words include: *ndakinna,* meaning "our land"; *bitawbagok* (the tribal name for Lake Champlain), meaning "the lake between"; *kuai,* meaning "hello"; *adio,* meaning "good-bye"; and *wliwni ni,* meaning "thank you."

RELIGION

The Abenaki were a deeply religious people. They believed that the Earth had always existed and called it their "Grandmother." They also believed that a being called the "Owner" had created people, animals, and all natural things, such as rocks and trees, and that each natural thing had an individual spirit. Their hero, Gluskab, who had created himself, could make life good or bad for the people. For example, he might bring them tobacco or affect the weather to their advantage.

The spiritual leaders of the Abenaki were healers called shamans (pronounced "SHAY-munz"). Shamans enlisted the aid of the spirits to heal the sick and solve problems. (See "Healing practices.")

During the sixteenth and seventeenth centuries French Catholic missionaries arrived on the lands of the Abenaki, seeking to convert the Indians to Christianity. Though at first feared and shunned as witches, the priests finally gained the trust of many Abenaki by learning their language and assisting in their health care needs. Protestant missionaries met with much less success in their conversion attempts. In time Roman Catholic churches and cemeteries became important parts of many Abenaki villages, and Catholic influences continued throughout the twentieth century.

LANGUAGE

The Abenaki language is part of the Algonquian language family. The eastern and western Abenaki people spoke different dialects (varieties) of the language. The best known of the many eastern dialects was the Penobscot, which is still spoken today. Many Abenaki place names remain in use in the New England area. For example, *Connecticut* means "the long river" and *Katahdin* (as in Mt. Katahdin, Maine) means "the principle mountain." The dialect of the western Abenaki continues to be spoken as a second language by some of the people.

During the nineteenth century Abenaki children were punished in American schools for speaking their traditional language; as a result, it almost become extinct. In the 1980s and 1990s the Abenaki tribes made great efforts to save their language, and it was even being taught in some Vermont schools.

GOVERNMENT

For the most part, at the time the Europeans arrived in the Northeast, the various Abenaki groups lacked a central governing authority. Issues such as whether or not to go to war were decided by all the adult members of a tribe, often under the loose leadership of a well-respected person called a sachem (pronounced *SAY-chem*) or chief. A sachem not only directed the war effort but represented the people in meetings with other tribes or different Abenaki bands. Even after the formation of the Abenaki Confederacy in 1670, though, French military officers complained that Abenaki leaders had a hard time controlling their warriors.

ECONOMY

The Abenaki economy was based originally on hunting, fishing, and gathering. After Europeans arrived on the scene, trade became more important. Wealthy Europeans who lived in drafty houses and castles were willing to pay large sums of money for furs to keep themselves warm in winter. The Abenaki and other tribes supplied European traders, especially the French, with a large number of the desired pelts. But by the mid-1660s the fur trade had fallen off because of overhunting. The British then allowed the Abenaki to buy European goods on credit, using their land for collateral (meaning the whites would have the right to take Native land if the Indians didn't repay the loan on time). After a while, though, the British refused to be repaid in animal skins and only accepted Abenaki land.

POPULATION OF ABENAKI TRIBES: 1990 CENSUS

The Abenaki tribe as a whole has never been federally recognized. This means that the U.S. government does not maintain official relations with the tribe. But three Abenaki groups in the state of Maine—the Penobscot, the Passamaquoddy, and the Maliseet—have achieved federal recognition. Maliseet people also live on seven reserves (the word Canadians use for reservations) located in New Brunswick and Quebec. Other people who claim Abenaki ancestry lost their lands but have continued to live throughout New England.

In the 1990 census, members of the various Abenaki groups in the United States identified themselves this way:

Tribe	Population
Abenaki	1,549
Maliseet	885
Passamaquoddy	2,466
Penobscot	2,407

SOURCE: "1990 census of population and housing. Subject summary tape file (SSTF) 13 (computer file): characteristics of American Indians by tribe and language." Washington, DC: U.S. Department of Commerce, Bureau of the Census, Data User Services Division, 1995.

By the late 1990s the surviving Abenaki tribes such as the Penobscot and the Passamaquoddy were supporting themselves through a variety of business ventures.

DAILY LIFE

Families

Typical Abenaki lived with extended families—families made up of a father, a mother, their children, grandparents, aunts, uncles, and cousins. Several related families lived together in the same large house, but each had its own living space and fire. Family members shared food and possessions, and children repaid their older relatives by taking care of them in their later years. In the summer the family groups lived in separate hunting territories that were inherited through the fathers. Abenaki villages rarely contained more than 100 people.

Buildings

Most Abenaki structures were made out of birch bark. The basic family dwelling for the western Abenaki was the longhouse, in which several families lived together. In winter, when food became scarce, families sometimes moved into cone-shaped wigwams covered with elm-bark mats that resembled the tepees of the Great Plains tribes. Wigwams were not as sturdy as longhouses but could be moved easily when a family was out tracking game.

Eastern Abenaki people built either dome-shaped houses or square houses with roofs shaped like pyramids. Many villages also had dome-shaped sweat lodges where purification ceremonies took place.

Clothing and adornment

The Abenaki made most of their clothing from tanned deerskin. In warm weather men wore breechcloths (flaps of material that were suspended from the waist and covered the front and back) along with sashes that were wrapped around the waist and knotted. Women wore wraparound knee-length skirts. Both men and women sometimes added leggings, buckskin sleeves, and moccasins as the weather got cooler.

In the cold winter months the Abenaki wore many of the same types of garments but made them from heavier materials such as moose hide; men often put on moose hide vests. Winter wear for both men and women included robes made from beaver pelts, fur hoods, and moccasins insulated with rabbit fur. A poncholike piece of skin with a hole or slit cut for the head provided extra warmth.

Both men and women wore their hair long, and women sometimes wore braids. The people wore decorated belts and necklaces and pendants made from shells or slate. Many men hung sheathed knives from their necks.

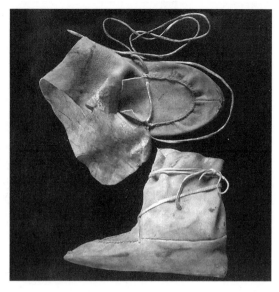

Abenaki moccasins.

Food

Most food was obtained by hunting and fishing along the streams and rivers of Abenaki tribal lands. In spring the people fished from the shore or from canoes for smelt, salmon, sturgeon, shad, alewives, and eels. Their fishing tools included nets, three-pronged spears, and weirs (fencelike enclosures used to trap fish). At night fishing took place by torchlight.

During the summer months coastal groups harvested the ocean for fish, shellfish, and sea mammals. In the fall the Abenaki used bows and arrows to hunt both large and small game. Inland Abenaki fished on frozen ponds during the winter. By wearing snowshoes made from wood and leather, the people could continue hunting moose, deer, bear, beaver, and otter throughout the cold weather. The Abenaki found a use for nearly every portion of a slain animal. Leftover fish were smoked over a fire for later use and extra meat was kept frozen in wooden containers.

Crops such as corn, beans, squash, and tobacco (mostly used for ceremonies) were raised near the rivers. In areas where the soil was less rich, the Abenaki used fish as fertilizer. Every February the western Abenaki collected maple sap, which they boiled to make syrup.

Women picked various greens and gathered food such as beechnuts, butternuts, hickory nuts, and berries that were eaten raw or baked into breads. After the men cleared land near the village, the women planted crops there—beans, corn, and squash among them.

Education

Abenaki children were often raised by their grandparents, aunts, or uncles. They learned tasks that were considered appropriate for their gender. Boys were taught the skills needed for hunting and warfare and began practicing with a bow and arrow at a very young age. By 12 they were permitted to go hunting with the men of the family. Girls were taught how to weave baskets, grow crops, gather foods, sew clothing, and tend to smaller children.

In the late twentieth century the Abenaki of Vermont began an Indian Education Program, a scholarship fund, a women's support group, and a children's dance company to educate their children in both the old and new ways.

Healing practices

Healers, or shamans, took care of the religious and medical needs in an Abenaki village. Most shamans were male. They used a variety of methods to cure the sick, including sweating and treatment with herbs, laxatives, teas, and salves (sticky substances applied to wounds or sores). European colonists learned about the use of plant medicines from the shamans; the use of these age-old treatments continues today.

If the use of herbs proved unsuccessful, shamans called upon special, magical remedies to treat illness. They might attempt to blow or dance an illness away, sometimes placing the patient on a surface covered with magical signs. If it became obvious that an afflicted person was near death, villagers brought the event about more quickly by letting the patient starve—a practice they considered kind.

ARTS

Birch bark boxes and baskets

The Abenaki were known for the objects they fashioned out of the bark of white birch trees that grew in their region. Birch bark was divided into flexible, waterproof sheets and shaped into such things as baskets, boxes, and canoes. Besides being useful, many of the objects were works of art. Sharp utensils were used to scrape the surface of birch boxes and expose the inner bark, producing contrasting patterns

A Penobscot woman in "Gala Day" apparel: a pierced metal hat with feathers, wampum necklace, and metal discs, 1884.

of dark and light woods. The Abenaki also created beautiful baskets by weaving strips of ash wood together or by twisting or braiding sweet grass. Such baskets are still sold throughout Maine and Quebec.

CUSTOMS

Games and festivities

Games have always played an important role in Abenaki culture. Boys began to race when they were small, and archery was considered an important part of a boy's development into an adult. Handball and lacrosse (a game played with a ball and netted sticks) were among the most popular games. The feats of ball players were central to many Abenaki stories, including one that tells of a fantastic game in which the players had lights of many colors on their heads and wore belts made of rainbows.

A Penobscot man in "Gala Day" apparel: feathered headdress, wampum tie, pierced metal arm band, and vest with ribbon and bead appliqué, 1884.

The Abenaki liked to sing and tell stories while carrying out their daily chores. They also enjoyed riddles and word games. Dancing and singing was featured at most major social events, including marriages, the coming of visitors, funerals, and the first corn harvest. At the end of the 1990s the Abenaki of Odanak, Quebec, still held an annual summer festival that revolved around storytelling, music, Native foods, and political and social discussions.

War and hunting rituals

When conflicts broke out with other peoples, the Abenaki war chief stood up with a red club in his hands and asked for volunteers to unite for the fight. Other men known for their leadership skills also stood up and asked for warriors to join them in forming battle groups of ten. Then the men feasted and danced well into the night. Before beginning a battle, they painted their faces red and drew pictures of past battle victories on their bodies.

Puberty

Around the time of puberty an Abenaki boy embarked on a vision quest—a long period of fasting in the woods, during which the young man waited alone for the appearance of the guardian spirit who was to guide him through life. Males were considered adults by the age of fifteen.

A girl's first menstrual period signaled the arrival of womanhood and her readiness for marriage. Menstruating women were isolated from others in a special wigwam and were not allowed to participate in their usual tasks because menstrual blood was considered powerful, even dangerous. Some girls also undertook vision quests.

Marriage

When a young man wanted to marry, he sent a representative to visit his intended bride with gifts to entice her into the marriage. If she refused the gifts, it meant that she rejected the proposal. If she and her parents agreed, the couple began a trial period of living together, although they were supervised by chaperons and were not yet allowed to engage in sexual relations.

Marriages became official when the groom's family accepted gifts offered by the bride's family and a wedding celebration was held. For western Abenaki it was customary for couples to live with the man's family after marriage; if the bride's family were wealthier, though, the couple would go to live with them. Eastern Abenaki newlyweds usually resided with the bride's family. Some chiefs of the eastern Abenaki were permitted to have several wives.

Funerals

The bodies of deceased Abenaki were dressed in their finest clothing, wrapped in birch bark, and tied with a cord. They were buried quickly so their spirits would not linger over the corpse and the village. Graves contained food for the deceased person's journey to the other world, as well as things such as weapons, tools, and personal items to use in the afterlife.

In winter the remains of the dead were placed on a high platform until the earth thawed in the spring and the corpse could be buried. If a man died during a hunting trip, his body was placed above ground; the first person to find the body in the spring was expected to bury it.

Widows wore hoods on their heads and did not participate in social events for one year after the death of a husband. After the death of a child, a grieving mother would usually cut off her hair and blacken her face. Relatives brought presents to the parents to help ease their pain; in return the parents sometimes held a feast.

CURRENT TRIBAL ISSUES

In the 1980s the Abenaki Indians of Vermont began a court battle for the right to hunt, fish, and travel on their traditional lands. In 1992 the Vermont Supreme Court ruled that all such Abenaki rights had ended. But the Vermont band fought on, and in the late 1990s the General Assembly of Vermont recognized the tribal status of the Abenaki people, meaning that an official relationship existed between the state and the Abenaki of Vermont. As a result, a commission on Abenaki affairs was created to work out matters of concern to both the tribe and the state and to aid the tribe in its efforts to achieve recognition by the U.S. government. When the federal government recognizes a group of Native Americans as an Indian tribe, special services such as health care and educational opportunities become available to them, and they usually are granted the right to use their homeland for hunting and fishing purposes. As of late 1998 the Abenaki were still working hard to attain this recognition.

NOTABLE PEOPLE

Joseph E. Bruchac III, Ph.D. (1942–), is an award-winning author and poet whose works reflect his Native American heritage. (He is also of Slovakian and English descent.) Bruchac's stories and poems emphasize the importance of spiritual balance and address environmental concerns as well. His books, which include many stories for children, have been widely published. The author has also launched a much-praised multicultural literary magazine.

A Penobscot named Louis Francis Sockalexis (1871–1913) was the first Native American to play professional baseball. He was an outstanding hitter for the Cleveland Spiders, but his career was cut short by a serious alcohol problem. He later worked as an umpire, basket weaver, canoeist, woodsman, and ferryman on the Penobscot River. In 1915 the Cleveland team was renamed the "Indians" in his honor (although in the 1980s and 1990s many Natives protested the use of Indian names in sports as demeaning and stereotyping.)

Samoset (1590–1653) was a sachem (chief) who lived on an island off the coast of present-day Maine. He served as a mediator (or go-between) between the Pilgrims and Native American groups. Samoset helped to create the first peace treaty between whites and the Wampanoag tribe (see entry). He also signed the first land deed in America, giving nearly 12,000 acres of Native lands to whites.

FURTHER READING

Information on the Abenaki language is available on the World Wide Web at http://www.hmt.com/abenaki/language/html.

Landau, Elaine. *The Abenaki*. New York: Franklin Watts, 1996.

Prins, Harald E. "Abenaki." In *American Indians*. Vol. 1. Edited by Harvey Markowitz. Pasadena, CA: Salem Press, 1995.

Iroquois Confederacy

For more information on an individual tribe within the Iroquois Confederacy, please see the Mohawk entry that follows.

Name

Iroquois (pronounced *EAR-uh-kwoy*) Confederacy. The Iroquois call themselves *Haudenosaunee* (pronounced *hoo-dee-noh-SHAW-nee*), meaning "people of the longhouse." The nations that were members of the Iroquois Confederacy, also known as the Five (later Six) Nations of the Haudenosaunee, thought of themselves as forming a longhouse (the typical Iroquois dwelling), with the different tribes at important corners of the jointly run central building.

Location

The tribes of the Iroquois Confederacy lived in west central New York in the early seventeenth century. They now own eight reservations in New York and Wisconsin, and two in Ontario, Canada, where members of the various tribes of the Iroquois Confederacy reside. There are also Iroquois living near Montreal, Quebec, Canada, along the St. Lawrence River.

Population

There were 5,500 Iroquois in the seventeenth century. In a census (count of the population) done in 1990, 52,557 people said they were members of Iroquois tribes, making the Iroquois the country's seventh-largest Native American group. In 1995, U.S. and Canadian census figures reported a total of 74,518 Iroquois in the two countries.

Language family

Iroquoian.

Origins and group affiliations

The six tribes of the Iroquois Confederacy are: Cayuga, Mohawk, Oneida, Onondaga, Seneca, and Tuscarora. Five of the six tribes that make up the Iroquois Confederacy probably originated in present-day New York. The sixth tribe, the Tuscarora, came from North Carolina.

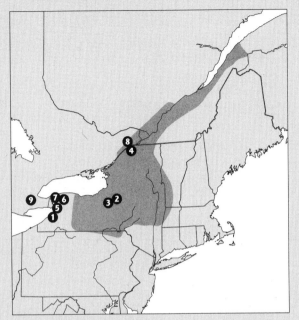

IROQUOIS CONFEDERACY

Contemporary Communities

New York

1. Cayuga Nation
2. Oneida Nation
3. Onondaga Nation
4. St. Regis Mohawk Tribe
5. Seneca Nation
6. Tonawanda Band of Seneca
7. Tuscarora Nation

Ontario

8. Mohawks of Akwesasne
9. Six Nations Reserve

Wisconsin

(Not on map) Oneida Nation of Wisconsin

Shaded area: Traditional lands of the tribes of the Iroquois Confederacy in present-day New York, and Ontario, Canada.

The Iroquois Confederacy was an association of five tribes (later six) who lived in the northeastern woodlands at the time of the first contact with Europeans. Theirs was a sophisticated society of some 5,500 people when the first white explorers encountered it at the beginning of the seventeenth century. The confederacy is said to be the only nation of Indians in the New World that was never conquered by white people. Today, Iroquoian tribes own seven reservations in New York state, one in Wisconsin, and more in Canada. The majority of the people live away from the reservations.

HISTORY

Legends of heroes

The legends about the formation of the ancient Iroquois Confederacy are probably composites of the many different actual people and events that brought about the peaceful union of the great tribes of the Haudenosaunee. As legend has it, sometime around the mid- to late-fifteenth century, the Mohawk, Onondaga, Seneca, Cayuga, and

Oneida nations engaged in near-constant warfare with one another and with neighboring tribes. This period, known as the "dark times," reached its lowest point during the reign of an Onondaga chief named Todadaho. People said that Chief Todadaho knew and saw everything, that his hair contained a tangle of snakes, and that he could kill with only a look. He was also reported to be a cannibal, in the Mohawk tradition in which eating one's victims in battle was thought to provide a warrior with their war skills.

Into this warlike era entered a heroic figure, Deganawida, a member of either the Huron or the Mohawk tribe. Frustrated with the warring going on in his own village, Deganawida journeyed far from home. He met up with Hiawatha (either Mohawk or Onondoga). Hiawatha spoke to him about rules of life, good government, and peace. Impressed, Deganawida brought Hiawatha back to his own village to teach his people these rules. Then the two men went to other nations, and soon the Mohawk, Oneida, and Cayuga nations had united, persuaded by these two messengers of peace. One day they came upon the home of Todadaho.

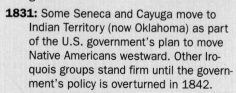

IMPORTANT DATES

1350–1600: The Iroquois Confederacy is formed.

1799: Handsome Lake develops the New Religion.

1831: Some Seneca and Cayuga move to Indian Territory (now Oklahoma) as part of the U.S. government's plan to move Native Americans westward. Other Iroquois groups stand firm until the government's policy is overturned in 1842.

1924: Congress passes legislation conferring U.S. citizenship on all American Indians. The Iroquois reject citizenship.

1942: As hostilities leading to World War II mount, the Iroquois exercise their powers as an independent nation to declare war on Germany, Italy, and Japan.

Todadaho sees the light

According to one legend, Deganawida watched through a hole in the roof as the cannibal prepared to cook his latest victim. Seeing Deganawida's face reflected in the cooking pot, Todadaho felt that, as a man with such a beautiful face, he no longer wanted to eat his victim. Going outside to dispose of the corpse, he met Deganawida. The stranger's words were so convincing that Todadaho became a loyal follower and helped spread the message of peace. In another legend, when Todadaho encountered the two messengers, his rage sprouted from him in the form of serpents growing from his head. Deganawida (or Hiawatha) asked the chief to join the confederacy, and then reached forward and combed the serpents from his head. In both versions, the Onondaga chief agreed to join the union.

So it was that sometime between the years 1350 and 1600, Deganawida and Hiawatha made peace among the five warring tribes and established the Iroquois Confederacy ruled by the Great Law. It was a league of nations that shared a positive code of values and lived in mutual harmony. The governmental structure of the Iroquois Confed-

An illustration of an Iroquois village on Manhattan Island before the Dutch arrived.

eracy was made up of the Grand Council of Chiefs, which included the Chief of the Chiefs and 49 other chiefs: nine chiefs from the Mohawk, eight from the Onondoga, ten from the Cayuga, and eight from the Seneca. The Great Law also established rules for settling blood disputes, thus gradually resolving some generations-old cycles of feuding.

Europeans affect Iroquois way of life

When the first white explorers arrived in Iroquois territory in the early seventeenth century, they found a settled agricultural (farming) society. Members of the Confederacy lived more or less peacefully among themselves, but continued to carry out raids against other tribes. During these raids the Iroquois were first introduced to European goods, acquired by the other tribes from French traders who had settled in Canada. European metal axes, knives, hoes, and kettles replaced traditional Iroquois implements of stone, bone, shell, and wood. Soon European woven cloth began to replace the animal skins used for clothing materials.

The tribes who were being raided by the Iroquois formed an alliance with the French and they attacked the Iroquois in 1609. In this way the Iroquois were introduced to French body armor made of metal (Iroquois armor was made of slatted wood). The French fought with firearms, far more destructive than the traditional Iroquois weapons—bows and arrows, stone tomahawks, and wooden war clubs.

In response to these European influences, the Iroquois gradually changed their fighting style. Instead of brute power, they used stealth, surprise, and ambush. Their motives for fighting also changed. In the past, they had fought for prestige or revenge, or to obtain goods or captives. Now they fought for economic advantage, seeking control over bountiful beaver-hunting grounds or perhaps a stash of beaver skins to trade for European goods.

The European presence in their territory proved disastrous for the Iroquois tribes. Diseases brought to North America by Europeans—smallpox, measles, influenza (flu), lung infections, and even the common cold—took a heavy toll because the Native people had developed no immunity (natural resistance) to these newly introduced diseases.

Sixth tribe joins Confederacy

Early in the eighteenth century the Tuscarora, an Iroquoian-speaking tribe living in North Carolina, moved into the territory occupied by the Confederacy. They were fleeing from European settlers and traders, who cheated them and took their people as slaves. Although they came from far away, the Tuscarora found they spoke the same basic language as the other Iroquois. In 1722 the Tuscarora became the sixth nation of the Iroquois Confederacy.

The eighteenth century saw the Iroquois involved in two devastating wars. The French and Indian War, which erupted in 1754, pitted the French and some Native tribes against the British. The American Revolutionary War began in 1775. Members of the Iroquois Confederacy did not agree on which sides to support in these wars. Most favored the British, seeing them as less a threat than the colonists who coveted Indian lands. When the Revolutionary War ended in 1783, the victorious Americans punished those tribes that had sided with the British. Many Iroquois were driven from their homelands, and the unity of the Confederacy was badly disrupted.

Cultures clash

Major changes in Iroquois culture took place in the 1800s. Alarmed that traditional Iroquois ways were giving way to European culture, many Iroquois turned to a religious movement called the New Religion (see "Religion"). It put new vitality into Iroquois culture, which was about to be severely strained by white settlers pushing westward onto Indian lands.

To make way for settlers, the U.S. government constantly devised schemes for opening Indian land for white settlement. One scheme was called assimilation, a process in which Native Americans were expected to give up their old ways and acquire white American ways, such as farming small plots of land rather than land in common. To further the goal of assimilation, members of the Quaker religion arrived to teach the Iroquois to read and write and to instruct them in modern farming methods. Men were encouraged to work on farms. Respected Seneca warrior Gaiantwaka, known as Cornplanter, helped bring about the change to a farming lifestyle, as did his half brother, Ganiodayo (Handsome Lake).

Throughout the nineteenth century, the Iroquois sold large amounts of land in exchange for trade goods. Shrinking land holdings made hunting increasingly difficult and left the men with little to do. Many men did not want to be seen doing the "women's work" of farming, but encouraged by Quakers, more and more Iroquois families left the longhouses and lived separately on small farms where the men could work in their fields unseen by their neighbors.

Iroquois resist

In 1830 the U.S. Congress passed the Removal Act, which directed that all Indians should be moved to "Indian Territory," the area of present-day Kansas and Oklahoma. In 1831 some Seneca did move to Indian Territory, but a core group of the Iroquois people continued to resist efforts to assimilate them into American culture or remove them from their home. Finally, the removal policy was overturned in 1842 and ownership of some Seneca land was restored.

In 1924 Congress passed legislation conferring U.S. citizenship on all American Indians; the Iroquois rejected such status. The Iroquois see themselves as a sovereign nation, which is a nation within a nation, with the right to make its own decisions. They do not see themselves as another ethnic group within the United States or Canadian population. (In fact, federal law and over 400 treaties grant U.S. Indian tribes the power to act as independent nations). The Iroquois have asserted their position in interesting ways. For example, when the United States declared war on Germany in World War I in 1917, the Iroquois Confederacy issued its own independent declaration of war, claiming status as a separate nation in the war effort. In 1949 a delegation representing the Iroquois as a nation attended ground-breaking ceremonies for the United Nations building in New York City. Iroquois statesmen and athletes use Iroquois passports when they travel around the world.

Canada's Iroquois today

The Iroquois in Canada published a Declaration of Independence in 1970. They were responding to efforts by the Canadian government to force Indians to become Canadian citizens, which would make them subject to Canadian laws and make their lands subject to taxes. The declaration stated in part: "we, the Lords, Warriors, Principle Women and People, do hereby proclaim to the Dominion of Canada and to the Nations of the World, that we, the People of the Six Nations Iroquois Confederacy of the Great League of Peace . . . [are] politically sovereign and independent in our rights to administer over our domestic concerns. . . . we are obliged by conscience to declare and proclaim the right and responsibility of our authority for our lands, our laws and our people."

Canada's Minister of Indian Affairs rejected the Iroquois claim of sovereignty. He stated: "It is impossible to have a nation within a nation. Our nation is Canada and the Indian people of Canada are Canadians." These opposing viewpoints continue to cause problems between the Iroquois people and the government of Canada.

U.S. IROQUOIS POPULATION BY TRIBE: 1990

In 1990, census takers asked American Indians in the United States to identify what tribes they belonged to. Those who identified themselves as Iroquois said they belonged to the tribes listed below; these numbers do not reflect Canadian Iroquois.

Tribe	Population in 1990
Cayuga	1,111
Iroquois	5,158
Mohawk	17,106
Oneida	11,307
Onondaga	1,729
Seneca	8,263

SOURCE: "1990 census of population and housing. Subject summary tape file (SSTF) 13 (computer file): characteristics of American Indians by tribe and language." Washington, DC: U.S. Department of Commerce, Bureau of the Census, Data

RELIGION

From ancient times the Iroquois believed that a powerful spirit some called Orenda created everything that is good and useful, while the Evil Spirit made things that are poisonous.

Many Iroquois were converted to Catholicism by French Jesuit missionaries in the seventeenth century. Quaker, Baptist, Methodist, and other church groups joined the effort to convert the Iroquois. An intense rivalry developed between those who clung to the old ways and the new Christian factions.

The New Religion

In 1799, the Iroquois way of life was eroding. Land had been lost and living conditions on the reservations were poor. Many Iroquois began to experience alcohol abuse, fighting, disintegration of family structure, and other hardships. At this time, a revival of the ancient

The title page of A Primer for the Use of Mohawk Children, *by Daniel Clause, 1781.*

Longhouse religion developed. It was led by a Seneca known as Handsome Lake (c. 1735–1815). He had spent much of his life in loose living and fell gravely ill when he was about sixty-five years old. He expected to die, but instead he experienced a vision and recovered. Inspired, Handsome Lake began to spread the Good Word among his fellow Iroquois. His New Religion was a combination of ancient Native beliefs and Quakerism.

The New Religion called for abstaining from alcoholic beverages (alcohol was introduced by Europeans and had become a problem for many Indians). The New Religion also called for abandoning witchcraft. The fact that Handsome Lake's message had come in a dream made a profound impression on his followers, because the Iroquois believed that important information was revealed to people in dreams. Handsome Lake's religion helped show the Iroquois how to retain their own culture while adapting to a world dominated by non-Indians.

The Code of Handsome Lake was published around 1850 and was revered throughout Iroquois nations in Canada and the United States. The Longhouse religion is practiced only by Iroquois nations. Today perhaps half of the Iroquois people are followers of the Code of Handsome Lake. Some practice only the Longhouse religion, while others maintain a simultaneous membership in a Christian church. Every other fall, members of the Six Nations come together for a traditional Longhouse religion ceremony.

LANGUAGE

The six Iroquoian dialects (varieties) are similar enough to allow members of different tribes to talk easily with one another. It has been noted that in the Iroquois language there might be many terms to describe characteristics of a single animal, but there would be no general word for animal. Or there might be words for a good man, good woman, or good dog, but no word for goodness.

The Iroquois language was written down in the twentieth century. Dictionaries and grammar texts have been developed for teaching the languages on the reservations.

GOVERNMENT

The Iroquois tribes were divided into clans (groups of related families), each with an animal name (Bear, Beaver, Turtle, and so on). In early times, each clan was led by the clan mother, who was usually the oldest woman in the group. In consultation with the other women, the clan mother chose one or more men to serve as clan chiefs. Each chief was appointed for life but the clan mother and her advisors could remove him from office if he failed to carry out his duties. Handsome Lake and his followers revived this traditional system of chieftainship, and today it is present on the Onondaga, Tuscarora, and Tonawanda Seneca reservations in New York.

Under the Iroquois Confederacy, forty-nine chiefs from the various tribes were chosen to act as tribal representatives at annual meetings of the Great Council. (This method of governing, as well as Iroquois ideas of political equality and freedom, separation of powers, and checks and balances between different parts of government, was used as a model by the founding fathers of the United States when they were forming a government for the new nation.) All decisions of the Confederacy were to be made by a unanimous vote of the chiefs, meaning they all had to vote the same way. However, if they did not reach unanimous agreement, then they agreed to disagree and the individual nations were free to act on their own.

When the Tuscarora Nation joined the confederacy at the invitation of the Oneida sometime after 1717, they were allowed no chiefs in the council, but the Oneida represented them in council. Thereafter, the Five Nations of the Iroquois Confederacy became known as the Six Nations.

In the 1800s, both the Mohawk and the Seneca living within the United States abandoned their traditional clan-based structure and established elective tribal governments. Other tribes eventually did the same, either abandoning their ancestral governments or modifying them to add elections. Traditionalists clung to the ancient structure, however, and today two competing sets of governments exist on several reservations.

ECONOMY

Even before the Europeans came to America, the Iroquois were an agricultural society. The primary crops were regarded as sacred gifts from the Creator. Corn, beans, and squash were called the Three Sisters: corn provided stalks for climbing bean vines, while squash plants controlled weeds by covering the soil. In addition to providing food, the corn plants were used to make a variety of other goods, for personal use or for trade with other tribes. After the Europeans came, the Iroquois traded furs, especially beaver, for European goods.

Today more than two-thirds of the Iroquois live in cities. Some work in construction, especially factory work, and in health, education, and retail professions. In a modern version of their ancient travels away from the village to hunt, Iroquois men today may support families living on the reservation by living and working in a city but returning home regularly. For example, many Mohawk live in Brooklyn, New York, during the week but return to their families on weekends.

Iroquois men, especially Mohawk, are famous as ironworkers in construction. They walk steel girders high in the air, and are known for showing little fear of heights. Consequently, they are in demand around the country for skyscraper and bridge building projects, which have included such landmarks as the World Trade Center in New York City and the Golden Gate Bridge in San Francisco, California. Fathers pass their ironworking tools on to their sons (or sometimes daughters) in a ceremony.

About half of those living outside cities actually live on reservations. There, unemployment and underemployment (lack of high-paying jobs) are constant problems. A large number of people on the reservations work for the tribal governments. About one-fifth of the Iroquois people on reservations who want to work are not able to find work.

DAILY LIFE

Families

The routines of Iroquois family life depended on the seasons. When the weather was right, for example, Iroquois men set out on hunting expeditions in dugout or bark canoes to provide meat and hides, while the women tended to the farming and other tasks associated with providing food. They also had primary responsibility for child rearing. Young girls were responsible for caring for younger brothers and sisters or for their cousins if they had no siblings.

Buildings

Extended families (including mother, father, and children plus relatives) of up to 50 people lived together in bark-covered, wooden-framed longhouses that were 50 to 150 feet long. Longhouses were constructed with a small entrance hall at each end that could be used

Iroquois steel workers in New York City on the steel frame of a building, 1925.

by all residents. Within the body of the house, a central corridor eight feet wide separated two banks of compartments. Each compartment was occupied by a nuclear family (father, mother, and children).

Within the longhouse compartment, a raised wooden platform served as a bed by night and chair by day; some compartments included small bunks for children. An overhead shelf held personal belongings. Every 20 feet along the central corridor, a fire pit served the two families living on its opposite sides. Bark or hide doors at the ends of the buildings were attached at the top; these openings and the smoke holes in the roof 15 to 20 feet above each hearth provided the only ventilation.

Villages of 300 to 600 people were protected by a triple-walled stockade, consisting of wooden stakes 15 to 20 feet tall that were buried in the ground. About every 15 years the nearby supplies of wild game and firewood would become depleted, and the farmed soil would become exhausted. During a period of two years or so, the men would find and clear another site for the village, which would then be completely rebuilt. While traditional longhouses are no longer built, buildings on Iroquois reservations reserved for religious activity are referred to as longhouses.

Clothing and adornment

The major item of traditional men's clothing was a breechcloth made of a strip of deerskin or fabric. It passed between the legs and was secured at the waist by a belt or sash. Decorated flaps hung in the front and back. The belt was a favorite article. Sometimes worn only around the waist, and sometimes also over the left shoulder, it was woven on a loom or on the fingers, and might be decorated with beadwork.

Items of clothing that were worn by both sexes included a fringed, sleeveless tunic, separate sleeves (connected to each other by thongs but not connected to the tunic), leggings, moccasins, and a robe or blanket. Clothing was adorned with moose-hair embroidery featuring curved line figures with coiled ends. Decorated pouches for carrying personal items completed the costumes.

By the end of the eighteenth century, cloth obtained from European traders replaced deerskin as the primary clothing material. Imported glass beads replaced porcupine quills as decorative elements. In the mid-1800s a sudden change occurred in the style of artwork used to decorate clothing with beads, quills, and embroidery. Rather than the traditional patterns of curving lines and scrolls, designs became images of plants and flowers, influenced by the floral style prominent among the seventeenth- and eighteenth-century French.

Food

Corn was the traditional staple of the Iroquois diet. It was baked or boiled and eaten on or off the cob; the kernels were mashed and either fried, baked in a kettle, or spread on corn leaves that were folded and boiled to form a dish called *tamales* (pronounced *tuh-MA-lees*). Some varieties of corn were processed into a concoction called hominy by boiling the kernels in a weak lye solution of hardwood ashes and water. Bread, pudding, dumplings, and cooked cereal were made from cornmeal. Parched corn coffee was brewed by mixing roasted corn with boiling water.

Besides corn and the beans and squash they raised with it, the Iroquois people ate a wide variety of other plant foods. Wild fruits, nuts, and roots were gathered to supplement the crops they grew. Berries were dried for year-round use. Maple sap was used for sweetening, but salt was not commonly used.

The traditional diet featured more than thirty types of meat, including deer, bear, beaver, rabbit, and squirrel. Fresh meat was enjoyed during the hunting season, and some was smoked or dried and used in corn dishes during the rest of the year. The Iroquois used the region's waterways to travel, but fish was relatively unimportant as food.

Education

Traditionally, mothers had primary responsibility for raising children and teaching them good behavior. Children learned informally by watching their family and clan elders. Girls learned practical skills by watching the women in the longhouse. Boys began learning to hunt with miniature bows and arrows and blowguns when they were about six years old. Lessons about life and Iroquois history were incorporated in the stories told around the fire.

Children were not spanked, but they might be punished by splashing water in their faces. Difficult children might be frightened into better behavior by a visit from someone wearing the frightening mask of Longnose, a cannibal clown.

Today, most children attend American or Canadian public and private schools. Some reservations operate their own Indian schools, where children (usually in the lower grades) can learn about the old ways as well as modern ways.

Healing practices

Traditional Iroquois rituals dealt with both physical and mental health issues. Medicine men or women were called shamans (pronounced *SHAH-munz* or *SHAY-munz*). They fought disorders caused by evil spirits, and they used herbs and natural ointments to treat physical ailments including fevers, coughs, and snake bites. They also cleaned wounds and set broken bones.

Another type of healer, known as a conjurer, used chants to fight ailments caused by witchcraft. The conjurer might remove an affliction from the patient's body by blowing or sucking. Twice a year, groups of masked people called False Faces visited each house in the village, waving pine boughs and casting out sickness.

In Iroquois healing practices, the soul was the source of a person's physical and mental health, and dreams were considered the language of the soul. Everyone in the community felt a responsibility to help solve others' problems by reading their dreams, a process called dream guessing.

ARTS

The Iroquois have a rich ceremonial tradition involving music and dancing. From the time of the first contact with Europeans until World War II (1939–45), many Native American dances were discouraged by missionaries and by government officials, who wanted the Natives to adopt the ways of the white society. Nevertheless, the Iroquois preserved some of their traditional dances, both social and sacred. Sacred dances celebrate the creation of the world, while social dances are for amusement. The dancers are accompanied by the music of drums and turtle shell rattles, which are still made by Iroquois artisans. Flutes are used in sacred dances but not for social dancing.

The Iroquois were especially skilled at carving masks. The use of masks, or "false faces," is still a part of their rituals. The masks symbolize spirit forces that are represented by the person wearing the mask at festivals or healing ceremonies.

Storytelling was a prized ritual, a way of teaching moral values and tribal history. In the winter, Iroquois families would gather around the fire to hear stories told by people who had perfected the art. (See the Mohawk entry for an example of Iroquois oral literature.)

CUSTOMS

Birth and naming

A hut located outside the village served as the birthing site. As her time drew near, the expectant mother and a few other women withdrew to the hut and remained there until a few days after the birth. Until the child could walk, it spent its days attached to a wooden board called a cradleboard, which the mother hung from a tree branch while she worked in the fields.

Iroquois mask and rattle.

The Iroquois tribes are organized into eight clans (groups of related families), and at birth each person becomes a member of the clan of his or her mother. Members of a clan are considered to be blood relatives, regardless of whether they are members of the Mohawk, Seneca, or other Iroquois tribes.

Traditionally, babies were named at birth, but when the child reached puberty, an adult name was given. Names referred to natural occurrences (such as the Moon or thunder), landscape features, occupations, and social or ceremonial roles. Some examples of Iroquois names are: In the Center of the Sky, Hanging Flower, He Carries News, and Mighty Speaker. A person was never addressed by name during conversation. When speaking about a person, especially to a relative, the name was only used if the person could not otherwise be clearly identified by using other words.

Puberty

Puberty marked the time of acceptance into adult membership in the society. On the occasion of her first menstrual period, a girl would retire to an isolated hut and stay there for as long as her period lasted. She was required to perform difficult tasks, such as chopping hardwood with a dull axe, and was prohibited from eating certain foods.

A young man had a longer trial. When his voice began to change, he went to live in a secluded cabin in the forest for up to a year. An old man or woman took responsibility for overseeing his well-being. He ate sparingly, and his time was spent in physically demanding activities such as running, swimming, bathing in icy water, and scraping his shins with a stone. His quest was completed when he was visited by his spirit, which would remain with him during his adult life.

Marriage

In the Iroquois tradition, a man and woman wishing to marry would tell their parents, who then arranged a joint meeting of relatives to discuss the suitability of the two people for marriage to each other. If there were no objections, a day was chosen for the marriage feast. On the appointed day, the woman's relatives would bring her to the groom's home for the festivities. Following the meal, elders from the groom's family spoke to the bride about wifely duties, and elders from the bride's family told the groom about husbandly responsibilities. Then the two began their new life together.

Divorce

In old times, when a woman was unfaithful to her husband, she was punished by whipping, but the man who was her partner in the unfaithful act was not punished. If a married couple decided to separate, both of their families would be called to a council. The parties would state their reasons for wanting a divorce, and the elders would try to convince the couple to stay together. If those efforts failed, the marriage ended. In ancient times, fathers kept their sons and mothers kept their daughters when a divorce occurred. By the early eighteenth century, however, mothers usually kept all of the children.

Festivals

Along with founding the Longhouse Religion, Handsome Lake revived the traditional Midwinter Ceremony, still considered by the Iroquois to be the most important of their ceremonies. Handsome Lake added four sacred rituals: The Feather Dance, Thanksgiving Dance, Rite of Personal Chant, and Bowl Game (also known as the Peach Stone Game).

The week-long Midwinter Ceremony, a time of renewal and thanksgiving, is held in late January or early February during the new

"Lacrosse Player," drawing by Seneca artist Jesse Cornplanter, 1908.

midwinter moon. To announce the beginning of the ceremony, medicine mask messengers appear at every house to stir the ashes of cold fires. At this time, names are announced for newborns or children adopting adult names. (Iroquois children are given a birth name and a new name when they are initiated into adulthood.) In former times, public confessions were part of the ceremony; those who admitted to failures pledged to reform.

In the spring, when the sap rose, it was time for the Thanks-to-the-Maple Festival. This one-day celebration included social dances and the ceremonial burning of tobacco at the base of a maple tree. In May or June, corn seeds saved from the previous year were blessed at the Corn Planting Ceremony. This was a half-day observance in which the Creator was thanked and spirit forces were begged for sufficient rain and moderate sun. Ripening strawberries in June signaled time for the Strawberry Festival. Dancers mimicked the motions of berry pickers. This one-day celebration was a time for giving thanks.

In August or early September, the corn was ready to eat. This event was marked by the Green Corn Festival, which involved ceremonies over four mornings. When all the crops had been harvested and stored away, and before the men left for the fall hunt, the Harvest Festival was held. This one-day celebration took place in October.

War etiquette

A strict code of honor governed warfare among the tribes. A tribe that was attacked was bound by the code to attack in return; if a tribe did not do so, its members were labeled cowards. Deaths had to be avenged. Before departing to conduct a war, the Iroquois held a war dance, a costumed event in which chiefs gave speeches about their past victories; the speeches were designed to excite a passion for revenge among the listeners. Then the warriors broke into a vigorous dance, featuring war cries by the chiefs and responses from the others. According to Lewis Morgan, an authority on the Iroquois who wrote in about 1850: "[A] well-conducted War dance is the highest entertainment known among the Iroquois."

Iroquois unearthing the bones of ancestors for reburial.

Death rituals

When a person died, everyone who had names similar to the deceased gave them up until a period of mourning was completed. Later, when new people were adopted into the clan, they were often given the name of the deceased person whose place they took. A wake was held the night following a death (a wake is a watch over the body of a dead person before burial). After a midnight meal, the best speakers of the village spoke about the deceased, and about life and death in general.

The body was placed on a scaffold (a raised platform) for several days on the chance that the person only appeared dead and might revive (which sometimes happened!). Eventually the remains were buried or the bones might be housed in or near the family lodge after they were picked clean by animals. When the village relocated, all of the unburied skeletons were placed in a common grave. By the end of the nineteenth century, burials were conducted according to European customs.

CURRENT TRIBAL ISSUES

Preservation of traditional values and artifacts

Much of the longstanding friction between the Iroquois and non-Indians has involved different attitudes toward land. During one land dispute, the grave of Seneca Chief Cornplanter had to be moved to make way for a dam. His descendant Harriett Pierce commented: "The White man views land for its money value. We Indians have a spiritual tie with the earth, a reverence for it that Whites don't share and can hardly understand."

For decades, the Iroquois have worked to reclaim articles they consider sacred and the remains of dead ancestors being held in museums. In 1972 archaeologists were ordered to stop digging up Native burial sites in New York state. Tribal members were notified to arrange proper reburials for any remains unearthed accidentally. Wampum belts (embroidered belts made from strings of white beads) held by the New York State Museum in Albany were removed from public display after Indians complained that they were being treated as curiosities, without proper respect being paid. The belts were finally returned to the Onondaga in 1989. Years of effort were rewarded in the early 1990s when the Smithsonian Institution in Washington, D.C., pledged to return human remains, objects buried with them, sacred objects, and other articles of importance to Indian tribes.

Traditional values are sustained on the various Iroquois reservations. The ancient languages are spoken and taught, traditional ceremonies are observed, and baskets are woven. Material wealth is not characteristic of reservation Indians, but Tonawanda Seneca Chief Corbett Sundown, keeper of the Iroquois "spiritual fire," denies that the people are poor. He told *National Geographic* writer Arden Harvey: "We're rich people without any money, that's all. You say we ought to set up industries and factories. Well, we just don't want them. How're you going to grow potatoes and sweet corn on concrete? You call that progress? To me 'progress' is a dirty word."

NOTABLE PEOPLE

Oren Lyons (c. 1930–) is an Onondaga chief who achieved recognition for his excellence in the traditional Iroquois sport of lacrosse as well as at boxing. (Lacrosse is a game of Native American origin. It is played on a field by two teams of ten players each. Participants use a long-handled stick with a webbed pouch to try and get a ball into the opposing team's goal.) An artist, author, publisher, illustrator, and tribal faithkeeper, Lyons works on behalf of indigenous (native) people around the world. In 1992 he became the first indigenous leader to address the United Nations General Assembly.

Ely Samuel Parker (1828–1895) (also known by the Seneca name Ha-sa-no-an-da) was a tribal leader descended from such major Seneca figures as Handsome Lake, Cornplanter, and Red Jacket. A man of many and varied talents, he served as a valued military assistant to General Ulysses S. Grant during the Civil War (1861-65) and helped prepare the terms of surrender that ended the war. He collaborated with anthropologist and author Lewis Henry Morgan on the first extensive study of Iroquois culture. After Grant was elected president of the United States in 1869, Parker was appointed Commissioner of Indian Affairs. He thus became the first Native American to head the office that controlled federal Indian policies.

John Napoleon Brinton Hewitt (1859–1937) was an influential Tuscaroran authority on American Indians. It was he who brought to the world's attention the fact that the Iroquois Confederacy inspired the framers of the U.S. Constitution. He wrote many articles and preserved dozens of Indian legends that might otherwise have been lost.

Gary Dale Farmer (1953–) is a Cayuga actor, producer, and activist who has spoken out against negative portrayals of Native Americans in the media. He has lodged protests against the casting of non-Natives to play Natives in the movies. Farmer has appeared in such films as *Friday the Thirteenth* (1980), *Police Academy* (1984), and *The Dark Wind* (1992).

Roberta Hill Whiteman (1947–) is an Oneida poet and teacher, best known for her 1984 book *Star Quilt*. The book contains her poem entitled "In the Longhouse: Oneida Museum," which describes Oneida history and traditions.

FURTHER READING

Graymont, Barbara. *The Iroquois*. New York: Chelsea House, 1988.

Parker, Arthur C. *Red Jacket: Last of the Seneca*. New York: McGraw-Hill, 1952.

Sherrow, Victoria. *The Iroquois Indians*. New York: Chelsea House, 1992.

Sneve, Victoria Driving Hawk. *The Iroquois*. New York: Holiday House, 1995.

Wolfson, Evelyn. *The Iroquois: People of the Northeast*. Brookfield, CT: The Millbrook Press, 1992.

Mohawk

Member of the Iroquois Confederacy; for more information on the Mohawk, please refer to the Iroquois Confederacy entry.

Name

Mohawk (pronounced *MO-hawk*). The Mohawk's name was given to them by the Algonquin people; it means "eaters of men" and refers to a Mohawk warrior's custom of eating the bodies of conquered warriors to ingest their strength. They call themselves *Kanien'Kehake,* which means "People of the Flint" (the meaning is uncertain, but may have something to do with making fire). The Mohawk were members of the Iroquois Confederacy and thought of the confederacy as being like a longhouse (the typical Iroquois dwelling). The Mohawks guarded the lands in the eastern part of the confederacy and were known as "the keepers of the eastern door."

Location

The Mohawk formerly occupied areas along the St. Lawrence River in Canada and the Mohawk Valley in central New York state. Today there are Mohawk reservations in central and upstate New York and there are several reserves in Canada. (See Iroquois Confederacy map on page 30.) A small group of Mohawks also resides on a reservation in Oklahoma.

Population

In 1755, there were an estimated 640 Mohawk. In a census (count of the population) taken in 1990 by the U.S. Bureau of the Census, 17,106 people identified themselves as members of the Mohawk tribe. An additional 8,500 or so Mohawks live in Quebec, Canada.

Language family

Iroquoian.

Origins and group affiliations

The Mohawk are descended from people who originated in present-day New York state. They are one of the few Native American peoples who still live on the land where they originated. The Mohawk are one of the six nations comprising the Iroquois Confederacy (the others are the Oneida, Onondaga, Cayuga, Seneca, and Tuscarora tribes). The majority of the Mohawk people still consider themselves one nation, even though their land straddles the border between the United States (at New York state) and Canada.

IMPORTANT DATES

1000–1450: Feuding among tribes over wild game and food resources ends with the founding of the Iroquois Confederacy by Deganawida, "the Peace Maker," and Hiawatha.

1776: Most Mohawk tribes side with the British during the Revolutionary War under the leadership of Thayendanégea, also known as Joseph Brant.

1989–90: Debates at Akwesasne Reservation about gambling on the reservation lead to violence.

1990: Attempt to build a golf course on sacred Mohawk land in Canada leads to violence.

The Mohawk Nation is one of six tribes making up the Iroquois Confederacy. Mohawk men were fierce fighters, easily recognized by the distinctive hairstyle that bears their name. The Mohawks have been in the forefront of the modern Native-rights movement and continue to defy all efforts to weaken their traditional authority and rights.

Distinguished in peace and war

The great peacemaker Hiawatha helped found the Iroquois Confederacy that brought five (later six) warring nations together under a peaceful, democratic government. Hiawatha may have been a member of the Mohawk tribe, though some historians say he was Onondaga.

The Mohawk from New York often hunted the wild game that was plentiful along the St. Lawrence River in Canada, long before their first encounter with French traders there. After they encountered the French in the 1600s, some Mohawk established permanent settlements to be near them. They enjoyed a lively trading relationship with the French, exchanging furs for European goods.

In the 1700s, Europeans arrived in Mohawk territory in present-day New York. There they found a large and thriving Mohawk community that the natives called Akwesasne (pronounced *ah-kwa-SAHS-nee,* which means "where the partridge drums," based on an ancient Seneca legend). Christian missionaries established a mission near Akwesasne in 1752 and called it St. Regis.

By the time the American Revolutionary War began in 1775, a bitter internal division arose among the members of the centuries-old Iroquois Confederacy. As the war began, many Iroquois, especially the Seneca and Onondaga, preferred neutrality. The Tuscarora and Oneida had a trade relationship with settlers and so fought on the side of the United States. A Mohawk leader by the name of Thayendanégea convinced some of the Six Nations to take the side of the British against the colonists in the war. The Mohawks at St. Regis chose to support the colonists.

The Iroquois League's Confederate Council, which operated only when there was agreement among all six nations, could not arrive at a plan of action. Since there was no agreement among the tribes, indi-

vidual nations, villages, and even families had to make their own decisions about alliance or neutrality. The division in the confederacy never fully healed.

Thayendanégea—also known as Joseph Brant because his mother married a man named Brant after Thayendanégea's father, a Mohawk chief, died—was both an officer in the British army and a Mohawk war chief. He led troops of Mohawks and British supporters on raids against the colonists' farms and villages, destroying food supplies for the Colonial armies. When the British were finally defeated, Brant retreated with a group of followers to Ontario, Canada. To reward him for his military services, the English gave him a retirement pension and a large tract of land along the Grand River in Ontario. Many Mohawk and other Iroquois followed him there, and the area eventually became the Six Nations Reserve.

Tribal lands under two governments

After the Revolutionary War, America became independent of the British, but Canada did not. The Mohawks found that their traditional lands were now part of two different countries, a situation that continues to cause conflict among various local and national governing bodies (see "Government").

In 1796, thirteen years after Brant fled to Canada, New York state signed a treaty guaranteeing the Mohawks a 36-square-mile reservation to include the village of St. Regis and other assorted lands. (Land that is set aside for the use of Native Americans is called a reservation; the Canadians call it a reserve.) Later, New York state purchased parts of the reservation but did so without the required consent of the U.S. government. This has led to numerous land claims (see below); some had still not been resolved at the end of the twentieth century.

Today, about 10,000 people, including Mohawks and members of other tribes, call the St. Regis Mohawk Reservation home (it is called the Akwesasne Reserve on the Canadian side). The people refer to themselves as the Akwesasne Mohawk tribe. They occupy 14,648 acres on the American side and 7,400 acres on the Canadian side of the reservation.

The Mohawk people consider themselves one nation in spite of the boundary line drawn through their lands by the United States and Canada. This line has caused many problems, including what Canadian and American governments call smuggling of goods such as cigarettes from one side of the border to the other. Many Mohawks condemn smuggling, but others claim they are not subject to international border laws inside their own nation.

U.S. land claims issues

Land claims issues (demand for the return of lands the Mohawk claim were illegally taken from them) have involved the Mohawks in the twentieth century. The Mohawk have a history of being outspoken in pressing these issues.

In 1953, Mohawk Chief Poking Fire sat outside the Vermont State House with about 200 Mohawks, demanding $1.2 million for the Vermont hunting grounds taken from them 154 years earlier. Then, in 1957, Standing Arrow, a Mohawk, led a group of Indians onto lands claimed by non-Indians on Schoharie Creek, near Amsterdam, New York. The Mohawk claimed the land under a 1784 treaty. They said that non-Indian claims to the land were illegal because the land was not bought from the Iroquois Confederacy but only from one group of Iroquois. To press their point, Mohawk militants occupied a 612-acre campsite for three years in the Adirondack Mountains, finally reaching an agreement with the state of New York in May 1977. The Mohawk were granted two sites totalling nearly 6,000 acres, located within Macomb State Park and near Altoona, New York.

In April 1980, the St. Regis Mohawk tribe in New York received more than 9,000 acres south of the reservation and $6 million in federal funds in an agreement with the federal government regarding lands the tribe claimed near the St. Lawrence Seaway.

Mohawk protest plans to expand a golf course onto a sacred Mohawk burial site, Quebec, Canada, 1990.

Mohawk in Canada

The Canadian Mohawk have been just as aggressive as those on the American side in asserting their rights. In 1899, 200 Mohawks on the Akwesasne reserve drove off a government police force that was trying to force the Indians to hold elections. In December 1968, forty-five Mohawks from that reserve, who were protesting a Canadian decision to charge them a duty (fee) on goods imported from the United States into Canada, were arrested as they blocked the bridge connecting Cornwall, Ontario, to New York.

There are about 8,500 Mohawks living in French-speaking Quebec, Canada. About 1,600 live in and around the small village of Kanesataké (near the town of Oka), and about 6,000 live on the Kahnawake Mohawk reserve, southwest of Montreal, Quebec's largest city. Relations between Mohawk residents and the citizens of Quebec have been uneasy for many years, and this hostility led to violence in 1990 after plans were announced to enlarge a golf course onto a sacred Mohawk burial site near Oka. In protest, Kanesataké Mohawks set up barriers near the site. When Quebec police tried to dismantle the barriers, one officer was shot and killed. Police surrounded the Mohawk reserve. Meanwhile, members of the Mohawk Warrior Society at Kahnawake Reservation blocked access to a bridge linking Montreal suburbs to the city to show their support for the Mohawk at

MOHAWK BAKED SQUASH

The three major crops of the Iroquois tribes, including the Mohawk, were beans, corn, and squash. They were called the "three sisters" and myths of the tribe connect them with stories of three beautiful maidens who walked through the moonlight. The three crops were planted together in one hill. Mohawk women used sticks to make holes in the ground to plant the corn. After the corn sprouted, the earth was piled around the base of the corn stalks to keep away predators. Finally, they planted squash, with its broad leaves, to keep the base of the other plants moist.

Put a squash in the ashes of a fire (or in a 350° F. oven) and bake until tender. Test the shell for doneness with a sharp stick. When it is soft, cut it open and remove the seeds.

From Evelyn Wolfson, *The Iroquois: People of the Northeast*. Brookfield, CT: The Millbrook Press, 1992, p. 30.

Oka. The action resulted in a 78-day standoff with the police and the military on one side and the Mohawk Warriors of Kahnawake and Kanesataké on the other.

White Quebecers gathered at the barricades and taunted the Mohawks; at one point a mob of 250 non-Natives stoned cars carrying about 100 Mohawk women, children, and elders who were fleeing the reserve. The events at Oka were shown every night on television news shows, and the terrible state of relations between Native and non-Native Quebecers shocked many people. The government later purchased the piece of land in dispute, but the tension still lingers.

GOVERNMENT

Today, Mohawk chiefs make up what is known as the Mohawk Nation Council. They represent each of the traditional clans at Grand Council sessions of the Iroquois Confederacy. This ancient body, considered by its supporters to be the true governing body of the Mohawk people, oversees the community as a whole, in Canada and the United States.

Representatives of various governing bodies in Canada, the United States, and New York state believe other agencies and governments should have a say in running the Mohawk Nation. As a result, in the 1990s eight government bodies claimed control over the small area of land at Akwesasne (or St. Regis). The situation has led to conflicts. In 1990, for example, two people were killed when arguments arose over whether to allow gambling on tribal lands.

ECONOMY

When the French arrived in what is now Canada in the 1600s, they were mainly interested in furs. Mohawk men acted as scouts for the French, searching out the best hunting territory. Others acted as fur traders, canoe guides, and partners in battles with the British. Through trade with Europeans, Mohawk women became internationally famous for their woven sweetgrass baskets. In the 1800s, some Mohawk men found work in lumber camps, while others continued with their traditional occupations.

SOME MOHAWK EXPRESSIONS

shé:kon (SHAY kohn)
. . . . . "hello"
kwé kwé (KWAY KWAY)
. . . . ."hello"
hén (hun) . . . . . "yes"
iáh (yah) . . . . . "no"
niá:wen (nee-AH wun) . . . . . "thank you"

At the end of the twentieth century, the Mohawk who remained on reservations were mainly employed in the service and tourist industries. The service industry includes a tribally-owned shopping center and other businesses such as construction. The Mohawk, taking advantage of the growing interest of tourists in Native American life, have opened arts and crafts galleries and allowed the public to attend and observe their celebrations.

Like many other tribes, gambling is a source of income for the Mohawk. They opened slot machines in the 1970s; today bingo is especially popular.

DAILY LIFE

Education

In the late 1800s and early 1900s, parents of Indian children across the country were encouraged to send their children to government-run boarding schools, where students were not allowed to speak their Native language or follow their customs. Public schools were so unresponsive to Indian needs that by 1968 the Mohawk student dropout rate was an astonishing 80 percent. Mohawk parents demanded that authorities pay attention to how schools were failing their children. They became actively involved in education reform, and twenty years later the 80 percent rate had fallen to below 10 percent.

In 1985 the Akwesasne Mohawk Board of Education was formed on the reservation; today it oversees three elementary schools. Some children attend the Akwesasne Freedom School in New York, which keeps traditional Mohawk culture and language alive for children from pre-kindergarten through eighth grade. In addition, the Mohawk Nation operates the Native North American Travelling

THE RABBIT DANCE

Mohawk stories often stressed giving thanks to the creatures and elements of the world, who gave the Mohawk people so much. An example of such a story follows:

Long ago, a group of hunters were out looking for game. They had seen no sign of animals, but they went slowly and carefully through the forest, knowing that at any moment they might find something. Just ahead of them was a clearing. The leader of the hunters held up his hand for the others to pause. He thought he had seen something. All of the men dropped down on their stomachs and crept up to the clearing's edge to see what they could see. What they saw amazed them. There, in the center of the clearing, was the biggest rabbit any of them had ever seen. It seemed to be a big as a small bear!

One of the hunters slowly began to raise his bow. A rabbit as large as that one would be food enough for the whole village. But the leader of the men held out his hand and made a small motion that the man with the bow understood.

He lowered his weapon. Something unusual was happening. It was best to just watch and see what would happen next.

The rabbit lifted its head and looked toward the men. Even though they were well hidden on the other side of the clearing, it seemed as if that giant rabbit could see them. But the rabbit did not take flight. Instead, it just nodded its head. Then it lifted one of its feet and thumped the ground. As soon as it did so, other rabbits began to come into the clearing. They came from all directions and, like their chief, they paid no attention to the hunters.

Now the big rabbit began to thump its foot against the ground in a different way. Ba-pum, ba-pum, pa-pum, pa-pum. It was like the sound of a drum beating. The rabbits all around made a big circle and began to dance. They danced and danced. They danced in couples and moved in and out and back and forth. It was a very good dance that the rabbits did. The hunters who were watching found themselves tapping the earth with their hands in the same beat as the big rabbit's foot.

Then, suddenly, the big rabbit stopped thumping the earth. All of the rabbits stopped dancing. BA-

College, founded in 1968. It travels throughout Canada and the United States to promote Mohawk/Iroquois culture and traditions. For information, write or telephone P.O. Box 273, Hogansburg, NY 13655 (613-932-9452) or (in Canada), R.R. #3, Cornwall Island, Ontario, Canada (K6H5R7); e-mail: nnatc@glen-net.ca.

Clothing and adornment

Mohawk men were known far and wide by their distinctive haircut, which is known today as a "Mohawk." Either just one side of the head was shaved or often both sides, leaving a central strip of hair running from the forehead over the top of the head to the back of the neck.

Mohawk people smeared their hair and bodies with grease to protect themselves from insect bites (such as fleas, mosquitos, lice, and black flies). Men painted their faces blue to express health and well-being, black for war or mourning, and red to represent either life or violent death.

BUM! The chief of the rabbits thumped the earth one final time. It leaped high into the air, right over the men's heads, and it was gone. All the other rabbits ran in every direction out of the clearing and they were gone, too.

Then men were astonished at what they had seen. None of them had ever seen anything at all like this. None of them had ever heard or seen such a dance. It was all they could talk about as they went back to the village. All thought of hunting was now gone from their minds.

When they reached the village, they went straight to the longhouse where the head of the Clan Mothers lived. She was a very wise woman and knew a great deal about the animals. They told her their story. She listened closely. When they were done telling the story, she picked up a water drum and handed it to the leader of the hunters.

"Play that rhythm which the Rabbit Chief played," she said.

The leader of the men did as she asked. He played the rhythm of the rabbits' dance.

"That is a good sound," said the Clan Mother. "Now show me the dance which the Rabbit People showed you."

The hunters then did the dance while their leader played the drum. The Clan Mother listened closely and watched. When they were done, she smiled at them.

"I understand what has happened," she said. "The Rabbit People know that we rely on them. We hunt them for food and for clothing. The Rabbit Chief has given us this special dance so that we can honor his people for all that they give to the human beings. If we play their song and do their dance, then they will know we are grateful for all they continue to give us. We must call this new song The Rabbit Dance and we must do it, men and women together, to honor the Rabbit People."

So it was that a new social dance was given to the Iroquois people. To this day the Rabbit Dance is done to thank the Rabbit People for all they have given, not only food and clothing, but also a fine dance that makes the people glad.

SOURCE: "The Rabbit Dance." Joseph Bruchac. *Native American Animal Stories*. Golden, CO: Fulcrum Publishing, 1992.

ARTS

The Mohawk talent for painting and wood carving can be seen in their elaborately carved and painted wooden cradleboards (for carrying babies), some of which survive and are widely admired by art experts. They feature relief carvings of plants and animals. Some Mohawk women still carry on the tradition of weaving baskets from sweetgrass.

The Mohawk Nation at Akwesasne ventured into the broadcast arts when they became one of only about two dozen Native communities to own and operate a radio station. The station, plus a newspaper and a magazine called *Akwesasne Notes* that are published on the reservation, help keep the culture alive.

CURRENT TRIBAL ISSUES

Along with land claims (see "History"), environmental issues are an ongoing concern for the Mohawk. The Canadian Mohawk resisted plans for a golf course on their lands partly, they claimed, because the extensive use fertilizers and pesticides on golf courses are ecological hazards. The Mohawk have been exposed to excessive air pollution, contaminated fish, and hazardous waste facilities that have damaged their health and their way of life. Both the Mohawk and government bodies are beginning to study and address these issues.

NOTABLE PEOPLE

Joseph Brant, also known as Thayendanégea ("He Places Two Bets"), was a Mohawk war chief and officer of the British army who led Indian troops into battle during the Revolutionary War (1775–83). He negotiated with both Canadian and American governments for the land rights of his people. He is credited with having translated the Bible into the Mohawk language.

Jay Silverheels (1912–1980) is best known for his role as Tonto, the Indian partner of the Lone Ranger, in a popular television series of the 1950s. Silverheels, whose real name was Harold J. Smith, first came to this country as a member of Canada's national lacrosse team in 1938. (The Mohawks excelled at lacrosse, a game of Native American origin.) A short time later he began acting in films. In 1950, he portrayed Geronimo in the movie *Broken Arrow,* hailed as the first film to portray Indians in a sympathetic light.

Kateri Tekakwitha (1656–1680) became the first Native American nun. Many miracles have been attributed to her, which led to her selection by the Catholic church in 1980 as a candidate for sainthood.

FURTHER READING

Ballantine, Betty, and Ian Ballantine, eds. *The Native Americans: An Illustrated History.* Atlanta, Georgia: Turner Publishing, 1993.

Bruchac, Joseph. "Otstango: A Mohawk Village in 1491," *National Geographic,* Vol. 180, No. 4, October 1991, pp. 68–83.

Came, Barry. "A Time for Healing: Emotions Still Divide Oka and Kahnawake," *Macleans.* November 12, 1990, vol. 103, no. 46, p. 26.

Mander, Jerry. "Our Founding Mothers and Fathers, the Iroquois," *In the Absence of the Sacred: The Failure of Technology and the Survival of the Indian Nations,* Sierra Club Books, 1991.

Mohawk Nation Council of Chiefs Home Page: [Online] http://www.slic.com/~mohawkna/

Menominee

Name

Menominee (pronounced *muh-NOM-uh-nee*). It means "Wild-Rice People." The French called them *Folle Avoines* ("Crazy Oat Indians") because of their heavy reliance on wild rice.

Location

The Menominee Indian Tribe of Wisconsin Reservation is located forty-five miles northwest of Green Bay. The reservation contains about 235,000 acres, most of them thickly forested. The reservation has two main villages—Neopit and Keshena—a smaller village called Zoar, and a somewhat scattered community called South Branch.

Population

In 1634, there were from 2,000 to 4,000 Menominee. In 1768, the number had dropped to 800, but was back up to 1,930 in 1854, and 2,917 in 1956. In a census (count of the population) done in 1990, 8,064 people identified themselves as Menominee. About 3,400 people live on the reservation.

Language family

Algonquian.

Origins and group affiliations

The Menominee are believed to have occupied areas in Michigan and Wisconsin for 5,000 years or more. The Menominee say they originated near Sault (pronounced *SOO*) Ste. Marie in Michigan's Upper Peninsula; around the year 1400 they were forced westward by the Potawatomi and Ojibway (see entries). Together with the Winnebago and Ojibway, the Menominee are the original tribes of Wisconsin and parts of Michigan. All three tribes share characteristics with newer arrivals such as the Sac and Fox (see entry) and the Potawatomi.

MENOMINEE

Contemporary Communities

Wisconsin

1. Menominee Indian Tribe
   of Wisconsin

Shaded area: Traditional lands of the Menominee along the present-day Michigan-Wisconsin state line.

At one time the Menominee controlled nearly ten million acres, lands that stretched from the Great Lakes to the Mississippi River. Mainly hunter-gatherers, they also did some hunting and fishing. The Menominee were a brave and generous people who managed to survive although surrounded by larger and more powerful tribes. However, American settlers and loggers took more and more Menominee land until the Natives were finally confined to a reservation after 1856. Today the Menominee are a relatively prosperous people whose traditional culture and language remain vital.

HISTORY

French disrupt peaceful existence

The Menominee have inhabited their territory for at least 5,000 years—the longest of any Wisconsin tribe. Their first encounter with Europeans happened when Frenchman Jean Nicolet (pronounced *JHON Nik-o-LAY*) passed through their territory in 1634, looking for a passage to China. Over the next thirty years, the Menominee had little interaction with French traders, but they suffered at the hands of other tribes who did, largely because of the fur trade.

The fur trade in Canada and around the Great Lakes resulted in intense rivalries among Native tribes. Eager to trade furs for French goods, some hunters began to expand their activities onto lands others regarded as theirs. Stronger tribes began forcing weaker ones westward. Refugees from the Ojibway and Potawatomi tribes crowded onto Menominee lands. The invasion was disruptive for everyone. Wars broke out among tribes competing for food and land. Many people starved to death or became victims of warfare and diseases.

IMPORTANT DATES

c. 3000: B.C.E.: Menominee inhabit homeland in Michigan.

1400: Menominee are pushed westward into their present homeland near Green Bay, Wisconsin.

1817–1856: Menominee make eight treaties with United States and move to a reservation.

1909–1930: Tribal sawmill provides employment but tribe must sue for managerial control.

1954: Menominee federal tribal status is terminated; it is restored in 1973.

Trading post established

Contact between the Menominee and the French really began when the French established a trading post at Green Bay, Wisconsin, in 1667. By this time, there were fewer than 400 Menominee left, and they were soon dependent on fur trading. French trade goods such as metal kettles, steel tools, cloth, needles, and scissors made life easier. Trade altered forever the Menominee's ancient way of life, turning a people who had once hunted only for what they needed into a people who hunted for profit. But trade may also have saved the tribe from dying out. The French maintained peace among rival tribes in order to protect trade, and the Menominee were spared more warfare. Eventually, however, over-trapping led to an over-supply of furs, and the French abruptly ended trade in the area in 1696.

Involvement in white men's wars

The Menominee resumed their hunting, fishing, and gathering lifestyle, but throughout the 1700s they found themselves caught up in warfare over and over again. This time the conflict was between the French, British, and American colonists, who all fought to dominate North America. When they could not avoid conflict, the Menominee sided with the French, who had never shown any desire to take over Native lands. After the French were defeated in the French and Indian War (1756–63), the Menominee became allies of the British. They fought with the British against the colonists in the American Revolutionary War (1775–83) and in the War of 1812 (a war between the

Menominee bark lodge built as a chapel for French missionaries, Green Bay, Wisconsin.

United States and Britain). By this time they had recovered to such an extent that there were at least ten Menominee villages.

The Menominee at last befriended the victorious Americans, who built a fort at Green Bay in 1815. Soon a trading post operated at the Menominee village of Minikani.

Treaty period

Americans wanted land. Vastly outnumbered, the Menominee surrendered more and more land, not always peacefully. Between 1817 and 1856, the Menominee made eight treaties with the United States. A treaty signed in 1831 granted them eight cents an acre for three million acres of wooded land. By 1850 nearly all tribal lands were in the hands of whites. The Menominee fought, but the pressure was too much for them. The Wolf Treaty of 1854 established a reservation in northern Wisconsin. Later, a small group of Potawatomi joined them on the reservation.

Loggers come

The Menominee sent 125 volunteers to the Union (Northern) Army during the American Civil War (1861–65), an amazing number considering that the tribe numbered only about 2,000. Menominee warriors fought at the Civil War battles of Vicksburg and Petersburg, and Menominee guarded the men who assassinated President Abraham Lincoln during their trial and execution.

After the Civil War, American timbermen came to Wisconsin, seeking to exploit the forests. They tried every means they could

think of—legal and illegal—to deprive the Menominee of their timber riches, but they failed.

By 1870 the Menominee had established three villages along the Menominee River, another eight or so to the south, and a Christian mission at Shawano. They successfully resisted efforts to turn them into farmers, opting instead to base their economy on logging. They were remarkably successful in this endeavor.

Logging success nearly destroys tribe

The Menominee were so successful in their logging operation that by 1890 they had built a hospital and school and had set up their own police and court system. At a time when most other Native American tribes were still trying to adjust to reservation life, the Menominee tribe was looked upon as a model of prosperity and modern thinking. Oddly enough, this success nearly caused their destruction when the U.S. Congress adopted a policy called termination in the 1950s.

Termination was part of the larger U.S. plan to assimilate Indians—that is, to make them more like white Americans. Termination of a tribe ended the special relationship that existed between the tribe and the U.S. government, thus bringing to an end certain government funding and services and making the tribes subject to state taxes. The effect of termination on the Menominee was very bad, because many were unable to pay their taxes and lost their land. It was not long before the Menominee were among the poorest people in the state of Wisconsin.

Anger over termination grew. In 1970, the Menominee formed a protest movement called Determination of Rights and United for Menominee Shareholders (DRUMS). Using tactics such as demonstrations and court actions, DRUMS was able to slow the sale of tribal lands. Finally, in 1973, President Richard Nixon signed the Menominee Restoration Act, which restored tribal status of the reservation. Today the tribe's enterprises are once again thriving.

RELIGION

The Menominee believed in a Great Spirit, who made the Sun, the stars, the Earth, and other spirits who took the form of animals. In their creation story, one of those spirits, Great Bear, asked the Great Spirit to transform him into a man. His wish was granted, but he soon felt lonely, so he asked a golden eagle to become his brother; the eagle became known as Thunderer. Great Bear then asked a beaver to join him, and she became Beaver Woman. This small family then "adopted" other spirits. These animal spirits who became people were the first Menominee. An All Animals' Dance was occasionally held to honor the characters of the creation story.

Like the Ojibway, the Menominee had a religious society called the Medicine Lodge Religion (Midewiwin), whose main purpose was to prolong life. The society taught morality, proper conduct, and a knowledge of plants and herbs for healing. Another religion, the Drum (or Dream) Dance Religion, holds that dreams can make a person sick if they are not acted out. Many Menominee retain elements of these two traditional religions, even those who belong to Christian churches.

"Model" community fails

In the 1800s, reformers decided the friendly Menominee should be converted and "civilized" (meaning they should adopt a more European American-based culture). In 1831 the reformers constructed a community called Winnebago Rapids. It was to serve as a model for future "civilizing" of other Native communities. Winnebago Rapids consisted of a dozen houses, a school, farm, blacksmith shop, and sawmill. But this experiment in peaceful coexistence through education and good example was a total failure. The Menominee rejected the model homes; some even used them to stable their horses. They tore up the flooring for firewood, and slept in their own traditional shelters pitched nearby. They refused to listen to the lessons of the teachers and preachers.

Today, Roman Catholicism, introduced by the French in the 1600s, is the most common religion among Menominee. The Native American Church (see box in Makah entry), has been embraced by some Menominee in rural areas. The church combines Christian and Native beliefs and practices, and features an all-night ceremony composed of chanting, prayer, and meditation.

LANGUAGE

The dialect (variety) of the Algonquian language spoken by the Menominee is most closely related to Cree and Fox. The Menominee used the language of the Ojibway in the fur-trade days as a second language for speaking with outsiders.

By the 1920s the Menominee language was going out of use, and by 1965 only 300 to 500 people spoke it. Today, the language is being used and taught at four tribal schools on the reservation and at the College of the Menominee Nation in Keshena.

The Menominee language frequently borrows from Ojibway, Siouan, and French languages. Having no word of their own for "warrior," the Menominee, Plains Cree, and Western Chippewa employ the Dakota word for warrior: *akicita as okiccita. Po So Na Mut* is a Menominee greeting.

GOVERNMENT

In the early days, the Menominee were loosely organized, with a tribal council that governed informally. After Native refugees from the fur-trade wars arrived and threatened the Menominee way of life, a more formal type of government became necessary. Members of the tribal council, usually elders from each clan (a group of related families), appointed a chief to take command during wars with the refugees. Later, the job of the chief evolved, so he was in charge of maintaining order, approving tribal policies, directing ceremonies, and generally looking out for the welfare of his people.

When the Menominee reservation was established in 1854, the tribe became subject to U.S. laws. Programs were set up to assimilate the people (cause them to adopt the white culture) and turn them into farmers so they would blend into the general population. The Menominee resisted, however. They became successful loggers and were able to establish their own police and court systems. They enjoyed success and prosperity until the federal termination policy enacted in the 1950s placed the tribal government in the hands of the state of Wisconsin. As a sovereign nation the Menominee had not been expected to pay taxes in the past. When their reservation lands became a county of Wisconsin, they were forced to sell valuable lake property to pay taxes. While struggling to keep their lumber operations going, they soon became impoverished.

In 1973 the Menominee Restoration Act was signed, reestablishing the former reservation. In 1977 the tribe adopted a constitution and in 1979 a tribal legislature was formed. The nine-member tribal legislature elects a chairperson, a body of judges, and a general council.

ECONOMY

Farming rejected

Before the coming of Europeans, the Menominee supported themselves mainly by hunting and gathering the abundant wild rice of their territory. They believed that to plant crops rather than gather rice would offend the Creator.

Reformers in the 1800s tried to turn the Menominee into farmers. The Menominee chose instead to sell white pine commercially. In 1909 the U.S. government supplied the Menominee at Neopit with a state-of-the-art sawmill, providing full tribal employment—but failed to turn over management of the mill to the tribe.

Economy based on forests

In 1930 the Menominee sued for greater tribal management of the mill. Thirteen lawsuits were filed but the Menominee received no satisfaction from the courts. Meanwhile, more than 200 Menominee served in World War II (1939–45), and back home, 50 women kept the tribal

National Guardsman with members of the Menominee Warriors group during the occupation of a building in a protest demonstration in Wisconsin, 1975.

sawmill going. In 1954, the Menominee tribal status was terminated by the federal government, resulting in a loss of certain federal benefits. The 2,917 Menominee were plunged into poverty. They were forced to sell prime lakefront sites to white developers. Upset Menominee united behind the organization called Determination of Rights and Unity for Menominee Shareholders (DRUMS). By 1973 they recovered their federal tribal status, and logging activities resumed in full.

The Menominee have become known for their successful forest management techniques. For every tree harvested, the Menominee plant one in its place. They have increased wooded acreage by 10 percent in the twentieth century. Sometimes called "Timber Indians," they manage the maple, beech, birch, hemlock, oak, basswood, black spruce, tamarack, cedar, and red, white, and jack pine trees that forest 220,000 acres of their 234,000-acre homeland. Menominee Tribal Enterprises limits the annual cut to 29 million feet.

The Menominee manage their land using three basic principles. They were described by Menominee President Lawrence Waukau when he spoke before the United Nations in 1995: "First, [forest land] must be sustainable for future generations. Second, the forest must be cared for properly to provide for the needs of the people. And third, we keep all the pieces of the forest to maintain diversity."

Several generations of a Menominee family in Wisconsin, 1931.

Recently the tribe has expanded their economic base to include gambling, which has provided much-needed jobs. Still, unemployment remains high on the reservation. Nearly 22 percent of the 1,000-member labor force there is unemployed (many Menominee work in the larger American economy throughout the Midwest). Per capita income on the reservation is only about $4,700, compared to about $20,000 for the American population. (Per capita income is the average income one person earns in one year.)

DAILY LIFE

Games

Because the Menominee had ample food to meet their needs, they also had ample leisure time. Lacrosse, a game of Native American origin, was a favorite pastime for Menominee men. It is played on a field by two teams of ten players each. Participants use a long-handled stick with a webbed pouch (a racket) to try and get a ball into the opposing team's goal. The Menominee played lacrosse with a deerskin ball stuffed with hair and a racket made of saplings.

Children played with dolls, bows and arrows, and hoops made of birch bark. In winter, entire families gathered around the fire to listen to stories.

Buildings

THEN... The Menominee traditionally lived in large villages in the summer. They built dome-shaped wigwams with frames made of sapling (young trees), covered with mats of cedar or birch bark.

Inside, mats made of cattails provided insulation and protection from rain; they were sometimes colored with dyes made from fruits and berries. Animal skins or grass mats were placed on the ground or on raised sleeping platforms. The Menominee preferred to cook and eat outside, weather permitting.

In the winter, smaller groups of extended families retreated to their hunting grounds, where they built dome-shaped wigwams similar to their summer homes. Outlying buildings included sweat lodges for purification before ceremonies or for curing diseases, a lodge where women retreated during their menstrual period, places for dreaming and fasting, and a lodge for the medicine man.

...AND IN THE TWENTIETH CENTURY As late as the 1950s, a few bark houses were still being used by elderly Menominee. An exhibit on display at the tribally-operated Logging Camp Museum in Keshena shows a restored Menominee camp typical in the early twentieth century. It features a bunkhouse, cook shanty, wood butcher's shop, blacksmith shop, saw filer's shack, horse barn, office, 100-foot cedar-roof shed, and a loggers' locomotive.

Today, most Menominee live in homes no different from non-Natives, with one exception: they post small family totem poles outside the front door.

Clothing and adornment

The early Menominee wore little clothing in warm weather. In cool weather they wore buckskin breechcloths (garments with front and back flaps that hung from the waist), leggings, and moccasins, with cloaks added for formal occasions, much like their Ojibway neighbors. Snowshoes made winter travel easier. They used oil and grease to soften their long hair and skin and sometimes painted their skin as well.

Much attention and skill were devoted to the decoration of clothing. It was adorned with satin ribbon and porcupine quills in geometric patterns including diamonds, triangles, leaves, crosses, deer heads, and thunderbirds. European glass beads were woven into hair streamers and sashes.

In the nineteenth century, full gathered skirts similar to those worn by white women became popular. Fashionable men's wear at the turn of the twentieth century included cotton shirts, sometimes with ruffles, silk ribbons, and decorative pins made of a cheap nickel alloy called German silver.

An early twentieth-century photograph shows Menominee men wearing checkered loggers' shirts and slouch hats intermingling with men in suits or feathered fur caps and elaborately embroidered robes. Women are dressed like their German-American neighbors, except for the addition of turquoise and silver or beaded jewelry.

Food

Menominee means "Wild-Rice People." Wild rice is actually a cereal grass that grows in lakes and streams and is harvested from a canoe. Menominee women stood in a canoe and reached for the tall, hollow rice stalks. They held them over the boat and shook them; the wild rice fell into the canoe. The Menominee considered harvesting wild rice to be both a spiritual and an economic activity. Wild rice was boiled and often flavored with maple syrup. Today some Menominee gather and sell both wild rice and maple syrup.

Women also gathered nuts, fruits, and berries. Menominee men supplemented the diet by hunting ducks and geese. They caught fish with spears and nets made of animal sinew; their favorite catch was sturgeon. All this combined to make a very healthy, well-rounded diet. Early explorers commented on the good health of the Menominee people.

Nineteenth-century Menominee who were willing to take up farming grew rye, potatoes, oats, corn, melons, fruit trees, and hogs in addition to beans, peas, turnips, wheat, and buckwheat. Farmers and wild-rice gatherers often shared the fruits of their labors.

Healing practices

Illness was believed to come from supernatural powers and evil witches, and a medicine man called a shaman (pronounced *SHAY-mun*) was the person to call. He brought to the sick person's home a bag of remedies that he had probably received from his father or his teacher. His bag might contain healing roots and herbs, charms such as deer tails, carved wooden puppets, and a medicine stick to be used as an offering to the spirits.

Herbal remedies were many and varied. From trees were derived treatments for swellings, sores, loose mucus, and colds. The Menominee used mint for pneumonia. They had herbal medicines for poison ivy and boils, female disorders and childbirth, urinary and venereal diseases, stomach and intestinal disorders, diarrhea, sleeplessness, and lung trouble. Insecticides, enemas, eyewashes, and pain-killers were important. The herb called Seneca snakeroot became so popu-

HOW YOUTH ARE INSTRUCTED BY TRIBAL ELDERS

George and Louise Spindler were anthropologists (they study human cultures) who had a close relationship with the people they called Menomini. In a book they wrote based on their work with the Menominee, the couple related the following example of how youth are instructed by tribal elders .

That old grandfather of mine tell me how to [hunt by circling around] . . . if you see no tracks you know he isn't there. Circle around again. The deer knows you circle, he stay still. Sure enough, the second time I circle, I see the deer hiding, laying against a windfall, ears down. So I shot him in the head. First deer I ever killed. Gee! I was happy! First deer I killed. I start whooping, run home. My mother and grandmother was surprised. "Is it really so?" they kept asking. We took pack straps, knives, a lit-tle hatchet. I took them up there, sure enough, there he was. The old lady [grandmother] was pretty good. She cut it up and we packed it home. That was pretty good.

The women sliced it up good. They made sticks to roast the meat close to the fire. Then they cook what they eat. The ribs and chest they boil, the best part for them. Then the men folks come. We waiting for them. When they come in, the grandfather come first. He had nothing, just his gun and pack strap. He say, "Who that is?" The old lady, she laugh, "I guess your grandson beat you!" The grandfa-ther say then, "Just for that we offer a prayer for to give thanks so this boy be a good hunter." So they all come; they was happy, for quite a while. We had a feast. We offer prayer . . . eat afterwards. I was fourteen when that happened. That I remember good.

SOURCE: George and Louise Spindler. *Dreamers with Power: The Menomini Indians.* New York: Holt, Rinehart & Winston, 1971.

lar as a healing remedy that the Menominee traded, over-collected, and almost exterminated it. They used skunk cabbage and wild or chokecherries on wounds.

During the French and Indian War (1756–63), Menominee war-riors brought smallpox back to their villages; more than one-quarter of their people died. U.S. soldiers carried smallpox and cholera into Wisconsin in the 1830s; another 25 percent of the population died. The Natives had no effective defense against the diseases until inocu-lation (shots) became widespread.

Education

Menominee children traditionally learned by example. Soon after moving to the reservation in 1854, the Menominee built a school, but they lost it when a 1954 law terminated the reservation. In modern times, with the profits acquired from timber, the Menominee have been able to build a college and four reservation schools attended by more than 500 children. The College of the Menominee Nation spe-cializes in forestry, health care, and gambling administration. Since the casino boom is not expected to last forever, tribal officials want their young people to learn management skills useful in any field.

CUSTOMS

Clan structure and rituals

The Menominee are divided into groups called Bear and Thunderer (see "Religion" section for the parts each of these figures played in the creation story). Each group is made up of clans whose members consider one another brothers and sisters. Membership is passed down through the father. The Bear symbol was a female bear with a long tail, and Thunderer was represented by an eagle, the most beautiful and powerful bird of the country, perched upon a cross.

Today's Menominee retain some of their ancient rites. For example, tobacco offerings are left at a stone called Spirit Rock to please the hero Manabozho, who turned a greedy warrior to stone for requesting eternal life. Menominee legend states that when Spirit Rock crumbles away, the Menominee will perish.

Festivals

Menominee of old held a Beggars' Dance in the fall, which celebrated the maple syrup season. Modern Menominee hold two annual powwows: the Veterans Powwow over Memorial Day weekend and the Annual Menominee Nation Contest Powwow the first weekend in August. At these powwows, members of several different tribes participate in dance contests and tribal drumming performances.

Hunting and gathering rituals

Before gathering wild rice, the Menominee threw tobacco (considered a sacred substance) onto the water to please the spirits. When hunting, they took only what they needed for food, clothing, and sleeping mats. They hunted with bows lubricated with bear grease and arrows made of pine or cedar. Bear was a favorite prey, and when one was killed, a special ceremony and feast was held, to which all a hunter's friends were invited.

Burial

The dead were buried and a spirit house marked the grave. Some Menominee still follow this burial custom.

CURRENT TRIBAL ISSUES

The Menominee find themselves engaged in quarrels with sportsmen and conservationists regarding how they use their ancestral lands. Some claim Indians should not be able to use modern technologies when fishing, for example. Others claim the Menominee gave up their fishing rights entirely. There is more at stake in this argument than the simple matter of what techniques are used, because the Menominee economy is partly based on fishing industries.

Menominee leaders are concerned about their environment and have objected to storage of nuclear waste on the reservation and to a planned copper mine that would degrade the Wolf River.

NOTABLE PEOPLE

Ada Deer (1935–) is a life-long advocate for social justice. She helped create Determination of Rights and Unity for Menominee Shareholders (DRUMS), which was instrumental in convincing Congress to reinstate the Menominee tribe after it was terminated in 1954. When Congress confirmed her nomination as the first woman to head the U.S. Bureau of Indian Affairs, she said: "I want to emphasize [that] my administration will be based on the Indian values of caring, sharing, and respect. . . . These values have been missing too long in the halls of government."

Tribal leader Oshkosh (1795–1858), also known as Claw, was known for his efforts to promote peaceful co-existence with white settlers. Despite his best efforts, Menominee lands were swallowed up and he was forced to oversee the removal of his people to a reservation that was only a tiny portion of their former homeland.

FURTHER READING

Ourada, Patricia K. *The Menominee.* New York: Chelsea House, 1990.

Paterek, Josephine. *Encyclopedia of American Indian Costume.* New York: W. W. Norton, 1994.

Sultzman, Lee. "Menominee History": [Online] http://www.dickshovel.com/men.html

Micmac

Name

Micmac (pronounced *MICK-mack*). Also called Mikmaque, Mi'kmaq, Migmagi, Mickmakis, Mikmakiques. The meaning of the name is uncertain; some scholars say it is a word for "allies," others believe it refers to the present-day Maritime Provinces of Canada. The Micmac call themselves Inu (pronounced *EE-noo*), a term they now apply to all Indians.

Location

The Micmac once thrived in the Maritime Provinces of Canada, including the modern provinces of Cape Breton Island, Nova Scotia, Prince Edward Island, New Brunswick, and the Gaspé (pronounced *gas-PAY*) Peninsula. Until recent years in the United States, the Micmac moved often and formed a landless and scattered community. Today, the people of the Aroostook Band of Micmac Indians live in communities in northern Maine. The twenty-eight bands of Micmac in Canada live on various reserves or in rural communities.

Population

The Micmac numbered about 4,500 around the year 1500, before the coming of the Europeans. By 1700, disease had reduced the tribal population to around 2,000. In the 1990s, the population of Micmacs in Canada stood at about 15,000. According to the U.S. Bureau of the Census, 2,726 people identified themselves as Micmac in the United States in 1990. (A census is a count of the population.)

Language family

Micmac is a branch of the Algonquian family of languages, and is related to the languages of the Abenaki (see entry) and Passamaquoddy tribes of New England.

Origins and Group Affiliations

The Micmac are members of a larger group of tribes called the Wabanaki (pronounced *wah-buh-NOK-ee*). According to a tribal legend, the Micmac hero and creator Glooskap brought the Micmac out of the earth and taught them how to survive in Canada's lands by the Atlantic Ocean. Just before the arrival of the Europeans in about 1500, the eight groups that make up the Micmac lived in scattered bands across northeastern and eastern Canada. The early Micmac also visited Anticosti Island, off the coast of New Brunswick, and Labrador, where they battled with Inuit (see entry) tribes.

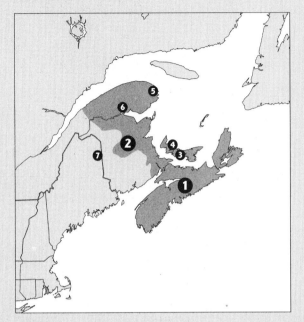

MICMAC

Contemporary Communities

1. ***Nova Scotia,*** 12 Micmac communities
2. ***New Brunswick,*** 9 Micmac communities

Prince Edward Island
  3. Abegweit Reserve
  4. Lennox Island Reserve

Quebec
  5. Gaspé Reserve
  6. Restigouche Reserve

Maine
  7. Aroostock Band of Micmac Indians

Shaded area: Traditional lands of the Micmac in the present-day Maritime Provinces of Canada.

The Micmac may have been hunting, fishing, and gathering in their northern region since the time of the last ice age, some ten to twenty thousand years ago. The wandering Micmac were so well adapted to their environment that their culture changed very little before whites arrived in the 1500s.

HISTORY

Early European visitors

Nearly one thousand years ago the legendary Icelandic explorer Leif Eriksson, son of the discoverer of Greenland, may have landed on Canada's Atlantic coast and traveled west, setting up a camp in a land he called Vinland in around 1001. A settlement believed to be his was discovered in the 1950s in Newfoundland, Canada, very near traditional Micmac territory.

The history of the Micmac people since the early sixteenth century was closely intertwined with that of the Europeans who arrived about that time. The Europeans came from France, Spain, Portugal, and other places, looking for the abundant fish and furs, especially beaver, to be found in and around Micmac territory.

The beginning of fur trade

In July 1534, the French explorer Jacques Cartier (pronounced *zhock kar-tee-AY*) arrived at the mouth of Canada's St. Lawrence River. He was on an expedition to find gold and also to locate the passage by water through the new continent to the Far East. Finding neither, Cartier did find furs. The Micmac were eager to trade with him. Europeans fell in love with beaver hats, and the Micmac enjoyed French goods, such as guns, metal kettles, steel tools, cloth, needles, and scissors they received in exchange for beaver and other furs. The fur trade dominated French-American relations for the next 250 years.

Cartier tried and failed to establish settlements in the lands of the Micmac, mostly because of the hostility of the neighboring Iroquois (see entry), who also wanted a trading relationship with the French. In time, however, the Micmac drove the Iroquois tribe out of the area. Cartier eventually returned to France. Because of religious wars at home, it would be three quarters of a century before the French again returned to the Gaspé Peninsula to resume trade with the Micmac.

The Micmac in New France

In 1604 the king of France granted control over the fur trade in the St. Lawrence River area to a French nobleman. The French called the area New France. The Frenchman founded the colony of Port Royal on the coast of present-day Nova Scotia in what was then Micmac territory. In around 1610, priests from the religious order the Society of Jesus came from France to convert the Natives to the Roman Catholic religion. A local Micmac chief was baptized and took the French name Henri Membertou (pronounced *on-REE mem-ber-TOO*). He was the first Native American to be baptized in New France. Membertou helped the French make the colony a success. In turn, they offered his people trading opportunities and French grain to use in the difficult months of winter.

IMPORTANT DATES

1534: French explorer Jacques Cartier meets the Micmac on the Gaspé Peninsula, beginning a long association between the French and the Micmac.

1590: The Micmac force Iroquoian-speaking Natives to leave the Gaspé Peninsula; as a result, the Micmac dominate the fur trade with the French.

1763: By the Treaty of Paris, France gives Britain the Canadian Maritime Provinces, including Micmac territory.

1775–83: Micmac support Americans in the American Revolution.

1960s: Micmac begin to recover some economic independence.

1982: Aroostook Micmac Council is established at Presque Isle, Maine.

The same year Membertou was baptized, the Micmac chief Panounias (pronounced *pa-NOO-nee-us*) became the guide and protector of French soldier and explorer Samuel de Champlain. In the spring of 1605, Panounias and Champlain traveled southward into the lands of the Abenaki tribe, looking for places to set up a trading post and colony. Violence erupted between the Micmac and Abenaki, and in 1606 several Micmac, including Panounias, were killed. In 1607, seeking revenge, Henri Membertou led a group of Micmac bands to raid an Abenaki village. With their superior French weapons, the Micmac were able to kill ten of the Abenaki; the rest fled. Soon the Micmac increased their power in the area and were able to start more favorable trading relationships with local farmers.

Europeans bring war and disease

In addition to goods and technology, the Europeans brought the Micmac deadly diseases. Between the time of Cartier's initial contact and the return of the French some seventy-five years later, the Micmac population dropped from an estimated 4,500 to around 3,000. European fishermen brought smallpox, throat infections, and intestinal diseases. The Micmac had little or no resistance to these diseases. Some tribe members, who were introduced to alcohol by the Europeans, became alcoholics and died prematurely. As a result of these problems, and with many warriors killed in battle, the Micmac population continued to drop well into the eighteenth century.

The Micmac remained close allies of the French throughout more than a century of intermittent wars with Britain over lands in present-day Canada. Micmac soldiers fought alongside French and Canadian soldiers from early wars in the seventeenth century until the French and Indian War (1754-63) decided the fate of New France.

The British take Canada

In 1760, the British, led by General James Wolfe, seized the city of Quebec in Canada. When Montreal fell the following year, the British took control over the entire area of New France, including Micmac territories. In 1763, Britain received Canada and the Maritime Provinces from the French as part of the Treaty of Paris that ended the French and Indian Wars. The Micmac lost a strong ally and trading partner when France withdrew from their territory.

In the 1760s British colonists, looking for land to farm, began to arrive in the Maritime Provinces. During the American Revolution (1775–83) the Micmac favored the Americans, perhaps in hopes that the overthrow of the British would restore French rule. After 1781 the British government granted land in the Micmac's territory to colonists who had lost their own lands farther south as a result of their loyalty to Britain during the American Revolution. During the War of 1812, a conflict between the British and American armies, the Micmac remained neutral.

Micmac in Canada

Over time, the Micmac were restricted in their land movements by the British government. Through a series of treaties, they were moved onto smaller reserves (the Canadian term for reservations) in their original Canadian territories. During the mid- to late nineteenth century, some of the Micmac who lived in the United States crossed the border into Canada to find work. By the early 1900s, many of these people had become permanent residents at Indian reserves or in small Canadian towns.

The economy of the Canadian Micmac declined during the nineteenth and early twentieth centuries, and their traditional way of life broke down. Micmac men had to take jobs in shipyards and railroads, and as lumbermen and loggers. The jobs were low paying and usually temporary. Commercial hunting of marine animals as a source of oil ended for the Micmac when petroleum products replaced porpoise and whale oil as a source of machine oil. Some Micmac joined the Canadian Army during World War I (1914–18) and World War II (1939–45).

During the 1960s the Micmac in Canada began to recover some economic independence. Many Micmac men discovered they liked construction work on high-rise buildings—work that paid well and satisfied their need for steady employment. Micmac women began training to become nurses, teachers, secretaries, and social workers. Although many of the reserves in Canada still reflect the rural poverty of the early twentieth century, the Micmac have begun to adapt to the changes of a new era.

The Aroostook Band of Micmac

In 1970, along with other off-reservation Native groups, some Micmac people in the United States, in an effort to fight poverty and discrimination, formed the Association of Aroostook Indians (AAI). They were recognized as a tribe by the state of Maine in 1973, and became eligible for Maine's Department of Indian Affairs services, Indian scholarships, and free hunting and fishing licenses. The AAI was dissolved and the group gained legal status as the Aroostook Micmac Council in 1982, with headquarters in Presque Isle, Maine. Today, without a reservation to live on, the Aroostook people are making efforts to retain their Native culture.

RELIGION

The Micmac shared many beliefs with other Algonquian-speaking tribes, including the belief in the Algonquian creator-hero called Glooskap, and in the Great Spirit Manitou. Glooskap, who did good deeds for the Micmac, was a giant who was said to have come from across the sea in a granite canoe. When he reached land there were no people to greet him so he split open an ash tree with his great bow and the first humans stepped from within the tree.

The main focus of Micmac belief was probably the Sun, which they prayed to twice a day in long ritual songs and identified with the Great Spirit Manitou. Another tribal god was Skatekamuc, a ghostlike spirit whose appearance in a dream indicated that death was near.

The Micmac also believed in witches, who could cause disease by casting spells. The Micmac spiritual world was inhabited by "little people" who played tricks that helped or hurt the Micmac according to their whim. They could be cast out with holy water or palm fronds saved from Palm Sunday (a Roman Catholic holy day).

The conversion of tribal members to the Catholic faith was largely complete by the late seventeenth century. Many Micmac converted because they hoped that European Catholic rituals could save them from the diseases that had been brought by the Europeans. The power of shamans (medicine men; pronounced *SHAY-muns*) probably also increased at this time as the Micmac's terror of the white man's diseases grew stronger. Today, most Micmac are Roman Catholics, the religion first introduced to them in the early 1600s by the French Jesuits (priests who are members of the Society of Jesus religious order).

LANGUAGE

The Micmac language is said to be the most northerly of the Eastern Algonquian languages. Some Micmac still speak it. In the seventeenth century, a Catholic missionary developed hieroglyphics (picture symbols) for the language, but in time the system fell out of use. In the eighteenth century the Micmac developed a writing system using the Latin alphabet. Catholic priests used it to translate the Bible into Micmac and to publish a Native-language newspaper. Another system of writing the language was developed in the 1970s and is still used. Today, most Micmac have French surnames (last names). Although the majority speak Micmac at home, they have French or English as their second language.

GOVERNMENT

The leader of the Micmac tribe was called the sagamore. His power was based on consensus (general agreement by the tribe) rather than force. He made peace between families, arranged for wars against common enemies, or helped settle disagreements. Some chiefs working in the French fur trade also resolved differences over trapping territories. The power of the chief could not be passed on to his heirs.

Today the Micmac Nation is made up of the Aroostook Band of Micmac Indians and twenty-eight other bands residing in Canada. The Aroostook Band is governed by a president and an eight-member board of directors who are elected for two-year terms. In 1991, the Aroostook Band of Micmacs Settlement Act was passed by the U.S. government. The act recognized the Micmac as a tribe, entitling members to various federal services and benefits. It also established a $900,000 fund to buy 5,000 acres of land for the tribe.

ECONOMY

For many centuries the Micmac were hunter-gatherers. They wandered the land, continuing this practice as they got involved in trading furs with the French. But they were forced to give up more and more land, and the numbers of fur-bearing animals decreased in the mid-1600s, so the Micmac had to find other means of survival. Some Micmac continued to hunt sea mammals in the Bay of Fundy. They processed and sold porpoise oil. That stopped around the mid-1800s when petroleum came into use. Still reluctant to end their hunting traditions, the Micmac found jobs as guides for sportsmen, and worked in commercial fisheries and logging camps. The Micmac strongly resisted becoming farmers. A few tried farming potatoes, but only for their own table.

By the early 1900s, many Micmac, after a long history of wandering in search of food and resources, settled on reservations. Women and children stayed behind while the men alternated between working away from home and returning to live with their families.

During the twentieth century, some Micmac have taken jobs as seasonal laborers. Families support themselves by selling crafts—especially splint baskets—and by government welfare. Some tribe members harvest ash trees that are used to make the baskets. In the past few decades, Micmac in the United States have been employed in logging, river driving, blueberry agriculture, and potato picking. Many have crossed into Canada to gain employment. Micmac people also manage and own several retail businesses.

DAILY LIFE

Buildings

The Micmac lived in small family groups instead of villages. Their homes were light and easy to move. The most typical residence was the cone-shaped wigwam, made of poles covered by bark, hides, woven grass mats, evergreen branches, or (in more recent times) tar paper and cloth. There was a hearth at the center and belongings were stored around the edges. For sleeping, furs were placed on top of boughs on the floor. In summer they probably lived in a longhouse that could hold several families. Even in the mid-nineteenth century the Micmac still lived in bark wigwams.

Clothing and adornment

In earlier times, the Micmac made clothes from moose or deer hides, bound together with sinew (animal tendons). Animal hair was also used to make clothing. Both men and women wore long hair and leather undergarments. The men dressed in loincloths and the women wore skirts. They covered their feet with moccasins and their legs with leggings of animal hide. In cold weather men also wore a traditional "eared" headdress that covered the scalp. It rose up in points like a bat's ears and draped over the top of their overcoats like a cape. When hunting seals they wore sealskin—with head and flippers attached—as a disguise that allowed them to get close enough to the seal herd to approach their prey. Men wore snowshoes in winter.

After the French came, the Micmac began to wear clothing of French broadcloth. They mixed it with garments of traditional Indian design. Micmac women wore caps that came to a peak, similar to hats worn by fifteenth-century Portuguese fishermen. Women used threads and quills to decorate overcoats obtained by trading furs with the French.

Foods

Before contact with Europeans, the Micmac hunted and gathered their food. Their only crop was tobacco, raised for ceremonial purposes. They brought in cod in January, young seals in May, and moose in September. Smelt, herring, Canada geese and their eggs, sturgeon, partridge, salmon, eels, elk, bear, and caribou also formed important parts of their diet. The Micmac used specialized weapons and containers to hunt. Barbed wooden spears were used for taking fish, usually at night by torchlight. The Micmac fished from hump-shaped canoes. They collected fat, which they often ate as a snack or stored for later use in birch bark and other types of containers.

The Micmac sometimes also ate roots, nuts, and berries that were made into loaves. They boiled and ate yellow pond lily, marsh marigold, wild leeks, milkweed flowers, and cattail, as well as various types of berries. They exchanged leather pelts for metal tools and dried peas, beans, and prunes.

Healing practices

Many Micmac relied on the spiritual powers of medicine people called shamans to combat deadly diseases. Shamans were respected for their powers, but were also sometimes hated and feared because they could use their powers for evil purposes. Herbal resources were also used to promote healing. Gargling with wild blackberry root helped sore throats. A concoction of unripened cranberries was used to draw out venom from poisoned arrows. Teas made from the bark of white oaks and dogwood eased diarrhea and fevers. A salve related to ginseng root was used to heal wounds.

Today, the Aroostook Band of Micmac receive health care services at the Aroostook Medical Center and Carey Medical Center.

ARTS

Micmac crafts

The Micmac were known for their elaborate and colorful beadwork and quillwork (feather crafts), which they used to decorate robes, moccasins, necklaces, arm bands, and other items. Micmac quillwork reached its peak in the Victorian era (1837–1901; the years when Queen Victoria ruled England), when the popularity of ornamental items like boxes, pincushions, and wall hangings was at its height among Americans. The Micmac also made attractive strings of beads called wampum from the shells they found on the shoreline.

CUSTOMS

Festivals

Like other Algonquian tribes, the Micmac traditionally held ceremonies to thank the tribal spirits for their generosity and to ask them for continued blessings. Such ceremonies may have included activities like dancing, feasting, sport, games, and gift-giving.

In August 1994 the Aroostook Band of Micmacs hosted its first annual powwow, a three-day festival that featured Micmac crafts, food, and games.

Family life

Because of the often harsh conditions in which they lived, the Micmac became a very self sufficient people, able to survive by their wits. In winter they scattered into small family groups to find what little food was available. In summer, they reunited in larger groups. The Micmac considered all members of the tribe as equals, and individual initiative was highly prized. Males were recognized as adults only after they had killed a large animal, such as a moose. In addition, a Micmac man could not marry until he had spent two years with his fiancée's father and proved his abilities as a provider.

Hunting

For the Micmac, each month was associated with the pursuit of a different wild resource. They hunted seals in January, smelt (a small fish) in March, and geese in April. They gathered eel or hunted for moose in September, sought elk and beaver for meat in October, and went ice fishing in December. While trying to capture seals, the Micmac sometimes disguised themselves in animal skins and stalked them, using clubs to kill their prey.

NOTABLE PEOPLE

Henri Membertou (c. 1580–1660) was an important Micmac chief, a Catholic convert, and an ally of the French. He was known as a shaman who could predict the future, walk on water, and cure people of diseases.

Micmac Chief Panounias (died 1606) guided the French explorer Samuel Champlain into the interior of North America (see "History").

Anna Mae Aquash, born Pictou, (1945–1976) was an American Indian Movement (AIM) activist who struggled to promote the rights of Indian people in North America. She was found murdered on the Pine Ridge Reservation in South Dakota at the height of Native American protests in the 1970s. Aquash became a symbol of American Indian protest and activism.

CURRENT TRIBAL ISSUES

In the mid-1990s, the Micmac Tribal Council in Maine began the Micmac Development Corporation to oversee tribal economic development, and was looking into the possibility of establishing a casino and resort business. They were also pursuing the ownership of a power station on the Penobscot River.

FURTHER READING

The American Indians: Algonquians of the East Coast, New York: Time-Life Books, 1995.

Calloway, Colin G. *The Abenaki*. New York: Chelsea House Publishers, 1989.

Whitehead, Ruth Holmes. *The Micmac: How Their Ancestors Lived Five Hundred Years Ago*. Halifax, Nova Scotia: Nimbus, 1983.

The Mound Builders:
The Poverty Point, Adena, Hopewell, and Mississippian Cultures

Name

The four known mound-building cultures of North America include the Poverty Point, Adena, Hopewell, and Mississippian cultures. Their names, usually taken from the place where relics of their societies were found, refer to a way of life and a cultural period, not a tribe. No Mississippian cultures survived the eighteenth century.

Location

The Poverty Point culture is named after the northeastern Louisiana plantation where remnants of it were discovered. Other communities of the culture existed along the lower Mississippi River. The Adena culture inhabited present-day West Virginia, Ohio, Kentucky, and Indiana. The Hopewell culture probably began in the Illinois Valley and spread into Ohio and then across the Midwest region. The vast Mississippian culture's territory extended from the mouth of the Illinois River in the north to the mouth of the White River in Arkansas in the south, and eastward along the Ohio and Tennessee Rivers to what is now North Carolina.

Population

The populations of the mound-building cultures are unknown, but at times they probably reached well into the millions. Population estimates for Poverty Point are about 5,000 inhabitants; the Adena culture is estimated to have been from 8 to 15 million; the Mississippian city of Cahokia alone is estimated to have had between 40,000 and 75,000 inhabitants during the twelfth century.

Language family

Unknown.

Origins and group affiliations

The relationship between the mound-building cultures is not clear. Scientists have not proved any direct descendancy from one culture to the next. It is clear, however, that the cultures were in contact, particularly through trade networks, and that the influence from one to the next was profound. The sequence of these cultures is as follows: The Poverty Point culture spanned the period from about 1500 B.C.E. TO 700 B.C.E.. The Adena culture appeared around 500 B.C.E. and flourished until about 100 B.C.E., and the Hopewell culture followed, from 100 B.C.E. to 550–750 C.E. The Mississippian culture was the last, existing from about 700 C.E. to 1751.

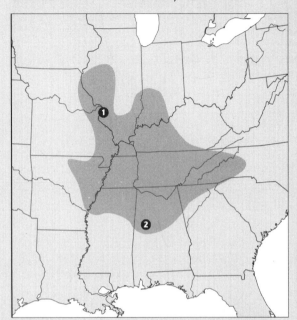

MISSISSIPPIAN CULTURES, 700–1751

Contemporary Landmarks

1. Cahokia Mounds, Illinois
2. Moundville, Alabama

Shaded area: Mississippian territory extended from the mouth of the Illinois River in the north to the mouth of the White River in present-day Arkansas in the south and eastward along the Ohio and Tennessee Rivers to what is now North Carolina.

W hile there are many things that will never be known about the mound-building cultures that thrived in vast territories of the Northeast and the Southeast for nearly 3,000 years, the mounds and artifacts left behind give a fascinating glimpse into some highly complex societies.

Evidence paints a portrait of peoples with complicated political systems, highly developed social customs and religious rites, and a thriving artistic community.

HISTORY

Types of mounds

The people of the mound-building cultures—the Poverty Point, Adena, Hopewell, and Mississippian cultures—left behind remnants of four types of mounds. Effigies (pronounced *EFF-a-geez*)—

mounds shaped like animals such as snakes, birds, or bears—were built along the Great Lakes and in Wisconsin, Michigan, and Iowa. Cone-shaped mounds were built in the Ohio River Valley. Flat-topped pyramids were built in the lower Mississippi region. Walls of earth (sometimes reinforced by stone) were constructed in the central Midwest.

Poverty Point culture (1500 B.C.E. to 700 B.C.E.)

Effigy mounds and dirt embankments that form six concentric circles extending about three-quarters of a mile in total length were found at the site of Poverty Point on the lower Mississippi River in Louisiana. Most can only be observed from the air. Other square, rectangular, and hexagonal mounds are also found at the site. It is estimated that 5,000 people lived at Poverty Point at its height.

IMPORTANT DATES

1400 B.C.E.: People of the Poverty Point culture are constructing large burial mounds and living in planned communities.

500 B.C.E.: The Adena people build villages with burial mounds in the Midwest.

100 B.C.E.: Hopewell societies are building massive earthen mounds for burial of their dead and probably other religious purposes.

700 C.E.: The Mississippian culture begins.

1200: The great city of Cahokia in the Mississippi River Valley flourishes.

1539–43: The Spanish treasure hunter Hernando de Soto becomes the first European to make contact with Mississippian cultures.

1731: The French destroy the Natchez.

People of the Poverty Point culture built large burial mounds and lived in planned communities. Important people in the tribe were buried in the mounds, which often had temples built on top of them. Archaeologists consider these communities the first chiefdoms (villages governed by one principal leader) north of Mexico. The reason for the decline of this civilization by 700 B.C.E. is unknown.

The Adena culture (500 B.C.E. to 100 C.E.)

The Adena culture, named after the estate in Ohio where its remnants were first discovered, had a population estimated at between eight and seventeen million at its height. The Adena were the first known people in the present-day United States to construct earthen mounds in which they regularly buried their dead. The mounds were often shaped in animal or geometric designs.

When the early American settlers first saw the Adena mounds, some ignored them, but others were fascinated. Some nineteenth-century writers theorized that they were built by the Toltecs or Aztecs of Mexico, while others thought the "First Empire Builders," as some called the Adena, might have been Hebrews, Greeks, Persians, Romans, Vikings, Hindus, or any group who had ever built a mound in the Old

An illustration of the Mound Builders gathering their crops.

World. The common belief was that the mounds could not have been built by Indians because at the time Americans made the erroneous assumption that Indians were incapable of planning and developing such vast monuments. In 1894 Cyrus Thomas, an ethnologist (a person who compares the practices and beliefs of different cultures) who worked for the Smithsonian Institution, published a paper showing that the mounds were the work of a number of different cultures that were part of the family of American Indian tribes.

Scholars disagree on whether or not the Adena were descendants of the earlier Poverty Point culture, but most believe that there was some interaction among the two cultures.

The Hopewell culture (100 B.C.E.–550 to 750 B.C.E.)

The Hopewell culture may have grown out of the earlier Adena culture. Discoveries there have included copper effigies of fish, birds, and serpent heads, as well as beads, axes, ornaments, a ceremonial antler headdress of carved wood, and tens of thousands of freshwater pearls and shell beads.

The Hopewell culture was more highly developed than that of the Adena, with richer burial customs, more sophisticated art, grander ceremonies, a stricter system of social classes, and more advanced farming practices. Items found at Hopewell burial sites included ear spools (a type of earrings) and skulls. The skulls showed that devices had been used to fashion the heads of infants, as they grew, into unusual shapes. The shapes showed a person's status in the society and were considered attractive.

The Hopewell people specialized in stone work and examples of it have been found as far away as Florida. The Hopewell extended their influence from New England to the lower Mississippi region. The culture began to decline around 550 C.E. for reasons unknown. Some theories suggest climate changes, crop failures, epidemics, and civil war, among other reasons.

Hopewell mounds rose from six to seventy feet. During the eighteenth and nineteenth centuries, there were fantastic theories about the origins of the Hopewell mounds. U.S. President Thomas Jefferson

(1743–1826) carefully examined a mound near his home at Monticello, Virginia, and proclaimed that the mounds were clearly built by American Indians.

Mississippian culture (700 C.E. to 1751)

The Mississippian civilization of Temple Mound Builders began in the Mississippi River valley around 700 C.E. It was at its height between 1000 C.E. and 1200 C.E., when the great cities of Cahokia and Moundville grew up.

Cahokia may have been the largest and most powerful city in eastern North America. Centrally located for both north-south and east-west trade exchanges, Cahokia flourished from about 900 to 1250 C.E. It was home to a gigantic 100-foot-high mound and more than 100 other mounds in its six square miles. Estimates of the population of the city of Cahokia alone ranged between 40,000 and 75,000 during the twelfth century. Nearby were many smaller towns and villages.

The 300-acre site of Moundville is located south of present-day Tuscaloosa, Alabama. Its 100-acre public square was surrounded by 20 pairs of mounds and enclosed by wooden fences. Moundville was the capital of a large prehistoric nation with a number of smaller district capitals that sent many of their resources and finely crafted goods to be enjoyed by Moundville's rich rulers.

Decline of Mississippian culture

Temple Mound Builders still lived in the Mississippi River valley in the sixteenth century when the Spanish first entered the region.

Over the next two centuries, the population of the region mostly perished. Many reasons are suggested for the decline. It may have been due to European diseases, to which the Indians had no resistance. Overpopulation and overcrowding—plus the problem of what to do about urban waste—might also have contributed. Massive crop failures possibly linked to changes in the climate may have played a part.

Some historians believe that when the Europeans first came to North America, a few of the tribes still living in the Mississippi and Tennessee River valleys were direct descendants of the Temple Mound Builders. But except for the Natchez tribe, one of the only remaining Mississippian culture societies known to the early European explorers and fur traders, few Native Americans had more than dim memories of the way of life of their probable ancestors. There is very little recorded about Mississippian tribes living at the time of European contact.

Sometime between 1539 and 1542, tribes who lived in the region where the Temple Mound Builders thrived forced the expedition of Spanish treasure-hunter Hernando de Soto to retreat down the Mississippi River. Over a century later, the French moved into the area and came into contact with the Natchez people, who lived on the Mississippi River in present-day west Mississippi. The French decided to impose taxes on the Natchez fur trade. From 1729 to 1731, the two cultures battled until the French, with the help of their Choctaw (see entry) allies, destroyed the Natchez nation and sold most of the survivors into slavery in the Caribbean. A few Natchez sought safety with neighboring tribes and continued their struggle against the Europeans. As the Natchez were absorbed into the other tribes, all that remained of the Mississippian culture was gone.

RELIGION

Not a great deal is known about the religion of the mound-building societies. While earlier societies generally built their mounds as burial memorials, the later Mississippian mounds became temples for an aristocratic priesthood. Priests in this advanced culture, as well as artists, could devote themselves fully to their professions, while their communities provided for them.

The Natchez, the last of the Mississippian people, may provide insight into the religion of the Mississippian culture. The Natchez credited their origin to the Sun God. According to their creation beliefs, a man and woman came to Earth to teach humans the proper way to live. The man was the younger brother of the Sun. He told the people to build a temple and to place inside it a sacred fire that was to be kept always burning; he explained that the fire was a piece of the Sun he had brought to Earth.

The sacred priest-leader of the Natchez was called the Great Sun and he was regarded as part-god. His primary duty was to maintain the sacred fire in the temple. The Great Sun dressed in rich clothes and was carried from place to place so he would never touch the bare ground. Only certain people were permitted into his presence and they had to follow strict rules when approaching him. No one was allowed to watch him eat or even touch the dishes from which he ate. During the few times that he walked, servants spread mats on the path before him. He rarely even used his hands. One French Catholic priest reported that if he wanted to give the remains of his meal to relatives, "he pushed the dishes to them with his feet."

Spanish explorers who wrote about the Natchez tell of the Great Sun's practice of greeting his elder brother, the Sun in the sky, with ritual song and prayer. Every month, the entire tribe went to the temple and paid tribute to the Great Sun. He generally appeared before them wearing a feathered crown and seated in an ornate chair that was carried by eight throne bearers. When the French destroyed the Natchez, they captured the Great Sun and sent him into slavery in the Caribbean.

LANGUAGE

It is not known what language was spoken by the Temple Mound Builders, or even if different groups of them spoke the same language.

Buildings

Adena mounds were usually cone-shaped and contained many burial remains. They were used over and over again for generations. The Adena mounds were probably also used for religious purposes besides burial. The most famous Adena earthwork is Serpent Mound in Adams County, Ohio, a five-foot-high, twenty-foot-wide mound shaped like a snake that measures 800 feet long from the mouth to the tail. If it could be stretched out in a straight line, it would measure about 1,300 feet. The snake has an egg-shaped object in its mouth. The mound cannot be fully viewed from ground level and lies on top of a 100-foot ridge. It may have been built as a message to the gods that lived above in the air or the sky.

The Hopewell's Grave Creek Mound in Moundville, West Village, is among the largest man-made earthworks ever created. It required three million basketloads of earth to build, and all of the earth was transported without horses or carts. Fort Ancient, near Lebanon, Ohio, has walls that extend more than three and one-half miles and stand from four to twenty-three feet high. The continuity of the walls is broken only by seventy openings. The Hopewell built it about three centuries before the arrival of Christopher Columbus.

The most impressive structures of the Mississippian culture were the temple mounds that loomed over their towns and villages. These mounds were built entirely of dirt carried to the site in baskets, a process that took a long time. Some mounds were massive. The one known as Monk's Mound at Cahokia, was built in a series of fourteen stages between 900 and 1150 C.E.. When finished it stood 100 feet high and covered more than 16 acres at its base.

The mounds were rectangular in shape and flat on top. They were used both as temples and as burial sites. When the mounds were filled with bodies, more room was made by leveling the top, adding another level of earth, and raising a fresh temple complex. The tops of other mounds became sites for trading, festivals, and other public functions.

Mississippian temples, like the society's houses, were built from wood and interwoven cane stalks or small branches covered with a plaster made from mud. Some farmers had two separate houses: an open home with good air circulation for warm weather, and an insulated home with a fireplace and areas dug beneath the floor to store food in cold weather.

Clothing

Members of the Adena, Hopewell, and Mississippian cultures wore decorated loincloths (flaps of material that covered the back and front and were suspended from the waist) and necklaces made from engraved stones. Mississippians often adorned their bodies with tattoos or painted their faces. Some very wealthy people wore headdresses decorated with feathers, animal fur, pearls, or even precious metals such as copper or galena, an ore of lead. The rulers of the Mississippian culture went to their graves in fancy dress.

Food

The Adena ate many native plants that we now consider weeds, such as goosefoot, giant ragweed, pigweed, hickory nuts, bottle gourds, squashes, and sunflowers. They did not eat corn, like the later Mississippian people, because at that time the only corn that could be grown in North America was not well suited to the climate where the Adena lived. The little bit of corn they grew was used only for ceremonies.

Much of the early Mississippian diet was based on hunting and fishing. When the people learned how to grow large supplies of corn and beans, their population was able to grow beyond what hunting and gathering alone allowed. A variety of corn that could withstand cold, wet weather was introduced to the Mississippi Valley between 800 and 1000 C.E. About the same time, fast-growing beans—kidney, navy, pinto, snap, and pole—were brought from Mexico. The beans were allowed to climb up the stalks of growing corn.

Healing practices

The Mississippian, like the Adena and the Hopewell, suffered from a variety of diseases, including arthritis, infections by parasites, and the ancient disease tuberculosis, a lung disease. Pictures on ancient pots show people with bent spines, a deformity that often is associated with tuberculosis. The pots might have been used to store herbal remedies to treat the ailment.

ARTS

Hopewell works of art showed a delicate, free-flowing style. Artists made shell drinking cups, gold silhouettes, and effigy pipes in the image of frogs, owls, and alligators. Artists used copper to fashion beads, collars, pendants, and effigies. At one grave site, a large headdress was discovered with imitation deer antlers made of copper-covered wood.

Mississippian mound builders expressed their culture through their pottery, which was often of outstanding quality and even displayed a sense of humor. One existing example is a jar shaped in the form of a very fat human leg and foot, while another depicts a face with a comical expression. Small statues have been found that were probably intended for use in their temples or as burial goods to accompany a Great Sun or a Lesser Sun into the afterlife. Such ceramics may have played a central role in the trade between the Mississippian and a large network that extended from the Gulf of Mexico in the south and the Great Lakes in the north, and from the Rocky Mountains in the west to the Appalachians in the east. Skilled artists made baskets, pottery, leather garments, and shell beads, as well as ornaments of copper and tools made of stone. The shell, copper, and various types of stone must have been imported because they do not naturally occur near the homeland of the Temple Mound Builders.

CUSTOMS

Social rank

The Natchez were the last of the Mississippian culture. Eighteenth-century French observers in the homeland of the Natchez described their social ranking system. The most important people were the Great Sun and his relatives, who made up the highest class. Below them were the nobles, followed by the honest men, and at the bottom were the despised commoners known as the "Stinkards."

The Great Sun could only marry partners from the lowest class of the society, the Stinkards. The Great Sun's brothers (the Lesser Suns) and his sisters (the Women Suns) also could only marry Stinkards. But the children of the Women Suns were permitted to keep their mother's social rank, and one of them would usually become the next Great Sun when his uncle died. The children of the Great Sun and the Lesser Suns did not retain their parents' high rank.

Stinkards who married into the top social class remained Stinkards all their lives. They could not eat with their spouses and had to stand in their presence. If they offended their high-ranking spouses in some way, they could be killed and replaced. The only way Stinkards could improve their own status was by showing extreme bravery during wartime.

Games

The Adena broke up the daily routine by playing games and holding athletic contests; the whole village probably participated.

Children had toys like dolls, little canoes, and sleds, and adults had dice made from bones to use for gambling.

The Mississippian culture shared some customs with modern Native American tribes. Experts who study the remains of ancient cities say that Cahokia contained large ball courts and special stones that were probably used for playing a game called *Chunkey*. In this game, stones were rolled across the ground while players threw spears at the spot where they believed the stones would stop. The winner was the player who landed his spear nearest the stone's stopping place. Chunkey was played by the Great Plains tribes during the nineteenth century.

Death and burial

During the earliest Adena period, bodies were wrapped in bark. In later times, bodies were sometimes left outdoors until predators, weather, or other natural processes had removed the flesh from the bones; then they were buried. Sometimes the bodies were cremated or buried without being left outdoors first. They were set in their graves either stretched out at full length or flexed, with the knees drawn up. Corpses of honored dead were coated with red dye or graphite (a type of soft lead) and covered with hundreds of delicate shell beads.

Adena mounds were designed to hold many bodies over a period of years. A mound might begin as a shallow pit grave, with a small pile of dirt heaped over it. As more corpses were added, more and more earth was also added to the mound, which sometimes reached a height of up to seventy feet.

The Hopewell built huge burial houses. Cremations were performed in clay-lined pits. The dead were surrounded with special grave goods, and individual graves were often covered with low earthen mounds. Spectacular burials were given for the top members of the society. Their corpses were surrounded with high quality artistic goods made of woods and metals.

The remnants of Mississippian pottery and sculpture show that the people of this culture thought often about death and the afterlife. Upon the death of the Great Sun or his relatives—his mother White Woman, his brothers the Lesser Suns, and his sisters the Woman Suns—some of their spouses and servants believed that it was their duty and a great honor to accompany the deceased into the afterlife. They willingly went to their own deaths; others were not quite so willing but were sent to their deaths anyway by Mississippian officials.

Some anthropologists (people who study ancient cultures) believe Mississippian officials may have given drugs to people who were about to become human sacrifices. The drugs made the victims unconscious; they were then killed and buried with their ruler to accompany him or her into the next life. However, unlike the people of the Adena and Hopewell cultures that came before, the Mississippian people apparently saw no need to bury their dead with fabulous treasures.

CURRENT TRIBAL ISSUES

Until about 1800, when they began venturing beyond the eastern area of the continent, most English-speaking colonists did not come into contact with Indian mounds. When white settlement expanded beyond the Appalachian Mountains, many mounds were plowed over. During the twentieth century, many more have been destroyed by farmers, vandals, and highway builders. The preservation of the mound builders' earthworks and relics has become the responsibility of the states in which they are found, and some are operated as historical sites by those states.

During the nineteenth century, many Adena mounds were saved from destruction through the efforts of scholars such as Frederic Ward Putnam, director of the Peabody Museum of Archaeology and Ethnology at Harvard University. In 1887, Putnam raised more than $5,000, which enabled Harvard to buy an important mound in Ohio from its owner. In 1900, Harvard University gave Serpent Mound to the state of Ohio on the condition that it would be preserved and opened to the public.

Several of the Hopewell mounds have become part of the current American landscape, without regard to, or respect for, their historical meaning. For example, during World War II (1939-45), the U.S. Army built a training camp near the Hopewell Culture National Historical Park, formerly known as "Mound City," and badly damaged the site. Grave Creek Mound in West Virginia has a racetrack built around its base and a saloon erected at the top. In Belpre, Ohio, there is a mound in the parking lot of a fast-food restaurant. In Newark, Ohio, part of the Newark Earthworks makes up a country club golf course. And in Huntington, West Virginia, visitors can pay $1.00 and observe a mound from a seat on a roller coaster ride.

Cahokia in Illinois is the site of the Cahokia Mounds State Historic Site and the Cahokia Mounds State Park. Many of the mound builders' sites are open to the public and feature museums and relics that celebrate and explain the region's mound building heritage.

Many existing earthworks have been worn down to rough shapes in overgrown rural fields and riversides, while others are being preserved. But, of more than 1,100 known sites in the state of Arkansas, only two remain relatively untouched. The still uncertain fate of the mounds remains in the hands of present and future generations.

FURTHER READING

Archaeological Parks in the Heartland (U.S.): [Online] http://krakatoa.uark.edu/misc/arts/heartland.html

Beck, Melinda. "The Lost Worlds of Ancient America." *Newsweek.* Vol. 118 (fall–winter 1991): 24.

Fowler, Melvin. *Cahokia, Ancient Capital of the Midwest.* Reading, Massachusetts: Addison-Wesley Publishing, 1974.

The National Park Service's "Ancient Architects of the Mississippi": [Online] http://www.cr.nps.gov/aad/feature.

Narragansett

Name

The name Narragansett (pronounced *nah-ruh-GAN-sit*) refers to both the people and the place where they lived. Some believe it means "people of the little points and bays." The name currently applies to living members of the Eastern Niantic and Narragansett tribes.

Location

At the height of their authority, the Narragansett occupied most of present-day Rhode Island. They lived mainly along the Atlantic Coast and in the valleys and forests west of Narragansett Bay. Today the Narragansett Indian Tribe owns a 1,943-acre reservation 45 miles south of Providence, Rhode Island. As of the mid-1990s, no one lived on the reservation; most Narragansett lived in Rhode Island and Massachusetts.

Population

Estimates range from 4,000 to 30,000 in 1600. In a 1990 census (count of the population) by the U.S. Bureau of the Census, 2,564 people identified themselves as Narragansett.

Language family

Eastern Algonquian.

Origins and group affiliations

The Narragansett are one of the oldest tribes in North America, dating back about 11,000 years. Powerful Narragansett chiefs controlled certain groups of Massachusett, Nipmuck, Pokanoket, Wampanoag (see entry), Coweset, Shawomet, Mashapaug, and Manissean Indians who lived in southern New England and New York state.

NARRAGANSETT

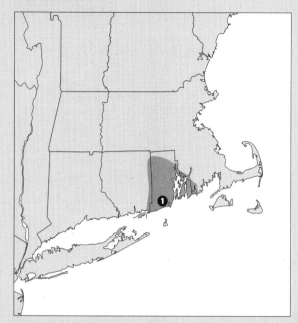

Shaded area: Traditional lands of the Narragansett in present-day Rhode Island.

Contemporary Communities

1. Narragansett Indian Tribe of Rhode Island

The Narragansett was possibly the largest and strongest Native American tribe in New England at the time British colonists arrived in the New World. They were a generous and friendly people. When Puritan minister Roger Williams made his way to Rhode Island after being expelled from Massachusetts in 1636, he was warmly welcomed. The Narragansett gave him land that became the city of Providence, Rhode Island. But other settlers followed, wars broke out, and in less than forty years, the Narragansett nation had been nearly destroyed.

HISTORY

Early contact with Europeans

Prehistoric Indians inhabited the northeastern United States at the end of the last Ice Age, around 11,000 B.C.E. They were wandering hunters of large mammals, but were forced to change their lifestyle when the great ice caps melted and the Arctic mammals died or moved further north. Those who settled along the coast, rivers, streams and bogs of New England between 10,000 and 700 B.C.E. were the ancestors of the Narragansett.

Italian explorer Giovanni da Verrazano visited the area in 1524 and lived among the Narragansett for fifteen days. He wrote that the people "have the most civil customs that we have found on this voyage. . . . Their manner is sweet and gentle." Over the next century, European contact with the Narragansett increased gradually; relations were usually friendly.

Seafaring Europeans came to Rhode Island because the nearby waters provided one of the richest fishing grounds in the world. They brought trade goods made of iron to exchange with the tribe. They also brought foreign diseases such as smallpox and plague. The Narragansett managed to escape the worst epidemics, which destroyed most of the Wampanoag (see entry) and others. Survivors joined the Narragansett, making the tribe even stronger than it had been before.

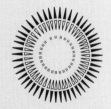

IMPORTANT DATES

1524: Italian explorer Giovanni da Verrazano visits the Narragansett, beginning European relations with the tribe.

1675: The Great Swamp Fight during King Philip's War nearly wipes out the tribe.

1880: The Rhode Island state legislature attempts to break up the tribe.

1983: The U.S. government officially recognizes the Narragansett tribe.

Settlers come—wars follow

In 1636 the Massachusetts Bay Colony banished Puritan minister Roger Williams and a few of his followers. Colonial officials objected because he spoke out against taking Native American land by force and against punishing people whose religious beliefs were different. Narragansett chief Miantonomi had heard of Williams, welcomed him and his followers, and gave them a place to build homes.

Over the next forty years, the Narragansett were frequently involved in wars with other tribes as they tried to maintain their dominance over New England. They also had to contend with more and more British settlers. In 1675, the United Colonies of New England began King Philip's War against the Wampanoag (see entry). They also declared war on the Narragansett because the great Narragansett Chief Canonchet, son of Miantonomi, refused to surrender Wampanoag refugees from the war.

On December 16, 1675, the colonial army laid siege to a Narragansett stronghold and destroyed it in what became known as the Great Swamp Fight. One participant of the battle estimated that between 600 and 1,000 Narragansett warriors died. Their parents, widows, and children were hunted down and brutally treated. By the end of the war in the summer of 1676, possibly as few as 200 Narragansett remained alive.

Survivors on the reservation

Of the surviving Narragansett, some were sold into slavery. Others merged with the Niantic, a related tribe; the combined group took the name Narragansett. They maintained themselves as a small independent unit on a 64-square-mile reservation in southern New England for more than 200 years. In 1880, however, the Rhode Island legislature purchased the reservation, hoping to break up the tribe. Despite this, the Narragansett remained a community and, in the 1920s, began a long struggle to win back their ancestral lands.

In 1978 the Narragansett finally won a lawsuit against the state of Rhode Island for the return of some of their traditional territory. In 1983 the Narragansett won recognition from the U.S. government. Federally recognized tribes are those with which the U.S. government maintains official relations. Without federal recognition, the tribe does not exist as far as the government is concerned, and is not entitled to financial and other help.

RELIGION

The Narragansett believed in a creator god called Cautantowwit. He made the first people from stone then smashed them, creating the ancestors of all other people. Second in importance to Cautantowwit was a spirit called Chepi, who was descended from the souls of the dead. His power could be called upon by specially trained healers. Chepi was feared because he could punish people who behaved improperly by causing them to become sick or die. Chepi warned Indians who followed the English lifestyle that evil consequences would result if they did not return to a Native American way of life.

The Narragansett also believed in many lesser gods and powerful spirits, such as the crow who gave them corn and beans—their staple crops—after he stole them from Cautantowwit's garden.

Many Indians in southern New England believed that an unusual or outstanding event had to be the work of a *Manittoo*, a god. Because of this belief, the white people coming into their territory with such unusual phenomena as European metallurgy, sailing technology, and printing and writing were often seen as gods. The English colonists had an easier time among the Narragansett because of this belief system.

LANGUAGE

All southern New England Indians, including the Narragansett, spoke related languages of the eastern Algonquian family. Both the people and the Narragansett language were destroyed by King Philip's War. A study done in 1861 declared that nobody had spoken Narragansett regularly since before 1816. According to the Summer Institute of Linguistics, no Narragansett person knew or used their native language in 1997.

Roger Williams, founder of Providence, Rhode Island, wrote a book published in 1643 called *A Key into the Language of America*. It remains the largest collection of Narragansett vocabulary. Later efforts, dating from 1769 to 1879, added 82 words, raising the total known to about 200. Isolated terms, such as *wigwam* and *powwow*, have become well known. Williams listed information about the tribal customs as well as their language and how it related to the Eastern Algonquian dialects of the Massachusett, Pequot (see entry), Mohegan, and Wampanoag tribes.

GOVERNMENT

The Narragansett lived under the authority of lesser chiefs called sachems (pronounced *SAY-chums*), who were under the command of a grand sachem who lived in the largest village. The position was hereditary (handed down to relatives), and often a sachem shared power with another person. The favorite arrangement was to share power with a nephew. When there was no close male relative, a female relative might become sachem.

The sachems ensured that all members of the tribe had enough land to support themselves. They were paid for their services in corn, deerskins, and food. Sachems were careful to treat their subjects well, because it was a matter of pride and wealth to have a large number of subjects. If a family disagreed with a sachem's decisions, it could join another tribe.

In the eighteenth century, the Rhode Island government abolished the position of sachem as it gradually began taking over tribal lands. The Narragansett ignored this arrogant action and continued to act under the authority of sachems and a tribal council.

At the beginning of the twentieth century, the U.S. government regarded the Narragansett tribe as extinct. In 1983, however, the remaining Narragansett won recognition from the federal government. Today the tribal government is run by a nine-member elected tribal council consisting of a sachem, a medicine man or woman, a secretary, a treasurer, and five members. The government also includes several government departments such as Housing, Health, Human Services, Natural Resources, and Finance.

ECONOMY

The Narragansett traditionally farmed, fished, hunted, and gathered to provide themselves with a varied diet. When they won recognition from the federal government in 1983, they became eligible for public education, health care, job training, and housing aid. They set about trying to make themselves self-sufficient.

Today, the largest single employer of the Narragansett is tribal government, which employs about three dozen members of the tribe. Others who are affiliated with the reservation maintain a community garden, harvest trees, or work in the building trades in nearby towns. Some work in the tourist trade at the Dover Indian Trading Post in Rockville and at the Narragansett Indian Longhouse, which offers lectures and tours. A planned casino will also generate jobs.

Among the Narragansett affiliated with the reservation, the per capita income was a relatively healthy $10,524 in the mid-1990s (the figure at most other reservations is lower). Compare this to a figure of about $20,000 for the American population. (Per capita income is the average income of one person in one year.)

DAILY LIFE

Families

For recreation, Narragansett men in traditional times enjoyed smoking and gossiping, playing games such as an early version of football, throwing dice, and dancing. Women were often busy at food cultivation and preparation, priding themselves on interesting recipes that combined several different foods.

Buildings

The Narragansett moved in both winter and summer. In summer they moved to take advantage of good lands for planting and gathering, and in winter they moved to get to a warmer place with good hunting. Sometimes they were forced to move when fleas and other biting insects became troublesome or to avoid infection when illness struck their village. Their wigwams had to be portable and easy to

SUCCOTASH

The Narragansett introduced the earliest European settlers to their native dish, called msickquatash by the natives and succotash by the settlers. The original dish consisted of corn and lima beans, picked fresh from the garden. New England housewives enlivened the dish by adding green peppers and other vegetables shipped in from the West Indies.

1 cup fresh or frozen baby lima beans

salt to taste

1 cup fresh or frozen corn kernels

4 Tablespoons (1/2 stick) butter OR
    1/4 cup heavy [whipping] cream

freshly ground pepper to taste

In a large saucepan, boil the beans in salted water to cover until nearly done. Add the corn kernels and cook until tender, just a few minutes. Drain, stir in the butter, and check seasoning, adding salt and pepper to taste.

From Frances McCullough and Barbara Witt, *Classic American Food Without Fuss.* New York: Villard Books, 1996, p. 151–152.

take apart and reassemble. Roofs were made of chestnut or birch bark attached to the top of bent poles, which were stuck in the ground. In the winter, they insulated the wigwams with mats or animal skins attached to the roof and spread on the floor. A hole in the roof allowed smoke from the fire to escape.

Two or more families sometimes shared the same wigwam. They also built shacks so family members could sleep near their crops to protect young plants from birds and other predators.

In the 1940s the Narragansett built a traditional longhouse on the reservation to serve as a community center. In the 1990s, plans were underway to build a new community center and homes on the reservation.

Food

Before the Europeans destroyed the Narragansett culture, New England food was plentiful and there was a great variety. Along the coast and in the swamps and streams, women caught spawning alewives, clams, oysters, lobsters, and other shellfish. In the woods they collected wild onions, chestnuts, wild strawberries, and other plants in season. Men prepared the fields for planting, and women planted and harvested the crops, including corn, beans, and squash.

Men hunted ducks, pigeons, deer, rabbits, squirrels, bears, and beavers. In the winter they fished through the ice. Men also grew their own tobacco and molded or carved their own special pipes for smoking it. To smoke a peace pipe with another person signified the formation of a new friendship.

Clothing and adornment

Little is known about the traditional clothing worn by the Narragansett. In summer, men probably wore breechcloths, a type of garment that is secured at the waist and passes between the legs. Women wore leather or woven skirts. We know that beads were popular; wampum—beads carved from the shells of local clams—acted as both decoration and money.

Healing practices

Narragansett healing practices went hand in hand with their religion. People known as *pawwaws* (this is where the term "powwow" comes from) presided over religious and healing ceremonies. To gain their respected positions, pawwaws had to be able to communicate with the spirit world and to heal or injure others. They might demonstrate their power by creating magic arrows from the hair of an enemy or by causing a real arrowhead to injure someone. However, pawwaws more often relied on massage and the laying on of hands to cure the sick. They were usually men. Women skilled at making medicines from plants were called in to attend the birth of a child.

Narragansett Pine Tree Medicine Man.

Today, medicine men and sometimes women still play an important role in tribal life. Their care is supplemented on the reservation by a tribally-administered Indian Health Program. Visiting nurses come to the reservation from hospitals in the Providence area.

CUSTOMS

Marriage

Historians believe that three generations of two different families lived together in one house. A woman probably moved in with her husband's family when she married. Sachems married only women of high rank, such as the daughter of another sachem. Sometimes sachems had two or three wives if they could afford to support them.

Festivals

The Narragansett honored Cautantowwit, the creator, with a *nickommo*, a special ceremony in which they sacrificed their most precious possessions by burning or burying them. They also honored him with a feast of thanksgiving in autumn; foods consumed at the feast included turkey, corn, beans, cranberries, and pumpkin pie.

Death and dying

Old men prepared the bodies of the dead for burial. First they rubbed them with mud or soot. Objects were placed in the grave to accompany the soul to Cautantowwit's house, where they lived much as they had on earth. Sometimes a sick or dead person's home was burned to prevent infection or a visit from the evil spirit who had afflicted the person. A dead person's name was never mentioned again.

CURRENT TRIBAL ISSUES

The Narragansett are striving for economic self-sufficiency. Housing projects are being designed to move the elderly and families onto the previously uninhabited reservation. A bingo parlor is also planned.

NOTABLE PEOPLE

The Narragansett sachem Miantonomi (d. 1643), who originally befriended the English colonists, was one of the first Native Americans to try to create a pan-Indian alliance against them (an alliance that would include members of different tribes). In a famous speech he said: "These English having gotten our land, they with scythes cut down the grass, and their hogs spoil our clam banks, and we shall all be starved." Miantonomi could not overcome rivalries among tribes, however. He was executed by the Mohegan tribe in 1643.

Other notable Narragansett include: Canonchet, Miantonomi's son and successor and a leader during King Philip's War (1675–76); Canonicus, Miantonomi's uncle, who governed internal matters in the tribe while Miantonomi dealt with external problems; and Quaiapen, a female sachem and Canonicus's daughter-in-law, who led part of the tribe in King Philip's War.

Narragansett sachem Miantonomi in captivity.

FURTHER READING

Algonquians of the East Coast. Alexandria, Virginia: Time-Life Books, 1995.

Beals, Carleton. *Colonial Rhode Island.* Camden, NJ: Thomas Nelson, 1970.

Simmons, William S. *The Narragansett.* New York: Chelsea House, 1989.

Summer Institute of Linguistics. Living Languages of the Americas: United States of America: [Online] http://www.sil.org/lla/usa_lg.html, March 7, 1997.

Through Indian Eyes: The Untold Story of Native American Peoples. Pleasantville, New York: Reader's Digest, 1995.

Ojibway

Name

Ojibway (pronounced *oh-jib-WAY*). It means "puckered up," and is thought to be derived from the way their moccasins were sewn gathered at the top. The Ojibway have been known by several different names. The traditional name is Anishinaubeg, which means "original people" or "first people." The people were also known as Chippewa, as a result of the mispronunciation of Ojibway by the French. The Ojibway are also known as Ojibwayy, Ojibwe, and Otchipwe.

Location

The Ojibway flourished north of Lake Huron and northeast of Lake Superior at the time of European contact. Today they live on about twenty-five American reservations located in Michigan, Wisconsin, Minnesota, North Dakota, Montana, and Oklahoma. In Canada, they live in Ontario, Manitoba, Alberta, and Saskatchewan.

Population

The French estimated there were about 35,000 Ojibway in the 1600s, but other historians say there may have been two or three times that number spread out over a wide area. In a census done in 1990, 103,826 people identified themselves as Chippewa, making this the third-largest tribe in the United States. About 60,000 Ojibway live in Canada.

Language family

Algonquian.

Origins and group affiliations

Algonquin peoples, including ancestors of the Ojibway, migrated from an area north of the St. Lawrence River westward into the Great Lakes region in about the year 900. After Europeans arrived, the Ojibway split up into several groups. Some joined in an alliance with the Potawatomi (see entry) and Ottawa in Michigan and Ontario. The Salteaux Ojibway in Michigan's Upper Peninsula met and were influenced by the Cree. In about 1830, a group moved to the Great Plains, took up local customs, and became known as the Plains Ojibway or Bungees.

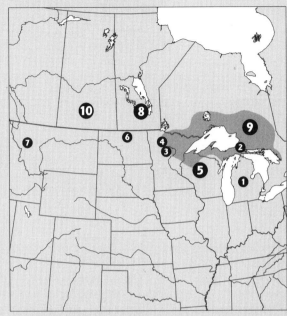

OJIBWAY/CHIPPEWA

Contemporary Communities

Michigan
1. Saginaw Chippewa Indian Tribe
2. Sault Ste. Marie Tribe of Chippewa

Minnesota
3. Minnesota Chippewa Tribe (6 tribes)
4. Red Lake Band of Chippewa Indians
5. **Wisconsin:** 6 reservations

North Dakota
6. Turtle Mountain Band of Chippewa

Montana
7. Swan Creek and Black River Chippewa
8. **Manitoba:** 32 reserves
9. **Ontario:** 78 reserves
10. **Saskatchewan:** 13 reserves

Shaded area: Traditional lands of the Ojibway in Michigan's Upper Peninsula and Ontario.

The Ojibway (often called the Chippewa) were a huge group who dominated the vast Great Lakes region for centuries. At one time they may well have been the most powerful tribe in North America. Today the Ojibway form the third-largest Native American group in the United States. Their attempts to adapt to a modern world while preserving elements of their ancient culture have been remarkably successful.

HISTORY

The Ojibway migrated with other Algonquin peoples from an area north of the St. Lawrence River in Canada westward into the Great Lakes region beginning around 900. No one knows exactly why the Ojibway left the Northeast. They may have been trying to escape diseases brought by Norse explorers who came in about the year 1000. Among the Ojibway the story of the move has been handed down from generation to generation. It describes how the Algonquin nations moved to the Great Lakes from a salt sea in the East—possibly Hudson Bay. The people suffered great hardship during their migration, which lasted several hundred years.

Encounters with the French

At the time of the first contact with Europeans, the Ojibway were concentrated in the eastern part of Michigan's Upper Peninsula. Frenchman Etiènne Brulé (pronounced *ET-ee-en BRU-lay*) arrived in 1622 looking for a water passage to the Orient. He encountered the Ojibway at a place known today as Sault Sainte Marie (pronounced *SOO Saint Marie*). Because of the rapids at the site, the French gave the Ojibway the name *Salteurs*, or *Salteaux*, meaning "people of the rapids." (Rapids is the name given to an extremely fast-moving part of a river.)

Fur traders and missionaries soon followed French explorers. By the late seventeenth century, the Ojibway had become heavily engaged in the fur trade with the French. They traded animal skins for European items like guns, alcohol, cloth, utensils, and beads. They became wealthy and powerful and dependent on French goods.

Now in possession of weapons, and wanting to range farther afield to take more furs, the Ojibway began to expand their territory. Between 1687 and the late 1700s, they expanded into the areas known today as lower Michigan, northern Minnesota, Wisconsin, and parts of Canada. They displaced many other tribes as they moved. It has been said that no other tribe has come close to controlling such a huge area.

French displaced by British

Between 1689 and 1760, France and England were repeatedly engaged in wars in North America. To protect their trade interests, the Ojibway sided with the French. Many Ojibway (mainly women) intermarried with the French. Their families, and those of Ojibway warriors fighting with the French, were often forced to travel from battle site to battle site, because it was far too dangerous to remain behind without protectors. This constant moving about disrupted traditional family life.

IMPORTANT DATES

1622: Frenchman Etiènne Brulé encounters the Ojibway at present-day Sault Sainte Marie.

1755–63: Ojibway ally with the French against the British during the French and Indian War to protect their trade interests.

1830: Many Ojibway move north to Canada rather than be forced to live southwest of the Missouri River. Others remain behind and work out ways to keep plots of land.

1968: Three Ojibway—Dennis Banks, George Mitchell, and Clyde Bellecourt—found the American Indian Movement (AIM) in Minneapolis, Minnesota, to raise public awareness of the violation of treaty rights by federal and state governments.

1983: In the Voight Decision, the U.S. Court of Appeals rules that Ojibway rights to hunt, fish, and gather on the lands of their ancestors are protected by past treaties.

1988: With the passage of the Indian Gaming Regulation Act, the Ojibway exercise their rights as a sovereign nation (a nation within a nation) within the United States by running gambling establishments on reservations.

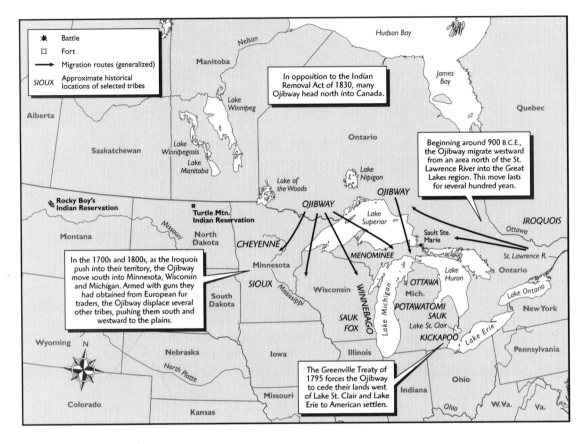

A map of the migrations of the Ojibway.

Map labels:

Legend:
- ✶ Battle
- ⊡ Fort
- → Migration routes (generalized)
- *SIOUX* Approximate historical locations of selected tribes

In opposition to the Indian Removal Act of 1830, many Ojibway head north into Canada.

Beginning around 900 B.C.E., the Ojibway migrate westward from an area north of the St. Lawrence River into the Great Lakes region. This move lasts for several hundred years.

In the 1700s and 1800s, as the Iroquois push into their territory, the Ojibway move south into Minnesota, Wisconsin and Michigan. Armed with guns they had obtained from European fur traders, the Ojibway displace several other tribes, pushing them south and westward to the plains.

The Greenville Treaty of 1795 forces the Ojibway to cede their lands west of Lake St. Clair and Lake Erie to American settlers.

French resistance to the British in Canada ended in 1760, leaving the British in control of Ojibway territory there. The British, who sought revenge for Ojibway support of their enemy, forbade trade between British businessmen and the Ojibway.

French influence in Michigan ended with their defeat by the British in the French and Indian Wars (1755–63). The Ojibway were left confused and angry because of their long dependence on trade and the disruption in their way of life.

American settlers in Ojibway land

The Ojibway decided to take the British side in the American Revolution (1775–83) because of an even greater threat—encroachment on Ojibway lands by American settlers. After the British lost the war, the Ojibway fought against American aggression, but were finally forced by a series of treaties to give up much of their land in Michigan to American settlers. A treaty era began, and each treaty worked to further strip the Ojibway and neighboring tribes of the best land, forcing them onto less desirable lands. Poverty and the spread of infectious diseases contributed to a hard life for the Ojibway.

More migrations

Around 1830 many Ojibway moved to the Plains and became known as the Plains Ojibway, or Bungees. Riding horses they acquired from the Spanish, they populated areas in what are now known as North Dakota, northeastern Montana, southern Manitoba, and southeastern Saskatchewan.

The Indian Removal Act was passed in 1830. It directed that all Indians should be moved to Indian Territory (present-day Oklahoma and Kansas), west of the Mississippi River. Many Ojibway moved north to Canada instead. Others remained behind and tried to keep individual plots of land that had been granted to them according to U.S. government policy of allotment. Allotment was adopted in the mid-nineteenth century in an attempt to eliminate the Native American custom of holding lands as a community. But taxes were levied on these plots; the Ojibway were often unable to pay the taxes for their plots and were forced to give up their land to American expansion. During the 1860s, many Ojibway were removed to Indian Territory along with other Native Americans.

American Indian Movement founded

Battles raged during the twentieth century between Native Americans and the U.S. government over issues such as forced removal, land use, and the freedom to practice ancient religions. The civil rights movement of the 1950s and 1960s, with its emphasis on the rights of minorities, led to a surge of activism (assertive action to support an issue). The Red Power Movement began as a series of public protests that focused the eyes of the world on American Indian issues. Then, in 1968, three Ojibway—Dennis Banks, George Mitchell, and Clyde Bellecourt, founded the American Indian Movement (AIM) in Minneapolis, Minnesota.

AIM is a vocal and controversial organization. During its 1973 seizure of the village of Wounded Knee in South Dakota, AIM organized Indians from many tribes to hold off federal forces in an armed standoff. Two Indian activists were killed and many others were wounded. AIM's goals are civil rights for all Native Americans and the revival of tribal religion. It also seeks to raise public awareness of the violation of treaty rights by federal and state governments.

RELIGION

Ojibway oral tradition teaches that the Creator, Kitche Manitou, created the world in five stages. First, the rock, water, fire, and wind were formed. From these four elements the Sun, Earth, Moon, and stars were made. During the third stage plants began to grow. Then, animals and later people emerged.

The Ojibway believe that the Sun is father and the Earth is mother of the people and other living things. The Sun and the Earth provide all that is necessary to sustain all life. As the *Anishinaubeg* or "first people," the Ojibway feel an obligation to care for and live in harmony with Mother Earth.

The Midewiwin ("good hearted") was the religious society of the Ojibway. It may have developed in response to diseases brought by the French. Members, who could be men or women, were called "Mides." They underwent a long training period before becoming members of the society. Their main purpose was to prolong life (see "Healing practices"). They acted as healers and taught morality and good conduct. Other names for the society are Grand Medicine Society, Medicine Lodge Society, and Mide Society.

French Catholic missionaries came in the 1600s and tried to convert the Ojibway, with little success. Two possible reasons for the lack of success are resistance on the part of the local Mides, and the fact that the people lived in remote areas and were not easy to get to. The Midewiwin maintained a strong hold over the Ojibway for a long time, but the society began to decline at the end of the nineteenth century, in part because of efforts to force Indians to conform to the larger American culture.

Today many Ojibway practice a religion that combines elements of their traditional beliefs with Christianity.

LANGUAGE

The Ojibway language, called Ojibway or Ojibwemowin, survived decades of educational policies that sought to replace it with English. The language once seemed to be heading for extinction, but is now taught on the reservations and at colleges and universities. The language is spoken by 40,000 to 50,000 people.

The mastery of spoken language is important to the success of an Ojibway adult. Children are encouraged to develop the art of oration by their parents and grandparents. The ability to speak well requires skills in describing things or events elegantly and in great detail.

GOVERNMENT

In the early days, Ojibway groups were not highly organized, because they were small and spread out over such a wide area. Each group had its own tribal leader and council. Election to the *ogima*, "leaders," was based on a person's merits rather than heredity. Leaders were usually men who had distinguished themselves in battle or who were wise and generous. Ogima candidates had to demonstrate outstanding speaking ability.

Today, most tribes operate under forms of government they adopted after the Indian Reorganization Act was passed in 1934. That act provided government loans and other services to reservations if they agreed to adopt new constitutions and reorganize their governments. Most did so, and they now have elective governing bodies.

ECONOMY

Living surrounded by lakes and forests, the Ojibway were skilled at fishing, hunting large game, gathering nuts and berries, and growing foods that required a short growing season, like squash and sunflowers. They gathered in summer villages to fish and plant gardens. They divided in winter and moved to their hunting grounds.

After contact with Europeans, the Ojibway became skilled traders. By the late seventeenth century, thousands of fur pelts were being shipped from Sault Sainte Marie and Detroit. The Ojibway became so dependent on trade that the beaver became overtrapped. This went against the Ojibway tradition of slaying animals only to provide food and clothing.

Economy under U.S. government

On the reservations later, the Ojibway earned money through the sale of their land and timber rights. They often received far less money for these rights than they were worth, and the money was barely enough to live on. Life on the reservations, which were often

OJIBWAY LANGUAGE

The Ojibway did not have a system for writing language. They communicated special events to future generations by drawing pictographs on birch bark or buckskin. The following are samples from the Ojibway vocabulary:

wi'giwam	"dwelling"
nasa'ogan	"tipi"
nenan'dawi'iwed	"one who treats the sick by administering remedies"
dja'sakid	"one who treats the sick by non-material means" (commonly called a juggler)
a'dikina'gun	"cradleboard"
ina'bandumo'win	"vision or thing dreamed"
mide'	a member of the Midewiwin
mide'wayan	"bag carried by a mide'"
Boozhoo	"hello"
Miigwech	"thank you"
Aaniin ezhi' ayaayan	"How are you?"
Nimino'ayaa	"I'm fine."
Mino'ayaag	"All of you be well."

An Ojibway man in a canoe race.

located in remote areas where the soil was poor, led to reliance on government welfare. Since the 1970s, however, lawsuits have led to decisions affirming Ojibway treaty rights and permitting them to support themselves off the land and lakes. In the 1983 Voight Decision, the U.S. Court of Appeals ruled that Ojibway rights to hunt, fish, and gather on the lands of their ancestors are protected by past treaties.

At the end of World War II (1939–45), most Ojibway moved to urban areas because they could not find work. They are employed in a wide range of occupations. Those who live on reservations have experienced high rates of unemployment (that is, those who wanted to work could not find work). They support themselves through seasonal work, including forestry, farming, tourism, trapping, and harvesting wild rice. Particularly since the 1970s, reservations also support small businesses: bait shops, campgrounds, clothing manufacturing, construction, fish hatcheries, hotels, lumber stores, marinas, restaurants, and service stations.

Gambling

Many tribes have turned to gaming casinos as a way to create jobs and make money. In Michigan and Minnesota, casinos generate tens of millions of dollars and employ thousands of Ojibway people who previously could not find work. Tribes have invested gaming income in the purchase of ancestral lands, road and home construction, and social services such as health and education. Some reservations have passed laws requiring employers on reservations to give preference to tribal members in hiring.

DAILY LIFE

Families

The Ojibway worked very hard to care for each other and their families. Sharing is a highly valued virtue, and those who are fortunate enough to acquire a wealth of goods or food are expected to share with those who have less. In spite of all this hard work, families found free time to embroider, carve, make and play with toys, tell stories, and play games.

Buildings

The traditional Ojibway dwelling, the wigwam, was made of birch bark or cattail mats covering an arched pole frame. Twine or strips of leather were used to tie poles together. The wigwam could be in the shape of a cone or dome, and was often built on a slope with ditches dug away from it to drain rain water. The Ojibway sometimes lived in tepees made of birch bark, buckskin, or cloth, stretched around a conical frame of poles and tied at the top.

Family members slept in the wigwam with their feet towards the fire. If the weather was very cold, an older person would remain awake to watch the fire. On warm nights, the family sometimes slept out in the open.

Other buildings in an Ojibway village included a sweat lodge for curing illness or for spiritual purification; a building used by members of the Midewiwin; and a wigwam for menstruating women.

Food

The Ojibway were mainly hunter-gatherers. Men used the bow and arrow and snares for hunting deer, moose, bear, beaver, lynx, mink, marten, otter, rabbit, and caribou in the North. Strips of meat were often smoked or dried to form a food called jerky. Dog meat was a popular menu item at feasts.

Women gathered berries and nuts and maple sap to make maple syrup and sugar in the spring. Wild rice was harvested from rivers and lakes in Minnesota and Wisconsin. If the climate permitted, they planted gardens of corn, beans, squash, and pumpkins.

Clothing and adornment

The Ojibway made clothing from green leaves, cloth woven from nettle-stalk fiber, and tanned hides. The green leaves were used for a head covering in hot weather. The nettle-stalk cloth was used for

CHIPPEWA WILD RICE

Wild rice was an important staple food for the Ojibway, because it could be stored and eaten during the winter when fresh foods were scarce. Wild rice is actually the seed of a special grass, a different species from white rice. One Ojibway (Chippewa) legend tells about Wenebojo, the trickster, who heard the grass in the lake calling to him. He made a canoe and paddled out into the lake with his grandmother, Nokomis. The grass told them it was good to eat, so Wenebojo and Nokomis tried it. The Chippewas have been eating wild rice ever since.

1 cup wild rice, washed well in cold water

2½ cups water

1½ teaspoons salt

4 strips bacon cut into julienne strips [thin strips about 1½–2 inches long]

6 eggs

1/4 teaspoon pepper

2 Tablespoons minced chives

Bacon drippings plus melted butter or margarine to measure 1/3 cup

Place the wild rice, water, and 1 teaspoon salt in a saucepan, and bring slowly to a boil. Reduce heat and simmer, covered, until all water is absorbed.

Fry the bacon in a large, heavy skillet. Drain bacon on paper toweling. Save drippings [the bacon grease left in the pan].

Beat the eggs with 1/2 teaspoon salt and the pepper until light. Pour into the skillet in which you browned the bacon, and brown the eggs lightly. Then turn gently, as you would a pancake, and brown on the other side. When eggs are firm, cut into julienne strips.

Lightly toss the bacon, julienne egg strips, chives, bacon drippings plus melted butter or margarine with the rice. Serve hot as a main dish.

Serves 4 to 6.

From Yeffe Kimball and Jean Anderson, *The Art of American Indian Cooking.* Garden City, NY: Doubleday, 1965, p. 107

women's underskirts. Hide was made into dresses, pants, breechcloths, shirts, and moccasins. Muskrat or rabbit skin or cattail down was put over the chest and inside moccasins during the cold winter months. Small children wore fitted hoods made of deer hide with a flap that could be brought forward to shade the eyes. Rabbit skins were used for making children's shoes, hats, and blankets.

After the Ojibway acquired blankets from traders, they made them into capes, winter coats (with a hood), and skirts (wrapped and fastened with a belt). Dark blue and black woolen cloth obtained through trade was a special favorite. Clothing made from this cloth was decorated with beads laid out in floral designs or with silk ribbons.

The Ojibway adorned themselves with elements found in nature and later with items acquired through trade. Necklaces were made of berries, small bones, animal claws, and wooden or glass beads brought by Europeans. Earrings, worn mainly by old men, were made of fur, bone, or heavy coins. Long ago, men wore large nose rings, and brass bracelets acquired from trade. Young men wore fur bands decorated with beading around the wrists and ankles. Dance costumes

were decorated with horsehair dyed red and made into a tassel covered with tin at the top. Nineteenth- and twentieth-century clothing has been adorned with sleigh bells, small mirrors, and pieces of tin. Beaded bands were used to hold men's leggings in place.

The Ojibway kept their hair long, and men usually wore some type of braids. Men might apply stripes of red and yellow paint to their hair or wear feather headdresses. Women might wind their hair in cloth or, on festive occasions, braid it in two braids with a long row of otter fur over each braid.

Healing practices

Illness was believed to result from displeasing supernatural spirits or from a social failure such as not hosting a feast after a successful hunting trip. The Ojibway believed that the sick should be treated both spiritually and physically. A sick person was carried to a healer's lodge by relatives, who brought tobacco, considered sacred, for the healer to smoke. The rising smoke alerted the spirits that the healer was thinking of them. Cedar was sometimes burned to purify the air, and to treat a contagious illness; sage was burned as a disinfectant.

The healer, who was usually a member of the Midewiwin society (see "Religion" above), might try to frighten the patient to start the healing process, or he might sing. Ojibway healers had an extensive knowledge of the use of plants and herbs to treat illnesses. It is said that they introduced European sailors to rose hip tea, which prevented the illness called scurvy caused by a lack of vitamin C.

NANABOZHO AND WINTER-MAKER

A character called Nanabozho appears in most traditional Ojibway stories, often getting into trouble through haste, rudeness, or attempting to disrupt nature. He sometimes showed great cunning by outwitting a natural or supernatural menace. Nanabozho teaches wisdom and medicine; he even teaches animals how to disguise themselves from predators. The following story offers an explanation for winter's appearance and disappearance.

Once upon a time this country was a big glacier. It was all ice and never was summer. The Indians lived here. They lived on and on.

One day Nanabozho came along. He said to the Indians, "How are you going to keep on living in this snow and ice? There must be something we can do to make it more productive." Nanabozho stirred them up.

The Indians then meditated. They made sacrifices and offerings, and fasted and prayed to the Great Spirit. They kept on meditating. They did not know what to do. They had been living comfortably before.

This problem was so great that they assembled again. They invited Nanabozho to sit in council at a feast to see what they could do about the great fear. When they were assembled, one old Indian, the wisest of the Ojibway, said, "There is only one thing we can do. We shall have a feast of wild rice and wild roots and invite Old Man Winter—the Winter-Maker—to it. Nanabozho will be our scout. He knows where Old Man Winter is." Nanabozho then prepared tobacco to take along to invite Old Winter-Maker to the feast.

Before the council began, the Indians huddled in secret. They planned to feed Old Man Winter a feast of boiling hot rice and herbs. They planned to keep him there and give him hotter and hotter food, so that he would grow fatter and sleepy, and sweat.

Finally Old Man Winter came. Oh, how the cold came when he came! Everything grew cold. The trees cracked and the forests cracked. The Indians kept on making the food hotter with hotter and hotter coals. Old Man Winter kept on eating and eating and growing warmer and warmer and perspiring more and more. At last, Old Man Winter said "You've got me. I believe I'll go."

He walked out into the north and disappeared. When the Indians looked out, they saw green grass and fields and fruit trees and birds. But they heard Old Winter-Maker calling, "I'm coming back; I'm coming back!"

SOURCE: Coleman, Sister Bernard, Ellen Frogner, and Estelle Eich. *Ojibway Myths and Legends.* Minneapolis: Ross and Haines, 1962.

Education

Children were considered to be a gift to all the people, and bringing them up properly was everyone's responsibility. Children learned by observing. Not listening to others, especially to elders, was considered extremely rude. Children were taught to choose language with care, to think before they spoke. Quarreling and bickering were not tolerated, and children were taught not to argue or to criticize others.

When the reservation system was established in the mid-1800s, the U.S. government took over control of education. Children went to day schools or to boarding schools where they were taught manual labor and housekeeping skills. Often they were separated from their parents and were severely punished for disobeying the rules.

Today, most Ojibway children attend public schools, although a few reservations have established Head Start programs, pre-schools, elementary schools, and special classes in Ojibway culture, history, and language.

ARTS

Music and dancing are important parts of Ojibway ceremonies. Their songs and dances look to nature for inspiration. Fred Benjamin, an Ojibway elder, explained, as quoted in *Circle of Life*: "[T]he Great Spirit [told them] to make songs out of what they saw. Like the leaves when the wind blows they're shaking; they make a little noise. That's how they got the idea to put bells on their legs. And sometimes you see a fowl, like an eagle, an owl, a chickenhawk. The Indian people looked at them, the way they'd swing their wings, how they'd go down and up. That's how they'd make the pitch of their songs...."

Ojibway elders, especially women, were often expert storytellers, sometimes acting out a story while telling it. The tradition of Ojibway storytelling has been kept alive through the works of notable modern authors such as Ignatia Broker, Maude Kegg, and many others. Ojibway people in Michigan and Minnesota keep their culture alive in many ways. They sponsor storytelling and arts and crafts exhibitions and stage powwows (special ceremonies in which members of several different tribes gather for singing, dancing, and feasting).

CUSTOMS

War and hunting rituals

Ojibway warriors were famous and feared. Before a war party left for battle, a ceremony called the Chief Dance was often held. During the Chief Dance, the spirits were asked to protect the departing warriors. Tobacco and food were offered and a special drum was played.

When Ojibway hunters killed a bear, a bear ceremony and feast was held. To show their respect for the bear, its body was laid out and carefully cut up. Foods that are popular with bears, such as maple sugar and berries, were placed next to the body of the "visitor," the bear. Everyone consumed some bear meat and promised the spirits that if another bear should come their way, it too would be treated with respect.

Birth and naming

When a baby was born, guns were fired to alert the village. A riotous feast was held to celebrate the occasion. It was believed that being born into a rowdy environment would make the child brave. Children were given six names; some names were revealed in dreams. The child was usually known by a nickname.

Puberty

The Ojibway practiced special rituals for boys or girls entering puberty. They believed that during a woman's menstrual period, or "moon time," the manitou (spirits) were a strong presence in her life, and she could easily harm herself or others. Therefore, a menstruating women was kept away from cooking and spiritual activities. When a girl had her first period, she was isolated for four days and nights in a little wigwam made for her by her mother. She was not to eat during this time and was instructed not to touch her body or face with her hands; she used a stick to scratch herself if necessary. Afterwards, a feast was given in her honor.

Boys entering puberty were required to fast and pursue a vision quest. A boy's father would take him into the woods and make a nest for him in a tree, leaving him there for several days, but checking up on him periodically. Sometimes a boy would have to perform the ritual several times before he had a vision of a spirit to guide him. A feast was held when a boy killed his first game.

Marriage

Ojibway people identify themselves by their clan (a group of related families). A man had to marry a woman from another clan, and their children belonged to the father's clan. When a man and woman and the woman's parents agreed to a marriage, there was no formal wedding ceremony. The couple lived with the woman's family for a trial period of one year. If the relationship was not satisfactory or if the wife failed to become pregnant, the man could return to his parents.

A couple who wished to remain together usually built their own lodge, or they might choose to live with the man's family. Marital separation was allowed, and after a time the parties could remarry. Men who could support more than one family might have more than one wife, each having her own section of the lodge. Some men designated a head wife, who was the only one to have children. Intermarriage (marriage to non-Ojibway, including non-Indians) was acceptable, and by 1900 most Ojibway were of mixed heritage, typically French and Ojibway.

Death and mourning

The dead were dressed in their finest clothing and wrapped in a blanket and birch bark. Sometimes the face, moccasins, and blanket

were painted with special substances. It was believed that the dancing ghosts who were the northern lights were also painted this way; the painted dead could join the dancing ghosts.

The body was removed from a wigwam through the west side and put into a grave, along with some food and other necessities for the spirit's journey to the afterworld. A close family member danced around the open grave. Then it was filled and a funeral ceremony was performed. Later, a bark house with a symbol of the deceased's clan was built over the grave.

Family members were expected to mourn for about one year. Special clothing was worn and a spirit bundle was made containing a lock of the deceased's hair. A widow placed food in front of her husband's spirit bundle and slept with the bundle. She could not be seen in public wearing cheerful clothing. When a baby died the mother carried the child's clothing in a cradleboard (a board onto which babies are strapped) for a year. A mourner's ceremony was held once a year and mourners were comforted and given gifts. Then loved ones were expected to stop grieving and join the community again.

CURRENT TRIBAL ISSUES

Casino gambling on reservations is a controversial issue. Those in favor point out that gambling boosts reservation economies. Those against argue that gambling proceeds end up in the pockets of a privileged few (even non-Natives) and do little to benefit entire reservation communities.

Key issues facing the Ojibway include economic development to reduce the numbers of unemployed, improved medical treatment to combat illnesses such as diabetes and alcoholism, better management of natural resources, protection of treaty rights, and an emphasis on higher education.

NOTABLE PEOPLE

Jane Johnston Schoolcraft (1800–1841) was the daughter of a Scots-Irish fur trader and an Ojibway woman from Sault Sainte Marie. She was one of the first Native American women to publish poetry; in her poems she described Ojibway culture, her love of nature, and her respect for piety and faith. Her husband, a mid-nineteenth-century government Indian agent named Henry Rowe Schoolcraft, wrote about the Ojibway with his wife's assistance. The 1855 poem "Hiawatha," by Henry Wadsworth Longfellow, is based on writings about the Ojibway by Mr. Schoolcraft.

Activist Clyde Bellecourt (1939–) was one of the founders of the American Indian Movement (AIM) and a powerful force in major activist struggles of the early 1970s. AIM was founded by Ojibway Dennis Banks (1937–), George Mitchell, and Bellecourt, in 1968. Leonard Peltier (1944–) also figured prominently in AIM. He has been in prison since 1976 after a conviction for killing two Federal Bureau of Investigation (FBI) agents. There has been widespread protest of his imprisonment, since many believe he did not receive a fair trial.

FURTHER READING

Brill, Charles. *Red Lake Nation: Portraits of Ojibway Life*. Minneapolis: University of Minnesota Press, 1992.

Broker, Ignatia, *Night Flying Woman: An Ojibway Narrative,* St. Paul: Minnesota Historical Society Press, 1983.

Circle of Life: Cultural Community in Ojibwe Crafts. Duluth: St. Louis Historical Society, Chisholm Museum and Duluth Art Institute, 1984.

Johnston, Basil. *Ojibway Heritage.* New York: Columbia University Press, 1976.

Kegg, Maude. *Portage Lake: Memories of an Ojibwe Childhood,* Edmonton: University of Alberta Press, 1991.

Morriseau, Norval. *Legends of My People.* Ed. Selwyn Dewdney. Toronto: Ryerson Press, 1965.

Tanner, Helen Hornbeck. *The Ojibway.* New York: Chelsea House, 1992.

Vizenor, Gerald Robert. *The People Named the Chippewa: Narrative Histories.* Minneapolis: University of Minnesota Press, 1984.

Vizenor. Gerald Robert. *The Everlasting Sky: New Voices from the People Named the Chippewa.* New York: Crowell-Collier Press, 1972.

Pequot

Name

The name Pequot (pronounced *PEE-kwot*) comes from an Algonquin Indian word meaning "destroyers," referring to the warlike nature of the group in early times. The Pequot call themselves "fox people." Today there are two Pequot tribes: the Mashantucket (Western Pequot) and Paucatuck (Eastern Pequot).

Location

Before Europeans arrived, the Pequots' lands covered all of southeastern Connecticut, from the Nehantic River to the Rhode Island border. About one-half of U.S. Pequot lived on or near two reservations in Connecticut: the Eastern Paucatuck Pequot Reservation in New London and the Mashantucket Pequot Reservation in Mashantucket. The other half lived mainly in Rhode Island and Massachusetts.

Population

In 1620, there were about 6,000 Pequot, including those who later became the Mohegan. Before the Pequot War of 1637, there were about 3,000. After the Pequot War, there were fewer than 1,500, and by 1762, the population was down to 140. In 1974, there were fewer than 55 Pequot, but in a census done in 1990, 679 people identified themselves as Pequot.

Language family

Eastern Algonquian.

Origins and group affiliations

Historians have different opinions about Pequot origins. Some say they moved from upper New York to eastern Connecticut in about 1500, while others say they have lived in Connecticut for a much longer time. In 1633, a group of Pequot that came to be called Mohegan split off from the Pequot and became their enemies. Several years later the Pequot lost the Pequot War of 1637. Many Pequot survivors were sold or given into slavery, while others took refuge with the Algonquin, Narragansett (see entry), Eastern Niantic, and Metoac tribes. They were soon absorbed into those tribes, and the Pequot tribe was called "perished." A few Pequot survivors of the war were forced by English colonists to join the Mohegan; those Pequot became the ancestors of the two current Pequot tribes: the Mashantucket and Paucatuck.

PEQUOT

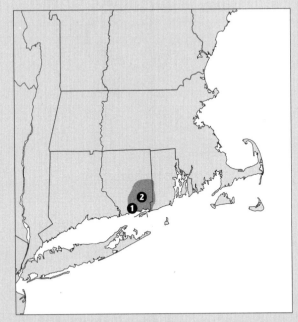

Shaded area: Traditional Pequot lands in present-day southeastern Connecticut.

Contemporary Communities

Connecticut

1. Eastern Paucatuck Pequot Reservation
2. Mashantucket Pequot Reservation

Before Europeans came, the Pequot controlled Connecticut, fiercely guarding their hunting grounds against other tribes. After Europeans started the fur trade, the Pequot tried to control it, which led to the bloody conflict and near-destruction of the tribe in the Pequot War of 1637. After that, for more than 300 years the tribe was rarely heard from. The story of how they went from power to poverty then triumphed to become owners of one of the world's richest casinos is truly astonishing.

HISTORY

Pequot expand control beyond own territory

Before their land was invaded by English settlers in the early 1600s, the Pequot farmed, hunted, fished, waged war, and dominated Connecticut. The tribe found some benefits in the presence of the French and English before they even saw any white men, because the newcomers diminished the powers of many of their rivals. Tribes to the north, who liked the European goods they got in exchange for furs, were waging wars for control of the fur trade with the French in what is now Canada. English slave ships were traveling along the Atlantic Coast, kidnaping Indians and leaving behind diseases like smallpox that killed many Natives. While other tribes were occupied with trade wars and sickness, the Pequot and Narragansett (see entry) became the two most powerful tribes in the entire Connecticut-New York region.

IMPORTANT DATES

1600: The first Dutch trading post opens in Pequot territory.

1637: Massacre at Mystic ends Pequot War and nearly destroys tribe.

1983: Mashantucket Pequot Indian Land Claims Settlement Act provides federal recognition and leads to Foxwoods Casino.

Relations with the Dutch

The first Pequot encounter with Europeans was with the Dutch, who built a trading post in Connecticut in 1622. The Dutch planned to trade with all tribes in the region, but the Pequot had other plans—they wanted total control. Their attacks on other tribes while trying to gain this control annoyed both the other tribes and the Dutch, who in 1622 took prisoner the Pequot Chief Tatobem. The Dutch said they would kill Tatobem if the Pequot did not mend their disruptive ways and pay a ransom for his release.

The Dutch expected the Pequot to bring beaver skins as ransom, but the Pequot brought wampum instead. The Dutch had no idea what value the Indian tribes placed on wampum, the small white or dark purple beads made from shells (see box on p. 140). The furious Dutch leader ordered Tatobem killed. When the Pequot heard of this outrage, they burned down the trading post.

The Dutch leader was replaced by a new one, who apologized to the Pequot and built a new trading post. Trade began again, with the Pequot firmly in charge. Soon, the Dutch were trading for both furs and wampum, and the Pequot resumed their attacks on neighboring tribes. Now they fought not only for control of other tribes' hunting grounds but also for control of the seashell beds along Long Island Sound—the best sources of wampum.

Massachusetts colonists want Connecticut

In 1620, Puritans (a Protestant group that opposed the Church of England) from England established a colony in Plymouth, Massachusett and began competing with the Dutch for control of trade in Connecticut. The colonists called Connecticut "paradise." They wanted Pequot territory, especially the Connecticut River valley, the only

UNCAS AND THE MOHEGANS

When the Pequot grand sachem died in 1631, the Pequot tribal council chose Sassacus to become the new grand sachem. Uncas (c. 1588–c. 1682), who was married to the daughter of Sassacus, had expected to be chosen, and he was angry. The quarrel between the two men escalated until Uncas finally broke off relations completely.

Accompanied by fifty Pequot warriors and their families, Uncas established a new village on the Connecticut River. The group took the name Mohegan, which means wolf, and set up a long and profitable trading relationship with English colonists. Uncas supported the English against his former Pequot kin in the Pequot War of 1637, and eventually under his leadership the Mohegan became one of the most powerful tribes on the Atlantic Coast.

The Mohegan proved to be as fierce as the Pequot had been, and many small tribes in Connecticut were swallowed up by them. When Uncas died, his sons carried on his policies. Historians agree that the fighting among tribes hastened the takeover of Indian lands in New England by white settlers. The Mohegan tribe eventually lost most of its land to the settlers.

In 1994 the Mohegan tribe finally reached an agreement with the state of Connecticut in which the state allowed the tribe to buy 700 acres of its former homeland (which had once included most of the state). The Mohegan Indian Reservation was established.

Uncas is probably most famous as a character in the book *The Last of the Mohicans*, published in 1826 by James Fenimore Cooper. Cooper seems to have been confused. He was probably writing about the Mahican (not Mohican) tribe of the Hudson River valley, but he took the name of the character Uncas from the Mohegan tribe of Connecticut.

waterway in the area that ran from the Atlantic Ocean into the rich Canadian hunting grounds. The Pequot Indians resisted English settlement, becoming one of the first of the New England tribes to do so.

In 1633, with rivalry heating up in Connecticut between the Dutch and the Massachusetts colonists, a bitter fight broke out among the Pequot. Chief Sassacus wished to maintain relations with the Dutch. His son-in-law, Uncas (see box), favored the English. Uncas and his followers broke off from the Pequot and formed a new tribe they called Mohegan.

Relations between the two Indian groups were very bad. They often attacked one another, thereby disrupting trade throughout the region. When a Boston, Massachusetts, trader was found murdered, the English blamed the Pequot. They demanded that Sassacus hand over the persons responsible; he refused. At about the same time, the Pequot were hit by a smallpox epidemic, and the English forced the Dutch to close their trading post and leave. Now very weak from disease, the Pequot had no Dutch allies they could count on. More Massachusetts colonists were welcomed into Connecticut by the pro-English Mohegan. Hostilities grew, with the Pequot on one side, and the

Mohegans, the Massachusetts colonists, and every tribe that felt unfriendly toward the Pequot on the other side.

Pequot War of 1637

In 1636 a second Boston trader was killed, and again the English blamed the Pequot. Puritan preachers spoke out in church against the tribe, calling the Pequot an evil force that must be destroyed. In response, a vengeful army of colonial soldiers destroyed a Pequot vil-

The attack on the Pequot fort, 1637. Hundreds of Pequot women, children, and elderly people were trapped inside the burning fort.

lage. Early in 1637, Sassacus led a raid against several Connecticut settlements, beginning the Pequot War.

Because the Pequot had made so many enemies fighting for control of the fur trade, no other tribe would come to their aid. One day, while 300 Pequot warriors from the village of Mystic were off on a raid, their former kinsmen, the Mohegan, joined with the English and the Narragansett tribe in a surprise attack on the undefended Pequot fort. Between 300 and 700 Pequot, mostly women, children, and the elderly, were trapped inside as the fort was set ablaze. Back in Plymouth, when the governor heard the news, he called the massacre a "sweet sacrifice."

When the Pequot warriors returned, they were heartsick to find their families dead and their village destroyed. Now broken in spirit and starving, they divided into small groups and fled. The colonists, not content with having won the war, were determined to destroy the Pequot tribe. They hunted down and killed many, with Sassacus as their main target.

Aftermath of war

With nowhere to turn, Sassacus sought refuge with his tribe's enemies, the Mohawk (see entry). They cut off his head and sent it to their friends, the English colonists. The remaining Pequot finally surrendered, and a peace treaty was signed in 1638.

Under the terms of the peace treaty signed with the colonists, the Pequot tribe was dissolved. Pequot warriors were executed. Women and children were sold into slavery in the West Indies or given as slaves to the Mohegan, the Narragansett, the Metoac, and the Niantic tribes.

The Pequot who were given in slavery to their relatives, the Mohegan, had an especially hard time. They were forbidden to call themselves Pequot, and they were treated so cruelly that in 1655, the colonists finally took them away from the Mohegan and moved them to eastern Connecticut. In 1666, 2,000 acres became the Mashantucket (Western) Pequot Reservation in Ledyard. About twenty years later, 200 acres called the Lantern Hill Reservation were set aside for the Paucatuck (Eastern) Pequot.

Most Pequot slowly drifted away from the reservations because they could not earn a living. By 1910 there were only 66 Pequot people living in Connecticut, and the state of Connecticut had illegally sold most of their land.

Revival

By the 1970s, only one tumbledown home remained on the Mashantucket Pequot Reservation. It housed the families of two half-sisters, Elizabeth George Plouffe and Martha Langevin Ellal. The two feisty old women struggled to hold on against white overseers who refused to let them use tribal money for repairs. Sometimes they were forced to chase off trespassers at gunpoint. When they died in the 1970s, their relatives realized they must take over their elders' dream—to hold onto their land—or watch it die. And so began a truly astounding American success story.

A lawsuit was filed in 1976 to recover Pequot land that had been illegally sold by the state. The case was settled in 1983. The settlement, called the Mashantucket Pequot Indian Land Claims Settlement Act, gave the tribe more than $700,000 and granted federal recognition. Federally recognized tribes are those with which the U.S. government maintains official relations. With federal recognition came the right to open a gambling casino.

And open a grand casino they did, in 1992. By 1998 Foxwoods was one of the world's largest and most profitable casinos. The few hundred individuals who were able to prove that they had Pequot ancestry suddenly found themselves the richest Native Americans in the United States.

Paucatuck Pequot

Matters have not gone as well for the Paucatuck Pequot. As of the mid-1990s, they were recognized by the state of Connecticut but had not been granted federal recognition. Without federal recognition, the tribe does not exist as far as the federal government is concerned, and is not entitled to financial and other help.

RELIGION

Little is known about the Pequot's traditional religious beliefs and practices, because the tribe was nearly destroyed soon after contact with Europeans. We know that their religion was based on a deep attachment to the land.

One Pequot achieved fame for his Methodist religious beliefs—nineteenth-century writer William Apess (1798–1839), the first widely published Native American author. His early books dealt with his own conversion to Christianity and the conversion of five Pequot women. Apess argued that Indians might be one of the "lost tribes of

PEQUOT WORDS

Thirty-five Pequot words were recorded in 1762:

uhpuckackip	"gull"
neuyewgk	"my wife"
muckachux	"boy"
squas or quausses	"virgin girls"
pouppous	"infant newborn"
nehyashamag	"my husband"
m'ssugkheege	"bass"
podumbaug	"whale"
sucksawaug	"clam"
muschundaug	"lobster"
yewt	"fire"
nupp	"water"
souchpoun	"snow"
sokghean	"rain"
mattuck	"trees"
wewautchemins	"Indian corn"
mushquissedes	"beans"
tommonque	"beaver"
kuchyage	"nose"
skeezucks	"eyes"
cottoneege	"mouth"
nahteah	"dog"
muckasons	"shoes"
cuzseet	"foot"
wuttun	"wind"
meeun	"Sun"
weyhan	"Moon"
tohcommock	"beach"
wumbanute	"white"
suggyo	"dark" or "black"
keeguum	"arrow"
teatum	"I think"
moche	"I will"
gynchen	"I kill"
mundtu	"God"
cheeby	"evil spirit" or "devil"

SOURCE: *News From Indian Country.* Vol. 8, No. 5 (March 1994): p. 10; Vol. 9, No. 17 (September 1995): p. 5B.

the Israelites," Hebrews who fled after being conquered by the Assyrians in the eighth century. Apess skillfully made his case that Native Americans, as lost tribes, were the chosen people of God.

LANGUAGE

The version of the Algonquin language spoken by the Pequot was also spoken by the Mohegan, Narragansett, Niantic, Montauk, and Shinnecock tribes.

GOVERNMENT

Because they were so often at war with other tribes, the Pequot had to be well organized under a strong leader. Pequot chiefs called *sachems* (pronounced *SAY-chums*) ruled with the advice of tribal councils. After the removal to reservations in the 1600s, the Pequot came under the control of the state of Connecticut, which mismanaged reservation affairs frequently. State officials allowed Pequot land to be leased and then lost to white colonists. By the 1940s, the Pequot people were forbidden to even hold gatherings or spend the night on the reservation without state permission. By the 1970s, there were scarcely any Pequot left on the reservation.

In the mid-1970s, Pequot Richard "Skip" Hayward and several other members of the tribe returned to the Mashantucket Reservation to re-establish the community. A constitution was adopted, and a seven-member elected tribal council was set up to oversee tribal affairs. More recently, the tribal council has had to be content with the huge number of non-Indian visitors to the casino on the reservation. Visitors become subject to reservation laws, which means the tribe has had to write laws and enforce them. A tribal court has been established, and the reservation has its own police force.

The Mashantucket Pequot tribe is skilled at dealing with the U.S. government. It passes this skill along to young people by funding an internship program, which pays college students a salary while they learn how to represent the interests of the Pequot and other Native American tribes before the U.S. Congress in Washington, D.C.

ECONOMY

The traditional Pequot economy was based mainly on farming, with hunting and fishing secondary. For the brief time between their first contact with the Dutch in 1600 and the near-destruction of the tribe in 1637, the Pequot carried on a lively trade in furs and wampum. At a time when metal money was rare even in the courts of European kings, the Pequot were largely responsible for making wampum an important trade item in the colonies (see box).

By the early 1800s, two-thirds of the Pequot people lived on the reservation, earning money by crafts such as basketry. They continued at these occupations until early in the twentieth century, when most of those who knew the crafts had died. Other Pequot worked in the American economy, first as servants or on whaling ships, and later in a variety of fields.

Casino brings huge economic benefits

A dramatic turnaround in the Pequot economy occurred with the opening of the Foxwoods Casino in 1992. Kevin Chappell described the personal effects of casino riches on tribal members in *Ebony* magazine: "The tribe's good investments have resulted in a grand lifestyle

A drawing of the expansion at the Pequot's Foxwoods Resort Casino in Ledyard, Connecticut, 1995.

for its members. Each person who proves . . . that he or she is at least one-sixteenth Pequot is given a new house, a managerial job or training paying a minimum of $50,000 per year, free education from private elementary school through graduate school (with a $30,000 annual [allowance] while in college), free health care and free daycare. And Pequot mothers are paid $30,000 annually with medical benefits for five years, even if they don't work and choose to stay home to raise their children."

The casino's success has had a tremendous impact on the state of Connecticut as well. In the early 1990s the state was suffering from an economic downturn because defense-related industries were shutting down and defense workers were being thrown out of work. Thousands of those workers found jobs at Foxwoods, which by the late 1990s was the largest employer in the state. Some workers went from building submarines to building boats to ferry gamblers from New York, while others perform the many other jobs necessary to host the casino's 40,000 daily visitors. The Pequots pay the state 25 percent, or at least $100 million, of the total money earned from slot machines each year.

The Mashantucket Pequot have been generous with casino profits. Millions of dollars have been donated to the Special Olympics;

other money has gone to finance playground equipment. A 1995 gift to the Smithsonian Institution's National Museum of the American Indian (NMAI)—$10 million—was the largest donation in Smithsonian history. "I guess you could call us wealthy people," tribal chairman Skip Hayward told a news conference. "We were wealthy before we had money, because we had a love of the land . . . our ancestors and our culture."

DAILY LIFE

Education

The Mashantucket Pequot Museum and Research Center, scheduled to open in 1998, presents the story of the Mashantucket Pequot Tribal Nation. It is the only American Indian-owned and operated institution of its kind. The complex promotes Indian heritage, scholarship, and preservation of the culture through a public museum and a research facility.

Buildings

For winter use in the old times, the Pequot built longhouses like those of the Iroquois (see entry). In summer, they lived in portable wigwams near their hunting and fishing grounds. Because they were so often at war, their villages were usually built on hilltops and were surrounded by sharpened sticks to keep out intruders.

By 1720 Pequot lived in fewer, larger, and more permanent communities. Most were combinations of frame structures and wigwams. Outbuildings included sweat lodges, animal pens, storage facilities, wells, stone walls, and small stone piles scattered over one or two acres.

Food

The Pequot grew beans and corn (the beans were allowed to twine up the cornstalks), squash, and tobacco. The land was stony and good soil was scarce, so women planted corn in scattered plots both near and away from their villages. The plots were heavily fertilized with dead fish. By 1732 the lands of the 250 or so Pequot who lived at Mashantucket Reservation were reduced to only 14 acres. There they cultivated apple trees and raised sheep and pigs.

Clothing and adornment

The Pequot dressed in buckskin clothing suitable to the colder climate of Connecticut. A favorite decoration was wampum beads.

THE IMPORTANCE OF WAMPUM

To the Indians of the Northeast, wampum was not simply "Indian money." It was used for many different purposes. Indians believed that the exchange of wampum and other goods established a friendship, not just a profit-making relationship.

To make wampum, wampum shells were ground and polished into small, cylindrical shapes like beads. A stone drill was used to make a small hole in the beads, which were then used loose or strung on strings made from animal tendons.

Wampum was used as personal adornment and often signified a person's rank in society—the more wampum one wore, the higher one's rank. Often people were buried with supplies of wampum—wealthier people were buried with more wampum than poor people.

Sometimes wampum was used to pay tribute to a more powerful tribe. After the Pequot War of 1637, the English forced the Mohegan to pay an annual tribute in wampum for sparing the lives of the Pequot who lived with the Mohegan.

Wampum was also given by tribal members to their sachems to help support them and to show gratitude for their services.

Wampum was also used to pass down a tribe's story from generation to generation. Designs were woven into belts as a way of recalling important historical events. The colors of the wampum beads used in this way had meaning: white was a symbol of peace, while black meant war or mourning. Wampum belts were sometimes used to communicate with other tribes. If the message communicated on a belt made the other tribe angry, members would kick the belt around to show their contempt for the message.

Among many other uses, wampum were used as ransom for captured prisoners, as prizes for winning at games or sports, as payments to healers for curing the sick, and as tokens of a young man's affection and his wish to propose marriage to a young woman. Warriors often wore necklaces made from wampum to remind them that they were fighting not only for their wives and children, but also for material goods. A person accused of murder might offer a gift of wampum to the victim's family; if the family accepted, the murderer's life would be spared.

Whereas in other Northeastern tribes only important people could adorn themselves with wampum, it was common for nearly everyone in the Pequot tribe to wear wampum ornaments. After trade began with Europeans, the Pequot added exotic feathers to their clothing.

CUSTOMS

Festivals

The Mashantucket Pequot tribe hosts an annual powwow. A powwow is a celebration at which the main activity is traditional singing and dancing. In modern times, the singers and dancers at powwows come from many different tribes.

Burial

The Pequot buried their dead with bows and arrows and great quantities of wampum beads. After their defeat in the Pequot War of 1637, the graves of Pequot dead were often ransacked by grave robbers, who stole the wampum. Learning of these crimes, many tribes gave up the custom of marking the graves of their dead.

CURRENT TRIBAL ISSUES

In the late 1990s the Paucatuck Pequot were still seeking federal recognition and were quarreling with the state of Connecticut over land and other rights.

Meanwhile the Mashantucket Pequot continue their efforts to add land to their reservation. Reservation lands are free from property taxes and other state and federal laws. This freedom is causing hostility among non-Native residents of Connecticut, especially business owners, who say it is unfair. Many neighbors object to the constant traffic and commotion at the casino. For their part, the Pequot say much of the anger is due to racism, because about half of the members of the tribe are African Americans. Tribal council member Gary Carter, who is black, put it this way: "Most of it is racial. There are people who believe that dark-skinned people shouldn't be making money, and they'll do anything they can to try to stop us. But what they don't realize is, to protect ourselves, we know how to play their games."

An illustration of a Northeast region Indian family wearing black-and-white wampum, 1653.

NOTABLE PEOPLE

Chief Sassacus (1560–1637) became Pequot grand sachem in 1632. Under his leadership, Pequot territory grew to include most of present-day Connecticut and Long Island. He bravely led his people through the Pequot War (1637) but was killed trying to hide from the English.

Other notable Pequot include: Sachem Robin Cassasinamon, who led the Mashantucket Reservation from its founding in 1667 to his death in 1693; minister and writer William Apess (1798–1839); and Elizabeth George Plouffe and Martha Langevin Ellal (d. 1970s), who fought to retain tribal land.

FURTHER READING

Chappell, Kevin, "Black Indians Hit Jackpot in Casino Bonanza." *Ebony*, June 1995, vol. 50, no. 8, p. 46.

Miller, Jay. "Blending Worlds." *The Native Americans: An Illustrated History.* Eds. Betty Ballantine and Ian Ballantine. Atlanta: Turner Publishing, 1993.

Sultzman, Lee. "Pequot History" (accessed 2/21/99). [Online] http://dickshovel.com/pequot.html.

Potawatomi

Name

The name Potawatomi (pronounced *pot-uh-WOT-uh-mee*) comes from the Ojibway "potawatomink," which means "people of the place of fire." The Potawatomi call themselves *Nishnabek,* meaning "true or original people."

Location

The Potawatomi originally lived on the east coast of the United States. Today they live on scattered reservations and communities in southern Michigan and the upper peninsula of Michigan, in northern Indiana, northeastern Wisconsin, northeastern Kansas, and central Oklahoma.

Population

In the early 1800s, there were an estimated 9,000 to 10,000 Potawatomi. In a census (count of the population) done in 1990 by the U.S. Bureau of the Census, 16,719 people identified themselves as Potawatomi. About 2,000 more live in Canada.

Language family

Algonquin.

Origins and group affiliations

The ancestors of the Potawatomi originally lived on the east coast of the United States, but according to their traditions, after receiving a message from the spirit world they began to migrate westward. Sometime before the early 1600s, they split into three factions near Michigan's Straits of Mackinac. The three groups came to be known as the Potawatomi, the Ojibway, and the Ottawa. After separating, the "Three First Nations" retained a special relationship, often living in the same communities and supporting each other in battles with Europeans and Americans.

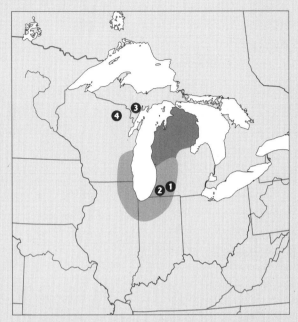

POTAWATOMI

Contemporary Communities

Michigan

1. Pokagon Band of Potawatomi Indian Nation
2. Huron Potawatomi
3. Hannahville Community

Wisconsin

4. Forest County Potawatomi Community

Shaded area: The traditional lands of the Potawatomi stretched from present-day southern Michigan, through Indiana and northeastern Illinois, around the southern end of Lake Michigan into southeastern Wisconsin.

Potawatomi history is marked by tribal expansion and transformations from a hunter-gatherer culture to a settled culture and then to a buffalo-hunting culture. Before Europeans came, they lived near the rivers and lakes of lower Michigan. After contact with the French, they replaced their canoes with horses and became fur traders and buffalo hunters. Due to a series of treaties and white encroachment on their land, many Potawatomi were relocated to the south-central states. Today, the Potawatomi are scattered throughout the Midwest and Prairie states; some live on reservations and many live in cities and other rural areas.

HISTORY

Pre-European contact

Early Potawatomi were hunter-gatherers living on the west side of the Great Freshwater Sea—Lake Huron. They clustered in what is now southern Michigan, living in villages beside streams and lakes, which provided abundant fish and waterways for traveling. By the end of the 1500s, the Potawatomi had settled in southern Michigan and northern Indiana.

In the 1600s, European settlers began to move westward from the Atlantic coast. As the white settlers pushed west, they displaced the tribes who, in turn, moved further westward themselves. Facing an influx of hostile tribes, the Potawatomi moved to the west side of Lake Michigan, into present-day Wisconsin. After a prolonged war with the invading Iroquois Confederacy (see entry), the Potawatomi yielded southern Michigan, moving further into mid- and northern Wisconsin and northern Michigan.

Alliance with the French

The move west brought the Potawatomi into contact with farming tribes, and they soon added farm crops to their diet. They also met the French for the first time. French fur traders and Catholic missionaries had arrived in about 1640. The tribe soon began to hunt furs for the French and some were converted to Roman Catholicism. A military alliance with the French made the Potawatomi stronger than their neighbors, and they began to control trade routes. By the 1670s, the Potawatomi were strong enough and had forged enough alliances with other tribes to begin pushing the Iroquois tribes out of Michigan.

When the Iroquois were driven from Michigan in the 1690s, the Potawatomi returned and tribal expansion began in earnest. From being farmers, the Potawatomi evolved into a traders and wide-ranging hunters.

Impact of horse and buffalo

Contact with white European settlers brought about two major changes to the Potawatomi economy. It introduced metal weapons and tools, such as hoes and rakes. It also encouraged the Potawatomi to replace their traditional means of travel, the birchbark canoe, with riding horses. Use of horses meant that the Potawatomi could participate in the autumn buffalo hunts on the prairies. Horses also extended their traveling range, bringing the Potawatomi into contact with new tribes and new territory. Sometimes this contact resulted in battles, as the Potawatomi clashed with the tribes already living in these areas.

The buffalo brought about another change in Potawatomi life, allowing them to become nomads who could roam more widely. The tribe was less dependent on living near rivers or lakes for food, since they now had an alternate source, the buffalo. They could build villages further inland, use the buffalo hides for shelter and clothing, and use other animal parts to make tools.

The Potawatomi used French-supplied weapons and horses to help them lay claim to an ever-expanding territory. At their height in the mid-1800s, the Potawatomi homeland stretched from southern Michigan, through northern Indiana and northeastern Illinois, and around the southern end of Lake Michigan in southeastern Wisconsin.

When the French lost control over the Great Lakes region around 1695, the Potawatomi allied themselves with the British, the new military force in the area. At British urging, the Potawatomi hassled the American settlers who were pushing their way into the Midwest. The Indians also fought as British allies during the American Revolution (1775-83). In 1795, battles between the Potawatomi and the Americans finally ended when the Potawatomi and other Native Americans signed the Treaty of Greenville.

Dealings with the U.S. government

The Treaty of Greenville began an era of decline for the Potawatomi, as the U.S. government desired their land for westward-moving American settlers. Their territory shrank, and food became scarce. Between 1795 and 1837, the Potawatomi signed thirty-eight treaties with the United States, yielding more than half their land in exchange for cash, food, goods, services, and eventually, reservations.

Along with this loss of land came the U.S. government policy called "removal." Under this policy Native Americans were relocated from their ancestral lands to places farther west. Relocating the tribes left their lands open to white settlement.

"Removal"

In the case of the Potawatomi, the Indian Removal Act of 1830 meant that the majority of Potawatomi left their homelands for reservations west of the Mississippi River. The Indiana Potawatomi were moved to Kansas during a forced march called the "Trail of Death." More than 150 Potawatomi died during this terrible journey, half of them children. The Potawatomi from Wisconsin and Illinois were removed to Iowa and then Kansas. In Kansas, the Mission band separated from the Prairie band and in 1867 they moved to a reservation in Oklahoma, where they now live as the Citizen band.

Not all Potawatomi were willing to go to the reservation, and some fled into Canada. Others hid out in Michigan, and eventually were given permission to settle on a reservation there. The relocation process lasted from 1835 to 1867.

The Potawatomi today

In the late 1990s, six distinct bands of Potawatomi live in the United States and a seventh band lives in Canada. The Canadian band numbers about 2,000 people who are descendants of the Potawatomi who fled from the United States during the time of removal.

Of the six U.S. bands, the Citizen band in Oklahoma is the largest (see box). The Citizen Potawatomi are the most assimilated (meaning they have been most absorbed, or have blended into white culture) and most are Christians. They are recognized by the federal government as a tribe. This means that the U.S. government negotiates with the tribe as if it were a distinct nation, just the same way it negotiates with other nations. Federally recognized tribes are also entitled to financial and other assistance.

The Forest County band, by contrast, is the most traditional, using the Potawatomi language and keeping alive tribal religious rituals and customs. The Forest County band live in northern Wisconsin and are a federally recognized tribe.

The Hannahville Potawatomi were recognized as a tribe by the federal government in 1936. They live in upper Michigan, where they settled after fleeing the forced removals of the 1830s.

The Huron Potawatomi moved from southern Michigan to Kansas during the removal period. Although they were once federally recognized as a tribe, recognition was withdrawn in 1902. Without federal recognition, the tribe does not exist as far as the government is concerned, and is not entitled to financial and other help.

Pokagon Potawatomi escaped removal because of a treaty. They have remained in southwest Michigan. Under the influence of French

IMPORTANT DATES

c. 1640: Potawatomi meet their first Europeans—French traders in search of beaver and missionaries seeking converts to the Roman Catholic faith.

1656: Iroquois win the war against the Algonquin confederation (which includes the Potawatomi). Potawatomi flee to northern Michigan and Wisconsin.

1690: Iroquois hold on Michigan weakens; Potawatomi resettle in lower Michigan and move into Illinois and southern Wisconsin.

1761: Potawatomi switch allegiance from the French to the British; they later help the British by attacking American settlers during the American Revolution.

1795: Representatives of defeated Potawatomi sign the Treaty of Greenville with the United States, ending hostilities. U.S. government proceeds to take over Potawatomi lands for white settlement.

1830: The Indian Removal Act is passed, allowing the United States to force Native tribes to leave their lands and resettle on reservations.

1953–54: The Prairie Band successfully fights to avoid termination of its federal tribal status under leadership of tribal chair Minnie Evans.

1990: Hannahville Potawatomi open the Chip-in Casino at Escanaba, Michigan.

1998: Prairie Band Casino opens, employing 750 people, and the Citizen band adds a radio station to their other holdings.

Potawatomi John Maskwas.

missionaries, many have become Roman Catholics. The Pokagons lost their tribal status with the federal government in 1934, but were finally re-recognized in 1994.

Prairie Band of Potawatomi, who now live in Kansas, were originally from the lands west of Lake Michigan. They were first removed to Iowa and later to Kansas as white settlement pushed ever westward. They are a federally recognized tribe.

RELIGION

Traditional Potawatomi religion is not a separate practice but runs through every aspect of tribal life. Religion connects the Potawatomi to their community, to nature, to their ancestors, and to the supernatural world. Potawatomi were connected to their ancestors through the Great Chain of Being (*Matchimadzhen*), which links past, present, and future generations. Supernatural beings include the culture hero Wiske and his more evil brother Chipiyapos. Potawatomi people communicated with the spirit world and gained protection and guidance through visions. The visions were achieved through fasting (not eating) and through the power of a personal medicine bundle, a collection of sacred objects. A number of religious leaders, ranging from various types of shamans to the priests of the Midéwiwin society, provided spiritual direction for Potawatomi communities. The Midéwiwin, or Medicine Society, was open to both men and women of any village who had special powers for foretelling and influencing the future. Each Potawatomi clan had its own sacred bundle, along with its own special dances, songs, and chants. The clan established its own rules of behavior for the members.

Contact with European settlers exposed the Potawatomi to Protestant and Catholic missionaries and some converted to the new religions. But others reacted to the white influence on their culture by joining movements they encountered in neighboring tribes that revived the old ways. One such movement originated with the Shawnee Prophet, a Kickapoo Indian who attracted many Potawatomi followers (see Shawnee entry).

One religious movement, the Dream Dance, began with the vision of a Santee Dakota (see Dakota entry) woman in 1876. In her vision she saw the end of U.S. expansion, and Indian domination of the land. By the 1950s, the Dream Dance found expression among many Native Americans who saw it as a message of hope and brotherhood. The Prairie Potawatomi, for instance, read the message as a need to express their cultural identity and to preserve their traditional values.

Today, religion in the Potawatomi communities embraces Christianity, the Dream Dance, and the Native American Church (see box in Makah entry). These beliefs are blended with the traditional emphasis on a balanced relationship with nature, respect for elders, and humility before the powers of the spiritual world.

POTAWATOMI POPULATION: 1990

According to the U.S. Census Bureau, 16,719 people said they were Potawatomi in 1990. They identified themselves this way:

Group	Population
Citizen Band	1,954
Forest County	333
Hannahville	63
Huron Potawatomi	88
Pokagon Potawatomi	48
Potawatomi	13,640
Wisconsin Potawatomi	593
Total	**16,719**

LANGUAGE

The Potawatomi spoke a version of the central Algonquin language that shares many sounds and words with the languages of the Fox, Sac, and Kickapoo tribes. In structure, the Potawatomi language is similar to southern Ojibway and Ottawa.

GOVERNMENT

Historically, each Potawatomi village was ruled by a chief, called a *wkema*, or leader. The chief, a senior member of the clan and a man of good character, was selected by his village. If he were strong and wealthy enough, he could rule over several villages, but this seems not to have happened often.

The chief was assisted by a council of adult males who approved the chief's decisions, and a society of warriors called the *wkec tak*. A man called the pipelighter carried announcements, arranged ceremonies, and called council meetings.

Relationships among the widely scattered Potawatomi villages (they had villages in four states) were kept strong through social ties such as marriage. As the Potawatomi nation expanded, new villages were founded, but the people retained close ties to their old villages and clans. The clans, such as the Bear Clan and the Wolf clan, were large extended family groups that originally had animal symbols.

Today, federally recognized Potawatomi groups are governed by elected tribal councils.

ECONOMY

Historic livelihood

In their earliest times, the Potawatomi were hunter-gatherers, living according to the seasons. They settled near rivers, streams, or lakes and hunted the creatures that flourished there. After European contact, the pelts of the small animals they captured were traded to the French and later to the British.

After the Potawatomi were forced to flee northward to escape the Iroquois in about 1640, they learned agricultural methods from their new neighbors, the Sac, Fox, Kickapoo, and Winnebago, and became farmers. Their crops were tended by the women of the tribe, as the men were still hunters. By now, however, the men were hunting the larger game abundant in the northern woods, such as elk, bear, deer, and beaver. The Potawatomi economy depended heavily on the trading of these animal hides for European weapons, tools, cooking utensils, and cloth.

The Potawatomi today

Today, the Potawatomi hold a wide variety of jobs. For instance, many of the Prairie band, who live on a reservation in Kansas north of Topeka, have turned to gaming (running gambling casinos) as an industry, and have opened a casino and bingo parlors. The Prairie Band Casino and hotel, a $37-million complex, opened in 1998 and employs 750 people.

In the first half of the twentieth century, the Hannahville Potawatomi in northern Michigan relied on farming and forestry. They farmed small plots whose crops included corn, squash, beans, pumpkins, and potatoes. Hunting and fishing rounded out their diet. Cash came from running sawmills, which turned the local timber into building materials. By the 1950s, the timber was exhausted and the tribe sought a new source of income. In 1990 they opened the Chip-in Casino in Escanaba, which provides the band with regular employment and money to invest in programs to help the tribe.

The Wisconsin Potawatomi, the Forest County band, relied on timber for jobs and income into the 1950s. When their forests were exhausted, they too turned to casinos and now own two, one in Milwaukee and the other in Carter. They also own a gas station, lease a smoke shop, and have their own logging crew.

The Potawatomi in southern Michigan, the Huron and the Pokagon, traditionally farmed and fished. Many of the Huron Potawatomi still live on the 120-acre Pine Creek Reservation. The Pokagon have no reservation, and many have assimilated—participating in the culture of the cities around them.

The Citizen Band Potawatomi in Oklahoma also have intermixed with the white culture, and many are of mixed blood. Tribal powwows (see "Festivals") are still held each June to preserve their Native heritage. The tribe owns and operates a golf course, a restaurant, gaming parlors, convenience stores, a bank, a museum and gift shop, and a race track. In 1998, the tribe purchased a radio station that broadcasts from Shawnee.

DAILY LIFE

Education

As children, Potawatomi were expected to learn to bravely accept hardships like hunger and danger. Both boys and girls played with toys that helped them prepare for their traditional adult roles in the tribe. The boys used bows and arrows, while the girls played with corn husk dolls.

Today, some tribes run Indian schools on their reservations, while other children attend public schools. Potawatomi people in the late twentieth century have turned their energies to the revival of Native language skills and cultural traditions. Many communities periodically hold powwows, where they express their spiritual beliefs through dancing, singing, and drumming. The Forest County group operates the Even Start program, which provides weekly language classes, as well as flash cards and videotapes for use in the home. It also runs the Fire Keeper School, an alternative educational facility that provides basic academic instruction as well as teaching cultural subjects such as language, singing, drumming, and crafts.

Buildings

Originally, Potawatomi summer homes were rectangular wigwams on the shores of lakes and rivers. They used the saplings that grew nearby as a skeleton for the wigwam, draping it with woven mats or sheets of bark. A smoke hole in the roof provided ventilation. Dome-shaped winter wigwams were made smaller to conserve heat. Later some Potawatomi lived in log cabins like their white neighbors.

A Potawatomi man and others in front of his Kansas home.

Food

Traditionally, fish was a staple in the Potawatomi diet. They also hunted wild game, which tended to be small animals such as muskrats, squirrels, raccoons, porcupines, turtles, ducks, geese, and turkeys. Wolves and dogs were featured at certain rituals. Later, large game such as buffalo and deer became common. The Potawatomi also gathered local wild foods, such as wild rice, red oak acorns, maple syrup, chokecherries, a large variety of berries, grapes, and plant roots.

Farm crops included corn, beans, squash, and tobacco. Modern Potawatomi crops vary according to the tribe's location and climate. A traditional meal might include meat, gravy, corn soup, frybread, boiled potatoes, and hominy (a dish made from corn).

Clothing and adornment

The Potawatomi wore clothing made from the hides of the animals they ate. They also wore woven fabric garments. Originally, they used shells found alongside streams as beads to decorate their hair, body, and clothing. Later they used metal decorations.

Both men and women wore their hair long. Women usually wore one long braid at the back. In times of war, warriors shaved their heads except for a scalplock (a long lock of hair left on the top of a shaven head). They put red and black paint on their faces.

ARTS

Oral literature

Before their contact with white settlers, the Potawatomi relied heavily on their spoken (oral) tradition to pass down stories and rituals from one generation to the next. They also used a system of pictographs (picture symbols) to help people remember complicated rituals and the details of stories. These pictographs were drawn on birch bark scrolls.

Potawatomi elders told stories to instruct Potawatomi children in how to live a respectful and spiritual life. Today many Potawatomi communities continue to share knowledge and cultural traditions through storytelling.

Potawatomi brave Wabuna, whose name means "large heart."

Potawatomi and Native American culture continue to fascinate people today. In 1994, Potawatomi dances were the subject of a ballet performed by the Milwaukee Ballet. The ballet was danced to an original composition based on Potawatomi legends.

CUSTOMS

Children

Potawatomi children were called by different names as they grew up. During its first year, a child was simply called "infant." On its first birthday, he or she was given a name by the clan. During childhood, the names used to refer to the child were "young boy" or "young girl."

Childhood ended for Potawatomi at puberty. A girl was considered a woman after she started her menstrual cycle, and girls typically married at a younger age than boys. Boys reached maturity through dream quests and hunting.

THE ADVENTURE OF A POOR MAN

The following story emphasizes the need to show respect for the dead by performing the proper rituals and reveals the importance of hospitality in Potawatomi society. The story begins with a poor man who has few friends going off on a hunting expedition. He kills a deer and sets up camp to cook it. Suddenly two strange, silent men appear.

"Hau," said the man, "My friends, you frightened me. . . . I am poor. No one brought me up to know what to do under such circumstances. I should like to know who you are, but I do not know how to ask." The two smiled and nodded to him in a friendly manner, so he went on: "Well, I shall feed you, and do what I can for your comfort." They nodded again. "Are you ghosts?" the hunter inquired. Again they smiled and bowed, so he began to broil meat on the coals, as one does for the souls of the dead.

Now it happened that this man was camped right in the midst of an ancient and forgotten cemetery, and, guessing something of the sort, he offered prayers to the dead in his own behalf, and for his wife and child. He offered to make a feast of the dead, and always to mention the names of the two visitors, or at least to speak of them.

The very next day he killed four bucks right in the trail and luck went with him wherever he traveled. When he got home, he told his wife what had happened, and how he had been frightened when these two naked, soundless men stood there. He told her to help him prepare a feast for them, although he did not know their names, for he hoped that these ghosts would help them to become accepted by society. He made a scaffold and invited one of the honorable men of the tribe, and told him of the strange adventure which had befallen him. He explained that he did not know how to go about giving a feast of the dead, and he turned it over to the elder.

The old man said that the poor man had done the right thing, and that the appearance of these ghosts was a good omen. So the feast was held.

A long time passed, and the poor man became a very great hunter, but he never forgot to sacrifice holy tobacco to the two spirits. He could even find and kill bears in the wintertime, something that no one else even thought of doing, but he could locate their dens at will. At length he even became one of the leaders of the tribe, and held the office of the man who was supposed to apprise the people of the arrival of visitors. He was the first to give presents to visiting strangers, and his name was N'wä'k'to, or "Keeps-on-even-with-everything."

SOURCE: Alanson Skinner. From "The Adventure of a Poor Man." *Bulletin of the Public Museum of the City of Milwaukee.* Vol. 6, No. 3. Milwaukee: 1927.

Festivals

The Citizen band Potawatomi in Oklahoma hosts one of the country's largest annual powwows, a several-day celebration of Native culture. Events include meals with traditional foods and storytelling. Also popular with Native and non-Native audiences are the highly competitive dance contests, with Native dances such as the Grass Dance (in which dancers wear a bunch of grass at their belts), and the Northern Shawl Dance.

Death and burial

Traditionally, Potawatomi funeral rituals were conducted by the clan of the deceased. They dressed the body of a man in his best clothing and laid him out with prized and everyday belongings, such as his moccasins, rifle, knife, money, ornaments, food, and tobacco.

The dying person decided how his body should be disposed of. Bodies could be buried, and in a variety of positions, such as standing, sitting, or lying down. Or the body could be placed above ground, in the fork of a tree. The burial site was marked with a post painted with pictograms to show the dead person's clan. After a death, the chief mourner adopted a replacement relative from the clan.

CURRENT TRIBAL ISSUES

As with many other Native American tribes, a major issue for the Potawatomi has been to convince the U.S. government of the legality of Potawatomi claims to land, fishing and hunting rights, and self-rule. The Potawatomi still struggle for federal recognition of each of the seven bands. Benefits of federal recognition include the right to determine how to use their land, how to use or sell the natural resources on that land, how to govern the people living on the reservation, and how to enforce the Native laws. Tribal status also gives Native Americans the rights outlined in treaties signed in the 1800s, promising them services and money for their land. The Huron Potawatomi, still unrecognized by the U.S. government, have devoted much time and money to obtaining federal recognition.

Other tribal issues include creating jobs that allow the Potawatomi to live on reservations so they can maintain their culture. Many Potawatomi continue to live in poverty on their reservations because of high unemployment. Their high-school dropout rates are higher than in the rest of the U.S. population, and many groups seek to bring job-training programs to the reservations. Social services include alcohol treatment programs, day care, and legal assistance.

The Potawatomi are concerned with protecting their natural resources. The Forest County community forms part of an action group that opposes the proposed establishment of a zinc-copper sulfide mine in northeastern Wisconsin. The Hannahville Potawatomi manages its own forest, farm, and wildlife.

NOTABLE PEOPLE

One of the most influential individuals in twentieth-century Potawatomi history was Minnie Evans, tribal chair of the Prairie Band of Kansas in the 1950s. In 1953 the U.S. government decided to terminate the federally recognized tribal status of this band of Potawatomi. Through the policy of termination, aimed at many

Native American tribes in the 1950s, the government sought to end its trust relationship with those tribes that were deemed capable of assimilating most easily into mainstream society. As termination would have ended vital government-provided services and threatened protection of tribal resources, Minnie Evans led the Prairie Band in fighting the process. Along with Prairie Band tribal members James Wahbnosah and John Wahwassuck, she testified before Congress in 1954, leading an opposition movement that eventually prevented the termination of her tribe.

Letourneau (Blackbird) was chief of the village of Milwaukee in the eighteenth century; he kept his people safe by convincing many of his warriors not to side with the British during the American Revolution. Main Poche (French for "withered hand") was a war chief and medicine man who led resistance to American colonization during the early 1800s.

FURTHER READING

Citizen Potawatomi Nation, http://www.potawatomi.org/

Landes, Ruth. *The Prairie Potawatomi: Tradition and Ritual in the Twentieth Century.* Madison: University of Wisconsin Press, 1970.

Pokagon Band of Potawatomi Indians Homepage: [Online] http://www. mich.com~pokagon

Sultzman, Lee. "Potawatomi History." : [Online] http://dickshovel. com.potawatomi.htm.

Powhatan

Name

The meaning of the name Powhatan (pronounced *pow-uh-TAN* or *pow-HAT-un*) is unknown. Powhatan was the name of an individual tribe and also the name of an alliance of thirty to forty tribes and groups united by their language, their location, and their political leader, Wahunsunacock (also known as Powhatan) and his family.

Location

The Powhatan lived in what is now the state of Virginia, in the area along the coastal plain known as the Tidewater. Their Northern boundary was the Potomac River; the southern boundary was the Great Dismal Swamp on the border between Virginia and North Carolina. Today descendants of the Powhatan live primarily in Virginia and New Jersey.

Population

In the early 1600s the Powhatan tribe was estimated to number about 135 to 165 people, while the Powhatan Confederacy consisted of between 3,900 and 10,400 people. In a census (count of the population) done in 1990 by the U.S. Bureau of the Census, 785 people identified themselves as members of the Powhatan tribe (see box entitled "Population of Powhatan Alliance Members: 1990").

Language family

Algonquian.

Origins and group affiliations

The Powhatan Alliance lasted only from about 1570 to 1650. Today, there are reservations in the states of Virginia and Rhode Island named for tribes who were part of the alliance. Along with the Powhatan tribe itself, some of the tribes of the confederacy were the Arrohatek, Appamattuck, Pamunkey, Mattaponi, Chiskiack, Chickahominy, Nansemond, Rappahannock, and Kecoughtan tribes.

POWHATAN

Shaded area: Traditional Powhatan lands in the area along the coastal plain of present-day Virginia known as the Tidewater.

Contemporary Communities

There are no official Powhatan communities today. Tribes once members of the Powhatan confederacy, not on map:

Virginia

Eastern Chickahominy Tribe, Providence Forge

Monacan Indian Tribe, Monroe

Nansemond Indian Tribe, Chesapeake

Pamunkey Indian Tribe, King William

United Rappahannock Tribe, Indian Neck

When the Europeans first arrived in the New World, several different, independent groups had formed a union with one another under the name of the Powhatan Alliance. In fact, the oldest treaty written in this country was among the Powhatan nations in 1646. For thousands of years the people had lived along coastal areas of the mid-Atlantic. After the coming of the Europeans, they struggled to survive war, illness, prejudice, and the disruption of their culture. In fact, diseases brought by the Europeans wiped out half the tribe by the late 1600s. But stories of the Powhatan remain popular, especially those about the historical figure Pocahontas.

HISTORY

Hostile contact with Europeans

The first contact between the Powhatan and Europeans took place around 1525 when Spanish explorers visited coastal Virginia. In 1560 the Spanish wanted to establish a Catholic mission in the area that would later be called the Tidewater. They kidnaped the son of a local chief, took him to Cuba, taught him Spanish and the Christian religion, and renamed him Don Luis de Velasco. In 1570 he returned to his homeland with several missionaries. Finding his people starving, he left the Spaniards and returned to his home. Later he visited the mission with a war party and killed the missionaries. In 1571 a group of Spaniards launched a raid in retaliation and killed thirty Powhatan people.

In 1584 the English created a colony on Roanoke Island in Virginia. Six years later a group of new British settlers arrived with supplies. They found that all the colonists had disappeared. There were rumors that the colonists had been killed by the Powhatan.

IMPORTANT DATES

1570: The Spanish attempt to establish a mission in Powhatan territory but are driven away or killed by the Native Americans.

1590: Powhatan consolidates his power over Tidewater, Virginia.

1607: The English colonists of the Virginia Company arrive in Powhatan territory.

1618: Powhatan dies and his title passes to his brother Opichapam.

1646: A treaty with the English ends the Powhatan Wars.

Powhatan extends his rule

Meanwhile, during the late 1500s the chief Powhatan was creating an empire in what is now Virginia. He had inherited from his father a confederacy of six tribes, but the ambitious leader quickly expanded his domain. Estimates of the size of the Powhatan Confederacy range from 128 to 200 villages, consisting of as many as eight or nine thousand people and encompassing 30 tribes. Communities under Powhatan's power received military protection and adhered to the confederacy's well-organized system of hunting and trading boundaries. In return, subjects paid a tax to Powhatan in the form of food, pelts, copper, and pearls.

Jamestown

In 1607 a group of English colonists established a fort on the James River near Chesapeake Bay in Powhatan territory. They did not know they were trespassing on a land ruled by a shrewd and powerful head of state. Powhatan remained highly suspicious of the newcomers while at the same time maintaining peaceful relations. In the first year of the new colony, the Powhatan captured John Smith, one of the colonists. Smith later wrote his account of the event, creating the basis for the continuing American legend of Powhatan's daughter Pocahontas. Smith said that he was threatened with execution but was rescued by Pocahontas. He also claimed that Pocahontas later persuaded her father to send food to the starving colonists. There are

An illustration from John Smith's General History *depicting Pocahontas saving him from execution at Powhatan's command, an event that many historians doubt happened.*

good reasons to doubt Smith's story, but by most accounts, the Jamestown settlers would have perished from starvation had it not been for the help of the Powhatan.

A group of descendants of the Powhatans, the Powhatan Renape in New Jersey point out that Smith enjoyed making up stories that made him look good. He only told the story about his rescue by Pocahontas after she had later gained fame. Previously, he never even mentioned a near-execution or Pocahontas. Many historians believe that the event Smith experienced was not an execution but a special ceremony that was going to make Smith a sub-chief under Powhatan.

The English later kidnaped Pocahontas and held her hostage in Jamestown to ensure the good behavior of her father, Chief Powhatan. She married the English colonist John Rolfe in 1614. Rolfe experimented with planting Brazilian tobacco in Virginia, and is often credited with successfully establishing tobacco as a cash crop. This contributed to making the colony financially successful. In 1616 the

Virginia Company, a major financial backer of the Jamestown colony, sponsored a trip to England for Pocahontas, John Rolfe, and their infant son, Thomas. On that trip Pocahontas was introduced to the British Queen Anne, wife of King James I, before whom she became a spokesperson for the Jamestown colony. While in England, Pocahontas caught an infectious disease (probably pneumonia) and died on March 21, 1617.

The First and Second Powhatan Wars

Powhatan died in 1618 and his title passed to his brother, Opichapam.

Opichapam was a weak leader, but his reign was short. His power passed to his brother Opechancanough in 1622. The new chief, who had headed the Pamunkey tribe for many years, considered the English his enemies. He attacked the colonists on March 22, 1622, hoping to drive them out of his territory. About a fourth of the colonists died in this First Powhatan War.

The struggle continued for about ten years, with time-outs when the Indians ran out of food and when the British ran out of gunpowder. The first war ended in 1632 when the Powhatan and the English colonists signed a truce, but warfare started up again not long after the truce and continued for many decades. The once powerful Powhatan began to lose force, and the once vulnerable colonists grew in strength and numbers. By 1675 the Powhatan Confederacy was demolished and the remaining Indians were forced to live under Virginia law.

The Powhatan people who survived began to speak English and adopt English ways. After 1646, the surviving Powhatan groups were sent by the increasingly numerous English to separate areas of tribal lands.

RELIGION

Worshipping the creator

The main god worshiped by the Powhatans was Okewas, sometimes called Okeus. Okewas, who appeared in the form of a young man, was a vengeful god who created the world. Anyone violating his

---

POPULATION OF POWHATAN ALLIANCE MEMBERS: 1990

In a census (count of the population) done in 1990 by the U.S. Bureau of the Census, 2,439 people said they were descended from Powhatan Alliance member tribes. No one identified themselves as Monacan or Nansemond, even though there are reservations named for those tribes in the state of Virginia.

Tribe	Population
Chickahominy	893
—Other Chickahominy	8
Pamunkey	400
Powhatan	795
Rappahannock	343
Total	**2,439**

strict moral code met with misfortune. Special priests made known to the people what Okewas wished from them. Those priests held ceremonies at his temples and made sacrifices to fend off his anger. The priests also healed the sick, identified criminals, and made sure Okewas's image was carried into battle. The priests could be identified by the way they wore their hair, which was shaved on the right side of the head except for a single lock of hair above the eyebrow.

The afterlife

The Powhatan believed the afterlife was a time of unending singing and dancing. In their traditions, upon dying, the soul traveled along a path lined with berries and fruit bushes eastward to the Sun, the home of the Great Hare. Halfway to the Sun, the soul entered the wigwam of a lovely female spirit, who provided corn and other refreshments. After reaching the Sun, the soul found its ancestors eating with the Great Hare. Eventually the soul re-entered the world of the living in a new form.

The Powhatan wars destroyed most of the group's traditional ways of life. By about 1800, most of the Powhatan people had been converted to Christianity, most likely by Protestant missionaries. In 1865 Powhatan people founded the Pamunkey Indian Baptist Church.

LANGUAGE

Most scholars believe that the language spoken by the Powhatans, a dialect (variety) of the Eastern Algonquian family, has become extinct. Although many Powhatans spoke the language around 1750, by 1800 it had almost died out. The modern Indians who live in Virginia speak English. Their identity as a tribe, which would entitle them to certain rights and benefits, has been challenged in the Virginia courts during the past two centuries because they did not speak a Native language.

GOVERNMENT

The Powhatan tribe was traditionally ruled by a male or female leader. Leadership positions were passed down through the women of the tribe. The common people of the tribe paid tribute to the leader in the form of corn, skins, game, and copper. As a result, the leaders could afford to wear elaborate clothing, eat the highest quality food, and live in larger-than-average houses. Leaders had almost absolute rule over their subjects. They could order the punishment or death of people who committed offenses. Priests ranked second in command.

Each village also had its individual leader. He or she paid tribute to superiors and received tribute from lower members of the tribe. Next came councilors, men who gained their position for accomplishing feats of strength or bravery. Along with priests and the tribal leader, these people made up the council that had power to declare war.

ECONOMY

In Powhatan families, duties were generally divided by gender. The women's major duty was farming, gathering, and drying food. They planted beans, corn, squash, and tobacco. Older children helped their mothers plant and weed gardens. Women were also were trained to weave mats and baskets, to prepare animal hides, and to make pottery.

Men did the hunting and fishing, and sometimes engaged in trade. The Powhatan had paths interlinking their villages. They carried out long-distance trade by receiving and passing items from far-off places along these trails. Women sometimes accompanied the men on journeys for trade and helped paddle their canoes so the men could keep their hands free to handle weapons.

DAILY LIFE

Families

Families usually consisted of a married couple, their children, and grandmothers and grandfathers from one or both sides. These extended families of from six to twenty people shared a Powhatan house. Sometimes a house was shared by the families of brothers too. Occasionally, a wealthy man had two or more wives and families. Chief Powhatan was said to have had a dozen wives.

Buildings

Powhatan houses were generally long and narrow. They were made by bending saplings (young trees) and covering them over with mats woven from marsh reeds, rushes, or bark. The bent saplings formed a semicircular roof. Poles buried in the ground helped support the roof. Houses usually had one room with a door at either end. In summer, the mat walls were rolled up or taken off to provide fresh air. Low platforms that lined the walls were used as work areas during the day and as beds at night.

The other main type of structure in a Powhatan village was a temple for the worship of their gods. Temples were often built on hills or ridges that overlooked the village. Constructed in the same way as the houses, temples were 60 to 100 feet long and faced in an east-west direction. At the eastern part of the temple, near the entrance, fires were kept burning. In a westerly-facing room the dried bodies of dead tribal leaders were guarded by wooden images of Okewas and other spirits. Temples were sometimes used for storage of food, goods, and other valuables.

Clothing and adornment

Because the area where they lived was very warm, the Powhatan kept clothing to a minimum. In summer children generally went naked until they reached puberty. Adults wore breechcloths (material that went between the legs and was fastened at the waist) made of deerskin or grasses. In winter they added deerskin cloaks, moccasins, and leggings. When it was very cold they wore a layer of animal grease for further insulation.

Hairstyles varied according to a person's social status and gender. Men shaved the right side of the head (to keep it from tangling in their bowstrings). Young women shaved the front and sides of the head and braided the hair that remained; adult women cut their hair just below the ears. Women also wore tattoos of animals and plants that were made by rubbing soot into cuts made in the skin with copper knives. Jewelry made of glass, copper, or bone beads was worn by both sexes.

Food

Most food came from hunting, fishing, farming, and gathering wild plants. The tribes moved upriver in the winter months to a place where deer, raccoons, and turkey were more plentiful. They fished with nets, hooks and lines, and bows and arrows. They also caught shellfish. In farming, they moved from one field to another as the soil became exhausted. The Powhatan grew corn, beans, and squash. In winter, women, children, and old men gathered walnuts, hickory nuts, acorns, and chestnuts. Native Americans collected nuts of all kinds, such as hickory, pecan, and pine nuts. Hazelnut trees were common throughout the wooded areas of the northeast. Hazelnuts were eaten raw or roasted, and were sometimes ground into flour and crushed for nut oil that was used in cooking. Some foods were stored in underground pits or elevated storage areas near the family home to prepare for winter.

Education

Powhatan children were trained for their roles in society beginning at a young age. Boys were taught to hunt by both their mothers

POWHATAN HAZELNUT SOUP

2¼ cups ground, blanched hazelnuts

2 packages (4½ gram) instant beef broth

2 scallions, washed and sliced

2 Tablespoons minced parsley

5 cups water

1 teaspoon salt

1/8 teaspoon fresh ground pepper

Place all ingredients in a large saucepan, and simmer together gently, stirring occasionally, for one hour. Serve hot. Make the servings small; the soup is rich.

From Yeffe Kimball and Jean Anderson, *The Art of American Indian Cooking*. Garden City, NY: Doubleday, 1965, p. 175

and fathers. Every morning the mother threw a piece of moss in the air. A boy had to hit it with his arrow before he was allowed to have breakfast. Boys also learned to make tools from stones and shells. They used the tools to carve bowls, make weapons, and hollow out logs to make canoes that could carry up to thirty people. Girls learned gardening and meal preparation. They also were taught to make pottery and prepare animal skins to be made into clothing and purses.

By the mid-1700s, Christian missionaries had taught many young men Christianity, English, and arithmetic. Much later, schools for Native American children were opened in Virginia, but they taught students little about their Native culture. For example, during the 1930s the white teacher of a pottery school on the Pamunkey reservation instructed students to use a pottery wheel, rather than learn the traditional Pamunkey technique of making pottery. Until an Indian high school was opened in 1950, none of the Virginia Indian schools went beyond seventh grade. In the 1960s Virginia schools ended their policy of segregation (separating the races in schools), marking the end of Indian schools there.

Healing practices

Powhatan priests used their influence with the gods to diagnose diseases and prescribe cures. They used rituals as well as herbs to treat sore throats, infections, diarrhea, fevers, and poisoning.

ARTS

Pottery

For more than 200 years, women of the Pamunkey tribe were famed for their pottery made of clay from their reservation. They strengthened the raw clay with crushed and burned mussel shells,

Pamunkey pottery, c. 1899.

and used their hands to shape a particular object. Then they smoothed the surface with a mussel shell. They sometimes etched a pattern on the surface before placing the piece in a fire to harden.

Dancing

The Powhatan danced for both religious purposes and amusement. Music accompanied the dancing. The Powhatan made rattles fashioned from dried gourds by filling them with pebbles or seeds. They also stretched animal skins over wooden bowls to make drums. Flutes were made from pieces of cane.

Dramatic production

Around 1880 the Pamunkey staged a production of the popular story of Pocahontas, a story that is more legend than historical fact. Rather than wear the scanty clothing that was traditional, they donned elaborately beaded costumes.

CUSTOMS

Festivals

The main harvest of the Powhatans took place each year from August through October. With food plentiful and the workload lightened, the people chose this time of year to hold their major religious ceremonies. Unfortunately, little is known about them because the English did not record the details.

Today, thousands of people gather in King William, Virginia, every Memorial Day for the annual Spring Festival. It is held at the

Sharon Indian School, which is located on Upper Mattaponi tribal grounds. This tribe was once part of the Powhatan Coalition. Festivities include sharing Native foods, storytelling, arts and crafts, Indian dancing, games and rides for children, and educational programs.

Naming

A person's name was very important in Powhatan tribes. A man who was known for his abilities in hunting and bringing food home to his family would obtain a name that reflected his skills. Throughout his life, a man's changing status was reflected in the way his name might change. At a celebration marking the birth of a new baby, the father would announce its name. Later, the mother gave the child a nickname. If a boy showed some special ability, like skills with a bow and arrow, his father gave him another name reflecting this ability. Later, if he performed a brave deed, the chief might give him still another, a name-title that singled him out as special.

Puberty

Powhatan boys who wanted to be leaders underwent a dangerous rite called *Huskanow*. The ceremony began with feasting and dancing. Then the older men took the boys out of the village and pretended to sacrifice them. The boys were expected to lie still for many hours. They stayed in the forest for several months, under the watchful eye of their elders. The boys were later beaten and had to drink hallucination-causing drugs; some became so agitated that they had to be kept in wooden cages. They were then "reborn" and allowed to return to their families. Any sign that a boy was reverting to the ways of boyhood required him to undergo a second Huskanaw. Few boys could endure the process a second time, and many died in the process.

Courtship and marriage

Young women were considered ready for marriage as soon as they reached puberty. Before they were permitted to marry, young men had to show they could hunt and fish and take care of a family. Young people courted each other with gifts of food. Parents generally bargained for the bride price—the goods a young man had to provide to a young woman's family to be permitted to marry her. He gathered the items, presented them to her family, and went home. The bride then traveled to his home and his father performed the marriage ceremony by joining their hands and breaking a string of beads over their heads.

Funerals

The bodies of the dead were wrapped in animal skins or rush mats and buried. Women served as mourners; they blackened their faces and wept for the entire day following the death. Some beads were buried with the body for use in the afterlife. Sometimes bodies were placed on a high scaffolding and allowed to decompose. Every few years all the bones were buried together in large pits.

CURRENT TRIBAL ISSUES

The biggest problem facing descendants of the Powhatan is gaining recognition from federal and state governments as Indian tribes. Before the 1960s, only two groups regained their status in Virginia as independent tribes within the boundaries of their traditional lands. The other tribes that made up the Powhatan Alliance were presumed to be extinct. However, during the 1970s and 1980s several other groups fought for and received recognition by the state of Virginia. In 1995 the Chickahominy tribe began seeking recognition from the federal government.

In 1971 many of the Tidewater Indians joined with other eastern tribes to form the Coalition of Eastern Native Americans. Membership in this group helped Powhatan Alliance descendants to gain access to federal funds that have been used for education, job creation, and housing improvements.

NOTABLE PEOPLE

Wahunsunacock (1550–1618), better known as Powhatan, led the Powhatan Coalition between 1570 and his death in 1618. A clever politician, he united the tribes of Coastal Virginia under his rule. Probably the best-known Powhatan was his daughter, Pocahontas (1595–1617), whose real name was Metoaka.

FURTHER READING

Feest, Christian F. *The Powhatan Tribes.* New York: Chelsea House Publishers, 1990.

McDaniel, Melissa. *The Powhatan Indians.* New York: Chelsea Juniors, 1996.

Mossiker, Frances. *Pocahontas: The Life and the Legend.* New York: Alfred A. Knopf, 1976.

Trigger, Bruce G., ed. *Handbook of North American Indians,* Vol. 15. *Northeast.* Washington, DC: Smithsonian Institution, 1978.

Sac and Fox

Name

Sac and Fox. The French called the Fox people "Foxes," after the name of one of the tribe's clans. The Fox called themselves *Meshkwakihug,* (or Mesquakie) meaning "red earth people," for the type of earth from which they believed they were created. The Sac called themselves *Osakiwung,* meaning "yellow earth people." Before it united with the Fox people, the tribe was also known as Sauk.

Location

Originally inhabitants of southern Michigan and Wisconsin, the Sac and Fox people now live, for the most part, on reservations in Oklahoma, Iowa, and Kansas.

Population

The Sac and Fox are two closely related but separate tribes. There were 2,500 Fox and about 3,500 Sac in the early 1600s. In a census (count of the population) done in 1990 by the U.S. Bureau of the Census, 3,168 people identified themselves as Sac and Fox.

Language family

Central Algonquian.

Origins and group affiliations

Members of the Sac and Fox tribe are descendants of the Sac (Sauk) and Fox peoples of the Great Lakes region. The Sac originally lived in the lower Peninsula of Michigan with their neighbors, the Fox. The Sac and Fox are now considered one tribe.

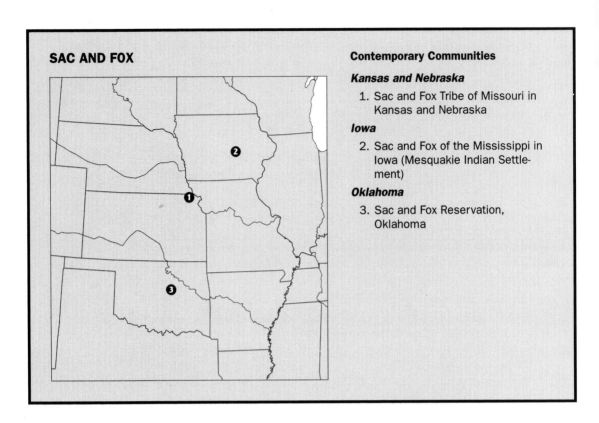

SAC AND FOX

Contemporary Communities

Kansas and Nebraska

1. Sac and Fox Tribe of Missouri in Kansas and Nebraska

Iowa

2. Sac and Fox of the Mississippi in Iowa (Mesquakie Indian Settlement)

Oklahoma

3. Sac and Fox Reservation, Oklahoma

The Sac and Fox people have shared a close association for centuries. They were outstanding hunters who were also known for their bravery. The Sac and Fox culture was based upon respect for life, people, communities, and all of creation. Although the people living on Sac and Fox reservations today participate in mainstream American life, they are doing their best to retain aspects of their traditional culture.

HISTORY

The Fox people probably originated in southern Michigan, and may have been a part of the Sac tribe centuries ago and then split off. When the French encountered them some time during the early- to mid-1600s, the Fox were divided into two groups. One group lived in central Wisconsin along the Fox River, and another lived in northern Illinois. The Sac people originated around Saginaw Bay in Michigan.

Trouble with the French

During the 1600s the Fox quickly grew hostile to the French traders moving into their territory, perhaps because the French traded with the Dakota, an enemy tribe. The Fox started to charge a toll for the French traders to cross their land along the Fox River, an important waterway between Lake Michigan and Dakota lands. The Fox placed a flaming torch on the riverbank, marking their territory as a signal to the traders to pay up or suffer the consequences—death. The Fox, who were allies of the Iroquois, also traded with the British. Conflicts with the French resulted in the French-Fox War (1712–37), a war that had disastrous consequences for the Fox.

The French-Fox War began as the result of an incident in 1712. The Illinois Fox and several other tribes friendly to the French had been invited to join a French settlement near Fort Detroit in Michigan. Misunderstandings developed among these groups, and the French and their Indian allies attacked the Fox, inflicting heavy losses on the tribe. The surviving Fox fled to join some other tribe members in Wisconsin. There, Fox harassment of French traders increased. The angry French sent two military expeditions against the Fox. They succeeded in winning all of the Fox tribes' allies to the French side and then nearly destroyed the Fox tribe.

The Sac were driven out of their territory near Michigan's Saginaw Bay at the same time as the Fox. They too relocated to Wisconsin. With the help of the Fox and other tribes, the Sac then drove the Illinois tribe from Illinois Territory on the Mississippi River and occupied it.

Fox join with Sac

As time passed, the Fox formed a close alliance with the Sac. The two groups were considered by outsiders as a single tribe, but between themselves they retained their individuality, as they still do today. During the 1760s, with their numbers declining, the Sac and Fox moved south. By the early 1800s, they occupied the land along the Mississippi, primarily on the eastern bank from the mouth of the Des Moines (pronounced *duh-MOYNE*) River to the Prairie du Chien (pronounced *doo-SHEEN*) in southern Wisconsin. Here they enjoyed abundant fishing and fertile farmland that produced plentiful harvests. They maintained a successful trading relationship with the French, Spanish, and British.

IMPORTANT DATES

Early 1600s: The Fox make their first contact with non-Natives with French traders.

1712: Losses in the French-Fox war drive the Fox to Wisconsin.

1733: Sac and Fox tribes merge.

1833: Sac and Fox are forced west of the Mississippi River.

1859: Members of the Fox tribe separate from the Sac and return to Iowa.

1993: Sac and Fox Nation defines its reservation as a "Nuclear Free Zone."

An illustration of a group of Sac and Fox Indians.

Division among the group

As the 1800s began, the Sac and Fox encountered increased pressure from white settlers. Internal disagreements caused one Sac group to move south to the Missouri River. They became known as the Missouri Band. In 1836 this group relocated to a reservation in Kansas on the Nebraska border. They remain there today as the Sac and Fox Nation of Missouri.

In 1825 the Sac people who lived along the Mississippi divided into two groups. One relocated to southeast Iowa. The other, followers of the Sac warrior Black Hawk, stayed with him at Rock Island, Illinois. They tried to reclaim the land of their ancestors east of the Mississippi but were stopped and defeated in the Black Hawk War (1832–33) by the U.S. Army and hostile Dakota Indians. The U.S. government then forced them to move further west to a reservation in Kansas. Some refused to leave Iowa and hid from U.S. troops.

Disputes developed between the Sac and Fox who had gone to Kansas. By 1860 some of the Fox had left Kansas and gone back to Iowa where they bought land near the town of Tama. A smaller group moved in with the Kickapoo, then later moved to northern Mexico.

The remaining Sac and Fox sold their Kansas land and relocated to a 750,000-acre reservation east of Oklahoma City. By 1891, most of this land had been given to white settlers by the U.S. government. The current Sac and Fox Reservation in Stroud, Oklahoma has less than 1,000 acres.

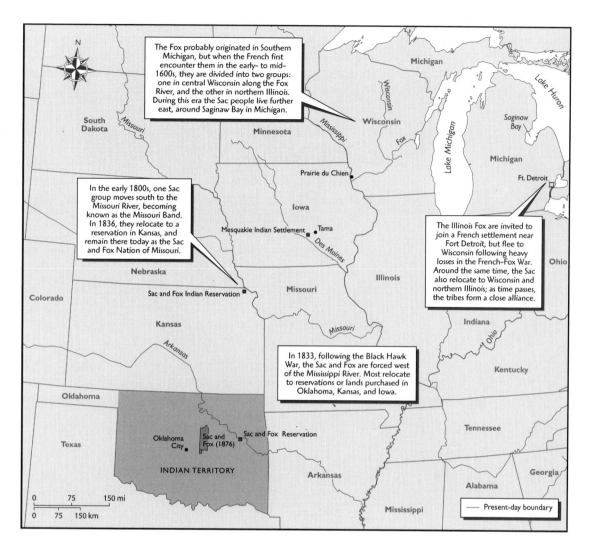

A map showing the migrations of the Sac and Fox through the mid-nineteenth century.

The Fox probably originated in Southern Michigan, but when the French first encounter them in the early- to mid-1600s, they are divided into two groups: one in central Wisconsin along the Fox River, and the other in northern Illinois. During this era the Sac people live further east, around Saginaw Bay in Michigan.

In the early 1800s, one Sac group moves south to the Missouri River, becoming known as the Missouri Band. In 1836, they relocate to a reservation in Kansas, and remain there today as the Sac and Fox Nation of Missouri.

The Illinois Fox are invited to join a French settlement near Fort Detroit, but flee to Wisconsin following heavy losses in the French–Fox War. Around the same time, the Sac also relocate to Wisconsin and northern Illinois; as time passes, the tribes form a close alliance.

In 1833, following the Black Hawk War, the Sac and Fox are forced west of the Mississippi River. Most relocate to reservations or lands purchased in Oklahoma, Kansas, and Iowa.

Present-day boundary

Members of the Sac and Fox Reservation in Iowa used their own money to buy lands that now amount to nearly 5,000 acres. Although their official name is the Sac and Fox of the Mississippi in Iowa, they prefer to be called the Mesquakie Indian Settlement.

RELIGION

Views on creation and the earth

The Sac and Fox believed that the universe was divided into two halves. The Great Manitou spirit ruled the Powers of the Sky, or Upper Region. Lesser spirits, such as the Earth, sky, waters, forests, and intelligent animals, ruled the Powers of the Earth, or Lower

Region. The Sac believed that the world was created by Gretci Munito, a powerful old man who lived forever.

Both Sac and Fox visualized the Earth on which they lived as a woman, who provided them with all their food. The Fox practiced a ceremony of apology for taking life when they cut trees, gathered plants, or took minerals.

Death, spirits, Christianity

The Fox believed that when a person died, the soul traveled through a series of villages to a final resting-place beyond the sunset. Only the souls of the good went further than the first village. Evil people were sent to the home of Machi Manitou, the chief evil spirit. Shamans (medicine men; pronounced *SHAY-muns*) could talk to the spirit world.

The Sac believed that the soul followed the Milky Way and crossed a river before entering the land of the dead. A figure called the "Brain Taker" tried to smash the head of anyone attempting to cross the river. If the soul crossed the river swiftly and safely, there would be feasting and rejoicing when it entered the land of the dead. If it were caught, its brains would be destroyed.

The Sac and Fox believed that human beings were both helped and hurt by spirits. During the great Indian ceremony called Vision Quest, the aid of spirits was eagerly sought. Many Sac and Fox today are Christians, or members of the Native American Church (see box in Makah entry), which was founded in the nineteenth century. The church combines Christian and Native beliefs and practices, and features an all-night ceremony composed of chanting, prayer, and meditation.

LANGUAGE

The languages spoken by the Sac and the Fox were Central Algonquian dialects (varieties), closely related to each other and to the language of the Kickapoo. During the early part of the twentieth century, much effort went into preserving the early language and tales of the people. As a result, there is a Sac-Fox dictionary, a Sac-Fox alphabet, and there are many books of Sac and Fox tales.

GOVERNMENT

The early Sac and Fox were governed by a clan system (clans are groups of related families). Some clan names were Fish, Ocean, Thunder, Bear, Fox, Indian Potato, Deer, Beaver, Snow, and Wolf. Separate societies were formed for games, ceremonies, and warfare. Members of those societies did not have to be of the same clan.

Three types of chiefs led the Sac and Fox tribes: a peace chief, a war chief, and a religious leader known as a shaman. Leadership roles were sometimes passed down from generation to generation. Other leaders were chosen on the basis of their merits. The tribal council made the final decision of who would serve as chief. The chief who could gather the most followers had the most influence.

Women were not permitted to be chiefs in the early days, but they participated in public meetings and gave advice on matters of importance. Times changed, however, and in the late 1990s Principal Chief Dora S. Young headed the Sac and Fox Tribe on the Oklahoma reservation near Stroud, Oklahoma. A business committee operates as the elected governing body for enrolled members of the tribe and transacts business on the tribe's behalf. The Sac and Fox Court, begun in 1885, tries cases involving members of the tribe.

ECONOMY

Pre-twentieth-century economy

The early Sac and Fox were village dwellers who followed an annual cycle of hunting, farming, and trading. Every year they traded thousands of dollars' worth of beaver pelts to the Europeans in exchange for horses, animal traps, firearms, blankets, and cooking utensils.

In the nineteenth century, the Sac and Fox who lived on the reservation in present-day Oklahoma were used to owning their land in common. In 1887, the U.S. government adopted an allotment policy and insisted that the people adopt the custom of individual land ownership. Most of the Indians could not raise sufficient food on their individual lots, particularly because they did not own the appropriate tools and had no money to buy them. Many ended up selling their property to whites.

Modern times

The tribe suffered economic hardship well into the twentieth century. Their homes often lacked heat and water, and medical and educational opportunities were very limited. Many ended up working as laborers on land they once owned.

Four Fox Indians, photographed in 1890.

Even today, unemployment remains a problem. In the mid-1990s unemployment on the reservation in Oklahoma ran about 22.5 percent—more than one-fifth of people who wanted to work could not find a job. Per capita income was about $6,204, only one-third of that of most white Americans. (Per capita income is the average income one person earns in one year.)

Today, individual members of the Oklahoma Sac and Fox lease their land for farming and grazing purposes. An important business operation is the tribe's Indian Country Bingo facility located in Stroud. In the mid-1990s members of the Sac and Fox Reservation in Oklahoma reacquired more than 4,000 acres of land that houses the Cushing Industrial Park. That complex includes a 25,000-square-foot building and a warehouse facility. The tribe also operates an arts and crafts outlet, a grocery store, a tribal museum, and a modern campground.

DAILY LIFE

Families

The basic unit of the Fox tribe was the extended family, made up of parents, children, grandparents, and other relatives. It usually consisted of between five and thirty members. Children spent most of their time playing. Boys were also taught hunting skills, while girls learned cooking and sewing.

Buildings

When first encountered by the Europeans, the Fox lived in summer camps consisting of several rectangular frame lodges surrounded by a fence of large pointed stakes. Their houses, called lodges, were very similar to those of the Sac. Lodges were up to sixty feet long and housed several families. They were covered with elm bark matting and had two entrances. The eastern door was called "where daylight appears," and the western door on the opposite side was called "where the Sun goes down." Wide benches covered with bark lined the sides of the walls and were used for sitting and sleeping.

Personal possessions and objects belonging to the clan were either hung from the ceiling or stored under the benches. Although campfires were sometimes made in the lodge, most of the cooking was done in temporary brush shelters set near the lodge.

In winter, as food became scarcer, Sac and Fox families usually left their villages and settled in smaller encampments. Their winter homes were small wigwams, no more than fifteen feet wide, that were built of poles and covered with reed mats. The doors and floors were covered with bearskins and buffalo robes. They used a central fire pit to prepare food and provide warmth.

While villages were usually small, a European visitor to a Sac village in 1766 described it as having ninety houses, many sheds for smoking meat, and regularly spaced streets.

Clothing and adornment

The Sac and Fox wore clothing decorated with buffalo hair or plant fibers woven in arrows or zigzags. Some garments were decorated with quills and ribbon work. In summer, the men usually wore moccasins and a breechcloth (a piece of material that went between the legs) of tanned deerskin or elk skin. Women wore wraparound skirts also made of tanned deer or elk skin with thong belts and moccasins. In colder weather, the men usually added leggings and a shirt. Women wore ponchos and leggings. Garters and belts were worn by both sexes. Summer clothing included lightweight robes made of deerskin or elk skin. Painted buffalo robes were worn in winter.

Accessories such as hawk and eagle feathers, long sashes worn around the waist, and animal-skin pouches were very popular. Griz-

The day school at the Sac and Fox Agency in Indian Territory, 1876–1896.

zly bear claw necklaces were highly prized because they were so hard to win. Both sexes pierced their ears and wore rings, hoops, and feathers through them. The use of body paint was common. Some Fox men dyed their hair blue. The women of both tribes wore their hair long, holding it in place with a decorated hair binder.

Food

The Sac and Fox hunted waterfowl, deer, and moose, following the animal herds during the winter months. Women farmed and gathered berries, nuts, honey, wild potatoes, fruits, and herbs, to supplement their diet. Crops included corn, beans, squash, pumpkins, and melons. Maple syrup was collected in winter and used to flavor food. Food was wrapped in bark and stored in a hiding place near the lodge.

The Fox held two organized buffalo hunts each year. When they found a herd, the hunters surrounded it and started a grass fire. Meanwhile a skilled archer killed the lead buffalo. With the herd leaderless and unable to escape because of the fire, the panicked buffalo were easy to kill. When the men returned with the carcasses, the women stripped, cleaned, packed, and dried the meat, and prepared the hides for making clothing and for trading.

Education

Sac and Fox boys were taught about making bows and arrows and hunting. Girls were taught how to cook, sew, and tend a garden.

In the late 1800s the U.S. government built boarding schools on the reservations. They separated children from their parents and tried to teach them to live like whites. The students learned about building fences, sewing, and tending cattle. Many parents did not like the system and its emphasis on manual labor; they refused to permit their children to attend the schools. Christian missionaries who taught at the schools tried with little success to convert the children to Christianity.

Today, children living on the Sac and Fox reservation in Oklahoma attend public schools in neighboring communities. The tribe sponsors a summer camp that teaches the Sac and Fox language to children. The Mesquakie Indian Settlement in Iowa has its own elementary and secondary school, where children can learn about their culture.

Healing practices

Tribal members learned their religious prayers and dances from shamans, who led ceremonies to ensure success in war and farming, or to cure illnesses. Medicine men and women were both respected and feared, because even "good" shamans were believed to have the power to put bad spells on people. Good shamans cured people by sucking out the illness-causing objects injected by bad shamans or witches. The Fox were afraid of witches, who became active at night, passing through the forest disguised as balls of blue-green light. Shamans gave their patients advice, charms, and remedies to counteract bad spells cast by witches; they also dispensed herbal remedies for illnesses.

ARTS

The Sac and Fox were known for combining form and beauty in everyday objects. They used feathers, plant fibers, wood, and stone to adorn such things as bags, boxes, and even weapons. The Fox made ribbonwork panels out of several layers of different colored ribbons and cutout floral or geometric shapes. After encountering Europeans, the Indians added European goods to their designs, including colored beads, woven cloth, and metal.

Today the Sac and Fox Tribe of Oklahoma operate the Sac and Fox Gallery, a retail store that sells arts and crafts made by members of the tribe.

CUSTOMS

Festivals

The Fox celebrated a successful harvest at great festivals that involved horse races and an early version of the game we know as

A FOX TALE

The Sac and Fox enjoyed gathering around a fire during the winter months to hear short tales about tribal practices and morality. Many of their stories, including the following selection, have been preserved.

Once upon a time there was a youth who blackened (his face) and fasted. He had been blessed by the manitous. And when he was visited by his father, "Come, O father, do let me eat!" he said to his father. Four days had passed since he had eaten.

"My dear son, I want you to fast two days more, but no longer." Then the old man went back home. He was implored by his son to let him eat, (but) he could not be prevailed upon by him.

So in the morning when the old man went to take another look at his son, lo, the youth had disappeared from the place where he was staying! There was a spring at the brook near by.

There the old man went. He went there to look over the bank, and behold! Lying there, on the flat of his belly, and drinking water, was his son. As he looked at him, lo, (his son) changed partly into a fish! He ran to his son to catch him, but he slipped hold of him and he lost his son.

Thereupon was the spring swollen with water, and the place where (the youth) escaped became a lake. For many a year it was common for the people, as they went canoeing about, to see catfishes down in the water. One catfish was white; it wore yellow ear-rings; that one was the youth who had fasted overmuch. One catfish was black, and that was his wife. And there were also four other tiny little catfishes; they were (all) white, (and) they wore yellow ear-rings. These went swimming past side by side, abreast and in line, these the offspring of him that had fasted overlong.

SOURCE: Jones, William, "Fox Tales." *Publications of the American Ethnological Society.* Vol. 1. Leyden: E. J. Brill, 1907.

lacrosse (a game of Native American origin played on a field by two teams of ten players each. Participants use a long-handled stick with a webbed pouch to try and get a ball into the opposing team's goal). They also played a ball game between two teams in which one hid a ball or stone under a blanket; the other had to find it.

The Sac and Fox tribes of Oklahoma host an annual powwow in mid-July that features Indian dancing and arts and crafts. They also host tribal feasts. Since the beginning of the twentieth century, the Sac and Fox Reservation in Tama County, Iowa, has hosted an annual powwow that celebrates their heritage and spirituality.

Puberty

As part of the puberty ritual, Sac and Fox boys were sent out to begin their vision quest. A vision quest involved praying and fasting alone, waiting for a special vision to be given by a spirit, and collecting special objects, like stones and feathers, that represented the new-gained power. They were then expected to accomplish a heroic deed. Males were considered full adults around age twenty. Female rituals began at first menstruation. The girl was sent to a lodge by herself and was allowed no visitors for ten days.

Courtship and marriage

Most young men married by about age twenty, to women three to four years younger. To court his intended bride, the man offered services and gifts. If the bride-to-be and her parents accepted, the couple was married and moved into the bride's family home. The young man then fulfilled his promises to the family. After two or three years, the couple usually moved to their own home and began having children. Marriage to more than one wife was allowed; usually a man married a sister or cousin of his first wife.

Death and mourning

Sac and Fox who died were either buried or placed on a platform. Sometimes a warrior might be buried lying or sitting on top of an enemy. Occasionally, a dog was sacrificed and buried with the dead person to be a companion in the afterlife. The mourning period for family members of the deceased lasted from six months to a year. During this time, the mourners blackened their faces and wore shabby clothing to demonstrate their grief.

War rituals

If an enemy tribe killed a Sac or Fox, the victim's family might organize a raid to get even. The man who was to lead a raid would fast from eating. He also built a special lodge with a strip of red cloth hung in front of it to signal that he planned a raid. Those who wanted to participate came in and smoked a pipe with him. Sometimes wives accompanied their husbands on a raid. As they approached the enemy, the leader rode in front carrying his sacred pack (a container with items such as animal teeth and eagle feathers that gave him special powers). If the raid was not successful, the warriors returned to their village separately. If it was successful, they returned together, sending ahead a messenger to announce their victory.

Sac and Fox braves wore special headdresses into battle. They were made of animal hair dyed red and tied to a strip of hair on their scalps. The rest of the head was shaved and colorful designs were painted on. Unless the weather was very cold, they kept their upper body bare. They sometimes painted human hands on their backs or shoulders with white clay paint. The hands showed how many enemies they had slain. After a successful raid, the Fox would paint their tribal symbol on a tree near where the enemy had fallen.

CURRENT TRIBAL ISSUES

In 1992, seventy-five-year-old tribe member Grace Thorpe, the daughter of Olympic athlete Jim Thorpe, led a fight against the construction on tribal land of a storage site for highly radioactive material. Using research that showed the harm that exposure to radiation could cause, Grace Thorpe began a movement opposing the facility. In February 1993 her tribe, the Sac and Fox Nation, voted against having the storage site built on their land. In so doing, they turned down $2.8 million that the U.S. government would have paid them and became the first tribe in Oklahoma to declare a "Nuclear Free Zone" on their tribal lands.

Recent Sac and Fox tribal leaders have asserted certain rights as a sovereign nation (a nation-within-a-nation, able to make its own laws). Those rights include taxing businesses, issuing license plates, protecting sovereign control over lands and resources, and governing according to Sac and Fox modern law.

NOTABLE PEOPLE

James Francis "Jim" Thorpe was born in 1888 on the Sac and Fox Reservation in Oklahoma. He played both professional baseball and football and made the hall of fame in both sports. In 1950 the Associated Press voted Jim Thorpe, an Olympic champion, the greatest athlete in the first half of the twentieth century. In 1954, a year after Thorpe died, a town in Pennsylvania was named in his honor.

In 1993 Jim Thorpe's daughter, Grace, known as Wind Woman, founded the National Environmental Coalition of Native Americans (NECONA) to fight the dumping of nuclear waste on Indian lands.

Sac leader Keokuk (1783–1848) rose to power because of his skills as a warrior, politician, and orator. He signed many treaties giving up Sac and Fox land to the American government, against the wishes of his rival, Black Hawk (1767–1838). He later skillfully defended Sac land interests against Sioux claims of ownership.

FURTHER READING

Bernotas, Bob. *Jim Thorpe: Sac & Fox Athlete*. New York: Chelsea House, 1992.

McDaniel, Melissa. *The Sac and Fox Indians*. New York: Chelsea Juniors, 1995.

Von Ahnen, Katherine. *Charlie Young Bear*. Minot, CO: Roberts Rinehart Publishers, 1994.

Shawnee

Name

The name Shawnee (pronounced *shaw-NEE*) is from the Algonquian term *sawanwa,* or "Southern people." Four separate divisions of the tribe exist today: the Eastern Shawnee, the Loyal Shawnee, the Absentee Shawnee of Oklahoma, and the United Remnant Band in Ohio.

Location

The Shawnee moved frequently and it is difficult for historians to trace their movements. Before Europeans arrived in the Americas, they lived mainly in southern Ohio, western Pennsylvania, and West Virginia. During the 1600s they scattered widely, and by the late 1600s and early 1700s, they lived mostly in eastern Pennsylvania and Ohio. Another scattering took place before 1750, and many returned to southern Ohio. A third scattering took place during the American Revolution (1776–83), when many Shawnee moved westward into Oklahoma. Today the Shawnee live mainly in Oklahoma and Ohio.

Population

In the 1660s, prior to contact with Europeans, there were anywhere from 10,000 to 12,000 Shawnee. In 1825, there were 2,500. In a census (count of the population) done in 1990 by the U.S. Bureau of the Census, 6,640 people identified themselves as Shawnee (see box on page 190).

Language family

Algonquian.

Origins and group affiliations

The Shawnee are thought to be one of the Algonquian tribes who moved from Canada's eastern coast during prehistoric times. They had connections with Sac and Fox (see entry), and Kickapoo tribes. Their closest associations were with the Delaware and Creek (see entry), and they had generally hostile relations with the Iroquois (see entry).

SHAWNEE

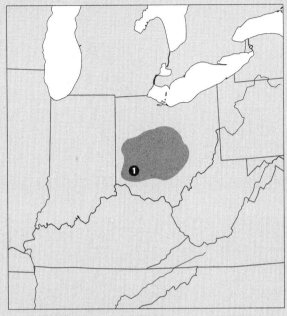

Shaded area: Traditional Shawnee lands in present-day Ohio.

Contemporary Communities

1. Shawnee Nation United Remnant Band, Ohio

(Not on map, Absentee Shawnee Tribe; Eastern Shawnee; and the Loyal Shawnee, all in Oklahoma)

For centuries the Shawnee wandered from place to place, becoming known far and wide for their skill as warriors. Beginning in the 1600s, they were often invited to settle among other tribes. In exchange for protecting those tribes, they received the use of harvest and hunting grounds. The Shawnee strongly opposed white settlement beyond the original thirteen colonies. Because of their ability to bounce back after bad times, they are currently one of the most prosperous Native American tribes.

HISTORY

Scattering of the Shawnee tribe

The Shawnee first made contact with Europeans in the early 1670s when French trappers and traders came to Tennessee and South Carolina. The Shawnee traded furs and hides to the French, and later the British, for European goods such as jewelry, glass beads, ribbons, pots, blankets, and steel weapons. By the late 1600s many Shawnee had moved northward into the Ohio Valley and eastern

Pennsylvania. There, some joined with groups of Delaware Indians and lived in what is present-day Indiana.

Return to the homeland

In the 1720s the Wyandot tribe offered the Shawnee a section of land to live on in southern Ohio. Shawnee from all directions welcomed the invitation and gathered there. It was excellent land for hunting and farming, and there was plenty of it. By 1730, most Shawnee had returned to this land in Ohio, on what were probably their original homelands. But because they needed huge tracts of open land for their wandering way of life, they saw the westward expansion by English settlers as a serious threat to their survival.

The French and Indian War

The French and Indian War (1754–63) broke out in 1754, as the British and French struggled for control of the American colonies. In 1755 the Shawnee were drawn into the war because of a misunderstanding over the murder of British General Edward Braddock (1695-1755) and half of his army of 2,200 men. Angry British colonists mistakenly believed that the Shawnee were responsible for the attack. As a result, when Shawnee representatives went to talk with British officials in Washington regarding another matter, they were hanged. The Shawnee then allied themselves with the French and went to war against the British. Shawnee war parties inflicted great punishment on English settlements. By the time the British finally won the war in 1763, the Shawnee knew that whites would soon retaliate and overrun the Shawnee settlements in the Ohio Valley.

Pontiac's Rebellion

Now firmly in control of the American colonies, the British began to treat Native Americans as a conquered people. They stopped supplying the gunpowder and rum that had become important to the Natives. To express their unhappiness, the Shawnee and other tribes burned white settlements and captured colonists. This led in 1763 to the Shawnee's involvement in the famous Indian uprising known as Pontiac's Rebellion. Pontiac was an Ottawa chief who, angry at the British for taking over Native American lands, united a group of warriors from different tribes in an effort to terrorize white settlers in Western Pennsylvania, Maryland, and Virginia. The Shawnee division was under the command of the most important Shawnee chief, Hokolesqua, and his primary war chief, Pucksinwah.

In an incident that has gone down in American history as one of the dirtiest tricks of warfare, the British military commander arranged to have smallpox-infected blankets delivered to the Indians. The terrible disease spread quickly and as a result thousands died.

Pontiac's Rebellion was not a military victory for the Indians, but it did result in an important agreement with the British. Called the Royal Proclamation of 1763, it set limits to the growth of the colonies, and directed that all lands west of the Allegheny Mountains in Pennsylvania were Indian Territory, where Indian people were to be left "unmolested." The document stated that Native nations had aboriginal title to their lands, and that only the British Crown—not the colonists—could buy land from them. The proclamation also described the proper way to make treaties and appointed two ambassadors to conduct relations between the British king and Native American leaders. But that agreement, like many other agreements between Natives and whites over the next century, did not last long, nor did British rule. White settlement continued to expand into Shawnee lands.

Whites adopted by tribe

The Shawnee did not give up their land without a fight. The tribe soon became feared for its practice of kidnaping and torturing whites who tried to settle on Shawnee land. Not all white settlers were killed, however. Some grew to appreciate the Shawnee way of life and were adopted by the tribe. One famous captive was the legendary frontiersman Daniel Boone (1734–1820), who stayed with the Shawnee for several months until he escaped. Another was a young man named Marmaduke Van Swearingen, who was adopted by Chief Pucksinwah and became the noted Shawnee warrior Blue Jacket .

Battle of Point Pleasant

In 1774, tensions between the Shawnee and the British heated up once again after the governor of the Virginia colony announced a plan to open land on both sides of the Ohio River to British settlers. The land he was talking about was the heart of Shawnee territory. The governor sent 3,000 soldiers with orders to invade Shawnee land and attack Shawnee villages. Before they could carry out this order, the British forces were attacked by a Shawnee war party led by Chief Pucksinwah and Blue Jacket. During the battle, later named the Battle of Point Pleasant, Chief Pucksinwah was killed. The battle ended without a clear victory for either side, and everyone's attention was then directed to the larger fight between colonists and the forces of the king of England.

American Revolution splits tribe

British colonists declared their independence from England in 1776, sparking the American Revolution (1776–1783). The Shawnee argued among themselves whether to support either side, but they could not agree. To avoid being drawn into the fight, nearly half of the Shawnee chose to move west into what is now Missouri. The rest decided to support England against the colonists. They believed that England would reward them after the war by protecting their homelands from white settlement. In the spring of 1782, Shawnee and Delaware warriors ambushed and defeated 500 colonial soldiers and tortured their leader to death. But their support of the British yielded them nothing, because the British lost the war.

Victory and retaliation

After the Revolutionary War, Blue Jacket and Chief Tecumseh (1768–1813), the son of Chief Pucksinwah, continued the fight against American settlement of Native lands. In 1791, Blue Jacket led a large force of Indians from several tribes in a surprise attack against American forces along the Wabash River in Indiana. The Indians killed some 630 men and wounded 300 more. Only 21 Indians met death, while 40 were wounded. This incident was the greatest victory in the history of Native American resistance to white settlement.

In response, President George Washington (1732–1799) in 1794 sent another army to put down the Indians. This larger force, under the command of General "Mad Anthony" Wayne (1745–1796), defeated Blue Jacket and his allies at the Battle of Fallen Timbers near present-day Toledo, Ohio. Wayne and his men burned Shawnee villages and destroyed the Indians' crops.

Prophet's Town

With the defeat at Fallen Timbers, Indian resistance to white settlement began to crumble. Now facing starvation at the hands of the

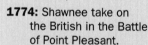

IMPORTANT DATES

1670: First contact is made with Europeans (French fur traders).

1774: Shawnee take on the British in the Battle of Point Pleasant.

1794: Shawnee are defeated by U.S. forces at the Battle of Fallen Timbers.

1795: Greenville Treaty opens Shawnee land to white settlement.

1811: Shawnee settlement of Prophet's Town is destroyed in the Battle of Tippecanoe.

1813: Chief Tecumseh is killed fighting the Americans at Battle of the Thames in the War of 1812.

1830: Most Shawnee leave Ohio.

1936: Two Shawnee groups in Oklahoma organize as one federally recognized tribe.

1937: A third Shawnee group in Oklahoma is federally recognized as the Eastern Shawnee Tribe.

1980: Ohio's Shawnee Nation United Remnant Band receives state recognition.

The Battle of Tippecanoe in which William Henry Harrison's troops wiped out Tecumseh's new community, Prophet Town.

American army, ninety-one Indian chiefs representing twelve nations were convinced to sign the Treaty of Greenville in 1795. The Shawnee lost more land as a result of the treaty than any other tribe. Many stayed in Ohio and agreed to abide by the terms of the treaty.

For the next ten years, the Shawnee, under the leadership of Chief Tecumseh, watched white settlers moving into their lands and their resources being depleted. In 1805 Tecumseh' younger brother, Lalawethika, started a religious revival that attracted large numbers of followers from various tribes to a community in Ohio he had established. He preached a return to traditional Indian values and a rejection of the ways of white people, and insisted that the whites had no right to take the lands they had taken. Lalawethika then changed his name to Tenskwatawa (pronounced *TENS-kwa-TAH-wuh,* meaning "the open door"). He was also known as the Shawnee Prophet.

Tecumseh joined his brother and worked to change the movement he had started from religious to political. The Shawnee leader wished to see all remaining Indian lands under the common ownership of tribes, and he wanted to form a military and political confederacy to unite many tribes under his leadership to fight the white invasion. A growing number of warriors moved into the new community, to the concern of government officials. In 1808, Tecumseh built a new village called Prophet's Town near Ohio's Tippecanoe Creek. To Prophet's Town came Native people who wanted to protect their homelands and preserve their Indian ways. Tecumseh traveled far and wide trying to recruit tribes to join his confederacy to halt the spread of white settlements.

While Tecumseh was away on one of these journeys, William Henry Harrison (1773–1841), governor of the Indiana Territory, put pressure on several chiefs to sell three million acres of Indian lands for white settlement. As word of this loss spread among the northwestern tribes, a flood of warriors decided to join Tecumseh's cause. When Tecumseh returned, he expressed to Harrison his anger and opposition to the sale. Harrison waited until Tecumseh left on another journey and set off with 1,000 men to attack Prophet's Town. In the battles that followed, Harrison burned Prophet's Town to the ground.

The death of Tecumseh

After the United States won the Revolution, the British retained territory in Canada and claimed a section of land in Maine. Relations between the United States and Britain were uneasy, and war between them broke out again in 1812.

During the War of 1812 (1812–14), the Shawnee once again fought on the side of the British. Tecumseh, still hoping the British would preserve Native American homelands against American settlers, led a force of warriors from many tribes. He was defeated and killed in 1813 at the Battle of the Thames in Ontario, Canada. So ended the last major combined Indian resistance to American expansion.

Shawnee move to Oklahoma

The Shawnee moved frequently and far after the War of 1812, often splitting up and then coming back together. Finally, most of them settled on reservation land in Oklahoma.

Life in Oklahoma was not easy for the Shawnee people, who tried to make their living by farming and ranching. Gas and petroleum were found on Indian land in the early 1900s, and many Shawnee were pressured into selling their land to whites. They were often paid less than

POPULATION OF SHAWNEE TRIBES: 1990

Most Shawnee live in Oklahoma, where they are divided into three groups. The Absentee Shawnee live near Shawnee, Oklahoma. The Eastern Shawnee live in Ottawa County in northeastern Oklahoma. The Loyal Shawnee mostly live in the town of Whiteoak in northeastern Oklahoma. In the 1990 census, Shawnee identified themselves this way:

Tribe	Population
Absentee Shawnee	1,129
Eastern Shawnee	762
Shawnee	4,749
Total	**6,640**

SOURCE: "1990 census of population and housing. subject summary tape files (SSTF) 13 (computer file): characteristics of American Indians by tribe and language." Washington, DC: U.S. Department of Commerce, Bureau of the Census, Data User Services Division, 1995).

its value, and they ended up in poverty. Tribal unity was badly disrupted as the people divided into the several groups in which they live today.

RELIGION

The Shawnee recognized a Great Spirit and worshiped the spiritual qualities in all natural things. The people believed they had been created by a female god, called Our Grandmother, who some day would gather them up in a huge net and take them to heaven. Each tribal group had a sacred bundle, which contained holy objects and was used to bring good harvests, success in battle, or help for the sick. Only the most important men and women in the tribe knew the contents of the bundles.

The people sought the aid of the spirits through dances, chants, and songs. Baptist missionaries in Oklahoma converted many Shawnee, and the Baptist religion remains a presence there.

LANGUAGE

The Shawnee language is still spoken by some Shawnee in Oklahoma, who are teaching it to Shawnee children.

GOVERNMENT

Tribal chiefs were men and women who had inherited their life-long positions. Peace chiefs served as spiritual leaders. War chiefs, who were chosen for their skill and bravery in battle, planned raids on the enemy. Decisions were made after discussions that continued until everyone agreed on a matter. Women served as important advisors during war and peacetime, and female elders were often put in charge of determining the fate of captives.

Today, each of the three Oklahoma tribes has its own elected tribal council that makes decisions for the tribe. Each tribe also has a chief who leads ceremonies.

ECONOMY

The Shawnee economy centered on hunting, farming, and food gathering. Beginning in the early eighteenth century, fur trading with the French became very important to the economy. Men hunted, traded, and fought in wars. Women gathered food, farmed, and made craft items used by the tribe. In springtime, men cleared fields, then women and children planted and tended the crops. Farming fields were owned by individual households.

Today, many Absentee Shawnee in Oklahoma receive income from farming and livestock, oil- and gas-related businesses, and other small businesses. A major source of funds is the tribe's Thunderbird Entertainment Center, which features bingo. The tribe also runs a site where several manufacturing plants are located, a medical supplies manufacturing plant, a shopping mall, smoke shops, and a convenience store. In the mid-1990s plans were underway for a motel, RV (recreational vehicle) park, and a boat storage facility.

UNITED REMNANT BAND OF OHIO

After the great Shawnee Chief Tecumseh was killed in 1813, some Shawnee remained in the Ohio Valley. Today their descendants are scattered throughout Ohio and neighboring states. They call themselves the Shawnee Nation United Remnant Band. They are recognized by the state of Ohio, but not by the federal government. (Federally recognized tribes are those with which the U.S. Government maintains official relations.) Without federal recognition, the tribe does not exist as far as the government is concerned, and is not entitled to financial and other help.

The Eastern Shawnee own a 700-seat bingo facility and maintain partial ownership in several oil wells near the reservation. They also operate two vision clinics that are open to the public.

The three Oklahoma groups are striving for economic self-sufficiency and meeting with success. They are better off than most tribes and have better housing.

DAILY LIFE

Families

The Shawnee lived in small groups of extended families, made up of mothers, fathers, their children, aunts, uncles, grandparents, cousins, and in-laws. They lived together in one big dwelling or in houses located near one another.

Buildings

In warm weather, the Shawnee lived in summer villages of 20 to 300 people. Each village had a large log council house used for religious and political gatherings; it provided protection when villagers came under enemy attack. Palisades—fence-like structures—surrounded the village for protection. Shawnee homes, large structures called longhouses, were made of saplings (small trees) tied into a

Shawnee brave Washawnow, "Swift Eagle."

frame and covered by sheets of bark or animal skins. A hole in the roof allowed smoke to escape.

During the fall and winter, the Shawnee set off on long hunting and gathering trips. Their cold-weather dwellings were similar to longhouses but were much smaller, often holding only one or two persons. Unlike other wandering tribes, the Shawnee did not carry their houses with them, because building materials could be found almost anywhere they went.

Clothing and adornment

The Shawnee wore buckskin clothing. In winter, men and women wore shirts, leggings, fur cloaks, and moccasins. Summer clothing for men consisted of simple breechcloths (flaps of material that covered the front and back and hung from the waist), and wrap skirts for women. Women also wore moccasins trimmed with bells that jingled when they walked. Children dressed like their parents. Most garments were decorated with dyed porcupine quills, beads, or feathers. After they began to trade for European goods, the Shawnee developed a fondness for silver pins, beads, necklaces, and bracelets. Shawnee men could be recognized by their silver nose rings and earrings.

Face and body paint was worn during ceremonies. Men wore headbands made of animal fur trimmed with one or more feathers from a hunting bird, such as an eagle, hawk, or owl. The women wore their long hair parted in the middle and rolled into buns, kept in place by silver combs. Some painted small red dots on their cheeks.

Food

Corn, the staple crop, was eaten as a vegetable or used to produce hominy (a hot cereal) or bread flour. The name "johnny cake," still used for corn bread, probably comes from the name "Shawnee cake." The Shawnee grew beans, squash, and pumpkins, and gathered wild rice. Women made maple syrup, and gathered persimmons, wild grapes, nuts, berries, roots, and honey. They used dried onions to season meat and cooked it over different types of wood. Maple, hickory, or cherry wood smoke added special flavorings.

Men hunted year-round, but especially during winter, for deer, elk, bear, turkeys, pheasants, and small fur-bearing animals. Shawnee hunters imitated animal calls. They disguised themselves so that they could approach their prey closely and shoot it with a bow and arrow or knock it on the head with a club. No part of an animal went to waste. Skins were used for clothing, bones to make tools, tendons for thread and bindings, and fat for cooking and skin ointment.

Education

The elders of the tribe were greatly respected. They formed close relationships with the children and taught them Shawnee ways. Children were taught that honesty was good and lying was a crime.

Today, Shawnee children attend public schools. The Loyal Shawnee of Big Cabin, Oklahoma, offer educational programs for children and had plans in the late 1990s to establish a museum and cultural center.

Healing practices

Shawnee healers used herbs and rituals to cure illnesses, which they believed were caused by evil spirits. The Shawnee "toughened" babies by briefly dipping them in cold water or snow every day for a few months. Both sexes purified themselves in sweat lodges where steam was produced by pouring water over hot stones. Then the bathers jumped into a cold river or stream.

Today, the Absentee Shawnee receive their health care mainly from a tribal clinic located on the reservation. The Eastern Shawnee have access to government-run facilities located near the reservation, and through Indian Health Care Service facilities located nearby.

ARTS

Oral literature

During winter, the Shawnee dressed in animal robes and gathered around the fire to hear elders tell stories of their past triumphs or tales about the gods.

An often-repeated story told of the Shawnee long ago crossing an ocean or "sea of ice." Anthropologists (people who study ancient cultures) believe the seawater could have been one of the Great Lakes or even a lake further north in Canada that they would have crossed as they journeyed southward.

Crafts

The Shawnee created baskets that were so tightly woven they could hold water. They also fashioned wampum (money) belts about five feet long and four feet wide decorated with symbols, designs, and special colors.

CUSTOMS

Social organization

Shawnee society had five divisions, each with its own particular purpose. For example, the Pekowi division took charge of religious duties, while the Kishpoko handled war duties, and the Mekoche took care of health and healing practices. Both the Thawikila and Chalaakaatha divisions took care of political matters. Tribal chiefs came from one or the other of these last two divisions.

Birth and naming

Women gave birth in a small hut where mother and baby remained for ten days until the baby was named at a special naming ceremony. Parents and tribal elders suggested names that would bring the bearer good luck or would guarantee certain skills.

Childhood and puberty

Children were not physically punished, but were encouraged to behave by being praised for good behavior and shamed for bad behavior

Many tribes sent boys on a vision quest at puberty, but Shawnee boys undertook their quest at a younger age, before reaching puberty. A boy on a vision quest went off by himself, usually under strenuous circumstance, to seek the spirit that would guide him through life. In one example of a vision quest, the boy rose each morning at dawn, ran naked through the snowy woods, dove to the bottom of a frigid pond (cracking the ice first if necessary), and then returned to camp. On his last day, he was told to grasp the first object he touched at the bottom of the pond—often a stone—and this became his "power object," which he then wore around his neck on a string. The object brought him courage, strength, and wisdom.

Festivals

Special ceremonies marked the changes in the seasons. The most important was the spring Bread Dance, when women were honored for their farming and gathering skills, and everyone prayed for an abun-

THE OKLAHOMA SHAWNEE

There are three groups of Shawnee in Oklahoma: the Absentee Shawnee, the Eastern Shawnee, and the Loyal Shawnee.

Absentee Shawnee

In 1845 a group of Shawnee left the Shawnee reservation in Kansas. They relocated to Indian Territory (now the state of Oklahoma) and came to be known as the Absentee Shawnee. In 1872 the U.S. government gave the Absentee Shawnee land on a reservation near present-day Shawnee, Oklahoma. The reservation was also occupied by the Citizen Band of Potawatomi. The Absentee Shawnee gradually split into two groups. One group, The White Turkey band, was more willing to adopt white ways, while the Big Jim Band refused to do so. Although relations between the two groups were troubled, in 1936 they organized as one tribe under the Oklahoma Indian Welfare Act.

Today, the Absentee Shawnee live in south central Oklahoma, about 35 miles west of Oklahoma City. The tribe remains divided into the Big Jim Band and the White Turkey Band. Members total about 2,000 people, and they live in two different Oklahoma counties.

Eastern Shawnee

In 1832, most of the Shawnee in Ohio moved to a reservation in Oklahoma, where they joined with a small group of Seneca (see Iroquois entry) to form the United Nation of Seneca and Shawnee. In 1937 this group of Shawnee officially separated from the Seneca and became the federally recognized Eastern Shawnee Tribe of Oklahoma. They claim to have about 1,700 members.

Most Eastern Shawnee lands are located in far northeastern Oklahoma near the Missouri border, with headquarters in West Seneca, Oklahoma.

Loyal, or Cherokee, Shawnee

The Loyal Shawnee were living in Kansas at the time the Civil War broke out in 1861. They received their name because of their loyalty to the U.S. (Northern) government during the Civil War (1861–65). But their loyalty benefitted them little, because after the war, U.S. officials forced them off their Kansas lands. In 1869 they purchased land from the Cherokee tribe (see entry) in northeastern Oklahoma and were made part of the Cherokee Nation. Today they are the largest Shawnee group, claiming a membership of about 8,000. The tribal headquarters is in Whiteoak, Oklahoma, but tribal members are scattered around the United States.

When the U.S. government is deciding who is eligible for government aid, the Loyal Shawnee are considered to be Cherokee citizens. While federal government officials and others sometimes call them the "Cherokee Shawnee," they refer to themselves as the Loyal Shawnee.

dant harvest. At the autumn Bread Dance, the tribe celebrated a man's role as hunter and gave thanks for the crops. A Green Corn Dance took place in August. During that seven-day celebration of the harvest, dances were performed to music from flutes, drums, and deer-hoof rattles, and all persons accused of minor crimes were forgiven.

In modern times, the Big Jim band of Absentee Shawnee holds Green Corn Dances during the spring and fall, and a ceremonial war dance is held in August. The Eastern Shawnee host an annual powwow during the third weekend in September. A powwow is a celebration at which the main activity is traditional singing and dancing.

War rituals

Warfare was a way to show courage and to gain honor. Shawnee councils gathered to decide whether or not the tribe would go to war. If the answer was yes, they sent tomahawks covered with red clay to neighboring villages as an invitation to join a war party. Dances and feasts were held before a battle. If prisoners were taken, they had to "run the gauntlet" past a line of warriors who beat them with guns and sticks as they passed.

Courtship and marriage

Marriage was usually arranged by families and the only ceremony was a gift exchange. The bride usually went to live with her husband's family. By the 1820s, Shawnee marriages no longer included a gift exchange.

Funerals

Attendants dressed a corpse in clean clothes and painted it. As payment, they received some of the deceased's possessions. Mourners grieved for twelve days and during that time did not engage in their normal tasks. Then a feast was held and the people returned to their daily activities. Spouses who lost a mate could not wear jewelry or body paint for a year.

CURRENT TRIBAL ISSUES

Despite the many migrations and upheavals of their history, the three Shawnee tribes in Oklahoma, the Absentee Shawnee, the Cherokee (Loyal) Shawnee, and the Eastern Shawnee, are known for their efforts to preserve their culture. In her book *The Shawnee,* Janet Hubbard-Brown states "While many other tribes in Oklahoma have completely forgotten their traditional ceremonies, the Shawnees . . . still know their complete annual cycle of ceremonial dances."

Recently, the Shawnee Nation United Remnant Band in Ohio has set about purchasing tracts of property associated with Shawnee history. They currently own 180 acres near their former homelands in Ohio. There they hold meetings, ceremonies, and youth education activities.

NOTABLE PEOPLE

Chief Tecumseh (1768–1813) is best known for organizing and leading Indian resistance to white settlement of America. An eloquent speaker and statesman, he urged Indians of all tribes to unite against the threat to their way of life. Tecumseh's younger brother, Tenskwatawa (called the Shawnee Prophet), began a religious revival movement that advocated returning to traditional Indian ways. Even though the two brothers managed to win the loyalty and support of more than fifty other tribes, many chiefs among the Shawnee became jealous of the brothers and they had few followers among their own tribe.

Other notable Shawnee include: Shawnee/Cayuga poet and teacher Barney Furman Bush (1945–), whose several books of poetry deal with nature and family; Tecumseh's father, War Chief Pucksinwah (d. 1774), who fought to help preserve Shawnee lands; and Shawnee-Sauk/Fox-Creek-Seminole professor Donald L. Fixico (1951–), a national expert on Indian issues and government policy towards Indians.

FURTHER READING

Flanagan, Alice K. *The Shawnee.* New York: Children's Press, 1998.

Hubbard-Brown, Janet, *The Shawnee.* New York: Chelsea House, 1995.

Gilbert, Bil, *God Gave Us This Country: Tekamthi and the First American Civil War.* New York: Atheneum, 1989.

O'Neill, Laurie A. *The Shawnees.* Brookfield, CT: The Millbrook Press, 1995.

"Shawnee History." [Online] http://www.dickshovel.com/shaw.html

Wampanoag

Name

Wampanoag (pronounced *wam-puh-NO-ag*). The name is probably a variation of *Wapanacki,* meaning "eastern people." The Wampanoag have also been called Massasoit, Philip's Indians, and Pokanoket (from the name of their principal village).

Location

The Wampanoag occupied about forty villages in northern Rhode Island and southeastern coastal Massachusetts and its offshore islands (now known as Martha's Vineyard and Nantucket) at the time of European contact. Today most live in southeastern Massachusetts.

Population

There were an estimated 15,000 Wampanoag in around 1600. In a census (count of the population) done in 1990 by the U.S. Bureau of the Census, 2,145 people identified themselves as Wampanoag.

Language family

Eastern Algonquian.

Origins and group affiliations

Ancestors of the Wampanoag had probably occupied the territory where the Pilgrims first encountered them for 12,000 to 15,000 years. The Wampanoag warred with the Narragansett tribe and allied with English colonists.

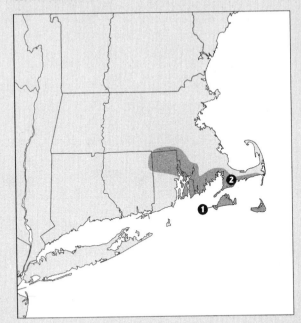

WAMPANOAG

Contemporary Communities

Massachusetts

1. Gay Head Wampanoag Indians
2. Mashpee Wampanoag Indians

Shaded area: Traditional Wampanoag lands in present-day northern Rhode Island and southeastern coastal Massachusetts and its offshore islands.

The Wampanoag were a peaceful agricultural people before Europeans arrived. Diseases from Europe nearly destroyed the tribe, while at the same time the newcomers were demanding more and more of their land. The Wampanoag welcomed the British colonists called the Pilgrims at the beginning of the seventeenth century and helped them through their first rough winters. The Pilgrims participated in a profound and permanent disruption of Wampanoag life.

HISTORY

Peaceful life begins to unravel

For thousands of years before Europeans came to the Americas, the Wampanoag occupied villages along the Atlantic Coast in southern New England, living comfortably off the fruits of agriculture, hunting, and fishing. Because the region was heavily populated even before the British arrived, the Wampanoag had made arrangements among themselves concerning who could hunt where. Their arrangement was different from Indian tribes in other areas of the country, where the land was less populated and hunters could range over very wide areas.

In the 1500s and 1600s, Europeans began establishing a presence along the Atlantic Coast. Even before they had much contact with Europeans, the Wampanoag were experiencing the effects of that presence. The French to the north, wanting more and more furs from their Indian trading partners, encouraged them to expand their territory into Wampanoag lands. War with the Narragansett (see entry) and other tribes was the result. At the same time, fishing and trading vessels sailed up and down the New England coast, bringing new diseases to Native peoples, who had no resistance to them. Some Wampanoag were taken captive by Europeans and sold as slaves in Europe.

IMPORTANT DATES

1621: Massasoit allies with Pilgrims.

1676: King Philip's War results in the destruction of life, loss of land, and the end of a way of life for New England tribes.

1928: Wampanoag Nation is reunified after living on separate reservations for more than 200 years.

1986: Gay Head Wampanoag get federal recognition.

The Pilgrims arrive

When the first Pilgrims (a group of English colonizers) landed in 1620 at a place they called Plymouth, the Wampanoag there had endured nearly a century of often terrible experiences with Europeans. In just the previous ten years, three disease epidemics, probably brought by Europeans, had killed as many as three-quarters of the entire Wampanoag population. Those who remained were forced to pay tribute to the Narragansett Indians, who were now the most powerful people in the region.

Still, the Wampanoag welcomed the English and gave them invaluable assistance, teaching them to hunt and fish and how to grow native crops by "hilling," a system of planting corn kernels in rows of small hills. Without this help, the Pilgrims would probably not have survived the punishing New England winter.

In 1621, Chief Ousemequin ("Yellow Feather"), called Massasoit by the Pilgrims, signed a treaty of friendship with the colonists. He hoped by doing so to secure their help against the Narragansett and Micmac tribes (see entries), who now had European weapons and were becoming troublesome. At some point Massasoit granted the colonists permission to occupy Plymouth colony; the colonists believed they now owned the land. That fall, after the first harvest, the Wampanoag and the Pilgrims celebrated the first Thanksgiving together.

The Wampanoag, like other Native groups, experienced tremendous suffering due to diseases brought over from Europe. In the ten-year period from 1610 to 1620, three epidemics killed as many as three-quarters of the Wampanoag population.

Fifty years of good relations followed, in which the British assisted the Wampanoag in skirmishes against other tribes. The friendship was so strong that just before his death, Massasoit (who was called "King" by the British) was granted permission by the General Court of Plymouth to give English names to his sons. Wamsutta became Alexander, and Metacomet became Philip. But the friendship that Massasoit carefully nurtured was already turning on him toward the end of his life, as new colonists arrived who saw Indians as little more than obstacles in the way of taking the land as their own.

Under Puritan influence

New settlers, called the Puritans, began to arrive in large numbers. The Puritans preached Christianity to the Wampanoag and tried to force observance of their laws. Natives were arrested for hunting on the Sabbath (the day of worship) or for observing ancient traditions the Puritans considered "savage." Natives who agreed to convert to Christianity were called "praying Indians." To keep them separate from their unconverted neighbors, they were resettled in new communities, called "praying towns." By 1675, there were about 2,500 "praying Indians" in New England.

Puritan efforts to convert the Natives did not cause nearly as much resentment as their expansion westward. They defeated Indian tribes and took over their lands. When Wamsutta (or Alexander) succeeded his father, Massasoit, as grand sachem (pronounced *SAY-shem*; chief) in 1661, Native resentment had reached a high pitch. The Puritans, who considered Wamsutta too arrogant, invited him to Plymouth for a conference. While there, he became ill and died suddenly; some historians believe he was probably poisoned. His brother Metacomet (called King Philip) succeeded him. By this time, it was obvious that the settlers had plans for unlimited expansion into Native territory. They had come close to destroying the Pequot (see entry) and had set up 14 reservations for Indians in the northeast that restricted Indians' rights and forced them off their lands.

King Philip's War

Metacomet was a military genius. Before launching King Philip's War in 1675, he declared: "Soon after I became *sachem* they disarmed all my people. . . . [T]heir land was taken. . . . *I am determined not to live until I have no country.*" Of all the revolts carried out against the colonists by Algonquian-speaking peoples, his war came the closest to succeeding. King Philip gathered an army made up of warriors from the Abenaki (see entry), Nipmuck, Narragansett (see entry), and Wampanoag tribes. The army attacked more than half of the English settlements in New England, and for a time held their own in the war against the Puritans. But the tribes were so weakened by epidemics that even their allied forces did not have the strength to win. By the time this tragic war was over, the colonists had nearly exterminated the Wampanoag, Nipmuck, and Narragansett tribes. Betrayed by his own people, including Wampanoag "praying Indians," and cut off from food, King Philip was forced to fall back into Rhode Island's cedar swamps. His defeat and death in July 1676 ended Native military action in southern New England.

After the war, colonial armies hunted and killed Native Americans, whether they were enemies, neutral, or friendly, and then divided their lands. King Philip was beheaded and his head was displayed on a post in Plymouth for twenty-five years as a warning to all who thought to resist colonial expansion. Widows and orphans were sold as slaves in the West Indies; "praying Indians" and enemy warriors alike were imprisoned, while many refugees fled. Only 400

Wampanoag survived the war. Gradually, over the next 200 years, the population climbed above 2,000. The Wampanoag people are concentrated on the Gay Head Reservation in Martha's Vineyard and on Cape Cod in Massachusetts.

RELIGION

Helen Attaquin, a Gay Head Wampanoag, described the Native American world view in her essay (from the book *Rooted Like the Ash Trees*) entitled "There Are Differences." She said: "'Indians do not believe in a 'universe' but in a 'multi-verse.' Indians don't believe that there is ONE fixed and eternal truth; they think there are many different and equally *valid* truths." This appreciation that there exists "more than one way to view this Earth of ours, and more than one way to share it" may have restrained the Wampanoag from simply ridding their shores of the Europeans with "their bristling armament [weapons] and the frightening aroma of death-causing diseases."

Wampanoag traditions center around the Great Spirit called Kiehtan, who made all things. *Manitou,* guardian spirits in the form of birds, fish, and animals, watch over the people. The spirit called Crow was believed to have been sent about one thousand years ago by the Great Spirit with gifts of corn and bean seeds in his ears. With these gifts the people were able to cease being wanderers, settle down, and plant gardens.

Early European explorers along the Atlantic Coast saw and wrote about religious ceremonies conducted by shamans (medicine men or women; pronounced *SHAY-mans*) at powwows. Powwow means "brings together." Explorers used the word to refer to the shaman and the ceremonies he or she conducted. Shamans performed magical feats the explorers called "juggling," made possible, the Natives said, by spiritual helpers or "devils."

The Pilgrims and Puritans brought Christianity to the Wampanoag. In the massacre of Native Americans that took place after King Philip's War, it was mostly Christian Wampanoag who were allowed to survive. Afterwards, more surviving Wampanoag turned to Christianity. Even as Wampanoag communities have died out or consolidated over the years, efforts to practice ancient ceremonies continued, and still do to this day. For example, the Wampanoag at Gay Head begin their annual celebration of Cranberry Day by giving thanks to the Great Spirit for the berries they are about to harvest.

LANGUAGE

The Wampanoag were speakers of an Eastern Algonquian dialect (variety) known as Massachusett. Most Eastern Algonquian speakers could understand other dialects, although some islanders had difficulty communicating with mainlanders.

GOVERNMENT

Prior to European contact

At the time of contact with Europeans, the Wampanoag lived in about forty villages with a Grand Sachem (Great Chief) at their head. Under him were lesser chiefs called sachems and sagamores. Colonists called the lesser chiefs "kings"; they actually had little authority but were highly respected. The position was handed down from father to son; if there were no male heirs, a woman could become a queen sachem. Sachems advised on the best areas for planting, hunting, and fishing. They devised punishments for those who broke rules. The sachem and a council of warriors (distinguished by extreme physical strength and special powers given to them by the spirits) decided when to make war.

After King Philip's War

By the early 1700s, many Wampanoag had been placed on reservations called "plantations." Today the two largest are Gay Head on Martha's Vineyard and Mashpee on Cape Cod.

In 1928, two Wampanoag men, Eben Queppish and Nelson Simons, brought together the Mashpee, Gay Head, and Herring Pond communities as the Wampanoag Nation. The Wampanoag reorganized in 1975, adding the Assonet and Nemasket people.

Gay Head is the only division of the Wampanoag Nation that has gained federal recognition (1987), which gives them certain legal rights and privileges in their relations with the U.S. government. For example, recognition brought Gay Head $3 million to build housing for the elderly and a hospital. Gay Head owns 485 acres of land and is governed by an elected tribal council; the council also has as members a traditional chief and a medicine man.

MASSACHUSETT PLACE NAMES

The Massachusett language survives mainly as Massachusetts place names and personal titles, often a mispronunciation of the original Native version. Gay Head was called *Aquinnah* ("land under the hill"); Hyannis was *Anayanough* ("warrior's place"); *Sakonet* ("black-goose place" or "rocky outlet"); *Pautuxet* ("at the little falls"), Cowasit ("pine place"), and *Mashpee* ("great pond or cove"). The first syllables of both "Massachusetts" ("big hill") and "Mississippi" ("big river") derive from the Algonquian superlative "massa-." *Massasoit* (translated loosely as "big chief" or "great commander") was the title given to Grand Sachem Ousemequin (Yellow Feather).

The Mashpee Wampanoag Tribe owns 55 acres and is governed by an elected tribal council. It is seeking federal recognition.

ECONOMY

After the Wampanoag became an agricultural people, they lived on corn, beans, and pumpkins, supplementing their diet by hunting and fishing. People helped one another prepare fields for planting in the spring. Women then took care of planting everything except for tobacco, which was considered a male specialty.

In winter the people moved inland to hunting camps, where individual extended families "owned" specific hunting territories and passed them down from father to son. Extended families include a father, mother, and children plus relatives.

The Wampanoag also traded with neighboring tribes. The favorite trade items were soapstone pipes and bowls and wampum beads. (Wampum beads are cut from shells. Long strings of the beads were used as money and for other purposes.) Trade items were gotten from the Narragansett and were in turn traded with the Abenaki, along with corn seeds, in exchange for birch bark to make canoes.

After the tribe was nearly destroyed in King Philip's War, the remaining Wampanoag worked as whalers, day laborers, domestic servants, farmers, soldiers, and basket makers. The Mashpee Manufacturing Company, incorporated in 1867, made and marketed brooms, baskets, and other wood wares.

Today, the Wampanoag of Gay Head do not live on a reservation. Gay Head lands include the Cliffs of Gay Head, a popular tourist destination on Martha's Vineyard; cranberry bogs; and a herring run. Some members of the tribe are employed by the tribal government; others are involved with tourism. In the 1990s the possibility of casino gambling was being explored.

The Mashpee Wampanoag own fifty-five acres, which are neither populated nor developed. The people live in the town of Mashpee in the popular resort destination of Cape Cod. The town's economy depends on tourism and summer visits by people who own property there. Some tribe members support themselves in construction, agriculture, and fish farming.

As is true with most Native American people, per capita income among the Wampanoag is fairly low. (Per capita income is the average income one person earns in one year). At Gay Head Reservation, the figure was $9,397 in the mid-1990s, while the figure for the Mashpee Tribe was $7,666. Compare this to a per capita income for the U.S. population of about $20,000.

DAILY LIFE

Families

In the summertime, Wampanoag families enjoyed a communal existence, with neighbor helping neighbor, and a fair amount of leisure time. Men often engaged other tribes in games of chance and endurance. During the long, cold months of winter, the people withdrew into smaller groupings of extended families. Men gathered around the fire and fashioned arrowheads out of stone. Women wove baskets and mats. Elders told stories and children listened.

Buildings

Before European contact, the Wampanoag built dome-shaped wigwams from long sapling poles, which were stuck in the ground, then bent and tied together. Walls were made of bulrushes woven into mats; similar mats were laid out on the floor or placed atop special raised racks for sleeping. A smoke hole at the top of the dwelling did not always keep the structure from becoming too smoky for comfort. Then the Wampanoag might sleep out under the stars.

Other buildings in a village were smokehouses, sweat lodges for purification, and dance houses for celebrating. When it was time for the seasonal move, a building's pole frame was left behind to be used again the following year.

After European colonization, fortified dwellings on hilltops provided safety. The Wampanoag eventually incorporated European hardware and furniture, and some moved to shingled homes similar to those of their European neighbors.

Food

Food in New England was plentiful and varied. The Wampanoag grew corn, squash, cucumbers, and beans. They gathered wild rice, nuts, and berries. Fish taken with hooks, lines, and spears included crabs, lobsters, eels, and whale. They used herring as fertilizer. They hunted fowl, beaver, and deer. They dried fish and meat on racks or smoked it, placed it in cedar baskets, then stored it in underground pits.

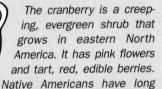

WAMPANOAG CAPE COD CRANBERRY PIE

The cranberry is a creeping, evergreen shrub that grows in eastern North America. It has pink flowers and tart, red, edible berries. Native Americans have long appreciated the cranberry both for eating and for its healing powers. Cranberries are very high in vitamin C. Cranberry juice is often recommended to prevent urinary tract infections.

Author E. Barrie Kavasch, an authority on Native American culture and cookery, reported that the Wampanoag Tribe of Gay Head, Aquinnah, on Martha's Vineyard (an island off southeast Massachusetts), celebrate a Cranberry Day Festival each October. Families gather to pick cranberries and picnic. This recipe for Wampanoag Cape Cod Cranberry Pie results in a dish that is a favorite at that celebration.

3 cups fresh cranberries

2 Tablespoons flour or fine cornmeal

1 cup sugar

1 cup maple syrup

1/4 teaspoon salt (optional)

1/2 cup boiling water

1 cup dark currants or raisins

3 Tablespoons freshly grated orange peel [see note]

2 Tablespoons butter

Pastry for a two-crust pie [homemade or store-bought]

Combine the first 8 ingredients in a medium saucepan and cook over medium heat, stirring thoroughly while you bring the mixture to a boil. Lower the heat to simmer, cover, and cook until the cranberries start to pop, about 5 minutes. Remove from the heat and stir in the butter. Set mixture aside to cool slightly.

Preheat oven to 425° F. Use your favorite pastry recipe to make pie crust [or buy a prepared crust]. Place bottom crust into a 9-inch pie plate. Pour cranberry filling into the pie plate. Slice remaining dough into long, thin strips, and arrange a latticework of pastry strips on top of filling in a basket-weave [pattern]. Crimp and flute [pinch] the pastry edges [so they don't hang over the edge of the plate].

Bake pie for 40 to 55 minutes until crust is just golden and juice is bubbling. Cool slightly on a wire race. Serve hot or chilled, with your favorite topping.

Makes one 9-inch pie.

[Note: The grated orange peel is called the zest; it should not include any of the white part underneath.]

From E. Barrie Kavasch, *Enduring Harvests: Native American Foods and Festivals for Every Season.* Old Saybrook, Connecticut: Globe Pequot Press, 1995, p. 50.

Clothing and adornment

Men generally wore breechcloths, garments with front and back flaps that hung from the waist and were often decorated with quillwork or embroidery. Animal-skin leggings and deerskin robes were worn. Women generally wore wraparound skirts with a belt. After European contact, they often wore dresses made from two skins sewn at the sides with straps at the shoulders.

Healing practices

Wampanoag religion and medicine went hand in hand. Illness was believed to be caused by angry spirits. Herbal treatments and sweat lodges (for ridding the body of poisons) were the remedies of choice.

Different herbal treatments were used by different groups. For example, the Gay Head Wampanoag believed that snake oil would heal stiff joints, while other groups used ground wintergreen leaves mixed with animal grease for this purpose. Remedies were administered by shamans, people who had received a vision in childhood telling them to become a medicine person.

During King Philip's War, the Wampanoag and their allies used fire against Europeans, because by then they knew them to be plague-bearers. They had observed during the plague of 1617 that the Pequot and Narragansett came through with little damage. Native Americans widely believed the sickness stopped at Narragansett country because of a burning ceremony that destroyed all plague victims' belongings—a ceremony the Wampanoag did not then share.

Education

Wampanoag children learned mainly by observing. Girls watched women plant, prepare, and preserve food; prepare skins to make clothing; and weave baskets and mats. Boys learned endurance by running, and by facing and surviving cold, pain, and hunger.

Wampanoag leader Metacomet, also known as King Philip of Pokonoket, led a fierce resistance to the colonial forces.

Certain boys were chosen by the warrior council to undergo tests to determine their fitness as warriors. If they passed the first round of tests, they fasted and were given a special cleansing drink that made them vomit. Warrior trainees learned to use war clubs and the bow and arrow in close encounters with the enemy. They learned the advantage of surprise and the techniques of the silent ambush. If they passed this second more rigorous round of tests and had reached the age of sixteen, they became members of the warrior council, known and admired for their courage, strength, and wisdom.

Today Wampanoag children attend American schools. In the late 1990s, the Gay Head Tribe hoped to eventually finance an elementary school with the proceeds from casino gambling if it is approved.

ARTS

Through the years the Wampanoag have retained contact with their heritage by learning and practicing traditional crafts such as

KING PHILIP'S PROPHECY

The following is part of a speech given by King Philip to his counselors and warriors. A prophecy is an oral or written prediction of things to come.

Brothers, you see this vast country before us, which the Great Spirit gave to our fathers and us; you see the buffalo and deer that now are our support. Brothers, you see these little ones, our wives and children, who are looking to us for food and raiment [clothing]; and you now see the foe before you, that they have grown insolent and bold; that all our ancient customs are disregarded; the treaties made by our fathers and us are broken, and all of us insulted; our council fires disregarded, and all the ancient customs of our fathers; our brothers murdered before our eyes, and their spirits cry to us for revenge. Brothers, these people from the unknown world will cut down our groves, spoil our hunting and planting grounds, and drive us and our children from the graves of our fathers, and our council fires, and enslave our women and children.

SOURCE: William Apess. "Eulogy on King Philip, as Pronounced at the Odeon, in Federal Street, Boston." In *On Our Own Ground: The Complete Writings of William Apess, a Pequot.* Ed. Barry O'Connell. Amherst: University of Massachusetts Press, 1992.

basketry, wood and stone carving, and making unusual pottery. The multicolored clays of Gay Head were shaped into pots, bowls, and jugs. Sometimes patterns were drawn into the clay with pieces of shell. The pottery was sunbaked because kiln firing dulled the colors.

CUSTOMS

Babies

Children were prized by the Wampanoag. At birth, babies were given a "true" name and a nickname. True names were sacred and were known only to the immediate family and to village leaders.

Puberty

A boy who had not been chosen for warrior training (see "Education") underwent a ritual in which he was blindfolded, led into the forest, and left there alone. He had to survive for an entire winter using only his wits, a bow and arrow, a knife, and a hatchet. Sometimes he had dreams; these were later explained by a medicine man or woman, who might decide from hearing about his dreams that the boy had the potential to become a medicine man himself.

Marriage

Men moved in with their wives' families after marriage. Wampanoag men sometimes chose wives from other tribes in order to make political alliances. Sometimes powerful chiefs married two or more wives.

War and hunting rituals

The Wampanoag went to war when wrongs were committed against them, such as trespassing on their hunting or fishing territory or on an especially productive berry patch.

To prepare for battle, warriors painted their bodies black, red, green, or white. The colors were obtained from charcoal or from berries and plants, so the choice of colors depended on what was in season. A war dance was held; sound effects included beating the ground with sticks and emitting piercing war cries. The help of the spirits was requested to make a warrior quick and cunning. A tea made from juniper berries was drunk to help the blood clot in case the warrior was wounded.

Once engaged in battle, it was every man for himself. Warriors fought independently, seeking personal honor and glory. Those who distinguished themselves earned eagle feathers to wear in their hair. Sometimes the widow of a slain warrior took up his weapons and fought in his place.

The help of the spirits was also sought for a good hunt. Hunters set off on an empty stomach because it gave them an incentive to find their prey more quickly. The Wampanoag killed only what they needed and all parts of the catch were used. The bones of a slain beaver were returned to the stream from which it came so the beaver could be reincarnated (it would come back to life) and be hunted again.

Burial

The dead were wrapped in furs or grass mats with their moccasins in their hands; food and other necessities for the journey through the after-world were buried with them. Mourners blackened their faces and an evening burial ceremony was held. Afterwards, the name of the deceased was never spoken again.

Festivals

A special week-long celebration was held at harvest time to thank the spirits for the gift of food. Everyone gathered at the dance house, and there was much dancing, singing, feasting, and playing of games. A pot of corn was placed on the fire, and its rising smoke joined the spirit powers where they dwelled.

Today, the Gay Head Wampanoag of Martha's Vineyard still celebrate Cranberry Day, now held the second Tuesday in October. In days gone by, the medicine man or woman decided when the cranberries were ripe and informed the people. The harvest could take days or even weeks, depending on the size of the crop. The Gay Head also hold a Spring Dance in April; the tribe's Noepe Cliff Singers and Dancers perform.

CURRENT TRIBAL ISSUES

Helen Attaquin, a Gay Head Wampanoag, has written that Native Americans care most about preserving their culture, land base, and their right as separate nations to make their own decisions. In recent years, the anniversaries of events such as the Pilgrim's landing and the First Thanksgiving have become opportunities for the Wampanoag and others to express their displeasure at the way their culture has been trampled upon. For example, 500 Native Americans once responded to a protest call to "bury Plymouth Rock." They demanded a National Day of Mourning, and a speech was given by Native American Frank Wamsutta James. In it he asked: "How can they expect us to sit and smile and eat turkey as they continue to dig up our graves and display our bones?"

NOTABLE PEOPLE

Weetamo led a group of warriors in battle in King Philip's War after the death of her first husband, Wamsutta. She was killed in a surprise attack on her village, and her naked body was found floating in a river. The Pilgrims beheaded her and posted her head on a pole alongside Philip's as a grisly warning to their enemies. Weetamo has become a romantic heroine in Native American lore.

Massasoit (1600–1661) was a Wampanoag chief who encouraged friendship with English settlers in the early 1600s. Because of this, Massasoit was forced to wage frequent attacks against hostile Indian groups not inclined to welcome the settlers. But even Massasoit eventually came to resent their growing encroachment. It was his son Philip (c. 1639–1676) who turned resentment into war in 1675–76.

Squanto (c. 1600–1623) was one of twenty Wampanoag from the village of Pautuxet who was kidnaped by English explorer Thomas Hunt in 1614 and sold as a slave in Spain. Rescued and set free, he finally made his way home, only to find that nearly his entire village had been wiped out in an epidemic. Squanto is remembered as the English-speaking guide and agricultural advisor to the Pilgrims at Plymouth colony.

FURTHER READING

Carlson, Richard G., ed. *Rooted Like the Ash Trees: New England Indians and the Land.* Naugatuck, CT: Eagle Wing Press, 1987.

Cwiklik, Robert. *King Philip and the War with the Colonists.* Englewood Cliffs, NJ: Silver Burdette Press, 1989.

Sewall, Marcia. *People of the Breaking Day.* New York: Atheneum, 1990.

Waters, Kate. *Tapenum's Day: A Wampanoag Indian Boy in Pilgrim Times.* New York: Scholastic, Inc., 1996.

Weinstein-Farson, Laurie. *The Wampanoag.* Indians of North America Series. New York: Chelsea House, 1989.

Southeast

Southeast

The Southeast region of Native American tribes was comprised of the warm, temperate part of eastern North America where there is sufficient rain for reliable agriculture, year after year. This includes not only the states south of the Mason-Dixon Line (the boundary between Pennsylvania and Maryland, once used to distinguish between the "slave states" of the South and the "free states" of the North) and east of the Mississippi River, but also west of the Mississippi in Louisiana and considerable portions of Arkansas and Texas. These areas are included in the Southeast region of tribes because the Caddoan and other native peoples who lived in them maintained a lifestyle very similar to Indian people east of the Mississippi, and quite different from the tribes of the Great Plains to their west.

Within the Southeast region, there were generally two types of Native economies. The interior peoples emphasized raising vegetables—corn, beans, and squash—supplemented by hunting and fishing. On the coast, where fish, shellfish, and marine mammals were plentiful, the tribes relied less on farming and more on collecting. Shellfish were a staple, and all around the coast, especially on the Gulf side of the continent, there are enormous mounds of shells discarded by hundreds of generations of coastal Indian people.

In the interior, there also exist the remains of great mounds, but these were earthen structures built as ceremonial and political centers. The oral traditions (knowledge, stories, and beliefs passed from generation to generation) of the Southeastern tribes say that the mound-builders were their ancestors, and in fact the 1540–1542 chronicles of Spanish explorer Hernando de Soto (c. 1500–1542) contain descriptions of the mounds and the temples built on top of them when they were in regular use. As late as 1740 the Natchez Indians, who lived near the present city of Natchez, Mississippi, were still using their mounds and temples.

Coastal Southeastern tribes encounter Europeans

The coastal Indians are not as well known as the interior tribes because they were quickly attacked, dispersed, and sometimes

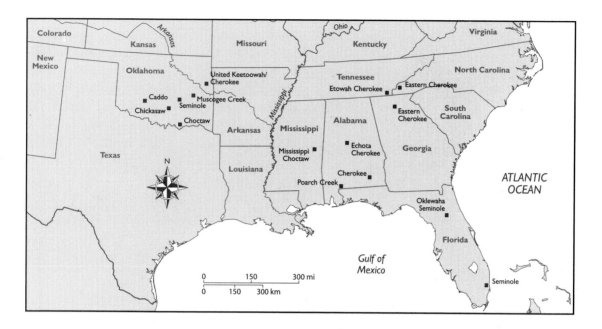

enslaved by the invading Europeans, beginning with de Soto. Along with the violence they met, they rapidly became victims of deadly European diseases to which they were unaccustomed. When he entered Florida searching for gold, de Soto brought with him chains and manacles for enslaving Indians to serve as porters, who were forced to carry the Spaniards' gear, and as concubines, women who were forced to serve as sexual partners and to take care of domestic tasks for de Soto's men. As they marched through Georgia, Alabama, and Mississippi, de Soto's soldiers killed thousands of Indian people. But the Indians fought back. In a well-coordinated night attack in 1541, the Chickasaw and their allies burned the dwellings of the Spanish, destroying much of their equipment and running off their horses. After wandering through Arkansas and Texas, de Soto died on the banks of the Mississippi River in 1542, leaving his men to flee down the river toward the Gulf of Mexico, pursued by thousands of angry Indians in canoes.

Farther north, British colonists also tried to enslave Indians, not as porters and concubines, but to work on their plantations. This attempt was unsuccessful, since the Indian workers could easily escape to join their own or other Indian tribes in the interior. So in the eighteenth century the remaining Indian slaves were sold or traded to Jamaica and other Caribbean islands, and were replaced by African slaves, who were more easily identified as slaves because of their skin color.

A map of some contemporary Native American communities in the Southeast region.

Around the mouth of the Mississippi River, the initial European presence was French. French traders served as go-betweens for furs and other goods sent down the Mississippi back to France. The French also established plantations on both sides of the Mississippi upriver toward the present city of Memphis, Tennessee. Meantime, the Spanish had mobilized many of the Florida Indians into a line of missions from St. Augustine, Florida, west across the peninsula toward the present city of Tallahassee. The tribes south of this line, especially the Timucua and Calusa, were so devastated by warfare and disease that the survivors joined other tribes or migrated to Cuba or other Caribbean islands. The three European powers—Britain, France, and Spain—then contested for control of the Southeast region from the middle 1600s until the United States took over the area in the beginning of the nineteenth century. In the meantime, the coastal tribes were being caught up, and chewed up, in the European struggle for control of "Greater Florida," which included everything south of Virginia and west to Alabama.

Interior Southeast tribes

While the Europeans fought for control of the coastal areas, the interior tribes were reorganizing to face them. The northernmost interior tribe was the Cherokee, related historically to the Iroquois of New York state, who at some point had migrated to the Appalachian Mountains. Living in the interior valleys of the Great Smoky Mountains, the Cherokee and their mountains got in the way of the expansion of British colonies toward the south in the eighteenth century, so that the coastal region was settled first.

The "fall line" of the major rivers is an important concept for understanding the history of this period. Essentially, coastal boats and some ocean-going vessels could only travel up the coastal rivers until they reached a waterfall or rapids. The locations of these falls in the various streams, connected together by a fall line on a map, essentially defined the areas where Europeans could live successfully, with a dock to receive supplies and to ship out their agricultural produce. Upstream from the fall line, trade goods and produce had to be carried in packs or on horseback, so this area was left to the Indians. In the early colonial period, then, the Cherokee occupied the area above the fall line in what are now the states of North Carolina and Tennessee.

Social and political organization

The interior tribes shared a kind of social and political structure that was useful for integrating their societies and creating alliances

"Village of Secota," an illustration by Theodor de Bry in his 1619 book, America pars decima. The drawing of the village, in present-day North Carolina, gives an idea of the ways of life that developed throughout the Southeast prior to European contact there.

with other tribes. The essential building block of the tribes was the matrilineal clan (a group of extended family members that trace their descent through the mother's line). All tribal members received their clan identity from their mother, and tribal law declared that one's mother and father had to be from different clans. Alliances among towns, and also among the different nations of the interior, were often based on intermarriage.

The Indian tribes of the interior tended to locate their villages along streams and rivers, needing access to water for drinking and bathing as well as for transportation in dugout canoes where possible.

The villages were arranged around a central ceremonial center. The center was usually an outdoor square surrounded by four arbors, with a large, enclosed central roundhouse on one side that served for tribal meetings and sometimes as a refuge during cold weather. Small log houses with small gardens were located near the center. Around the village were large cultivated fields, some of which belonged to families while others, called "town fields," were cultivated for the benefit of the whole village. Periodically, the entire village had to move when local soil and other resources had been depleted.

The interior tribes had elaborate military organizations. Typically, war leaders were assigned ferocious military titles, which were carried as personal names. For example, a recent principal chief of the Cherokee is Wilma Mankiller, who bears a personal name derived from a military title. As a Southeastern warrior gained more experience and performed brave deeds, he was awarded higher and more prestigious titles, and given the responsibility of leading war expeditions.

Adopting new members into tribes

Wars inevitably created refugees, and while all Southeastern tribes occasionally adopted such people, this became a matter of national policy with the Creek Indians. Under the rules of the Creek Confederacy, families, villages, and even whole tribes could be adopted and take up residence with the Creek. The remnants of the Calusa, Timucua, Yamasee, and later the Natchez were taken in as individuals and families. Larger groups of Alabama, Coushatta, and Hitchiti were given the status of clans or towns, depending on size, while multiple villages of the Yuchi and Shawnee were taken in so that they became "nations within nations," but subject to the laws of the Confederacy.

Similarly, people of European and African ancestry acquired citizenship in the Indian nations of the Southeast. In early colonial times, European indentured servants broke the bonds of servitude by "running away to join the Indians." Later, African American slaves escaped to form "Freedman" communities among the villages of Southeastern Indians.

One special circumstance among the Creek was the birth of the Seminole nation. Originally constituting the southernmost villages of Creek in southern Alabama and Georgia, the Seminole experienced a large increase in population when they took in refugees from the Creek Wars of the early-nineteenth century. Migrating farther into the Florida peninsula when the Spanish withdrew, they became a separate nation and are the ancestors of the present-day Seminole of Oklahoma and Florida.

Languages in the Southeast region

The Creek and Seminole both speak languages that are quite different from the Cherokee language, which is part of the Iroquoian family of languages. The Creek and Seminole, along with the Choctaw, Chickasaw, Alabama, and several other Southeastern tribes, speak languages from the most prominent language family of the Southeast—the Muskogean family. Besides the Muskogean family and the Iroquoian, other language families represented in the Southeast region include Caddoan, Algonquian, and Siouan, as well as four languages that are not related to a language family. Some scholars believe that the Southeast region probably represents the ancient homeland of the Siouan peoples, who migrated north and west in prehistoric times, finally spilling out onto the Plains as Lakota and Dakota people.

The Choctaw and Chickasaw were originally one people, and the languages are still only dialectically different. Sometime in the late prehistoric period, according to oral tradition, the Chickasaw withdrew from their brethren in central and southern Mississippi and Alabama, and established themselves as traders in the area south of present-day Memphis, Tennessee. From that location, they traded up and down the Mississippi River, dominating other groups not only by their economic power, but also their military power. As a disciplined, well-organized military force, the Chickasaw not only defeated de Soto in 1541, but also repulsed an Iroquois invasion and a French invasion in later years. Their automobile license plates still proclaim them to be the "Unconquered Chickasaws."

Trade and other relations

As soon as European trade goods became available in the seventeenth century, the Chickasaw became allied with the British, establishing a busy trade route toward the east, just north of Creek territory in Alabama and Georgia. The Choctaw, on the other hand, established trade relations with the French in New Orleans, and were allied with them in wars against the Chickasaw, the Creek, and other tribes of the vicinity.

The Choctaw, who were much more numerous than the Chickasaw, were never able to unite themselves as strongly as the other Southeastern tribes, largely because of geographical problems. The watersheds of the Pearl and Tombigbee Rivers contain numerous swamps, which divided the Choctaw towns from one another, and made it difficult for them to act collectively in war or politics.

West of the Mississippi, the Quapaw, or Arkansaw Indians, are often included as part of the Southeast Region, as are the Caddo of the west and the various tribes of Louisiana, notably including the Houma and Chitimacha. The Quapaw are a small tribe whose cultural relationships are with the Osage and Kansa to the northwest. The Caddo and their ancestors built mounds in earlier times and relied on agriculture, just like other Southeastern peoples, but later they lived in earthen lodges, kept horses, and hunted buffaloes, although still maintaining their corn fields. Their cultural relationships were with the Wichita and Arikara to the north.

Two tribes that moved around in this period were the Shawnee, sometimes considered as part of the Northeast Region, and the Alabama. Originally located on the Savannah River, the Shawnee for a time occupied the area of Kentucky. Then, some of the Shawnee towns joined the Creek Confederacy. Later, the Shawnee preceded the other Southeastern nations westward, ultimately coming to occupy reservations in Oklahoma and Kansas. The Alabama and the Coushatta, in early historic times, occupied the area near the mouth of the Alabama River, where they were strongly allied with the French. After the French withdrawal, the Alabama and Coushatta towns migrated singly toward the west, coming to rest in Louisiana and Texas, although several towns joined the Creek Confederacy.

Traders and mixed bloods

As soon as there were Europeans in North America, there were traders. Most were British traders, who traveled among the Indian nations, bartering guns, knives, and kettles for furs, deerskins, and other products of the forest. Some of these men married the daughters of chiefs. Their offspring became members of a newly created mixed-blood aristocracy, which is still important in the culture and politics of the Southeastern Indian nations. Familiar with the ways of the white man, and most often bilingual in English and a native language, the mixed bloods came to dominate trade. They soon established farms and ranches in their tribal areas and hired their tribesmen as workers, or they purchased African slaves from the colonies. The status of black people within the nation was always a source of political dispute.

Although one might expect that mixed bloods in the various nations would be sympathetic toward European interests, this was not always the case. Some of the most militant Indian leaders had white ancestry, including John Ross of the Cherokee and Alexander McGillivray of the Creek. Such leaders were instrumental in navigating their Indian nations through the treaty period, when the interior tribes gradually gave up land in exchange for peace and the benefits of trade.

Land crises

A crisis point was reached in the Southeast region just after 1800, when the Indian nations were crowded onto small parcels of land, and were surrounded by a steadily increasing number of land-hungry white people. By that time, each of the interior nations had matched its own army and defenses against those of the United States and been forced to withdraw farther into the interior. The Cherokee had been defeated in the war of 1794, and the Creek in 1814. The Chickasaw were firm U.S. allies, while the Choctaw were in political disarray, with their French sponsors withdrawn from North America after the Louisiana Purchase of 1803.

By this time the Indian populations had been devastated, but there were still enough Indian warriors available to cause some worry on the part of the U.S. government. By 1800 the Cherokee numbered about 25,000 persons, the Creek about the same, the Choctaw 20,000, and the Chickasaw about 3,000.

The Indian Removal Act and Indian Territory

Even including wars and disease, perhaps the most traumatic injury inflicted on the Southeastern Indians was the passage of the Indian Removal Act in 1828. Although negated by a ruling of the U.S. Supreme Court, the Act was nonetheless implemented by President Andrew Jackson, on behalf of the land-hungry frontier people who elected him to office. The federal government demanded that eastern and midwestern tribal groups be moved to an area west of the Mississippi River. The administration set aside an area in what is now Oklahoma that was established for Indian settlement and came to be known as Indian Territory.

Although all Indian people removed to Indian Territory suffered death and disease along the "Trail of Tears" in the period 1831–1848, some groups suffered more than others. The least affected tribe was probably the Chickasaw, who were by that time a highly integrated and sophisticated group, with important allies in the federal government. Anticipating the certainty of removal, they explored Indian

Territory, the eastern half of what is now Oklahoma, and selected an area at the western edge of the Territory where they could establish themselves as traders with the Plains Indians, while farming and ranching along the creeks and rivers near what is now Tishomingo, Oklahoma. After a period of thoughtful negotiations with the federal government, they made an orderly migration in 1837.

The Choctaw were a much larger group and politically divided among themselves about whether to resist emigration or not, and if they did emigrate, which lands they wanted to occupy in Indian Territory. The mixed-blood elite wanted to occupy lowlands along the Red River where they could take their slaves and start plantations. Ordinary Choctaw wanted to occupy the rolling hills farther north, where they could establish small family farms. For the entire decade of the 1830s, each Choctaw town was embroiled in controversy and, although Choctaw migration began in 1831, it did not end until 1847. Many Choctaw avoided removal by retreating to the hills and valleys of Mississippi, just west of Philadelphia.

The Creek essentially formed two factions—the mixed-blood elite on the one hand and the ordinary Creek and their Freedman allies on the other hand. The elite proceeded to move in wagons with their slaves and supporters to organize plantations near the Arkansas River, while the other or "traditional" faction built family farms and ceremonial grounds farther south and west.

This kind of factionalism between "traditionals" and "mixed-bloods" was even more emphatic and much more complicated among the Cherokee, who were split among regional as well as class, clan, and marriage alliances. Treaties between the Cherokee and the U.S. government had promised the Cherokee a permanent homeland and self-government on that part of their ancestral territory that was located in Georgia. When faced with the prospect of losing their rights and lands, the Cherokee Nation sued in federal court. Having important friends in the federal government and among the Christian clergy, they fully expected to win their case before the Supreme Court and stay in the East. So when President Jackson sent federal troops to remove the Cherokee by force, they were not ready to go. Many were dragged from their houses by soldiers and set on the road to walk 600 miles to Indian Territory. Thousands of Cherokee and other Indian people, especially the very young and very old—and the people who had no horses or wagons—died along the way.

The special targets of Indian Removal were those Indian people occupying desirable farmland or mineral resources. After they had been removed, the government became less thorough in searching for Indians in rough, mountainous terrain. Several thousand Cherokee hid in the Great Smoky Mountains, feeding themselves from small gardens. They gradually emerged from their hiding over the next several decades. In Mississippi, the pattern was the same, as the Choctaw became recognized by the federal government in 1918. In addition, other small groups of Indian people had avoided removal because they occupied state reservations, such as the Catawba in South Carolina, or because they were so dispersed into the general population, like the Lumbee of North Carolina.

The Seminole were a special case. Living in the wetlands of Florida at the time other groups were being removed from the Southeast, they occupied land that was not especially desired by Euro-Americans and therefore might not have been subjected to any forced removal. But the Seminole continued to open their doors to escaped slaves. To all the people who benefitted from the slave system, this was intolerable, and so the Seminole were invaded by a series of federal armies between 1830 and 1845. The Seminole turned the forces back and inflicted great casualties to the U.S. troops, finally forcing the federal government to pay off certain bands to remove themselves to Indian Territory, while the other bands were left in peace in Florida, like the Chickasaw, still unconquered.

Life and culture after removal

In Indian Territory, the Southeastern nations got themselves reorganized, although in different ways. For the Cherokee, the struggle was over a national government, as the different factions contested for power. The elite struggled against the emerging traditional or "Keetowah faction" and they quarreled among themselves in other complex ways. The polarization of the Creek continued, with periodic outbreaks and protests of the traditional faction during the "Green Peach War" and the "Crazy Snake Rebellion." The traditional Choctaw, living in the eastern Oklahoma hills, essentially abandoned the federally-sponsored tribal government and left it to the mixed-blood elite. The Chickasaw remained united, but increasingly were married and mixed with the local white population. The Seminole tenaciously maintained the chief-and-band political system they had developed in Florida.

In Indian Territory, the Southeastern Indians adopted plows instead of hoes for agriculture, and they raised increasing numbers of horses, cattle, and hogs. Their diet and economy improved and their

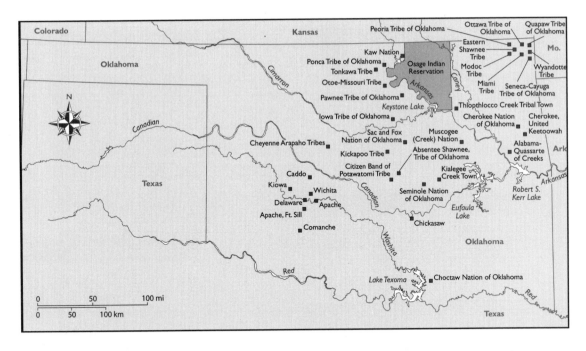

A map of Oklahoma reservations today.

populations increased. Solicited by Christian missionaries, they experienced patterns of conversion that reflected their political structure. The Creek traditionalists became Baptists, while the elite became Methodists. The traditional Choctaw became convinced, tee-totaling (not drinking any alcohol) Methodists while the elite Choctaw joined a variety of Protestant denominations in the small towns. The Keetowah (traditional) Cherokee remained non-Christian and even took to burning Christian churches and punishing anyone who became baptized.

Southeast Indian nations today

After settling in Indian Territory or back in their eastern homes, the Southeast Indian nations faced more disruptions at the hands of inconsistent government policy with respect to Native peoples. The Civil War forced an adjustment of reservation boundaries, depending on whether a group had sided with the Confederacy or the Union. More traumatic was the government's allotment policy. The 1887 Dawes Act required that communally held tribal land was to be partitioned into lots owned by individuals. The Curtis Act of 1898 dismantled tribal governments in Oklahoma. On the brighter side, the Indian Reorganization Act (1934) and the corresponding Oklahoma Indian Welfare Act of 1836 brought some civil rights and religious freedom to Indians—although the constitutional Bill of Rights was not extended to Indian citizens until 1968. In the last several decades, tribal governments have been built up by federal funds, so that they supply social services to their citizens. And some tribes have benefited by sponsoring bingo halls and other gaming facilities.

Meanwhile the eastern remnants of recognized Southeastern tribes have become more organized and have likewise attracted federal funds. In addition, new groups have emerged and sought formal acknowledgment from the federal government. The Bureau of Federal Acknowledgement of the Bureau of Indian Affairs now has a list of 20 or more groups located in the Southeast region that claim ancestry among the aboriginal tribes of the area, and who seek official recognition of their status. And so, after a long period of hardship and oppression, the immediate prospects of the descendants of the aboriginal tribes of the Southeast region seem very bright. Not only are there more Indian people than there have been since the seventeenth century, but also more tribes.

John H. Moore, Ph.D.
Anthropology Department
University of Florida, Gainesville

FURTHER READING

Crawford, James M., ed. *Studies in Southeastern Indian Languages.* Athens: University of Georgia Press, 1975.

Foreman, Grant. *Indian Removal.* Norman: University of Oklahoma Press, 1972.

Hudson, Charles. *The Southeastern Indians.* Knoxville: University of Tennessee Press, 1976.

Kniffen, Fred B., Hiram F. Gregory, and George A. Stokes. *The Historic Indian Tribes of Louisiana.* Baton Rouge: Louisiana State University Press, 1987.

Paredes, J. Anthony, ed. *Indians of the Southeastern United States in the Late 20th Century.* Tuscaloosa: University of Alabama Press, 1992.

Porter, Kenneth W. *The Black Seminoles.* Gainesville: University Press of Florida, 1996

Wallis, Michael, and Wilma P. Mankiller. *Mankiller: A Chief and Her People.* St. Martin's Press, 1994.

Wright, Muriel H. *A Guide to the Indian Tribes of Oklahoma.* Norman: University of Oklahoma Press, 1951.

Caddo

Name

The name Caddo is an abbreviation of the Caddoan word *Kadohadacho*, meaning "the real chiefs." The term comes from the word *Kaadi* (chief), and designates not only the Caddo people, but the Caddoan language family, the original group of 25 tribes within the Caddo Nation, and the lands they occupied.

Location

Caddo groups lived in parts of Arkansas, Louisiana, Oklahoma, and Texas, with the Red River Valley at the center of their territory. Present-day Caddo people live in Oklahoma (near Fort Cobb and Fort El Reno) and in other southwest central states.

Population

In the 1700s, there were about 8,000 people from Caddo nations, including about 2,500 Caddo, 3,000 Hasinai, and 1,800 Natchitoches (the three main tribes in the Caddo Nation). In 1910, there were only 452. In a census (count of the population) taken in 1990 by the U.S. Bureau of the Census, 2,935 people identified themselves as Caddo; an additional 49 people identified themselves as Oklahoma Caddo. In 1998 the Caddo Tribe of Oklahoma claimed 3,200 enrolled members.

Language family

Caddoan.

Origins and group affiliations

Most experts agree that the Caddo Nation lived in the Red River region since at least 800 C.E., if not longer. The nation consisted of about twenty-five tribes with similar languages and cultures that lived along the Red and Arkansas rivers in present-day Oklahoma, Texas, Louisiana, and Arkansas. But until they were removed from their homelands in the nineteenth century, the tribes were not united and operated mostly on their own. The three powerful members of the Caddo confederacies were the Hasinai, the Natchitoches, and the Kadohadacho, or Caddo proper.

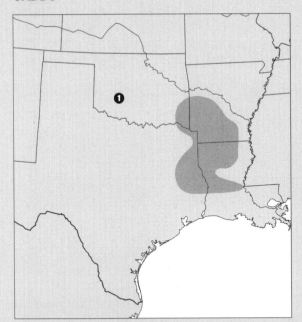

CADDO

Contemporary Communities

1. Caddo Indian Tribe of Oklahoma

Shaded area: Traditional Caddo lands along the banks of the Red River in present-day Texas, Arkansas, Oklahoma, and Louisiana, and in east Texas along the Texas River.

The Caddo lived comfortable lives as farmers and livestock tenders in the beautiful, fertile lands along the Red River before Europeans arrived in their lands. According to their tribal legend this was the place where they had lived since the beginning of time. After the Europeans came, the Caddo became embroiled in three centuries of disputes. Through it all, these intelligent, adaptable people remained true to their treaties and to their traditions. Though brave when they had to fight, they preferred to live in peace.

HISTORY

Before Europeans

Early writings about the Caddo describe the people as "industrious, intelligent, sociable, and lively; courageous and brave in war, and faithful to their . . . word." These writings also told of the friendly welcome the Caddo extended to European visitors, giving them the best food and places to sleep.

The Caddo built their homes, temples, and burial mounds in villages with central open areas for social gatherings and ceremonies. These were the villages found by the first Europeans who explored their region.

Around the mid-1500s the Caddo acquired horses from other tribes who had gotten them from Spanish explorers. They learned to hunt buffalo on the western Plains. This changed Caddo life, and the tribe adopted some traits of the Plains cultures. They became skilled horsemen and hunted farther west than ever before.

Relations with the Spanish and the French

In 1541 when Spanish explorer Hernando de Soto led his treasure-hunting expedition into Caddo territory, the tribe controlled lands in Louisiana, Arkansas, Texas, and parts of Oklahoma. De Soto did not mention in his journals that he had seen the Caddo people. When French explorer René-Robert Cavelier de La Salle arrived in 1686, he began a French association with the Caddo that would last until 1762.

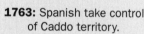

IMPORTANT DATES

1714: French found a trading post in Caddo territory and begin a half-century of control.

1763: Spanish take control of Caddo territory.

1803: United States takes control of Caddo territory with Louisiana Purchase.

1835: A treaty is signed giving Caddo territory to the United States. Some Caddo move to Texas, where a reservation is established for them in 1846.

1859: Caddo relocate to Indian Territory to escape murderous white Texans.

1872: Wichita Reservation is established for Caddo and other tribes.

1890: Wichita Reservation is dissolved and allotment policy is established.

1938: Caddo organize as the Caddo Tribe of Oklahoma.

1963: Caddo, Delaware, and Wichita tribes are given land in Oklahoma, which the three tribes now hold in common.

From the beginning of their arrival in Caddo territory, France and Spain vied for control of the land and its people. The French sought to do this by trading and giving gifts, while the Spanish felt the best way to control the people was to convert them to the Catholic faith. The Caddo preferred the French approach and established friendly relations with them, thwarting Spanish efforts to control the tribe for the time being.

Between 1714 and 1719 several French trading posts and forts were built along the Red River. The Caddo learned to speak the French language, and the French developed a great respect for the tribe. There were troubles back in France, though, and the French never succeeded in building up the Louisiana territory and attracting settlers. A war that raged between France and Spain was carried over into Caddo territory. Caddo villages became European forts, and European soldiers marched along Caddo trails. The Native people suffered and died from European diseases; survivors were sometimes forced to abandon their villages.

In 1763 France gave up Louisiana to Spain, and the Caddo came under the control of the Spanish. The Caddo were angry at being "given away" by the French as if they were cattle, and they threatened to resist Spanish control. The Spanish were quick to realize that they had to adopt French ways of dealing with the Caddo. They built up a relationship based on trade, the giving of gifts, better treatment, and friendship with the Indians. But the relationship between the Caddo and the Spanish was not to last long.

Under U.S. control

Caddo territory passed into the hands of the United States with the Louisiana Purchase of 1803 (when France sold to the United States territory extending from the Mississippi River to the Rocky Mountains and from the Gulf of Mexico to British North America, an area that doubled the area of the United States). The Caddo were enthusiastic about the change, not because they had disliked the French or the Spanish but because the Americans paid more for furs. The U.S. government continued the policies of their European predecessors by giving the Caddo gifts, and they promised that no whites would be allowed to settle on their lands.

Meanwhile Indians from the East were being driven out of their lands by American settlers, who never seemed to have enough land to satisfy them. In the 1820s the U.S. government began allowing small groups of displaced Indians to settle on Caddo lands. At first the Caddo did not object—they could use the help of the Choctaw, Delaware, and Cherokee peoples against the Osage, who raided Caddo hunting expeditions and camps, stole horses, and killed Caddo people. But the Caddo did object when the U.S. government worked out a treaty in 1825 that would require thousands of Indians from many different tribes to move onto Caddo lands and become part of the tribe.

Next, white settlers set their sights on Caddo lands and began to move there, even though it was against the law. The game supplies in their traditional hunting territory were now seriously depleted, and Caddo tribes were still experiencing losses of population due to war and disease. For the first time Caddo people began to think about moving away from their ancient villages.

Caddo sell their homeland

The Caddo signed a treaty with the United States in 1835, selling about a million acres of land in Louisiana for $80,000 worth of cash and goods. They agreed to move within one year—at their own expense—to land outside the boundaries of the United States, never to return.

Some Caddo moved to join their relatives in Texas, which was then part of Mexico. In the 1820s Mexico had invited American settlers to move to Texas because it was sparsely populated. By the mid-1830s those settlers were revolting against Mexican rule. Before more Caddo could move to Texas, white settlers there asked the U.S. government to prohibit Indian movement to the territory. They feared that angry Natives who had been forced out of their homelands would join together to fight against Americans in Texas.

A short residence in Texas

By 1836 the white settlers had won control of Texas. Some Caddo joined the Texas Cherokee, who battled the Texans in 1839 and lost. A series of peace treaties followed, the last being the Council Springs Treaty (1846) between the Caddo and the U.S. government. In exchange for "perpetual peace," the Caddo agreed to move to a Texas reservation.

The Caddo lived peacefully on the reservation for a short time, but white Texans' resentment and hostility toward all Native Americans was growing stronger. In 1858 white men attacked a group of Indians who were simply grazing their horses. The U.S. government decided to move the Caddo to Indian Territory for their own safety. (Indian Territory was the land that now forms most of the state of Oklahoma.) During the 1800s many tribes were moved to Indian Territory as part of the government's plan to make the area into a state governed by those tribes.

White Texans did not think the government was acting fast enough to rid Texas of its Indian population, and they threatened to massacre every Indian on the Caddo reservation. To avoid such a tragedy, Indian Superintendent Robert S. Neighbors hurriedly took 1,500 Indians across the Red River in the scorching heat of the summer of 1859. In 15 days they marched to what would become the new Caddo County along the Washita River in Oklahoma. There, the Wichita Agency and Reservation was established near Fort Cobb. (The Wichita were Caddoan speakers.) Superintendent Neighbors was murdered when he returned to Texas.

Settling in Oklahoma

At the Wichita Reservation the Caddo began to cultivate land and build homes. But whites began to cast their eyes on Indian Territory, demanding that it be opened up for settlement. The U.S. government

Caddoan leader George Washington, a delegate to Washington, D.C., in 1872 when the boundaries of the Wichita-Caddo Reservation were being decided.

finally gave up efforts to keep settlers out of the territory. In 1890 the government passed a law that divided Indian land into 160-acre parcels, one parcel for each family. Instead of tribes cultivating their land as a community, as was traditional, families would cultivate their own parcels. This policy was called allotment, and the idea behind it was to turn "savage" Indians into farmers so they could assimilate, or become more like the rest of American society. After the parcels were allotted, the leftover land was opened to white settlers. Thousands of acres of Indian land passed into their hands in the early 1900s.

The Caddo managed to retain much of their culture throughout the allotment period, which lasted until the 1930s. At that point the U.S. government finally concluded that allotment was not working. Laws were passed to end the policy, to restore Indian lands to the Indians, and to organize tribal governments so tribes would govern themselves. The Caddo organized themselves in 1938 as the Caddo Tribe of Oklahoma. In 1963 land in Oklahoma was restored to the Caddo, Wichita, and Delaware tribes. The land, which is owned by the three tribes, is now a 487-acre reservation spread throughout Grady, Canadian, and Caddo counties. About 900 Caddo live there, and more Caddo live on land their families received long ago as allotments.

RELIGION

Traditional beliefs and practices

The Caddo worshiped a Great Spirit they called Ayanat Caddi ("the great captain"), as well as many spirits and powers, including the Sun, the Moon, and animal spirits. They believed that long ago the Great Spirit placed a family (carrying corn and pumpkin seeds) near a lake in Caddo territory, and from that family sprang all the Caddo people.

According to Caddo belief, everything in nature had power that could be used for both good and evil. Natural forces had to be kept happy so they would not turn their powers against the tribe.

The religious leader of the community was a priest known as the *xinesi*, who informed the people of the wishes of the spirits. The xinesi conducted ceremonies, maintained the temple, and performed religious services. Fire was especially sacred to the Caddo, and a perpetual fire was kept burning in the temple, tended by the xinesi.

Modern religions

Missions were started by the Baptists after the Caddo moved to the Oklahoma reservation, and an Indian Baptist church is still maintained there. The Caddo began performing the Ghost Dance in 1890. The Ghost Dance was a revitalization movement that had arisen in the 1870s and aimed to bring back traditional life styles. Ghost Dance practitioners hoped they could also bring back the buffalo and their dead ancestors and free the continent of the white invaders through their devotions. The Caddo held the Ghost Dance two or three times a year, usually during the summer months, in an effort to rid their land of white people and white ways. By 1921, though, the Ghost Dance religion had lost some of its power.

Meanwhile, a man named John Wilson (c. 1840–1901) was spreading the Peyote (pronounced *pay-OH-tee*) religion among the Caddo and many other Native groups. (Peyote is a cactus plant that causes hallucinations when chewed and eaten.) Wilson was of mixed Delaware, Caddo, and French parentage but considered himself Caddo and spoke only that language. He claimed to have had several visions while under the influence of peyote, and these visions allegedly revealed the "right way" for Native Americans to worship Jesus Christ. According to Wilson, those who followed the Peyote Road would be set free from their sins.

A Caddo named Enoch Hoag (c. 1856–1920) served as Wilson's assistant, then developed his own version of Wilson's Big Moon Peyote ceremony. Hoag began a 30-year reign as a Caddo chief in 1896.

LANGUAGE

Varieties of the Caddoan language were spoken by many tribes, including the Wichita and the Pawnee (see entry.) The Caddo were the southernmost tribe speaking the language. They also used a sign language, and many Caddo spoke several other Native American dialects to communicate with other tribes.

There are two different forms of the Hasinai language: (1) a common form that is used in ceremonial songs, and (2) a prayer language that only a few Caddo men now living in Oklahoma are allowed to use. Since the 1970s the common form of Hasinai has been taught outside the home in places such as the Caddo Tribal Complex in Oklahoma.

GOVERNMENT

The Caddo Nation consisted of 25 small, loosely organized tribes with similar languages and cultures. The Caddo were not united as a people before being removed from their homelands in the nineteenth century. Each tribe remained independent of the others.

Village leadership and power passed through the mother, making it a matrilineal society. Each tribe was ruled by several officials, led by the xinesi, or priest. Beneath him were the *caddi* (the village headmen or chiefs) and the *canahas* (subchiefs and village elders). The caddi governed the community, making important political decisions. The canahas assisted the caddi, performing tasks like lighting their pipes and making sure their beds were ready during a hunt.

Caddo war leaders were called *amayxoya*. They were elected from those who had achieved success in combat. When the tribe was engaged in war, the war leader had absolute authority.

The Caddo Nation of the late 1990s was a union of the Kadohadacho, the Hasinai, and the Natchitoches peoples. The Caddo are governed by a constitution and an eight-member elected board, although every tribal member has a say in the decision-making process. The tribe is headquartered in Binger, Oklahoma, where it oversees a senior citizen's center, a community center, and indoor and outdoor dance grounds. The Caddo also co-own land (they own it with the Delaware and Wichita tribes) spread over three counties, where a school, a Bureau of Indian Affairs Office, and an Indian Baptist church are located.

ECONOMY

Throughout history the Caddo have been noted for their work ethic (a guiding philosophy that stresses the importance of hard work). No one was allowed to be idle, and those who refused to work were punished. Long ago the Caddo economy was based mostly on agriculture, although the people did do some hunting and fishing. After about 1700, when the Caddo became expert horsemen, hunting and trading grew even more important than farming. The Caddo traveled as far north as Illinois to trade with other tribes. Their most prized trade items were salt they extracted from boiled spring water and a certain type of wood that was popular for making bows.

The Caddo are working with the Delaware and the Wichita to help members of all three tribes achieve economic independence. They jointly own WCD Enterprises, which is in charge of leasing the oil, gas, and grazing lands that provide much of their income. The tribe manages farming operations, a factory, a smoke shop, and a bingo enterprise.

Caddo people work in fields such as health care, education, banking, ranching, farming, sports, and construction. Yet unemployment for people living on the reservation is extremely high, with as many as 40 percent of job seekers unsuccessful in their efforts to find work.

DAILY LIFE

Families

Several Caddo families—as many as eight to ten—lived in the same house in traditional times. Each family had its own space within the dwelling, but the entire household owned and cultivated the land around the house. Food supplies were distributed to each family by an elderly woman in the household who was in charge of that task.

Buildings

The Caddo built two kinds of houses: grass- and earth-covered. Houses were conical in shape and could be as large as 60 feet in diameter. Villages were arranged around a central open area used for ceremonies and other gatherings. Caddo communities also held a variety of public buildings, including the temple for the sacred fire and meeting places for tribal leaders.

Clothing and adornment

The Caddo made their clothes out of deerskin and buffalo hide. In summer both men and women wore only breechcloths, garments with front and back flaps that hung from the waist. They often went barefoot, wearing moccasins only for travel. In winter they wore leggings, buckskin shirts, and moccasins that they painted with intricate designs. The Caddo also decorated their clothing with fringe and adorned themselves with bead necklaces, collars, nose-rings, and earrings.

Some Caddo tribes removed their body hair completely, including their eyebrows. Hair on the head might be cut short with one long section tied off to the side, or it could be allowed to grow uncut and untended. The Caddo wore tattoos with designs featuring animals and birds. At puberty, Caddo girls received tattoos of large, brilliantly colored flowers.

Food

Caddo life revolved around farming, hunting, fishing, and gathering wild plants. Corn was their most important crop, with two harvests per year. The early crop, "little corn," was much like modern-day popcorn; it was planted in April and picked in July. "Flour corn" was planted in June and harvested in September in a celebration called the "Harvest of the Great Corn."

The Caddo ate corn baked as bread and in a variety of other ways. They also cultivated squash and beans, melons, sunflowers, and tobacco. The tribe hunted deer, buffalo, bears, raccoons, turkeys, and other animals and gathered nuts, acorns, berries, and fruits such as pomegranates and wild grapes. At some point before the turn of the nineteenth century the Caddo began to raise livestock.

Farming, Caddo-style

An early European onlooker once wrote down his observations of the Caddo style of farming. He said that when it was time to make the fields ready for planting, word went around the entire village. On the chosen day the men gathered their tools and met at one family's field and prepared it, while the women went to the home to prepare a feast. If there was no meat, he wrote, "they [would] bake Indian bread in the ashes, or boil it, mixing it with beans." After the feast the men socialized until the next day, when they moved on to the next household's field. The women of the house did the planting.

Education

The Caddo prized the virtues of honesty, fair dealing, and hospitality, and they passed these beliefs on to their children. In the late twentieth century a Caddo cultural center stood as a reminder to tribal members of their proud and ancient heritage.

Healing practices

Aside from their roles as political and religious leaders, the xinesi served as the tribes' healers. They cured the sick or wounded with a variety of aids, including fire, snakeskins, feathers, necklaces, and musical instruments. Another aspect of the xinesi healing ritual involved sucking foreign objects and blood from victims to purge (or rid) them of disease-causing evil spirits. Illnesses, called *aguian* (meaning "arrow tip"), were thought to stem from an object shot into a victim by an evil spirit or a witch.

The Caddo also practiced a limited number of natural remedies with special brews and used sweat baths to cure the sick. As Elsie Clews Parsons wrote in her article "Notes on the Caddo," different doctors had different rules for curing, depending on their supernatural guide. For example, she wrote: "Tsa'bisu . . . [was] a famous doctor. His supernatural partner was a red-headed woodpecker." The powers these animals provided to the doctor helped him in curing the sick or wounded.

Modern-day Caddo are treated by the Indian Health Service at two facilities located on tribal territory. The people also have access to hospitals in nearby towns.

ARTS

Caddo women were skilled at crafts; they decorated their houses with handmade, beautifully colored rugs, baskets, and clay pottery.

Oral literature

The Sun and fire were central characters in the stories of Southeast tribes. Sacred fires were often the centers of their towns and homes, and their tales reflect the importance of the Sun as a figure of power. Like many other North American tribes, the Caddo told stories that centered on the trickster figure, Coyote.

Tribal history was shared largely through song. The song that accompanies the Drum Dance tells of the tribe's beginnings, while the song that accompanies the Turkey Dance tells of events both ancient and modern. These and other songs have been recorded and preserved in the collections of the Hasinai Cultural Center and the Duke Oral History Collection of the Western History Manuscripts Collection of the University of Oklahoma.

CUSTOMS

Festivals and ceremonies

Of all the Caddo ceremonies, the most important had to do with hunting, warfare, and harvest. The Turkey Dance celebrates victory and must be performed in the daylight. A Drum Dance began an evening ceremony and a Morning Dance ushered in the dawn. Since corn was the major crop, it was often the central focus of ceremonies.

The Caddo have worked hard to maintain their culture and still perform traditional dances and ceremonies. Since the 1970s the

Caddo Culture Club has worked to preserve stories, songs, dances, and customs, and they hope to continue this project of preservation well into the twenty-first century.

War and hunting rituals

Before going to war some Caddo warriors sang and danced around a fire for a week or more, offering gifts to the Great Spirit such as corn or bows and arrows. Warriors rubbed their bodies with smoke from the fire so that the Great Spirit would grant their wish to slay their enemies.

Some Caddo groups tortured prisoners of war, then killed and ate them. This practice was considered necessary to "feed" the Caddo gods. Caddo warriors also took scalps from their enemies and sometimes heads for trophies.

The Caddo took special care with the burial of dead warriors. Those who died at home were buried with the scalps they had taken from enemies in life; this was believed to grant them power over their foes in the House of the Dead. They were also buried with food, water, tools, and weapons. A fire burned near graves for six days, until the spirit passed on to the next world. Those who died in battle were either cremated (their bodies were burned) or left to be eaten by wild beasts, which was considered a great honor.

Before a hunt, Caddo men prayed to animal spirits, asking that the animals allow themselves to be slain.

Courtship and marriage

A Caddo man who wished to marry would present the woman of his choice with the finest gift he could manage. If she accepted it, then they were married. Sometimes these marriages lasted only a few days. If a man came along and offered a better gift, a woman was free to leave her husband and marry the new man. Men only had one wife at a time, though few stayed with their wives for long.

NOTABLE PEOPLE

Carol Hampton (1935–) is a teacher, tribal historian, writer, and activist for the Caddoan people. She has taught Native American Studies at the University of Science and Arts of Oklahoma. Hampton has also been active in the Caddo tribal council since 1976 and in many state and national programs concerning education and Native American development.

Other notable Caddo include Enoch Hoag (see "Religion"); highly regarded Caddo-Kiowa artist T. C. Cannon (1946–); Richard Donaghey, who operates the internationally known First Nations Dance Company; and Dayton Edmonds, a Methodist minister and storyteller whose tales combine elements of Native American spirituality with Christian teachings.

FURTHER READING

Berlainder, Jean Louis. *The Indians of Texas in 1830.* Washington, DC: Smithsonian Institution, 1969.

Bolton, Herbert Eugene. *The Hasinais: Southern Caddoans as Seen by the Earliest Europeans.* Norman: University of Oklahoma Press, 1987.

"The Caddo Indian Tribe of Oklahoma." http://www.caddonation.com.

Carter, Cecile Elkins. *Caddo Indians.* Norman: University of Oklahoma Press, 1995.

Glover, William B. "A History of the Caddo Indians." Formatted for the World Wide Web by Jay Salsburg. Reprinted from *The Louisiana Historical Quarterly,* vol. 18, no. 4, October 1935.

Newkumet, Vynola Beaver, and Howard L. Meredith. *Hasinai: A Traditional History of the Caddo Confederacy.* College Station: Texas A&M Press, 1988.

Parsons, Elsie Clews. "Notes on the Caddo." *Memoirs of the American Anthropological Association.* No. 57. Menasha, WI: American Anthropological Association, 1941.

Smith, F. Todd. *The Caddo Indians: Tribes at the Convergence of Empires, 1542-1854.* College Station: Texas A&M Press, 1995.

Weslager, C.A. *The Delaware Indians: A History.* New Brunswick, NJ: Rutgers University Press, 1972.

Cherokee

Name

Cherokee (pronounced *CHAIR-uh-key*). The name comes from the Creek word *chelokee,* which means "people of a different speech." The Cherokee refer to themselves as *Ani'-Yun'wiya',* meaning "the real people" or "the principal people" or *Tsalagi,* which comes from a Choctaw word for "people living in a land of many caves."

Location

The Cherokee originally lived in parts of eight present-day southeastern states: North Carolina, South Carolina, Virginia, West Virginia, Kentucky, Tennessee, Georgia, and Alabama. In the late 1990s most Cherokee lived in northeastern Oklahoma, North Carolina, and Tennessee.

Population

In 1674, there were an estimated 50,000 Cherokee. From the mid-1600s to the 1730s, there were about 25,000. In a census (count of the population) conducted in 1990 by the U.S. Bureau of the Census, 369,979 people identified themselves as Cherokee, making the tribe the largest in the United States. (See box.)

Language family

Iroquoian.

Origins and group affiliations

Many historians believe that the very early ancestors of the Cherokee moved from territory that is now Mexico and Texas to the Great Lakes region. Then, between 3,000 and 4,000 years ago, after enduring conflicts with the Iroquois (see entry) and the Delaware tribes, the Cherokee moved again—this time to the southeastern part of the present-day United States. Their traditional enemy was the Chickasaw tribe (see entry). In the late 1990s there were 3 major tribal groups and more than 50 other organizations in at least 12 states that claimed to have Cherokee origins.

CHEROKEE

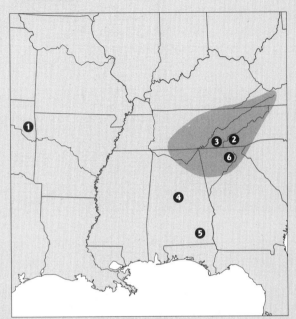

Contemporary Communities

1. United Keetoowah Band and Cherokee Nation of Oklahoma
2. Eastern Cherokee Tribe, North Carolina
3. Etowah Cherokee Nation, Tennessee
4. Echota Cherokee Tribe of Alabama
5. United Cherokee Tribe of Alabama
6. Georgia Tribe of Eastern Cherokees

Shaded area: Traditional Cherokee lands in the Appalachian Mountains in present-day North Carolina, South Carolina, Virginia, West Virginia, Kentucky, Tennessee, Georgia, and Alabama.

Before the arrival of Europeans in their territory in 1540, the Cherokee were an agricultural people numbering about 50,000 who controlled 40,000 square miles of land. Over the years the tribe lost many of its people to wars and the white settlers' diseases. The Cherokee became known as one of the "Five Civilized Tribes" along with the Chickasaw, Creek, Choctaw, and Seminole nations (see entries). White people coined this term because these groups had formed institutions that white culture valued, such as constitutional governments and school systems. This, however, did not help them when settlers wanted their land.

During the nineteenth century many Cherokee were forced by the U.S. government to move westward, away from their homeland on the sad journey known as the Trail of Tears. They formed new government and school systems in Indian Territory, but the government abolished these when the state of Oklahoma was created in 1907. But the Cherokee rebounded from their misfortune. At the end of the twentieth century they made up the largest Indian group in the United States and enjoyed a high standard of living.

HISTORY

Trade with Europeans

The Cherokee people were actually a confederacy consisting of as many as 200 separate towns nestled in the river valleys of the southern Appalachian Mountains. The people in these towns shared a common language and customs, but each town had its own chief, and there was no overall chief or government for the confederacy. The Cherokee had been farming in the southern Appalachian region for 1,000 years when they first encountered Europeans in 1540 as Spanish explorer Hernando de Soto led a party through Cherokee lands. After that, the Cherokee had very little contact with outsiders until the 1600s, when white traders began moving into the region. The tribe traded with them for manufactured goods such as metal tools, glass, cloth, and firearms. In exchange they supplied the whites with deerskins, which became an important source of leather in Europe. This partnership changed the Cherokee culture. The people no longer farmed and hunted for survival. Instead, they engaged in buying and selling, and hunters replaced priests as the leaders of Cherokee society.

For generations the tribe had shown great respect for nature, but eighteenth-century Cherokee hunter-traders killed as many deer as they could to keep up with the booming fur trade. One report shows that the number of deerskins the Cherokee sold in a year increased from 50,000 in 1708 to around one million in 1735. Further changes took place when white traders built stores near Cherokee towns and married Cherokee women. Instead of remaining with their people, the women often went to live with their white husbands. Traditional Cherokee people did not accumulate possessions, but the children of these couples began to inherit personal wealth.

The Cherokee were allied with the British traders, and so fought with the British in the French and Indian War (1755–1763) and the American Revolution (1775–83). In the peace treaties that followed each of these wars, the Cherokee lost large portions of their lands.

IMPORTANT DATES

1540: The Cherokee are first visited by Europeans.

1821: Sequoyah's method for writing the Cherokee language is officially approved by tribal leaders.

1827: The Cherokee adopt a written constitution.

1838: Cherokee leave their homeland on a forced journey known as the Trail of Tears.

1907: With the creation of the state of Oklahoma, the government abolishes the Cherokee tribal government and school system, and the dream of an Indian commonwealth dissolves.

1984: The first modern-day meeting between the Eastern Band and the Cherokee Nation is held.

CONSTITUTION

OF THE

CHEROKEE NATION,

MADE AND ESTABLISHED

AT A

GENERAL CONVENTION OF DELEGATES,

DULY AUTHORISED FOR THAT PURPOSE,

AT

NEW ECHOTA,

JULY 26, 1827.

—————

PRINTED FOR THE CHEROKEE NATION,
AT THE OFFICE OF THE STATESMAN AND PATRIOT,
GEORGIA.

The title page of the Constitution of the Cherokee Nation, July 26, 1827.

Divisions among the Cherokee

Between 1790 and 1817 several groups of Cherokee moved westward in an attempt to hold their culture together against the threat of increasing numbers of white settlers. One group settled in Arkansas and became known as the Western Band (today's United Keetoowah Band). By 1820 this group had 5,000 members. But the majority of the Cherokee people stayed in their southeastern homeland. Terrible smallpox epidemics (uncontrollable outbreaks of disease) raged in the mid-1700s, killing nearly half the Cherokee population, and a series of treaties between 1785 and 1806 resulted in the loss of even more Cherokee land. Christian missionaries joined with government forces in trying to make the Cherokee assimilate (blend) into white culture. Many Cherokee had already turned away from traditional ways in the hopes that the government would let them stay in their homelands.

Two conflicting factions arose within the Cherokee nation. One was called the "Treaty Party." Its members, who were mostly well-to-do slave-holders, merchants, and plantation-owners, believed in assimilation. They thought the Cherokee should sell their homelands in Georgia to the U.S. government and voluntarily move to lands west of the Mississippi River. Resistance, they warned, would be a disaster for the Cherokee.

The "Ross Party" of Cherokee, led by Principal Chief John Ross, thought the Cherokee should negotiate with the government and use the U.S. court system to stay in what was left of their ancestral lands. They created a law under which selling or bargaining away Cherokee land was an offense against the tribe punishable by death.

The fight for the southeastern homelands

In the 1820s a warrior named Sequoyah (pronounced *suh-KWOY-ah*) showed tribal leaders a method he had invented for writing out the Cherokee language. His system used a syllabary—a writing code using symbols for syllables rather than for single letter sounds as in the English alphabet. Many Cherokee quickly learned to read and write in the Cherokee syllabary. From 1828 to 1835 the

Cherokee Phoenix, a weekly newspaper printed in both English and Cherokee, was published and widely read.

In the early 1820s the Cherokee established a capital in New Echota, Georgia. They wrote a constitution for a government in 1827 that was, in many ways, similar to the U.S. Constitution. They wished to establish their own government and the right to preserve their homelands in Georgia, Tennessee, and Alabama. The Georgia legislature, however, passed a series of laws that abolished the Cherokee government and appropriated (took for itself) Cherokee land.

When the state of Georgia tried to remove the Cherokee from their lands, the Cherokee took the case to the U.S. Supreme Court. They based their case on a clause in the Constitution that allows foreign nations to seek redress (compensation or remedy) in the Supreme Court for damages caused by U.S. citizens. The court ruled that Indian nations are not foreign nations but dependent, domestic nations. Up until that time, U.S. law had treated Indian nations as separate, or foreign, nations. Although the Cherokee lost this case, in a case in 1832 the Supreme Court ruled that Georgia could not remove the Cherokee from their land, stating that only the federal government had the right to regulate Indian affairs; states could not extend their laws over Indian governments. But this Cherokee victory was temporary.

THE CASE

OF

THE CHEROKEE NATION

against

THF STATE OF GEORGIA:

ARGUED AND DETERMINED AT

THE SUPREME COURT OF THE UNITED STATES,

JANUARY TERM 1831.

WITH

AN APPENDIX,

Containing the Opinion of Chancellor Kent on the Case; the Treaties between the United States and the Cherokee Indians; the Act of Congress of 1802, entitled 'An Act to regulate intercourse with the Indian tribes, &c.'; and the Laws of Georgia relative to the country occupied by the Cherokee Indians, within the boundary of that State.

BY RICHARD PETERS,

COUNSELLOR AT LAW.

Philadelphia:

JOHN GRIGG, 9 NORTH FOURTH STREET.

1831.

The title page of the Cherokee Nation case against the state of Georgia, argued in the U.S. Supreme Court, 1831.

The dispute deepens

In 1830 the U.S. government passed the Indian Removal Act, which required the Cherokee and other Indians living east of the Mississippi to trade their homelands for property in Indian Territory. (Indian Territory at the time was comprised of what are now Oklahoma, Kansas, and parts of Colorado, Nebraska, and Wyoming.) During the 1800s the U.S. government moved many tribes to Indian Territory, where, they were told, they would govern themselves and not be bothered by white settlers.

In 1832 Cherokee Principal Chief John Ross argued before the U.S. Supreme Court that the Removal Act went against the terms of

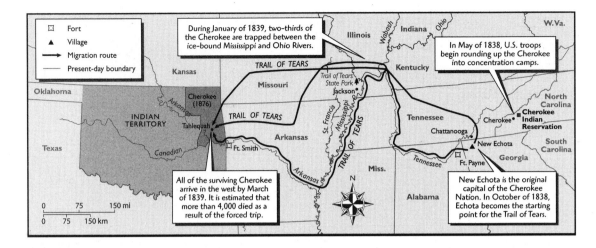

The routes taken by the Cherokee on the forced trip to their new home in Oklahoma, now known as the Trail of Tears, 1838–1839.

the U.S. Constitution. Although the Supreme Court agreed with Chief Ross, President Andrew Jackson refused to accept the Court's decision. Instead, he made plans to enforce the Removal Act. Angry Cherokee leaders refused to talk with government agents about an exchange of their land for land in Indian Territory.

In direct opposition to the wishes of most Cherokee, the Treaty Party signed the Treaty of New Echota in 1835. The treaty agreed to the exchange of the tribe's land in the East for property in Indian Territory and some money to aid the relocation process.

The majority of the Cherokee people were outraged at the signing of such a treaty. The Treaty Party was a small group with neither the authority nor the right to represent the entire tribe. In response, Chief Ross and 16,000 tribal members signed a petition of protest against the treaty. But the U.S. Senate passed the treaty anyway, and the tribe was ordered to move west within two years. Most of the Cherokee refused to leave voluntarily.

The Trail of Tears

In 1838 an appalling and discriminatory program of forced removal was launched against the Cherokee. Seven thousand government troops removed the Cherokee from their homes, gathered them in disease-infested camps, and then forced them to travel about 800 miles (many on foot) for three to five months to reach what was to be their new homeland.

The Indians set off on their journey without food, supplies, or shelter. Once on the trail they were attacked by whites, who stole the

few possessions they managed to carry along. At least 13,000 Cherokee began the tragic march, and before it was over a quarter to a third
of them had died. Some were left unburied at the side of the road. The
route of the forced march—a painful reminder of an agonizing experience in Native American history—was later named the Trail of Tears.

In North Carolina about 1,000 Cherokee escaped removal with
the help of state officials who were sympathetic to them. One North
Carolinian, William H. Thomas (called Wil-Usdi by the Cherokee),
bought land in his name for the Cherokee, went to court in their
defense, and even visited Washington on their behalf.

Conflicts followed by "Golden Age"

Once moved into Indian Territory, conflicts among the Cherokee
were initially intense. On June 22, 1839, three Cherokee leaders—
John Ridge, Major Ridge, and Elias Boudinot—who had signed the
despised removal agreement, were killed. As the Cherokee groups
settled into their new home, a new leadership arose—sometimes
called the National Party—and worked to establish an effective form

*"Trail of Tears," a painting by
Robert Lindneux.*

of government. The National Party invited the full participation of the two other Cherokee groups already living in Indian Territory: the Treaty Party and the Old Settlers, the group of Cherokee who had moved to Arkansas from North Carolina in the early 1800s, hoping to settle there permanently. In 1828 whites had forced them to move farther west to Indian Territory, where they set up their community according to their old ways.

The Old Settlers resented the arrival of the newcomers, and the three Cherokee groups could not reach any agreement. Several years of violent conflicts came to an end with a ceremonial day of unity in 1846, when the Cherokee people dedicated themselves to making the best of their circumstances. They did this to avoid being divided into two tribes by the U.S. government. Although tensions persisted, the differing groups enjoyed a period of peace and prosperity known as the "Golden Age" of the 1850s.

America's Civil War divides Cherokee people

The U.S. Civil War (1861–65) threatened to divide the tribe once again. Chief John Ross at first favored neutrality (not taking sides). In time, however, he agreed to fight on the side of the South (the Confederacy)—a move encouraged by wealthy Cherokee landowners who held a lot of power in the Cherokee Nation and favored the South. But the Old Settlers and many others joined the Northern (Union) army. Experts estimate that 25 percent of the entire Cherokee population died in the Civil War.

More broken promises

At war's end the U.S. government punished Cherokee supporters of the South by invalidating (no longer honoring) all treaties made with the Cherokee people. In new treaties signed in 1866 and 1868, large portions of Cherokee lands were taken for use by the railroads, for white settlements, and to house other Indian tribes. The U.S. government had promised the Cherokee people that land in Indian Territory would be set aside solely for Indian use—that no non-Indians would be allowed to settle there. Thus began a series of broken promises made by the government to the Cherokee. Within 15 years whites outnumbered Natives in Indian Territory.

For years the Cherokee had earned money by providing grazing land to white ranchers for their cattle. Without explanation, the government halted the grazing land practice in 1890. The poverty-stricken Cherokee were forced to sell their land to white settlers.

FROM INDIAN TERRITORY TO THE STATE OF OKLAHOMA

As part of the Indian Removal Policy of 1830, the Western Territory Bill called for the establishment of an Indian commonwealth or territory in the removal area. It was to be governed by a confederation of tribes and was to be composed of present-day Kansas, Oklahoma, parts of Nebraska, Colorado, and Wyoming. As other states were organized, the area reserved for Indians was reduced until its boundaries were almost identical to present-day Oklahoma. By 1868 this territory, known as Indian Territory, was the only unorganized territory (without a state government) in the lower 48 states.

In 1890 the Oklahoma Organic Act reduced Indian Territory to the eastern portion of the territory and established a U.S. territorial government called Oklahoma Territory in the western portion. After much dispute, the U.S. government made Oklahoma into a state in 1907. The promise of a free Indian state had dissolved.

In *Chronicles of Oklahoma,* historian Edward E. Dale described one Cherokee woman's pain as she spoke of the passing of her nation to statehood. Thirty years later, with tears in her eyes, she recalled "It broke my heart. I went to bed and cried all night long. It seemed more than I could bear that the Cherokee Nation, my country and my people's country, was no more."

Since Oklahoma became a state, Indian tribes have kept their status as self-governing and independent communities, except for limitations placed on them by treaties, agreements, or laws. Oklahoma Indians have the lowest income level and the highest unemployment rates of any of the population of Oklahoma.

Indians once owned all the land in the state of Oklahoma, but their lands were greatly reduced. At the turn of the century the "Five Civilized Tribes" owned 19.5 million acres of land. In 1975 Oklahoma tribal lands amounted to only 65,000 acres. Individual Native Americans owned about one million acres.

Today, about 600,000 Oklahomans identify themselves as Indians—more than in any other state. In a 65-mile radius around the city of Tulsa, there is the highest non-reservation population of Indians anywhere in the world.

Worse luck followed when terrible dust storms forced many Cherokee farmers to leave Oklahoma in the 1930s.

In the 1970s, after years of hardship for the Cherokee, the U.S. government began to make federal money available to Indian tribes. Since that time the Cherokee tribe in Oklahoma has become a national leader in education, health care, housing, and economic matters. The Cherokee Nation of Oklahoma adopted a new constitution in 1975, elected its own officials, and began governing itself once again.

Eastern Band of Cherokee Indians

While the Cherokee Nation was adapting to its western home, the Cherokee that had remained in North Carolina were organizing in the East. The people called themselves the Eastern Band of Cherokee Indians. In 1924 the tribe reached an agreement with the U.S.

government to make sure that Eastern Cherokee lands would remain forever in the possession of the tribe.

In 1984 more than 30,000 people attended a two-day meeting at which representatives of the Cherokee Nation of Oklahoma and the Eastern Band discussed common concerns. Such meetings are now held every two years.

United Keetoowah Band

The United Keetoowah Band (UKB) traces its history back to 1817. At that point in time a group of Cherokee refused to adopt the white way of life and instead agreed to trade their lands in North Carolina for lands farther west in Arkansas, where they lived for the next 11 years. But in 1828 the federal government removed them from Arkansas to Indian Territory, where they set up their headquarters in Talequah, Oklahoma. Because they did not intermarry with whites as other Cherokee groups did, the descendants of the UKB represent the largest group of full-blood Cherokee people in the United States. (They prefer the name Keetoowah to Cherokee). The UKB have retained traditional ways to a greater extent than other Cherokee groups, and many still speak the Keetoowah language.

RELIGION

As far back as the 1600s the Cherokee tribe was divided in its religious beliefs. The majority believed that the world had been created by several "beings from above," who then abandoned it. The Sun took over and created plants, animals, and people, then continued to watch over and preserve the Earth. The Cherokee holding these beliefs worshiped various heavenly bodies, animals, and fire.

The other group of Cherokee believed in "three beings who were always together and of the same mind." The three beings created all things and were present everywhere. They had messengers who visited the world to take care of human affairs.

The two groups of believers participated in the same ceremonies. For both, the primary god was the Creator, who was called *Yo wah* or *Ye ho waah*. Where there was order, there was goodness; where there was disorder and confusion, there was evil, represented by *Uktena*, a creature who was part snake, part deer, and part bird.

Religion was part of the Cherokee people's daily life and a part of nature. The annual cycle of festivals followed the Earth's seasonal rhythms. During times of peace, a town's head priest also functioned as its chief. Cherokee ways changed when Europeans came, and many Cherokee converted to Christianity; today many belong to Protestant Christian churches. The Keetoowah in Oklahoma, who have retained more of the old ways, practice the Stomp Dance religion. They are associated with several active stomp grounds where traditional Native ceremonies are held. (See "Festivals.")

CHEROKEE WORDS

OH-see-yoh. . . . . "hello"

gog-GEE. . . . . "summer"

wah-DOH . . . . . "thank you"

HOH-wah . . . . . "you're welcome."

LANGUAGE

The Cherokee language is the southern branch of the Iroquoian language. It is quite different from northern Iroquoian languages like Mohawk. In the Cherokee language verbs and nouns are not single words, but phrases that include descriptions of an action or object. For example, *so qui li*, the term for "horse," is translated as "he carries heavy things." Some words have several meanings, and meaning is sometimes shown by the way a word is spoken.

Cherokee differs from English and other European languages by placing the subject of a sentence after the object. For example, in the sentence "The girl caught a fish," "girl" is the subject, "caught" is the verb, and "fish" is the object. If the sentence were in Cherokee, "girl" would appear after "fish" in the sentence. This is in keeping with the belief that humans (often the subjects of sentences) are not superior to other living things (often the objects of sentences) but rather are equal to and partners with all creation.

The Cherokee language has its own unique written form. In the early 1800s a Cherokee man named Sequoyah invented a system for writing the Cherokee language. Most Cherokee were soon able to read and write their language.

In the late 1990s Cherokee was spoken by at least 14,000 people, and schools in Cherokee communities offered classes in both English and Cherokee. Those who sought to preserve the language have shot video footage of Native speakers, who are careful to pronounce words properly and assume the correct facial expressions as they speak.

GOVERNMENT

In traditional times, each Cherokee town had a chief who led in wartime and a priest who led in peacetime. Chiefs sought the guidance of a town council, made up of men and women who debated issues until they reached an agreement. In the early times the Chero-

POPULATION OF CHEROKEE PEOPLE IN THE UNITED STATES

The Cherokee live in nine major groups throughout the United States. In 1990 the members of the various Cherokee tribes identified themselves to the U.S. Bureau of the Census this way:

Tribe	Population
Cherokee	352,680
Cherokee of Northeast Alabama	87
Cherokee of Southeast Alabama	196
Eastern Cherokee	5,968
Echota Cherokee	3,773
Etowah Cherokee	85
Northern Cherokee	285
United Keetoowah Band	145
Western Cherokee	5,811
Other Cherokee	5
Cherokee Shawnee	944
Total	**369,979**

kee did not have a single chief who ruled over all, and the entire group came together only for ceremonies and wars. The post of principal chief was created in the nineteenth century to unify the nation, especially in its dealings with whites.

The Eastern Band of Cherokee was formed in 1889. Its current government is made up of a principal chief, a vice-chief, and a 12-member tribal council whose members are elected to two-year terms. The council deals with tribal issues, while another group runs the court system.

Before removal, the Cherokee Nation had formed a constitutional government based on the U.S. government's model. A couple of decades after removal, the Cherokee formed a new government with an executive, legislative, and judicial system. This government successfully led its people, providing many high quality services, particularly in education.

In 1906, as Oklahoma was about to be made a state, the U.S. government dissolved the government of the Cherokee Nation and took over tribal affairs. From then until the 1970s, when a new government was formed by the Cherokee Nation, principal chiefs of the tribe were appointed by the presidents of the United States and had little authority.

At the end of the twentieth century the Cherokee Nation tribal government consisted of a 15-member elected tribal council, whose members served four-year terms and worked with a principal chief. The Cherokee Nation District Court handled judicial matters. An agreement made with the U.S. Congress in 1990 gave the tribe even more control over its own affairs.

ECONOMY

The pre-contact Cherokee economy was based on farming and hunting. Women did most of the farming, took care of the animals, prepared the food, made clothing, and cared for the house and children. Men served as warriors and hunters. They cleared fields for farming and built houses and canoes. They also hunted many types of animals.

The Cherokee used all parts of a captured animal. For example, bears supplied meat and grease for food, fur for clothing, and claws for jewelry. The flesh of deer was used for food, the skin and the hide (tanned with a solution made from deer brains) were used to make clothing and other objects, the bones and antlers were used for tools and ornaments, the tendons for thread, and the hooves for glue.

Before the trade era with Europeans, the Cherokee did not generally accumulate possessions or wealth. But by the 1820s many Cherokee had intermarried with whites and become landowners. Many had even become slave owners. They raised cotton and other crops on large farms and plantations and sold the crops for profit. For most Cherokee, the period of removal meant the loss of most of the wealth they had accumulated.

The creation of the Great Smoky Mountains National Park in the 1930s helped to improve the economic condition of Cherokee living in North Carolina. After World War II ended in 1945, the park had become the main industry at the Eastern Cherokee Reservation in North Carolina.

In the late 1990s both the Cherokee Nation in Oklahoma and the Eastern Band of Cherokee in North Carolina were operating bingo parlors to help finance tribal services. In addition, the tribally owned Cherokee Nation Industries employed nearly 300 Oklahomans, mostly tribal members, in its electronic parts factory. (The company also operates a variety of other businesses, including ranches, poultry farms, tobacco shops, arts and crafts outlets, a cabinet factory, and a construction company.) The Eastern Band of Cherokee, in its efforts to broaden the economy, invested in a mirror factory and a fish hatchery. Cherokee people work in many professions within the American economy.

DAILY LIFE

Families

The Cherokee people were organized into seven clans (family groups) according to the ancestry of the mother. Usually a woman lived with her husband, their children, her parents, her sisters, her sisters' children, and any unmarried brothers. Fathers felt close to their children but were not considered their blood relatives.

Women's roles

The Cherokee were a matrilineal society, meaning that descendancy was determined through the mother's side of the family.

Cherokee fields were controlled by women, and women often worked behind the scenes to help make major decisions. Women also often served as warriors in battle. Women who had great influence or power were known as *Ghighua,* or "Beloved Women." The most noted Cherokee Beloved Woman was Nan'yehi, or Nancy Ward, a brave warrior and tribal leader of the late seventeenth century who tried to warn her people against signing away their land rights to the invading white culture.

Buildings

A Cherokee town was made up of a council house, a town square, and 30 to 60 private homes. The entire town was surrounded by a fence made of vertical poles placed close together to protect the people from attack. The circular council house was large enough to hold all 400 to 500 citizens for council meetings and major religious ceremonies. The square was used for ceremonies, meetings, and social events.

It remains unclear whether traditional Cherokee dwellings consisted of a single building or multiple buildings. It is known, however, that the walls of the structures were formed by weaving small tree branches between support posts and then plastering clay and grass over the framework. The roofs were thatched with bark shingles. By the nineteenth century the log cabin had become the most popular type of house among the Cherokee.

Clothing and adornment

Deerskin was the most common material used to make clothing and moccasins, and the members of the tribe who made the clothing used bone needles and animal tendons to sew garments together. Cherokee men wore breechcloths—garments with front and back flaps that hang from the waist. In cold weather they added deerskin leggings, fringed shirts, and robes made of fur or feathers. Beneath their deerskin dresses, women wore long, fringed petticoats (slips) that were woven or knitted from the wild hemp plant.

For festive occasions the Cherokee wore accessories made from turkey or eagle feathers, dyed porcupine quills, mulberry-root bark, or thread spun from the hair of bears or opossums. They also wore wristbands and arm bands hung with horn and shell rattles. Shells, bones, and copper were used to make jewelry.

Men often decorated their bodies and faces with paint or tattoos. They wore earrings and elongated their earlobes by cutting holes in them and inserting stones or bone in the holes. In early times Cherokee men grew beards, sometimes braiding them in three sections. By the time the Europeans arrived, though, it was common for the men of the tribe to pluck out all of their facial hair.

Hairstyles for Cherokee men were quite distinctive. They grew a palm-sized section of hair on the crown of the head and then plucked out a two-inch-wide ring around it. The long top section was pulled through a decorated, two-inch-long section of hollowed deer antler, and any loose ends around the topknot were decorated with a thick, colored paste. The hair below the plucked ring was cut short. Women used bear grease to make their hair glossy and decorated it with yellow or red dust. It was either worn loose or tied in a high knot.

Food

The Cherokee in traditional times farmed, hunted, and gathered their food. They grew beans, squash, sunflowers, melons, pumpkin, other food crops, and tobacco on their group farms. Wild nuts, roots, and fruits were gathered from the surrounding countryside, and food was preserved for winter months by drying it.

Women of the Cherokee tribe kept a kettle of soup or stew bubbling at all times. It was their method for using up leftovers. A particular favorite was a mixture of game or fowl, usually squirrel, rabbit, or turkey, with corn, beans, and tomatoes. The settlers in Jamestown, Virginia, called it Brunswick Stew.

Corn was the primary Cherokee crop. One variety was used for roasting, another for boiling, and a third for grinding into cornmeal. Ingredients like dried beans and chestnuts were often added to cornmeal bread, which was topped with bear grease or oil from pounded nuts. *Kanuche,* a rich broth made by boiling crushed hickory nuts in water, was a special food that could be mixed with corn or rice.

Fishing provided much food for the tribe. Various fishing techniques made use of hooks, nets, traps, bows, even poison designed to stun the fish long enough for the men to simply pick up the ones they wanted. Although the Cherokee ate bear, turkey, rabbit, and other small game, deer was the most important source of animal food. When hunting deer, Cherokee men disguised themselves by wearing entire deerskins with antlers. This allowed them to sneak up on their prey without being noticed. Using blowguns, they could hunt small animals from a distance of 60 feet or more. A blowgun was made by hollowing out a seven- or eight-foot long cane stem. Wood splints, balanced with feathers or thistles, were used to make darts.

MARY O'BRIEN'S APRICOT BLUE-BERRY COOKIES

Native Americans enjoyed eating berries raw and preserved them for winter use by drying them. The dried berries were sometimes boiled and seasoned with maple sugar. Cookbook author E. Barrie Kavasch was given this recipe by a Cherokee woman named Mary O'Brien. She suggested many variations using whatever fresh fruits are in season.

1½ cups flour

1/2 cup white cornmeal

1 teaspoon baking soda

1 teaspoon cinnamon

1 teaspoon salt

1/2 cup butter

2/3 cup sugar

1 egg, beaten [with a fork]

1 cup apricot purée (use jarred preserves or mashed and pitted fresh apricots)

1 cup dried or fresh blueberries

1/2 cup chopped pecans

Preheat oven to 350°F.

In a medium bowl measure and stir together the flour, cornmeal, baking soda, cinnamon, and salt.

In a smaller bowl cream together the butter, sugar, beaten egg, and apricot purée. Add these wet ingredients to the flour mixture bowl and blend well. Then add blueberries and pecans. Blend all ingredients well.

Drop by teaspoonfuls onto a lightly greased cookie sheet. Bake for 15 to 20 minutes until just barely golden in color. Remove and cool slightly before serving.

Makes about 3 dozen cookies.

From E. Barrie Kavasch. *Enduring Harvests: Native American Foods and Festivals for Every Season.* Old Saybrook, CT: Globe Pequot Press, 1995, p. 169.

Education

From the time they were small, Cherokee children were taught lessons in bravery by having to endure hunger and pain. They were also taught to respect the Earth and other creatures and to honor their elders. A boy was instructed in male roles by his mother's brothers. From them he learned how to hunt, make war, and carry on ceremonies. A girl learned how to care for the house and children by assisting her mother and her mother's sisters. She also learned to weave, garden, and make baskets.

In the late 1700s, the Cherokee Nation developed their own schools. When Sequoyah's writing system spread through the nation, the Cherokee people had a higher literacy rate (meaning more people could read and write) than the settlers who lived nearby in the Southeast. After being forced to move to what is now Oklahoma, the Cherokee reestablished their unique educational system. In the 1840s they started 144 elementary schools and two high schools (called seminaries)—one for men and one for women. The Cherokee Female Seminary was modeled after the very modern-thinking Mount Holyoke Seminary (later Mt. Holyoke College) in Massachusetts. Unfortunately, financial problems later led to the closing of both Native high schools. When the state of Oklahoma was created in the early 1900s, the U.S. Congress abolished the Cherokee school system.

The modern-day Cherokee Nation offers job training and assistance, vocational-technical schools, and child, teen, and adult programs. An Education Department oversees educational opportunities for Cherokee students of all ages. Many Indian groups in the late twentieth century have modeled their own community schools on the school systems created by the Cherokee.

Healing practices

The Cherokee believed that illness came into the world when animals became angry with humans for intruding on their territory and killing them for food. Plants friendly to humans helped cure these animal-caused diseases. The root of white nettle, for instance, was used on open sores; a tea brewed from witch hazel bark was said to cure fevers; tobacco juice was used to treat bee stings and snake bites. Tobacco was looked upon as a powerful medicine—so powerful, in fact, that a lotion made from it could make unhappy wives fall in love with their husbands again.

The Cherokee believed that spiritual help promoted healing. Priests served as doctors; they knew all the proper prayers and chants and the correct methods of applying medicines to the sick. Healers sometimes massaged patients with hands warmed by sacred fire, told them to plunge into a cold stream immediately after a sweat bath, or scratched the victim's body and sucked out the cause of the illness.

The arrival of Europeans in the New World brought a variety of new diseases to which the Indians had no natural immunity. After a series of epidemics killed half the Cherokee population in the first half of the eighteenth century, many Native people lost confidence in their doctor-priests. Tribal members began seeking medical treatment from non-Indian doctors, believing that it took a white doctor to cure a white illness. Still, many of the traditional medicines were effective and are still in use.

The Indian Health Service now operates a hospital on the Eastern Cherokee Reservation. A number of health clinics and community health programs serve the people of the Cherokee Nation, who have access to 30 hospitals in the area where they live.

ARTS

Oral literature

The Cherokee have always used legends to teach children about the history of the tribe and the proper way to live. Stories also explain the workings of the natural world. To preserve this storytelling past, the Tsa-la-gi Library of the Cherokee Nation puts on puppet shows, telling tales of the tribe using Native characters.

Carving and basketry

The Cherokee were known for the beauty of their carvings and basketry. They made tools, pipes, and canoes from materials such as stone and wood. For baskets, they used honeysuckle vine, cane, and a vine called wild hemp, then painted the finished baskets with dyes from various plants and roots.

Theater and museums

Unto These Hills, a modern-day pageant honoring Cherokee history, is performed every year at the Eastern Cherokee Reservation in Cherokee, North Carolina, which also operates the Qualla Arts and Crafts Center. The Cherokee Nation of Oklahoma presents the drama *Trail of Tears* at their open-air theater in Tahlequah, Oklahoma. The Sequoyah Birthplace Museum is Tennessee's only Indian-owned historic attraction; it celebrates the life of the man who invented the Cherokee writing system.

CUSTOMS

Festivals

The Cherokee held six major ceremonies each year, following the course of the Earth's growth and resting periods. The major ceremony, the Green Corn Dance, took place at harvest time and celebrated harmony and renewal. At this time all crimes of the past year (except murder) were forgiven.

Cherokee ceremonies are celebrated at "stomp grounds," sites for religious Stomp Dances. During Stomp Dances, people of all ages perform songs and rhythmic movements that create a sense of peacefulness. The dance is a type of prayer that is performed before a fire. The flame is lit from an ember of a sacred fire—one that never goes out. The stomp ground chief begins a dance and the dancers follow, moving in a winding line and twisting into a spiral as they circle the fire. Girls and women provide the rhythm by shaking turtle shell rattles attached around their legs.

In the late 1990s the annual Cherokee Fall Festival was held on the Eastern Cherokee Reservation. Cherokee Holiday, a week-long celebration of Cherokee history and culture, takes place each year in Tahlequah, Oklahoma. It includes a parade, rodeo, crafts, traditional singing and dancing, Native games, sports tournaments, and Indian feasts.

War and hunting rituals

Dances were held before hunting expeditions. For example, the Buffalo Hunt Dance and Bear Dance, performed by both men and women, showed respect for the animals that would soon be killed.

Cherokee war parties consisted of two to a hundred men. Before going off to war, the Cherokee prepared for several days. Warriors performed special songs and dances and drank a beverage high in caffeine known as "black drink," which was believed to purify their systems by causing them to vomit.

The Cherokee warriors had a reputation for excellence. When staking out an area, they often sent ahead a team of spies wearing animal disguises. The spies scouted the territory and, when they spotted the enemy, made the sounds of the animal whose costume they were wearing, thus alerting their companions to the locations of their foes.

In times of war, Cherokee women could take their husband's place in battle. Women warriors were known as "War Women."

Marriage and divorce

Men and women were required to marry people outside their clan. If a couple decided to divorce, the husband moved back to the home of his mother. Adultery (cheating on one's mate) was considered a very serious offense. Those found guilty of it were subjected to a public whipping by a town official.

Birth

Two days after its birth, a baby was passed over a fire four times by a priest, who asked for blessings for the child. Four to seven days after the baby's birth, the priest took it to a creek or river, offered it to the Creator, prayed for its long and healthy life, then plunged the infant into the water seven times. An elder woman of the tribe would then give the child a name that reflected some physical or personality trait of the infant or that recalled an event that happened at the time of the birth. The child might keep the name for life or take another later, after some great personal achievement.

Funerals

Burials among the Cherokee took place promptly after death, and mourning was a very dramatic affair. Female relatives cried long and loudly, wailing the name of the departed one, and male relatives put on old clothes and placed ashes on their heads. Relatives observed a seven-day mourning period, during which they ate little and could not show anger or good cheer. The deceased's belongings were either buried with the body or destroyed.

A priest performed a cleansing ritual at the house of the deceased and supervised the family's ceremonial bathing. A special hunting party set out to get meat for a feast to help ease the mourners' sorrow. The meal was prepared by family and friends and eaten seven days after the death. Widows were expected to mourn for several months and to neglect their personal grooming. Friends decided when a widow had grieved enough; then they washed her hair and dressed her in clean clothes.

CURRENT TRIBAL ISSUES

According to some Native sources, growing numbers of whites are falsely claiming Cherokee ancestry—posing as descendants of the Cherokee just to take advantage of federal government programs designed for tribal members. Efforts are being stepped up to make sure that such imposters are caught. Meanwhile, the Cherokee Nation of Oklahoma and the Eastern Band of Cherokee are working together to ensure that their language and culture will stay alive for centuries to come.

Since the 1890s the United Keetoowah Band in Oklahoma has set itself apart from the Cherokee Nation. In 1978 the Cherokee Nation tried without success to make the unwilling Keetoowah people part of their tribe. In the late 1990s, as part of their efforts to keep their identity separate from other Cherokee, the Keetoowah were planning a move back to Arkansas, the territory from which they had been forcibly moved more than 175 years earlier.

NOTABLE PEOPLE

Sequoyah (c. 1770-1843), who is believed to have been the son of a part-Cherokee woman and a white man, went by the English name George Guess. He grew up without any formal education and spoke no English. Despite a crippled leg, he fought in two European-led wars. Later he observed whites using written forms of communication. He decided to give his people the same advantage and invented a written language. Sequoyah traveled far and wide teaching the language to his people, and soon thousands of Cherokee could read and write.

Wilma Mankiller (1945–) was elected principal chief of the Cherokee Nation of Oklahoma, making her the first woman to lead a major Indian tribe. She was reelected twice. Robert Latham Owen (1856–1947) was the second Native American elected to the U.S. Senate, serving from 1907 to 1925, and one of the first two senators to represent the state of Oklahoma.

FURTHER READING

Claro, Nicole. *The Cherokee Indians.* New York: Chelsea House Publishers, 1992.

Hoyt-Goldsmith, Diane. *Cherokee Summer.* New York: Holiday House, 1993.

Landau, Elaine. *The Cherokees.* New York: Franklin Watts, 1992.

Perdue, Theda. *The Cherokee.* New York: Chelsea House Publishers, 1989.

Sneve, Virginia Driving Hawk. *The Cherokees.* New York: Holiday House, 1996.

Chickasaw

Name

The name Chickasaw (pronounced *CHICK-uh-saw*) may come from a story of two brothers, Chisca and Chacta, from whom the Chickasaw and the Choctaw tribes are said to be descended (see Oral literature). The English called these Indians "Flat Heads."

Location

The Chickasaw thrived in northeastern Mississippi at the head of the Tombigbee River. They controlled the entire Mississippi River valley as well as parts of western Tennessee and Kentucky and eastern Arkansas. One group was invited by South Carolina officials to settle on the Savannah River near Augusta, Georgia, and did so in 1723. At the end of the twentieth century most Chickasaw were scattered throughout a multi-county area of southern Oklahoma.

Population

In 1693 there were an estimated 10,000 Chickasaw. In 1890, there were 6,400. In a census (count of the population) conducted in 1990 by the U.S. Bureau of the Census, 21,522 people identified themselves as Chickasaw, although the Chickasaw Nation has 35,000 enrolled members. The Chickasaw is the thirteenth largest Native American tribe in the United States.

Language family

Muskogean.

Origins and group affiliations

The Chickasaw tell stories of originating in the West, possibly the Red River valley in Texas, where they were part of the Choctaw tribe. Around the year 1300 c.e. they crossed the Mississippi River and separated from the Choctaw, who became their enemies. In fact, the Chickasaw had few friends; they fought with nearly every tribe that came in contact with them, including the Creek, Caddo, Cherokee, Iroquois, Menominee, Potawatomi, and Shawnee (see entries).

CHICKASAW

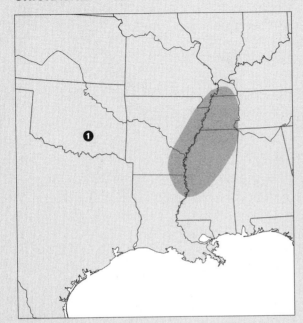

Contemporary Communities

1. Chickasaw Nation, Oklahoma

Shaded area: Traditional Chickasaw lands along the Mississippi River Valley in present-day Mississippi, as well as parts of western Tennessee and Kentucky, and eastern Arkansas.

The Chickasaw were a fierce, warlike people who struck fear into the hearts of all who crossed their path. Their longtime allies, the British, recognized their courage and willingness to take on any foe, no matter how superior the enemy's numbers. The British supplied the Chickasaw generously with weapons and relied on their help to win control of the North American continent. In the late 1700s, when American colonists seized control of the eastern part of North America, the tribe was driven from its ancestral lands. The Chickasaw became part of a group known as the "Five Civilized Tribes," which was forced to move to Oklahoma.

HISTORY

Bad times with Spanish explorers

Long before the arrival of the Europeans, the Chickasaw defended their fertile territory in the Mississippi River valley against any newcomers who dared set their sights on it. Chickasaw men thought of themselves first as warriors, then as hunters, and last as farmers.

In the late winter of 1540 Spanish explorer Hernando de Soto led an expedition into Chickasaw territory, making the first recorded contact with the tribe. The relations between the two groups were uneasy; there was distrust on both sides. The Spanish demanded food and a place to set up a winter camp. Chief Miculasa reluctantly agreed. According to historian Lee Sultzmann, the Spanish shared some of their roast pork from the herd of pigs that traveled with them. The Chickasaw reportedly "loved it" and began to help themselves to Spanish pigs. The Spanish retaliated (paid them back) by killing two of the thieves and cutting off the hands of the third. Tensions mounted, and eventually the Chickasaw launched a surprise attack on the Spanish, driving off de Soto's party. Their victory over the Spanish earned the Chickasaw a reputation across Europe as blood-thirsty warriors. The Spanish left the region in March 1541, never to return.

Allies of the English

English traders based in South Carolina established trading posts along the Mississippi River in 1700, and the Chickasaw became their allies and trading partners. The traders had heard of the tribe's superior fighting ability. In exchange for animal skins and slaves, they supplied the Chickasaw with guns, metal tools, knives, and cotton cloth. The Chickasaw people used the guns for hunting and for carrying out assaults on the French, who were battling Spain and England for control of the North American continent.

To get more skins for trade, the Chickasaw expanded their hunting expeditions into the territory of neighboring tribes, kidnaping their women and children to trade as slaves as they went along. Meanwhile, distant tribes who were being pushed westward by American colonists tried to take over Chickasaw land. Throughout the eighteenth century, the Chickasaw people engaged in almost constant fighting. Frequent contact with the English led many Chickasaw to adopt white ways. The makeup and culture of the tribe changed dramatically as many Chickasaw women married English men and gave birth to children of mixed blood. More cultural changes took place as the tribe willingly adopted refugees from other tribes that had been defeated by the French.

The Chickasaw remained allies of the English (but saw little actual fighting) until England's defeat by the freedom-seeking colonists in the

American Revolution (1775–81). After the war the tribe signed a treaty with the victorious Americans. The Treaty of Hopewell (1786) established the boundaries of Chickasaw territory, and American settlers were to stay off the land. But future conflicts with white settlers—who never seemed to have enough land—were almost guaranteed.

A half-century of treaties reduce homeland

The Chickasaw were struck by a 1784 measles epidemic that killed many of their leaders. Weakened, but still ready to defend their territory, the tribe engaged in a four-decade-long battle with the Creek, the Osage, and others, who were stealing from them and attacking their hunting parties.

Southern tribes had been assured that Americans did not want their land—the white settlers already had plenty. In time, however, all confidence in this pledge to respect Native land rights was dashed. First, neighboring tribes such as the Cherokee, Choctaw, and Creek gave up land to the U.S. government. Then in 1801 the Chickasaw agreed to grant Americans permission to build a road through their homeland. Within eight years some 5,000 Americans were living on Chickasaw land illegally. The U.S. government pressured the Chickasaw to leave and make way for whites. The tribe could see that their control of the region was nearing an end.

In 1832 the first in a series of treaties was signed giving all Chickasaw lands east of the Mississippi River to the U.S. government. The treaties called for the removal of the Chickasaw to "Indian Territory," the land that now forms most of the state of Oklahoma. Over the remaining decades of the nineteenth century the U.S. government moved many tribes to Indian Territory as part of its plan to make the area into a state governed by those tribes (see box in Cherokee entry, "From Indian Territory to the State of Oklahoma").

The Chickasaw wanted their own land in Oklahoma but could find nothing to suit them. They finally decided to lease a portion of land from the Choctaw, their old enemies. And so the Chickasaw became part of the movement of the "Five Civilized Tribes" to Indian Territory. (The Five Civilized Tribes were the Chickasaw, Choctaw,

Seminole, Creek, and Cherokee. They were given this name by their white neighbors because they had established institutions that were valued in white society.)

Removal to Indian Territory

The removal of the five tribes to Indian Territory took nearly 20 years to complete. The Chickasaw were the wealthiest of the five tribes and had greater access to wagons and other time-saving equipment that facilitated relocation efforts. They accomplished their move more quickly than other groups, in only two years (1837–38). A count of the tribe's population taken just before their departure showed 4,914 Chickasaw and 1,156 black slaves. The Chickasaw also took 5,000 horses with them and were plagued most of the way by would-be horse thieves. Throughout the journey many of the tribe's members died from smallpox, malnourishment, or illness brought on by eating spoiled government-supplied food. Among the dead was Chief Tishomingo, the last great Chickasaw war chief, who had lived to the age of one hundred and two.

Conditions in Indian Territory were far from ideal. The region was filled with unhappy ex-warriors from numerous different tribes, many of them longtime enemies. An atmosphere of tension and chaos reigned. Living in Indian Territory on Choctaw land, the Chickasaw argued among themselves and with the Choctaw, who they feared would come to control them. The conflicts were resolved in 1855, when the Chickasaw signed a treaty with the United States that created the land boundaries of an independent Chickasaw district. The next year the Chickasaw people formed their nation. They adopted a constitution and laws, elected Cyrus Harris as their first governor, established a capital city at Tishomingo, and erected various government buildings.

Division over America's Civil War

Though unified as a tribe by 1856, the Chickasaw people soon found themselves divided by conflicting political views. Some members of the tribe were mixed-blood slave holders who had attained great wealth in American business. Others were more traditional full-blooded Chickasaw who took a strong stand against the enslavement of blacks. Matters came to a head with the outbreak of the U.S. Civil War in 1861. Many Chickasaw joined the Northern Union forces to fight against slavery, while the "official" Chickasaw Nation—dominated by so-called mixed-bloods—signed a treaty with the Southern

Confederacy. Many Chickasaw warriors lost their lives in the bloody struggle.

After 1865, with the Civil War no longer a distraction, white settlers cast their eyes on Indian Territory and began to move in, despite laws restricting such actions. They called for a reevaluation of the reservation system, arguing that too much land was being set aside for Indians and that the assimilation process (the Natives' adoption of white American ways) was moving far too slowly.

Allotment of Chickasaw lands

The Chickasaw were the wealthiest and most advanced of the five nations living in Indian Territory. They had developed their oil resources and moved into the cattle industry. But feuds still turned the Chickasaw against each other. After one conflict-filled election, intermarried white Chickasaw citizens were stripped of their citizenship in the Chickasaw Nation. These conflicts did not last long, as the U.S. Congress moved forward with its allotment plans. Allotment called for the division of reservations into small parcels of land. Each Indian would be given an allotment (an individually owned parcel of land) to tend on his or her own, instead of large plots being tended by an entire tribe, as was their custom. Leftover land would be opened up to white settlement.

Chickasaw lands were allotted in 1897. Each full-blood Chickasaw (then 1,538 of the 6,319 Chickasaw population) received 320 acres of land. In 1907, Oklahoma was admitted as the forty-sixth state of the United States. Just prior to this, the Chickasaw Nation was dissolved by the federal government, along with the governments of all five nations of the Civilized Tribes. By 1920 about 75 percent of Chickasaw lands had been either sold to whites or leased. The Chickasaw Nation continued only as a tribal council led by a federally-appointed governor. Many of the Chickasaw people moved away or were assimilated into the local population.

Finally in 1970 Congress granted the Chickasaw tribe the right to elect its own leaders, and the people were able to regroup. Only in the 1990s did the tribe begin to recover from the blow of losing its land to allotment.

As the twentieth century drew to a close a majority of Chickasaw lived scattered throughout several counties in southern Oklahoma. The modern-day Chickasaw Nation is federally recognized, but no Chickasaw reservation exists. (Federally recognized tribes are those

Members of the Chickasaw Nation on the White House steps waiting to present a petition in the 1950s.

with which the U.S. government maintains official relations. Without federal recognition, the tribe does not exist as far as the government is concerned and therefore is not entitled to financial aid or other assistance.)

RELIGION

Everything in the Chickasaw world was filled with religious meaning. Tribal members were closely tied to the Moon and its phases and celebrated the beginning of each lunar cycle. The Chickasaw believed in a supreme being called *Ababinili,* a combination of the Four Beloved Things Above: Sun, Clouds, Clear Sky, and He That Lives in the Clear Sky. The tribe also recognized a host of other lesser powers, witches, and evil spirits. In the old times a priest called a *hopaye* conducted religious ceremonies and explained to his followers the meaning of signs, symbols, dreams, and other events.

The Chickasaw believed in a life after death. They buried their dead facing west—toward the pathway to judgment. The good were said to journey on to a world where they were rewarded for their life's work; the evil, however, would be trapped between worlds, destined to wander in the Land of the Witches.

Baptist, Presbyterian, and Methodist missionaries worked among the Chickasaw after 1819, and today most Chickasaw belong to either the Baptist or Methodist churches.

The Chickasaw came into contact with a variety of religious philosophies late in the nineteenth century. Among them were the Ghost Dance and Peyote (pronounced *pay-OH-tee*) religions. The Ghost Dance movement was initiated by a Pauite named Wovoka. Among the messages it spread were that Indians should love and help one another and return to their traditions. Followers hoped that its dances would bring back to earth dead ancestors and game and that someday things would be restored to the way they were before the white settlers arrived. Followers of the Peyote Religion developed their own ceremonies, songs, and symbols. Peyote is a cactus native to the Southwest. When eaten, it brings on a dreamlike feeling and often produces visions, which followers of the Peyote religion felt moved them closer to the spirit world. Peyote was taken as a sacrament and followers vowed to follow the Peyote Road. They promised to be trustworthy, honorable, and community-oriented. Chickasaw people probably participated in Ghost Dance and Peyote ceremonies held by other Oklahoma tribes.

LANGUAGE

In the eighteenth century the Chickasaw branch of the Muskogean language was the common language used between whites and all Indians living along the Lower Mississippi River. Only about 550 people spoke this language in the 1990s, but many of these speakers were working to teach and preserve the language.

GOVERNMENT

Traditional Chickasaw villages and towns were fiercely independent—only during times of war did the people manage to put aside their differences and unite. Villages were led by a chief called a High Minko, whose position was inherited, and a war chief called a Tishu Minko. Tribal elders and priests served as advisers.

After 1800 Chickasaw leaders authorized mixed-blood members of the tribe to oversee dealings with Americans. The mixed-bloods were well versed in the ways of the whites, and throughout the nineteenth century they advocated the idea of giving up Chickasaw lands to white settlers. Some mixed-blood supporters even received money from the U.S. government for their backing of the plan.

The Chickasaw Nation was dissolved in 1906 by the U.S. government, despite protests by the Chickasaw and even an attempt to form a separate state. Tribal governors were appointed by the U.S. government until Congress granted the Chickasaw the right to elect their own in 1970. At that time the Chickasaw elected Governor Overton James, and under his leadership the modern Chickasaw Nation was born. (See "Economy.")

The Chickasaw Nation describes its current government as a democratic republic, modeled after that of the federal government. Registered voters elect a governor and lieutenant governor to four-year terms. The voters also elect 13 members to the tribal legislature. Three supreme court justices perform duties much like those of the justices of the U.S. Supreme Court (the highest court in the States). The seat of the Chickasaw government is located in Ada, Oklahoma.

ECONOMY

In traditional times, the Chickasaw were mainly hunters; farming was a secondary occupation. After the British arrived, though, the tribe's way of life changed. Extensive trading was carried on, and Chickasaw hunter-warriors became dependent on British guns for their livelihood. The Chickasaw developed their own breed of horse (the Chickasaw Horse, known for its endurance and its long, graceful stride) for conducting trade with the British. In addition, some mixed-blood Chickasaw grew very wealthy running large plantations (farms) powered by black slave labor.

Chickasaw life was thoroughly disrupted after the tribe's removal to Indian Territory, and again by allotment and the abolishment of the tribal government. After a period of readjustment, though, some Chickasaw prospered as the wealthiest and most advanced members of the Five Civilized Tribes. Many remain farmers or cattle and horse raisers.

In the 1970s and 1980s, under the strong leadership of Governor Overton James, the Chickasaw took advantage of state and federal loan programs to encourage tribal self-sufficiency through business ownership. The Chickasaw Nation now operates several gaming centers with bingo—a primary source of money and employment. About 1,300 people are employed by the nation in its various enterprises, which also include a motel, restaurant, smoke shops, a computer equipment and supply company, and trading posts. Businesses cater to tourists at the tribe's historic capital city, Tishomingo, and at sites such as the Chickasaw National Recreation Area, Oklahoma's only national park.

DAILY LIFE

Families

The Chickasaw is a matrilineal tribe; family lines are traced through the women of the tribe. Children usually take their mother's house or clan-name. Men and women of the same house or clan-name are not allowed to marry.

Buildings

Centuries ago Chickasaw families usually owned three buildings: a winter house, a summer house, and a storage building. Some also built special steamrooms called sweat houses, used for purification rites.

The winter house was dug three feet into the ground. Its frame was constructed from pine logs and poles, then covered with clay and plaster made from dried grass for added protection against the cold. These houses were so warm, in fact, that British traders visiting on business often complained about the heat.

The Chickasaw summer house was rectangular. Walls were made of a combination of woven mats and clay plaster, and roofs were made of thatch or bark. The houses had porches, balconies, and a central partition dividing the interior into two rooms. This design was later adopted by the pioneers of the West for their log cabins.

A house at the center of the community was used for meetings and ceremonies. The grounds surrounding this house were used for ceremonies, ball games, and other gatherings.

Chickasaw villages changed in size based on the politics of the time. In times of peace the villages tended to spread out. In times of war, however, the houses and buildings were clustered more closely in fewer, larger villages, often situated in the hills to discourage attackers.

COMANCHE CHICKASAW PLUM BARS

2 eggs, well beaten [with a fork]
1 cup light brown sugar
1/2 cup buttermilk
1 teaspoon vanilla extract
2 cups all-purpose flour
1/4 teaspoon each of salt and allspice
1 cup cooked wild plums, mashed (pits removed)
1 cup chopped pecans or hazelnuts
Powdered sugar to sift over baked plum bars

Preheat oven to 325°F. Grease a 13 x 9-inch baking dish or pan.

In a medium mixing bowl mix the beaten eggs with the brown sugar, buttermilk, and vanilla until the mixture is creamy. Add the flour, salt, and allspice, beating together, then stir in the cooked plums and chopped pecans. Pour this batter into the greased baking dish; spread evenly. Bake for 35 to 40 minutes until golden brown.

Place cooked cake on wire rack until cooled completely. Cut into about 30 bars and dust them well with finely sifted powdered sugar.

Makes about 30 bars.

From E. Barrie Kavasch. *Enduring Harvests: Native American Foods and Festivals for Every Season.* Old Saybrook, CT: Globe Pequot Press, 1995, p. 287.

Clothing and adornment

Europeans noted that Chickasaw men were uncommonly tall for Native Americans, averaging six feet in height, while the women were a foot shorter. Heads were flattened in infancy—this look was considered attractive. The British called the people "Flat Heads."

Men wore breechcloths, garments with front and back flaps that hung from the waist. They were topped with deerskin shirts, robes of bear fur, and deerskin boots in cold weather. Deerskin leggings protected them when they rode through the underbrush. During special ceremonies and when preparing for war, men painted their faces. The most outstanding warriors wore a capelike garment made from swan feathers. The men usually removed their body hair and shaved away the hair along the sides of their heads, leaving a tuft of hair down the center that they kept fixed in place with bear grease. In contrast, Chickasaw women simply tied up their long hair and wore dresses made of deerskin.

Food

In traditional Chickasaw society the men hunted and the women gathered food and raised crops; some Chickasaw women also supervised slaves. The men of the tribe were extremely skilled trackers and trappers. They used animal calls and decoys to lure wild game such as deer, buffalo, and bear. Fish were coaxed out of deep waters with poisoned nuts, then easily speared or netted.

The women gathered and cultivated a variety of wild foods, including strawberries, persimmons, onions, honey, and nuts. They also dried fruits and made tea from different wild roots and herbs.

Education

At birth infant boys were placed on a panther's skin in the hope that they would acquire the animal's fierceness and power. This ritual marked the beginning of their training as warriors. Male children were trained and disciplined by their mother's brother.

At the turn of the twenty-first century the Chickasaw Nation was placing a strong emphasis on the education of its people. Children and adults attended public schools, vocational training centers, and colleges.

Healing practices

The Chickasaw believed that evil spirits caused sickness. Traditional Chickasaw healers, known as *aliktce,* fought these spirits with potions, teas, and poultices (soft, moist substances that are heated, spread on a cloth, and applied to inflamed parts of the body). Healers also conducted the Picofa Ceremony, performing special rites over the sick person four times a day for three days. During the ceremony a fire was kept before the victim's front door; it usually faced east, opposite the Land of the Dead. Only the family members of the sick person were allowed at the service, and they danced around the fire at night. The name "Picofa" is taken from the cracked corn and pork casserole that participants would eat on the third day of the ceremony.

ARTS

Oral literature

Like many other Native peoples, the Chickasaw have a long storytelling tradition that centers on tales of world-ending floods. The Chickasaw also tell creation stories—stories of their origin in the Far West and their migration from there to the New World in ancient times. Tribal lore holds that the Choctaw and the Chickasaw—then one tribe known as the Chickemacaw—migrated over a long period of time, not all at once. They were following two brothers, Chisca and Chacta, who carried a magical pole that leaned eastward. The people settled on the eastern side of the Mississippi River, the place at which the pole stopped its eastward leaning. In *The True Story of Chief Tishomingo,* Cecil Sumners traces the origin of the name "Mississippi" to the cry of a tribal elder. Upon seeing the river the elder is said to have shouted, "Misha-sipo-kni," meaning both "beyond the ages" and "father of waters."

CUSTOMS

Festivals, games, and ceremonies

Like the Seminole and other Southern tribes, Chickasaw men performed a purification ceremony in which they consumed a "black drink"—a potion that contained a large amount of caffeine and made them vomit. In the summer they entertained themselves by playing a particularly violent type of football. The games lasted a full day and involved hundreds of players.

Two major annual festivals are now held by the Chickasaw. One, called the Renewal of Traditions, lasts for two days in July and features the Stomp Dance (a nighttime dance originated by the Seminole), ball games, storytelling, and traditional foods and crafts. The Chickasaw Festival and Annual Meeting—a week-long affair held each September—includes a Princess Pageant, Chickasaw Nation Junior Olympics, and a powwow (a traditional song and dance celebration).

War and hunting rituals

Chickasaw war parties in traditional times were small, consisting of 30 to 50 men. The warriors were best known for their sneak attacks on the enemy. Even after acquiring horses, Chickasaw warriors often traveled on foot because the landscape was heavily wooded.

It was believed that the ghost of a dead warrior would haunt his family until his death was avenged (the person responsible for his death was punished). Often the widows of warriors killed in battle slept directly over the tombs of their dead husbands.

Courtship and marriage

All marriages were arranged by women. If a man decided to take a bride, he sent his mother and/or sister to the chosen girl's family, carrying enough cloth to make at least one dress. If her family agreed to the proposal, the bundle of cloth was presented to the bride-to-be, who sealed the pact by accepting the material. Then a marriage ceremony was held.

When a Chickasaw man married a woman, in a sense he married all of her sisters as well. He could choose to live with all of them. Likewise, if a man died, the man's brother had the right to marry his brother's widow.

The tribe had a strict moral code. Unfaithfulness to a spouse was a serious offense among the Chickasaw—especially if the wife did the cheating. And women who bore children out of wedlock (without being married) were considered a disgrace to their families.

Funerals

In many ways Chickasaw traditions were nearly identical to those of the Choctaw, but the tribes differed in their way of burying the dead. Chickasaw dead were buried beneath their houses among all their worldly possessions. The faces of the dead were painted red, and the bodies were arranged in a sitting position, facing west (the direction of the land of the afterlife).

CURRENT TRIBAL ISSUES

It was only in the last quarter of the twentieth century that the landless Chickasaw Nation was able to move toward self-sufficiency and away from interference by the federal government. The tribe is making great strides in employing its people and educating its children.

NOTABLE PEOPLE

Esteemed Native American Studies professor Linda Hogan (1947–) is a writer and poet whose works reflect ideas and images of Chickasaw life. Other notable Chickasaw include Cherokee/Quapaw/Chickasaw writer and educator Geary Hobson (1941–), a staunch supporter of Native American writing; Puc-caiunla (c. 1760–1838), the last Chickasaw chief to inherit his position from his father; painter and sculptor Bert D. Seabourn (1931–); and anthropologist and museum curator Towana Spivey (1943–).

FURTHER READING

Official Web site of the Chickasaw Nation: [Online] http://www. chickasaw.com/~cnation/index.html.

Sultzmann, Lee. "Chickasaw History." [Online] http://dickshovel. com/chick.html.

Sumners, Cecil L. *The True Story of Chief Tishomingo*. Amory, MS: Amory Advertiser, 1974.

Choctaw

Name

The Choctaw (pronounced *CHOCK-taw*) traditionally called themselves the Chata'ogla or Chata'. The name is apparently a proper name and cannot be translated.

Location

The Choctaw nation thrived in what is now the southeastern United States, largely east central Mississippi. Today, major Choctaw communities are found in southeast Oklahoma and Mississippi; there are smaller ones in Louisiana and Alabama.

Population

There were about 20,000 Choctaw before the coming of the Europeans. In a census (count of the population) done in 1990 by the U.S. Bureau of the Census, 65,321 people identified themselves as Choctaw.

Language family

Algonquian.

Origins and group affiliations

The Choctaw ancestral homeland is in east central Mississippi. During the 1830s a majority of the tribe moved to a large block of land west of the Mississippi. A popular theory holds that many of the Native groups of the southeastern United States were once Choctaw.

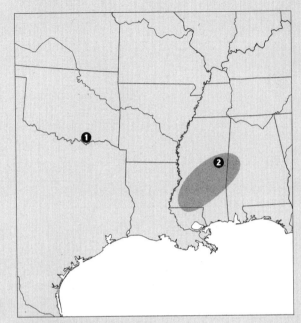

CHOCTAW

Contemporary Communities

1. Choctaw Nation of Oklahoma
2. Mississippi Band of Choctaw Indians

Shaded area: Traditional lands of the Choctaw in east central Mississippi.

The Choctaw were known as a peaceful people. Although ready to defend themselves when challenged, they seldom initiated warfare against neighboring tribes. At one time, Choctaw territory covered more than 23 million acres in Mississippi and in parts of Alabama and Louisiana. As a result of their forced move to Oklahoma in the 1830s, the people now live on two main reservations in Oklahoma and in Mississippi.

HISTORY

A popular Choctaw legend tells how in the distant past a Choctaw leader named Chata led his people on a journey. Chata carried a sacred pole that he placed in the ground at the end of each day's journey. Each morning they found the pole leaning eastward and they continued on, eventually crossing the Mississippi River. One morning they awoke to find the pole standing upright. There they made their sacred mound by burying the remains of their ancestors, which they had carried along with them. Archaeologists (people who study the cultures of ancient peoples by looking at the artifacts, or things they left behind) believe that the mound was the site of tribal political and religious meetings for centuries up until the early 1700s.

The Spanish explorer Hernando de Soto was the first European known to encounter the Choctaw. De Soto and members of his expedition came upon the Choctaw in the 1540s. De Soto demanded women and baggage carriers of the Choctaw, and a fight broke out. Having never seen horses before, the Choctaw were frightened by those of the Spaniards and Choctaw losses were heavy in the battle, but they inflicted some heavy wounds on the Spanish as well. Afterwards, the Spaniards crossed Choctaw land without further incident.

Relations with the French and the Americans

The Choctaw had a better relationship with the French, who established their colony of Louisiana in 1700. The English had made a terrible impression on the Choctaw when their slave raiders operating out of the Carolinas had taken thousands of Choctaw into slavery in the early eighteenth century. But in the 1730s the French wiped out the Natchez, a neighboring tribe. The Choctaw took the survivors in with a newly wary view of the French.

A Choctaw Civil War occurred from 1747 to 1750, pitting those tribal members who wanted to maintain trading relations with the French against those who wanted to begin trading with the English. The war was so severe it wiped out entire villages and severely weakened the Choctaw.

During the American Revolutionary War (1775–83) the Choctaw sided with the Americans. They entered into their first treaty of friendship with them in 1786. When a second treaty was signed in 1801, Americans began to appear in Choctaw country in increasing numbers. In 1805 Americans began to pressure the Choctaw to accept the idea of removing themselves to new homes west of the Mississippi. But the Choctaw remained loyal to the United States. In 1811 the tribe expelled Shawnee leader Tecumseh from their lands when he tried to get them to join a confederacy against the United

IMPORTANT DATES

1540: Hernando de Soto encounters the Choctaw and a battle arises between them.

1786: The Choctaw enter into their first formal treaty with the American government.

1820: Some Choctaw agree to trade a portion of their land for territory west of the Mississippi River.

1830: The Treaty of Dancing Rabbit Creek is signed, resulting in the forced migration of the Choctaw to lands west of the Mississippi.

1918: The Bureau of Indian Affairs establishes the Choctaw Indian Agency in Philadelphia, Mississippi.

1975: Choctaw national administrative offices are established at a historic school building.

1983 : The 1860 Choctaw Constitution is ratified, by which the Choctaw Nation of Oklahoma governs itself.

THE PROMISE

The Choctaw were forced to give up the rest of their lands east of the Mississippi River and move as a nation to Indian Territory by the terms of the Treaty of Dancing Rabbit Creek. Article IV of that treaty secured them this guarantee:

The Government and people of the United States are hereby obliged to secure to the said Choctaw Nation of Red People the jurisdiction and government of all the persons and property that may be within their limits west, so that no Territory or State shall ever have the right to pass laws for the government of the Choctaw Nation of Red People and their descendants; and that no part of the land granted them shall ever be embraced in any Territory or State.

States. They then fought against the Creek in a war that arose when a faction of Creek decided to join Tecumseh's confederacy. They also fought with General Andrew Jackson's army against the British. Despite all this, in 1816 the United States demanded that the Choctaw people give up a great deal of their tribal land.

A painful journey

By 1820, many of the Choctaw agreed to trade some of their traditional territory and move to a large tract of land west of the Mississippi River. However, about 6,000 chose instead to remain on the more than ten million acres of original homeland they retained east of the Mississippi. But in 1830, under the terms of the Treaty of Dancing Rabbit Creek, the Choctaw were forced to give up those remaining lands east of the Mississippi and move as a nation to the West. Their relocation spanned the years from 1831 to 1834. It was part of a larger forced Indian journey from the southeast that came to be known as "The Trail of Tears" for the terrible suffering it imposed on Native peoples. During their journey westward to Indian Territory (land that now forms most of the state of Oklahoma where the U.S. government once planned to move all Indians) many Choctaw children and adults endured starvation and faced bitter cold. Nearly one-half of the tribe died along the way.

During the mid-1850s, the Choctaw in the West were able to build a stable economy, started a public school system, and governed themselves by their own laws, in a process similar to that of their American neighbors.

Choctaw resettle in Oklahoma

Because they had sided with the southern states during the American Civil War (1861–65) the U.S. government forced the Choctaw to sell their western lands. The treaty they signed in 1866 granted a right-of-way for railroad companies to build tracks that crossed over the territory where the Choctaw lived. News of a railroad brought more white settlers. By 1890, American settlers on Choctaw land outnumbered tribal members by three-to-one.

Around 1900 the Choctaw, along with other tribes, were forced to resettle in a different region of the rapidly changing territory. Each nation was forced to accept individual allotments, rather than holding the land in common as was the long-held tradition. By 1907, when Oklahoma became a state, the Choctaw Nation was dissolved and its members were required to become citizens of that state.

Choctaw in the twentieth century

Once they settled in Oklahoma, the language and culture of the Choctaw flourished. However, the outbreak of influenza (a fast-spreading, often fatal illness at that time) during World War I (1914–18) killed twenty percent of the Choctaw population in Oklahoma. The country's allotment policies, which broke up tribal lands into individual parcels that could be sold, proved to be disastrous for the Choctaw. Within one generation most of the allotted land passed from Choctaw ownership to white ownership, and often through fraud.

The Mississippi Choctaw

While the majority of Choctaw were forced to move west by the Indian Removal Act, about 6,000 Choctaw stayed in Mississippi. Under the terms of the removal treaty, the remaining Choctaw could take individual parcels of land (only 69 Choctaw heads of households, however, were allowed to register for the Mississippi land). Most of the Choctaw in Mississippi lost everything they owned and became squatters in their former land. Many eventually moved west to join the relocated tribe.

In 1918 the Bureau of Indian Affairs opened the Choctaw Indian Agency in Philadelphia, Mississippi. The agency established schools in impoverished Choctaw communities and offered other forms of financial assistance. During the early twentieth century, the boll weevil (a type of beetle that destroys cotton plants) infested the crops in east central Mississippi, bringing down the economy of the region and inflicting great hardship on the Choctaw who lived there. In the second half of the twentieth century, wise and dynamic tribal leadership helped improve the economic conditions of tribal groups in both the East and West.

Choctaw today

During the 1970s the Choctaw chief Hollis Roberts struggled to reestablish the sovereign (independent and self-governing) political authority of the Choctaw Nation. In 1975 Choctaw national administrative offices were established at the historic Presbyterian College building in Durant, Oklahoma, which had once served as a school for

COMMON CHOCTAW EXPRESSIONS

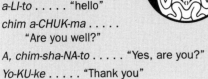

HO-ka hay . . . . .
    "all right"

a-LI-to . . . . . "hello"

chim a-CHUK-ma . . . . .
    "Are you well?"

A, chim-sha-NA-to . . . . . "Yes, are you?"

Yo-KU-ke . . . . . "Thank you"

Indian youth. In 1981 the federal government finally recognized the 1860 Choctaw Consititution and it was ratified (approved) by the Choctaw people in 1983. Today the Choctaw Nation of Oklahoma provides programs for its 80,000 people in areas such as economic development, housing, the environment, job training, health, food distribution, and recreation, as well as programs for the elderly. Money earned from their tourist facilities helps the tribe today in its efforts to survive and flourish.

RELIGION

Although the Choctaw believed in spiritual beings, they did not worship a single Supreme Being. They considered the Sun to be a very powerful force. Tribal members often consulted with certain people who were said to possess special powers. These included healers, rainmakers, and prophets. Medicine men were expected to predict future events, instill bravery in warriors, and help inspire a successful hunt.

The Choctaw believed that two kinds of souls survived after a person's death. The first frightened survivors at night or assumed the form of an animal. The second was an inner spirit, which began its journey to the afterworld immediately after death.

The afterworld had two sections, a good and a bad, separated by a mountainous barrier. An individual could be damned to the bad section for offenses such as murder, telling lies that led to another person's committing murder, divorcing a pregnant wife, or gossiping.

LANGUAGE

The Choctaw language is also called Choctaw-Chickasaw. It is closely related to the Creek language. Both are classified as Western Muskogean and are part of the Great Algonquian language family. When they were questioned in 1987, half of the Choctaw people (about 12,000) said they still spoke their native language.

The Choctaw have always excelled at public speaking. They often indicate their agreement to a proposal by saying "hoka hay." A popular legend claims that during negotiations with the Choctaw, President Andrew Jackson, imitating this phrase, would frequently say "okay," and that expression is now used by people all around the world.

GOVERNMENT

The traditional Choctaw tribe had many subgroups or bands. The eldest male of each band, or *ogla,* was recognized as the chief. The ogla was consulted to provide wisdom and teaching, and played a major role in ceremonies and celebrations.

Today, the government of the Oklahoma Choctaw is run by the tribal council, made up of a chief and twelve representatives. The Mississippi Choctaw Reservation is governed by a sixteen-member council. The chief, who is also the chief executive, serves for four years and presides over meetings of the council, which take place four times a year.

ECONOMY

For centuries, Choctaw men, women, and children cultivated the river floodplains on which they lived. The Choctaw tribe held all their land in common, but individuals could claim a field as long as they could cultivate it and did not interfere with fields already claimed by other members of the tribe. If a field was abandoned by an individual, control over it reverted to the tribe.

Today, the tourism industry employs many Choctaw. The greatest economic gains to the two major Choctaw tribes have been provided by high-stakes bingo. The Oklahoma Choctaw Nation's Choctaw Bingo Place in Durant, Oklahoma, draws busloads of bingo players every day from as far away as Dallas, Texas. Begun in 1994, the Mississippi Choctaw tribe's Silver Star Casino generates about $100 million annually. Their Arrowhead Resort, with its 2,000-seat convention center, was under construction in the late 1990s. Mississippi tribal members are also employed in manufacturing and agriculture, and operate an industrial park.

Tribal industries of the Oklahoma Choctaw include a fishing plant, a shopping center, a travel plaza, and the operation of a health center. The Choctaw Nation also runs a tribal newspaper called *Bishinik.* The tribal government employs more than 1,400 people, making it the largest single employer of Choctaw.

In the mid-1990s the unemployment rate on the Oklahoma reservation stood at more than 13 percent (this means that 13 percent

CHOCTAW POPULATION: 1990

The U.S. Census reported 82,299 Choctaw in the United States in 1990, with 26,884 living in Oklahoma. The Mississippi Band of Choctaw reported 9,050 Choctaw in its territory in 1995. Choctaw identified themselves as follows:

Tribe	Population
Choctaw	65,321
Mississippi Choctaw	2,624
Mowa Band of Choctaw, Alabama	947
Oklahoma Choctaw	17,323
Other Choctaw	16

A Choctaw family living at an ancient site in 1961.

of people who wanted to work could not find work). The per capita income was very low—about $6,200, compared to about $20,000 for the United States population as a whole. (Per capita income is the average income one person earns per year.)

DAILY LIFE

Families

The rhythm of Choctaw family life was based on the growing season. In midwinter, the men cleared the growing fields by burning the underbrush. In spring, they planted crops using cedar spades and shovels, and hoes made of flint or bone. When they were not farming, the men fished and hunted wild game. Boys were trained to hunt with bows and arrows. Children, women, and old people gathered fruits, plants, and nuts.

Daughters were brought up by their mothers. Sons were brought up by their mothers' brothers, because they were the closest of the boy's male relatives within his clan (a group of related families that forms the basic social unit of the Choctaw society).

Buildings

The Choctaw lived in circular lodges. The frames were made of sticks, and palmetto thatches covered the tops and sides. Each lodge had one door that generally faced south. There was an open fire in the middle of the structure, and an opening in the roof allowed smoke to escape. Many persons lived in one lodge.

Clothing and adornment

Choctaw men wore belts and loincloths, adding moccasins, leggings, and garments from feathers or mulberry bark in winter. Women wore short deerskin skirts, adding deerskin shawls and moccasins when the weather got colder. The Choctaw wore decorated garments, earrings, and feathers of bright colors. Both men and women wore face paint and tattoos. Below their knees, men wore strings of bells they obtained from traders. Men wore their hair long, with bangs and braids. Women had long hair and wrapped it into a roll on the backs of their heads.

Food

The Choctaw hunted bear, turkey, deer, and other animals. They also caught trout and shrimp, which, along with bear, were eaten fresh or were dried for future consumption.

The Choctaw people gathered berries that were eaten fresh, and grapes and crabapples that were dried. Their primary crops were squash and corn, which were used in their most common dishes.

Education

In earlier centuries, Choctaw boys and girls were trained in the use of blowguns for hunting small game, such as squirrels, rabbits, and birds. The blowguns were pieces of cane, about seven feet long, out of which they blew sharp cane darts. Until firearms were introduced, Choctaw youth were taught how to use bows and arrows to hunt larger game. They also learned to catch fish with traps.

From the mid- to late-1800s, the Oklahoma Choctaw group had a thriving school system. Unfortunately, when the Choctaw Nation was abolished in 1907, the Choctaw became citizens of Oklahoma, and their good school system also ended.

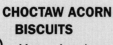

CHOCTAW ACORN BISCUITS

Many American tribes, including the Choctaw, harvest acorns. They are gathered when the brown-shelled nuts start falling from the trees. Sweet acorns, like those from the white oak, can be eaten raw. Other varieties contain a tannic acid, which tastes bitter. It must be leached out of the acorns. You cover the acorns with water and bring them to a boil. Boil them for 30 minutes, drain, add fresh water, and continue the process several times until the boiling water becomes very light in color and the bitter taste is gone. Then dry the nutmeats in the sun or in a 150° F. oven. When dried, the nutmeats should be chopped into a coarse meal for use in the recipe.

1/2 cup acorn meal

1/2 cup whole wheat flour

1 1/2 teaspoons baking powder

1/4 teaspoon salt (optional)

2 Tablespoons lard, chilled, or 1 Tablespoon each, chilled butter and vegetable shortening. About 3 Tablespoons milk.

Preheat oven to 400° F.

In a mixing bowl, combine dry ingredients. Add lard and crumble with fingertips or a pastry blender until mixture resembles coarse meal. Stir in milk. Turn dough onto a lightly floured work surface and pat out until 1/2 inch thick. Cut out 1 1/2-inch biscuits.

Reduce oven to 375° F. Place biscuits on a greased baking sheet and bake for 12 to 15 minutes, until golden.

Serve with jelly. Makes 10 to 12 biscuits.

From Beverly Cox and Martin Jacobs, *Spirit of the Harvest.* New York: Stewart, Tabori & Chang, 1991, p. 37

The U.S. government started schools for the impoverished Mississippi Choctaw people in the 1920s. Still, the educational level of the average Mississippi Choctaw remains low. Gambling casino profits have helped the Mississippi Band to establish a Choctaw school, which offers courses in Choctaw language, history, and arts.

Healing practices

The Choctaw treated diseases with plants and herbs, sometimes through the aid of medicine men. They boiled various roots to make medicines, wash wounds, treat snake bites, fight pneumonia, treat fever, and guard against smallpox.

The Choctaw wrapped themselves in several layers of cloth and drank hot tea to sweat disease out of the body. To cure stomach pains and arthritis they pressed a small compress onto the area of discomfort. They treated broken bones with wraps and splints.

ARTS

Choctaw music stresses the importance of living in harmony with nature. Most Choctaw dances took place in an open field to the beat of drums and striking sticks. Three major types of Choctaw dances have been preserved. Animal dances are dances held to honor various birds and animals. The Green Corn Dance, held in late summer, looks forward to a bountiful corn harvest. Both men and women participate in the Choctaw war dance, which in past centuries took place for the eight days prior to a battle. A chanter, often a young man, leads songs for dances. He begins with a shout and the other dancers join in the dance song.

Collectors prize Choctaw swamp cane baskets. The double-weave basket, a sort of basket within a basket, is the most favored. Family members usually pass down basketry skills. For centuries, Choctaw women have created a unique style of beadwork design that features double-curved scrolls and other elements of prehistoric Choctaw ceramics and shells.

CUSTOMS

Festivals

Traditionally, the Choctaw did not go in for spectacular ceremonies, religious or otherwise. Today, though, they host one of the top Native American events in the Southeast, July's Choctaw Fair, held in Philadelphia, Mississippi. The fair features traditional tribal ceremonies and dances, ethnic foods, stickball games, and a craft fair. Oklahoma's Annual Choctaw Festival draws nearly 10,000 visitors. It takes place at the historic Old Capitol building that now serves as a Council house and museum. Activities include a princess pageant, cultural ceremonies, Native foods, arts and crafts, sports, and musical entertainment.

Commemoration

Every year in Skullyville, Oklahoma, on the first Saturday of June, members of the Choctaw tribe meet to commemorate the forcible removal of their people from their eastern homelands in Mississippi and Louisiana. They honor the thousands of Choctaw people who suffered and died in the early 1830s during the relocation journey that is called the "Trail of Tears." In addition to a symbolic reenactment of the walk, present-day Choctaw listen to speakers, eat Native American foods, and perform tribal dances.

Women

Choctaw culture was, in many respects, matriarchal (the mother ruled the family). Although men were warriors, war chiefs, and diplomats, women did the decision-making during times of peace.

Tul-Lock-Chísh-ko, "He Who Drinks the Juice of the Stone," a Choctaw ball player in full dress.

Speech-making

The Choctaw were especially accomplished public speakers. When a formal debate was to take place, a large brush arbor was constructed with a hole in the center of the roof. Those wishing to speak stood beneath the hole in the full heat of the southern sun, while the audience remained comfortably seated in the shade. The idea was that audience members could bear to listen as long as the speaker could stand in the heat and speak.

Games

Recreation was very important to the tribe. *Ishtaboli,* or stickball, was (and still is) a favorite sport and was sometimes used to settle disputes. The object of the game was to sling a leather ball from a webbed pocket at the end of a long stick so that it hit the opponent's goal at the end of the playing field, which was often a mile or longer. Tackling was one way of stopping the opponent. The Choctaw were very adept at handling, throwing, and passing the ball. The games were rough and sometimes resulted in serious injury or death, but no one was punished.

Courting and marriage

According to their courting customs, when a young man found himself alone with the woman he loved, he would come within a few yards of her and toss a pebble. If she smiled, it meant she approved of the courtship. If she disapproved, she gave him a scornful look. Another method a young man might use in courting was to enter the woman's lodge and lay his hat or handkerchief on her bed. If she approved, she would allow the item to remain. If she disapproved, she removed it from the bed. If they both agreed to the union, the couple arranged a time and place for the marriage ceremony.

During a marriage ceremony, the families of the couple stood about 100 yards from one another. The brothers of the woman approached the man and seated him on a blanket. The man's sisters went to the woman and did likewise. Sometimes, for fun, the woman pretended to run away and had to be brought back. The woman's family set a bag of bread near her, and the man's family set a bag of meat next to him (indicating the man's role as hunter and the woman's as gatherer). Friends and relatives of the man then showered gifts over the head of the woman, which her family members grabbed and distributed among themselves. The gifts usually consisted of clothing, money, and household items. The couple, now man and wife, then rose together and everyone went to a feast. Afterwards, the man took his wife to his lodge.

Death

The Choctaw believed that the soul was immortal, and that the spirit of the deceased person lingered near their corpse for some days after death. In ancient times the body at death was wrapped in skins and bark and placed on a platform with food and drink nearby. After some days, people who grew long fingernails especially for the task would thoroughly remove the rotting flesh from the bones of the dead person. The bones were then given to grieving relatives, who painted the skull red and placed it in a coffin. The flesh and platform were often burned, or the flesh was buried.

In more recent times, a Choctaw person after death was dressed in special ceremonial clothing that was worn for viewing by the community. The clothes, which were handed down from one generation to another, were not buried with the person. Often, a hunter's gun was placed in his grave next to his body. Mourning periods were based on the age of the deceased and varied from three months for children to up to a year for parents.

CURRENT TRIBAL ISSUES

Although the two largest Choctaw groups—the Choctaw Nation of Oklahoma and the Mississippi Band of Choctaw—have received federal recognition, other Choctaw groups, such as the Mowa Choctaw of Alabama, are seeking federal recognition.

The Mississippi Choctaw have been successful in luring industries and businesses to the reservation, since the construction of an industrial park in 1973. Large corporations have opened businesses there that employ about 1,000 Choctaw. The Oklahoma Choctaw have also established successful tribal industries.

Both the Mississippi and Oklahoma Choctaw have established housing authorities that have provided the reservations with affordable modern housing. The greatest economic gain on both reservations has been high-stakes bingo.

NOTABLE PEOPLE

Pushmataha (1764–1824) was a Choctaw warrior, statesman, and chief. Pushmataha was very loyal to the United States. He refused to join the Shawnee Chief Tecumseh in an Indian confederacy against the whites, and signed a treaty ceding lands in Alabama and Mississippi to the United States. Rosella Hightower (1920–), an internationally known ballerina, has also directed ballet and opera companies. Educator Linda Lomahaftewa (1947–) is a painter whose works highlight the culture of the Plains Indians. Her artwork has been featured at a variety of exhibitions throughout the country.

Choctaw Chief Philip Martin (1926–) has promoted the self-sufficiency and economic development of the Choctaw. Chief Hollis E. Roberts fought for his people to become a self-governing nation. As a result of his efforts, the Choctaw Nation of Oklahoma, composed of more than 80,000 people, is governed by the terms of their 1860 Choctaw Constitution.

FURTHER READING

"Choctaw Nation History." Choctaw Nation Home Page: [Online] http://www. toners.com/choctaw/history1.htm.

Lepthien, Emilie U. *The Choctaw.* Chicago: Children's Press, 1987.

McKee, Jesse O. *The Choctaw.* New York: Chelsea House Publishers, 1989.

Creek

Name

Creek. The Muscogee (as they called themselves) were named "Creek" by the English because they lived along the fertile creeks of Alabama and Georgia. The term Muscogee identifies them with land that is wet or likely to flood.

Location

The early Creek, a union of several tribes, lived on lands in present-day Alabama, Georgia, Florida, and South Carolina. By 1832 the U.S. government pressured the tribes to move west of the Mississippi River. While some of the people remained in Alabama (and live there today as the Poarch Creek Band), many eventually settled in Oklahoma, where members of the largest group, called the Muscogee Nation, now reside.

Population

There were about 10,000 Creek in the early 1700s. In a census (count of the population) done in 1990 by the U.S. Bureau of the Census, 44,168 people identified themselves as members of the Creek tribe, the tenth most-populous Native American tribe in the country.

Language family

Muskogean.

Origins and group affiliations

The early Creek may have been descendants of prehistoric people of what is now the southeast United States. The original Creek Confederacy was made up of the Alibamu, Coushatta, Muscogee, and other groups. Modern Creek live in Alabama, and are scattered around the southeast. Oklahoma is home to four main groups of Creek.

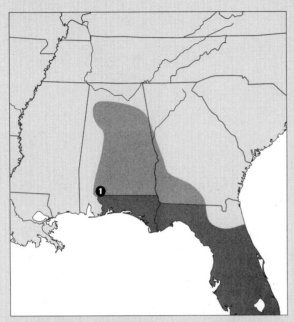

CREEK

Contemporary Communities

1. Poarch Creek Indians, Alabama

(Not on map: Muscogee Creek
Nation, Oklahoma)

Dark Shaded area: Traditional Creek lands in present-day Alabama, Georgia, and South Carolina.

Light Shaded area: Creek land in Florida that became the land of the Seminole.

The Creek were one of the "Five Civilized Tribes," a name the Europeans gave to the Cherokee, Chickasaw, Choctaw, Creek, and Seminole because they established many institutions valued by Europeans. The Creek were farmers and traders and were once one of the dominant tribes in the mid-south. The Creek Confederacy, an alliance of independent tribes, was established to resist attacks by other Northern tribes. The size of the alliance changed constantly as tribes entered or left it. Because of this, historians can't make general statements about a "typical" Creek tribe. It is known that Creek society was balanced and harmonious, and members had a large degree of personal freedom.

HISTORY

Settling in the Southeast

Old legends of the Creek tell of ancestors who migrated to the Southeast from the Southwest. Many archaeologists (people who study ancient cultures by looking at artifacts, or the things that were left behind) believe that the Creek are descendants of people who moved into North America thousands of years ago. They may have been Maya Indians from Mexico and Central America who merged peacefully with other Native American people already living in what would become the United States.

The first contact with Europeans took place about 1539, when Spanish explorer Hernando de Soto came to their region. Disagreements arose between the Spaniards and the Natives. Chief Tuscaloosa of the Choctaw (see entry), a member of the Creek confederacy, organized an ambush. Even though it ended in a defeat for the Natives, it still dealt a severe blow to the Europeans.

IMPORTANT DATES

1539: Creek are defeated in their first encounter with Europeans.

1775: Many Creek support the British during the American Revolutionary War.

1814: With the end of the Red Stick War, the Creek lose much of their remaining land.

1830: The Indian Removal Act authorizes the U.S. government to move the Creek off their land.

1971: The Muscogee (Creek) Nation conducts its first federally recognized principal chief election in the twentieth century.

Creek lands reduced

In time, the Creek found themselves in the midst of territories claimed by the Spanish, the French, and the English. English traders frequently married Creek women and their wives taught them Native customs and language. The children of these mixed marriages, who understood both cultures, often rose to positions of leadership in the tribe.

Because some of the Creek became allies of the British during the American Revolution (1775–83), the new U.S. government demanded the tribe give up some of their land. An agent was appointed to influence the Indians to adapt the white lifestyle and become "civilized." A violent split developed between the Creek factions who were willing to cooperate and those who were not. The Red Stick War (1812–14) between the Creek and the whites turned into a Creek civil war, waged between those who opposed the U.S. government's "civilization" program and those who supported it. The war ended with the Battle of Horseshoe Bend in 1814. In that conflict some Creek joined American forces and defeated the Creek who opposed being forced to assimilate, or blend into the white culture. In the peace treaty that followed, the Creek had to give up 23 million acres of land, two-thirds of what they possessed.

Creek people move west

Treaties signed by the Creek in 1832 and 1836 gave the United States possession of virtually all Creek lands. In exchange the Creek

The Creek Council House, Indian Territory, c. 1880.

were given lands in present-day Oklahoma in what was then called "Indian Territory." Once again, Creek opinion was divided. Some people refused to leave their homes, while others, believing they had no choice, voluntarily left the Southeast. Finally, in 1836 and 1837, the U.S. Army oversaw forced relocation of most of the remaining Creek. Dressed in clothing that was inadequate for the winter weather, the Creek walked hundreds of miles. Thousands died—some on the journey and some during the first few months in their new home. Eventually they learned how to adapt to the unfamiliar weather and lived peacefully beside the Plains Indians.

Muscogee adopt constitution

Historically, Creek communities had been divided geographically into upper and lower towns. The Creek lower towns in Oklahoma were located closer to Euro-American settlements. The greater interaction with the newcomers led the people of the lower town to become more open to changes in traditional ways. The upper town Creek remained more loyal to the old ways.

Opothleyaholo, an Upper Creek chief, worked hard to make the removal process to Oklahoma as successful as possible for his people. The American Civil War (1861–65) interrupted the settling-in process. Although Opothleyaholo spoke up for neutrality (non-involvement), attacks by the Southern Army against his people forced the Creeks to become involved in the Civil War. Once again the Creek were divided. Most Lower Towns allied themselves with the South while the Upper Towns generally supported the North. After the war, the Creek were forced to give up half of their land in Indian Territory for supporting Southern soldiers.

Tribal land broken up

Two pieces of legislation by the U.S. Government disrupted Creek society. The Dawes General Allotment Act of 1887 required shared tribal land to be allotted (divided into lots owned by individuals, a departure from traditional Creek practice of owning land in common). The tribal government in Oklahoma was dismantled by the Curtis Act in 1898. This act enforced allotment, did away with tribal courts, and required that all laws that were passed by tribal governments be approved by the president of the United States.

Chitto Harjo and the Crazy Snake Uprising

Tribal spokesperson Chitto Harjo was outraged at the notion that an external organization could dissolve his nation. Demanding that the federal government honor the Treaty of 1832 that promised the Creek a specified amount of land and self-government in Oklahoma, Harjo became part of a movement to organize an alternative government. The Crazy Snake Uprising (named after an English translation of the name Harjo) was an effort to resist further encroachment by the white settlers and government policies. Several years of turmoil followed, in which Harjo presented his opposition directly to a select Senate committee. But tension mounted until Harjo's death in 1911 or 1912.

During the mid-1930s the federal government did away with some of its policies designed to dissolve Indian tribes. A 1970 law opened the way for adoption of a new Creek Nation constitution in 1979. The Creek people were divided between those who supported the 1979 constitution and those who wanted to keep the 1867 constitution. Supporters of the new constitution won.

Today the Creek are thriving, though most must leave the reservation to work. The social services the tribe provides to its members are described by the Bureau of Indian Affairs as "the best in the nation."

RELIGION

The Creek religion centered on a single god known as the Master of Breath. All creations (such as the Sun, Moon, and planets) and living creatures were considered different forms of this Great Spirit. The Creek believed that living a good life would be rewarded. They had special prophets who conferred with the gods to diagnose disease and predict the future. Daily bathing in a nearby stream was an important part of their religious rites.

After Europeans arrived, missionaries of various denominations tried to convert the Creek to Christianity. Many of those who were converted during the eighteenth century either concealed their conversion or left the community to escape punishment by people who honored only the old ways. Eventually, some Creek towns accepted Christianity. At that point, the church replaced the town square as the focal point of activity, and the Christian town preacher replaced the town chief. Today, Creek are still divided between those following their ancestral religion and those who have adopted Christianity. Most Christian Creek are members of the Baptist, Methodist, or Presbyterian churches.

LANGUAGE

The Creek language is part of the Muskogean group, which includes the languages of the Chickasaw, Choctaw, Tuskegee, Alabama, Natchez, Miccosukee, and Seminole tribes. It was the most common tongue among members of the Creek confederacy. Early European traders had to learn the melodious language, for most Creek showed no interest in adopting the harsh tones of English. Early Creek words had few vowels and most contained the letter "k." During the early eighteenth century, some Creek stopped speaking their language. To be recognized as Indian meant being forced to leave their homes, and therefore some tried to hide their Indian identities.

A system for writing the Creek language was devised by missionaries in the 1840s. The first published works were the Bible and other religious books. The Creek started a cooperative publishing company that printed a periodical called *Indian Journal,* which addressed the tribes' viewpoints on current events. The Poarch Creek in Alabama no longer speak the Muscogee language, but some groups in Oklahoma continue to speak it.

GOVERNMENT

For centuries Creek towns were governed by a chief. His duties included greeting official visitors, overseeing the storage of the food supply, and representing the town before other groups. A council made up of older men assisted the chief in ceremonies and helped him make decisions about warfare.

In 1867 the Muscogee Nation adopted a new constitution. It was made up of an executive branch headed by the principal chief, a legislative branch composed of a House of Kings and a House of Warriors, and a judicial branch. In 1971 the Muscogee (Creek) Nation elected a principal chief who was recognized by the federal government (that is, the federal government agreed to have dealings with him). In 1979 they ratified a new constitution. The principal and second chief are elected every four years. Members of the national council are elected every two years. A judicial branch of the council operates a tribal court system.

ECONOMY

From the early days, the labor of men and women was considered equally important. The women worked in the fields, tilling the soil with sharp sticks and hoes fitted with points made of stone or sharpened bone. Children helped the women to gather berries, roots, nuts, herbs, and plants. Men caught fish with bows and arrows. They also trapped fish, sometimes stunning them with a special poison. Groups of men also hunted in the forests for deer, bear, and rabbit. During the seventeenth century the Creek began to trade deerskins for guns, ammunition, cloth, metal pots, and other items.

As of the 1990s one of the major sources of employment and money within the Muscogee Creek Nation has been gambling in its three bingo halls. Profits have provided the people with college funds,

POPULATION OF CREEK TRIBES: 1990

There are four main groups of Muscogee in Oklahoma. The largest group of Creek, the Muscogee (Creek) Nation, is a non-reservation tribe whose people are located in ten counties across the state. The other three are the Alabama Quassarte Tribal Town, the Kialegee Tribal Town, and the Thlopthlocco Tribal Town. The Poarch Creek Indians are descendants of the original Creek who remained in the southeast. The Poarch Reservation is located in Porch, Alabama. Other small groups are located throughout the Southeast.

In the 1990 census, members of the various Creek tribes identified themselves this way:

Tribe	Population
Alabama Quassarte	180
Creek	44,168
Eastern Creek	589
Lower Muskogee	180
MaChis Lower Creek Indian	64
Poarch Band	498
Principal Creek Indian Nation	56
Thlopthlocco	102
Other Creek	35

SOURCE: "1990 census of population and housing. Subject summary tape file (SSTF) 13 (computer file): characteristics of American Indians by tribe and language." Washington, DC: U.S. Department of Commerce, Bureau of the Census, Data User Services division, 1995.

programs for the elderly, and youth activities. The Nation operates about 400 acres of farmland, raising mostly soybeans. Tribal grazing lands feed about 200 cattle. Manufacturing provides jobs for twenty Natives. The tribal government, which employs about 850 people, is the largest employer.

The Muscogee Nation has also undertaken such economic development projects as operating a farm and running stores selling tobacco-related products. During the mid-1990s the unemployment rate stood at about 9.3 percent (more than 9 people out of 100 who wanted to work were not able to find work). This is a fairly low figure compared to other reservations. The per capita income for the tribe was $8,372, compared to about $20,000 for the average American worker. (Per capita income is the average income one person earns in one year).

The federally recognized Poarch Band of Creek Indians community in Alabama is seeking access to more jobs, and trying to provide members with the necessary education and training to do the jobs.

DAILY LIFE

Families

Families, who lived together in groups of buildings called compounds, all belonged to the same clan (a group of related families). Creek clans included the Wind, Bird, Alligator, and Bear clans. Creek traced their family lines through the mother. Children were counted as part of their mother's clan. They were considered related to her relatives, but not to the relatives of their father.

The duties in Creek families were assigned by gender. Women performed household chores and made cooking utensils, storage vessels, and clothing. Men built houses, provided materials for clothing, and performed military functions. Women raised the children, but fathers maintained an emotional tie to their children. Hide and fur trading was a cooperative effort, with men hunting the animals and women tanning and dressing the skins.

Buildings

The heart of every Creek town was an open square. The square was known as the "stomp grounds." It was the site of warm-weather meetings of the town council, the Green Corn Ceremony, and other ceremonial dances. In winter, town council meetings were held in a circular structure about 40 feet in diameter with a cone-shaped roof rising 25 feet into the air. It served as a social gathering place during bad weather and a shelter for the aged and homeless. Each town had a 200- to 300-yard-long playing field where a lacrosse-style game was played. (Lacrosse is a game of Native American origin. It is played on a field by two teams of ten players each. Participants use a long-handled stick with a webbed pouch to try and get a ball into the opposing team's goal.) The games were also used as a way of settling disputes between towns. A pole about 40 feet tall stood in the center of the game field. A target on the top was used for spear or archery practice.

Each Creek family home was made up of a cluster of buildings. They may have included a kitchen, a granary/storehouse, a building for sleeping during the summer, and another for sleeping during the winter. Some had a separate warehouse. Vertical poles supported the building's peaked roof made of grass or cypress bark shingles. Walls were sometimes added by weaving split saplings (young trees) between the poles and coating this framework with several inches of plaster made from clay and straw. Beginning in the late eighteenth century, the Creek began building log cabins.

Clothing and adornment

Because of the warm climate, the Creek generally did not wear much clothing. Even in winter, their windowless houses were kept so warm with their hearth fires that there was little need for additional garments. The men wore breechcloths (deerskin pieces that hung from thin rawhide belts). They might add grass blankets or deerskin leggings in colder weather. Women wore shawls and skirts made from grass, deerskin, or bark, sometimes adding fur blankets in winter. Most children wore no clothing until they reached puberty. After seeing European products brought by traders, the Creek quickly added cotton, linen, and wool textiles to their wardrobes. They also learned to weave and dye cloth.

Although their clothing was simple, the Creek used a great deal of body ornamentation. Both men and women used porcupine needles dipped in dark blue dye to tattoo designs over most of their bodies. They also liked to paint their faces and bodies. Men removed facial hair by plucking; some also plucked hairs from their head, leaving a long lock down the middle that they braided with feathers or other decorations. Deerskin turbans were also popular among men. Women wore their long hair wrapped around the head, fastened with silver jewelry. Neck ornaments and earrings for both genders were fashioned from shell, coral, bones, silver, and copper. Beads, silk

A SWEET AND NUTTY FINISH TO DINNER

Wild foods such as hickory nuts were a Creek staple. Author E. Barrie Kavasch offered this recipe for a custard-like dessert. He concocted it based on the recollections of a noted Creek artist, Acee Blue Eagle, and others.

Simi Chumbo

1 pint whole milk

4 heaping Tablespoons fine yellow cornmeal

2 Tablespoons honey or maple syrup

1 cup hickory nuts, finely chopped

1/2 cup pecans, coarsely chopped

1/4 teaspoon each of salt and allspice

2 Tablespoons sweet [unsalted] butter or walnut oil

3 large eggs, well beaten [with a fork]

Place the milk in a medium saucepan over medium heat and bring almost to a boil. Sprinkle the cornmeal over the top; stir it in well. Add the honey, nut meats, seasonings, and butter or oil. Simmer, stirring, until it thickens, about 15 minutes. Remove from the heat and cool.

Whisk in the well-beaten eggs. Pour this mixture into a 10x10x3-inch buttered baking dish. Bake in a preheated oven at 350° F. for 30 to 40 minutes. Cool slightly. Cut into squares or bars and serve. This is good with pecan or maple-nut ice creams or fresh whipped cream and seasonal berries like Juneberries and strawberries.

Serves 4 to 6.

From E. Barrie Kavasch, *Enduring Harvests: Native American Foods and Festivals for Every Season.* Old Saybrook, Connecticut: Globe Pequot Press, 1995, p. 259-60.

ribbons, bells, and lace obtained from European traders were added to clothing, moccasins, and hair arrangements.

Food

Most Creek families had their own small gardens. Crops were also grown in shared fields, with each family receiving the harvest from its assigned section. Both men and women helped with the communal farming. A portion of the community harvest was set aside to provide for visitors and needy families. Originally, the Creek grew, gathered, and hunted only what they needed for their own use. As trade with the Europeans developed, they became commercial hunters, selling the Europeans deerskins and furs.

Corn, eaten fresh or dried, was the main Creek crop. *Sofkey,* a sour broth made of crushed corn and sometimes flavored with deer meat, was also a staple of their diet. They also raised beans, squash, pumpkins, melons, peppers, peas, cucumbers, rice, and sweet potatoes. Creek women gathered wild foods, including berries, peaches, apples, herbs, roots, hickory nuts, and acorns. Cooking oil was obtained by boiling mashed nuts and skimming off the oil. Deer was the most popular meat. They also ate wild hogs and such small game as squirrel, opossum, and turkey. Meat was preserved by drying or smoking it. Fishermen caught catfish and sturgeon.

Abuskee, a drink made of roasted corn, was a popular beverage. People also enjoyed ah-gee-chum-buh-gee, a combination of boiled cornmeal, dried fruits, and brown sugar, served in corn husk packets like dumplings.

Education

Traditionally, a woman's brothers educated and counseled her male children in such skills as hunting, fishing, and building boats and houses. Young boys were taught a game called chunkey to sharpen their skills at spear throwing. One player pushed a stone disk that rolled down the field. Other players chased it with a long stick that curved at one end. They hurled their sticks to the point where they thought the disk would stop. Sometimes whole families played the game together. Girls were taught by their mothers, their mother's sisters, and their grandmothers to cook, weave baskets, sew, and sing songs as they searched for edible plants.

Although the Muscogee Creek Nation now operates a boarding school, most children attend local public schools, vocational schools, and community colleges. During the 1990s the Muscogee Nation undertook development of a language program for its elementary school students.

Healing practices

Creek doctors used parts of many different plants to make medicine. Tobacco was thought to be powerful and was used for healing and in ceremonies. For example, tobacco mixed with boiled red sumac was smoked to treat head and chest ailments; mixed with water, it was both drunk and rubbed on the body to cure stomach cramps. Other items used as medicines were roots, tobacco blossoms, bark, milkweed, spider web, and charred coals. Medicine men concocted teas and ointments to treat burns, insect bites, fever, indigestion, diarrhea, and other diseases. Some of these potions contained morphine and salicylic acid (the active ingredient in aspirin). Doctors also helped people deal with emotional distress.

The Indians had no immunity or medicine to deal with diseases brought by Europeans, such as smallpox, measles, cholera, and malaria. Many people died during epidemics. Alcohol abuse became another European-introduced problem, as many Creek had no physical tolerance to drinking. When the Indians lost their original lands, their food supply was disrupted. Diet-related health problems, like diabetes, became more common.

HOW THE CLANS CAME TO BE

The basic units of Creek society were the clans. Often, a person felt closer to members of his own clan who lived in a distant town than he did to members of other clans who lived in his own town. The following tale points out that the Wind Clan was the most powerful; in fact, the ruling chief of each town was chosen from this group.

In the beginning, the Muscogee people were born out of the earth itself. They crawled up out of the ground through a hole like ants. In those days, they lived in a far western land beside tan mountains that reached the sky. They called the mountains the backbone of the earth. Then a thick fog descended upon the earth, sent by the Master of Breath, *Esakitaummesee*. The Muscogee people could not see. They wandered around blindly, calling out to one another in fear. They drifted apart and became lost. The whole people were separated into small groups, and these groups stayed close to one another in fear of being entirely alone. Finally, the Master had mercy on them. From the eastern edge of the world, where the sun rises, he began to blow away the fog. He blew and blew until the fog was completely gone. The people were joyful and sang a hymn of thanksgiving to the Master of Breath. And in each of the groups, the people turned to one another and swore eternal brotherhood. They said that from then on these groups would be like large families. The members of each group would be as close to each other as brother and sister, father and son. The group that was farthest east and first to see the sun, praised the wind that had blown the fog away. They called themselves the Wind Family, or Wind Clan. As the fog moved away from the other groups, they, too, gave themselves names. Each group chose the name of the first animal it saw. So they became the Bear, Deer, Alligator, Raccoon, and Bird Clans. However, the Wind Clan was always considered the first clan and the aristocracy of all the clans. The Master-of-Breath spoke to them: "You are the beginning of each one of your families and clans. Live up to your name. Never eat of your own clan, for it is your brother. You must never marry into your own clan. This will destroy your clan if you do. When an Indian brave marries, he must always move with his wife to her clan. There he must live and raise his family. The children will become members of their mother's clan. Follow these ways and the Muskhogeans will always be a powerful race. When you forget, your clans will die as people."

SOURCE: "How the Clans Came To Be." *Creek Lifestyles, Customs and Legends.* September 18, 1996. Creek Home Page: (http://www.edumaster.net/schools/ryal/creek.html), December 31, 1996.

During the latter part of twentieth century, attempts were made to improve the health of the Creek; the Muscogee Nation began to manage its own hospital and a group of clinics.

ARTS

Weaving

Creek women learned a special type of weaving technique called finger weaving. Bands of fabric were created by weaving braided multiple strands of yarn with the fingers, sometimes with beads attached. The ends were often left unbraided to form tassels. Because they did not use looms, the women could make only those garments that

could be fashioned from narrow fabric strips. These included scarves, sashes and other types of clothing.

Marion (Wild Horse) McGhee, Creek Fluff Dancer, picks up feather with his teeth, 1964.

CUSTOMS

The Creek confederacy was made up of people from a variety of backgrounds who joined either for military protection or because they had been conquered by the Creek. Each group was an individual community. As a result, traditions and ceremonies varied among the towns. However, the customs described below were fairly common.

Festivals

The Creek held "stomp dances" to celebrate special occasions, such as planting season, hunting season, weddings, and the approach of medicine men. A leader began the stomp dance by moving around the fire counter-clockwise. Dancers engaged in a non-stop chant. Around their legs women wore pebble-filled turtle shells. Their shuffling feet set the rhythm for the dance. Dancers were arranged in a circle; men and women alternated.

Summer's Green Corn Ceremony, which lasted eight days, celebrated the ripening of the corn and signaled the beginning of a new year. People sang, danced and played games. A special feature was the Ribbon Dance, which is still performed by women today at Green

Corn Ceremonies. Three or four women are selected for life to perform this function. The women fast before the dance. Then, wearing rattles and shells fastened to their legs, they wave special sticks in a certain rhythm and are accompanied by male singers and gourd players.

Special fires holding sacred power were prepared for the ceremony. Adults drank a black herb potion that purified their bodies, and they fasted before tasting the new corn. Dances and feasting then followed. In the spirit of renewal, forgiveness was granted to any person who had not yet been punished for an offense (except murder) committed during the past year.

Today, the Creek National Festival and Rodeo takes place annually on the third weekend in June at the Creek Nation Complex. Events include stomp and other dances, a parade, a rodeo, sporting events, and a fine arts and crafts festival. Native American food is in great abundance. A powwow takes place each year over Labor Day Weekend. A powwow is a celebration at which the main activity is traditional singing and dancing. In modern times, the singers and dancers at powwows come from many different tribes.

Naming

A Creek man's first name identified his town or clan, while the second name described some personal characteristic. For example, the name of the famous historical figure Chitto Harjo came from the facts that he was a member of the Snake clan (*chitto* means "snake,") and *harjo* that he was "recklessly brave."

Hunting rituals

Before the coming of the Europeans, the Creek hunted deer to use for food and clothing. They painted their cheeks with ocher (dirt containing iron deposits) because they thought it improved their vision. They also sang special songs to bring the deer closer. Then they attacked them with bows and arrows, wooden spears, and blowguns.

Courtship and marriage

When a Creek man wanted to marry, he or his female relatives proposed to a woman's mother and aunts. Before the bride-to-be could accept, she had to get approval from her clan elders. The wedding could not take place until the man had proved his abilities by building a house and killing a deer. Likewise, the woman had to prove she could cook. The couple lived together for a year before deciding whether to make the marriage permanent. After that time, divorce was possible but it was rare among families with children. If his wife gave her permission, a man could marry other women. He had to provide separate homes for each of them. People who were unfaithful to their spouses were punished by severe beatings or having their ears or nose cut off. Offenders who remained hidden until the annual Green Corn Ceremony period of forgiveness, however, could escape this punishment.

Funerals

In past centuries, burials took place on the floor of the deceased's home. The body was wrapped in a blanket and placed into a circular pit in a sitting position. Later, graves were dug outside near the family home. The body was kept in the home for a four-day period, which ended with an all-night wake. Family members put the deceased person's favorite clothing into the casket, along with bits of food and tobacco. After they lowered the casket into the ground, they built a fire at the head of the grave and tended it for four days, until the soul began its passage to the sky. After the burial, family members washed themselves with an herbal compound prepared by a medicine man. This was supposed to help ease the pain of their loss. Creek Christians have abandoned most of these funeral customs, although an all-night service is still held in a church before a burial.

CURRENT TRIBAL ISSUES

Most Creek are members of the Muscogee Nation in Oklahoma. The early groups that made up the Creek were diverse, though, and a few groups desire to be organized separately from the Muscogee Nation.

The Creek are trying to retain their cultural heritage, especially their language and customs. They are also trying to maintain economic independence and gain access to ancestral lands with spiritual significance to them that are located away from tribal property.

NOTABLE PEOPLE

Chitto Harjo (1846–1912), also known as Crazy Snake, formed a group of Creek known as the Snakes. They believed that the Creek Treaty of 1832 guaranteed the Creek self-government and refused to recognize U.S. authority over them. In resisting U.S. troops, Harjo was seriously injured and died from his wounds; afterwards, the Snake movement quickly weakened.

Opothle Yoholo (around 1780–1863), a skilled Creek orator, negotiated land agreements with President John Quincy Adams, and later with President Andrew Jackson. For a time he resisted the government's enforced removal of the Creek, but he finally accepted relocation. In 1836 he led 2,700 people to Indian Territory. He became head chief, and tried to preserve the traditions of his ancestors.

FURTHER READING

"How the Clans Came To Be." *Creek Lifestyles, Customs and Legends.* September 18, 1996: [Online] http://www.edumaster.net/schools/ryal/ creek.html, December 31, 1996.

Newman, Shirlee P. *The Creek.* New York: Franklin Watts, 1996.

Scordato, Ellen. *The Creek Indians.* New York: Chelsea House Publishers, 1993.

Seminole

Name

The name Seminole (pronounced *SEH-muh-nole*) may be from the Spanish word *cimmarrón* meaning ("wild one") or from the Creek word meaning "runaway" or "lover of the wild."

Location

The Seminole people originally lived in Alabama and Georgia but migrated to Florida in the seventeenth century to escape American colonists and traders. Today, there are six Seminole reservations in Florida; the Oklahoma Seminole live in fourteen different towns in that state. Other Seminole reside in California and some are scattered in small groups around the United States.

Population

In 1821, there were an estimated 5,000 Seminole. In a census (count of the population) done in 1990 by the U.S. Bureau of the census, 15,564 people identified themselves as Seminole (see box).

Language family

Muskogean.

Origins and group affiliations

Seminole was a name given to a group of Creek, Yamasee, Oconee, Apalachicolas, Alabamas, and other Indians who fled to Florida in the 1700s from several areas in the southeastern United States. In the 1830s, most of the Seminole were forced to leave their homelands and relocate in present-day Oklahoma, where they formed new relationships with other southeastern tribes also relocated there, including the Cherokee, Chickasaw, Choctaw, and Creek (see entries).

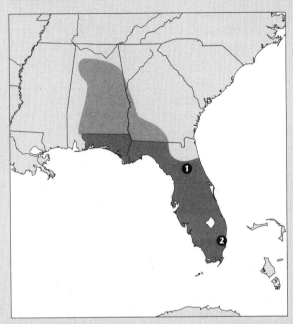

SEMINOLE

Contemporary Communities

Florida

1. Oklewaha Band of Seminole Indians
2. Hollywood Reservation Headquarters of the Seminole Nation of Florida, which includes:
   Big Cypress Reservation
   Brighton Reservation
   Immokalee Reservation
   Tampa Reservation

Oklahoma

(Not on map; the Oklahoma Seminole live in 14 different towns in that state.)

Light shaded area: Traditional lands of the Seminole prior to their migration to Florida.

Dark shaded area: Homelands of the Seminole after the early 1700s.

The Seminole did not even exist as a tribe until the late 1700s, when a group of Creek Indians moved to northern Florida and settled there to avoid trouble, find better soil, and seek skins for trading. This core group was joined by members of other tribes, as well as runaway slaves, to form the Seminole population. The history of the Seminole has been marked by conflicts, forced removal to the western United States, and great adversity. Through it all the people have shown self-sufficiency and a fierce independence.

HISTORY

Move to Florida

The early people whose descendants now make up the Seminole tribe as well as the Creek resided at the fifteenth-century site of Etowah in Georgia. They lived in clans (large groups of related families) that enjoyed an abundant food supply. They also engaged in warfare with the neighboring tribes of Cherokee, Chickasaw, and Choctaw. In the 1700s, some people moved to Florida to avoid being caught up in these conflicts. They founded communities along river or stream banks.

Peace shattered by War of 1812

The eighteenth century was mostly a peaceful time for the Seminole in Florida. They had good relations with Spanish military troops stationed there. For nearly 100 years, the people hunted and gathered in the wilds, often trading their goods at the Spanish forts. Runaway slaves from the American slave plantations farther north often hid among the Seminole, who warmly accepted them.

This period of peace ended during the War of 1812 between the United States and Great Britain. Although America had won independence from Great Britain in 1781, the western boundary of the new United States extended only to the Mississippi River. In 1812 American settlers were pushing beyond the Mississippi onto land claimed by the British.

Creek Wars

During the war, some of the southeastern Indians sided with Britain and some sided with the United States. In 1813, a group of Creek Indians captured an American army post near Mobile, Alabama, and massacred the soldiers. The U.S. army retaliated. In the conflict that followed, called the Creek Wars of 1813–1814, some Creek joined with the United States to fight against other Creek. Many Indians died and many of their towns were destroyed. The Indians had to sign a peace treaty giving all their lands in Georgia and some in Alabama to the U.S. government. Rather than be ruled by the U.S. government, many more Creek fled to Florida and joined the Seminole, thereby tripling the Seminole population.

The First Seminole War

Ever-larger numbers of white settlers were also moving southward, some onto land claimed by the Spanish. A clash between these settlers and the Native inhabitants of the area was almost sure to take place sooner or later. Fighting between American settlers and the

IMPORTANT DATES

1700s: Creek settle in Florida, forming the core group of a new Seminole tribe.

1817: First Seminole War occurs when soldiers from neighboring states invade Seminole lands in Florida looking for runaway slaves.

1832: The U.S. government attempts relocation of the Seminole to Indian Territory in Oklahoma, leading to Second Seminole War.

1932: Florida Seminole move to reservations.

1957: Florida Seminole Tribe of Florida is established and gains federal recognition.

Seminole caused the United States to declare war on the tribe in 1817 in a conflict called the First Seminole War. U.S. troops invaded Florida in search of runaway slaves who had sought refuge with the Seminole. This was a violation of the boundary between the United States and Spain, but Spain was too weak at that time to fight back. As a result, U.S. military raids increased and American troops under General Andrew Jackson, who later became president of the United States, seized Florida from Spain, burning Native villages and killing their inhabitants. In 1821 Spain gave up Florida to the United States. American settlers began taking over the prime farming land and hunting grounds of the Seminole.

Southern plantation owners continued to travel into what was now American territory in search of the escaped slaves they considered their "property." Many of the escaped slaves, who were living under the protection of the Seminole, formed themselves into a black Seminole clan and were adopted into the tribe. Armed soldiers from the southern states accompanied the plantation owners and took many prisoners, not caring if their prisoners were former slaves or full-blood Seminoles.

Seminole move to reservations

In 1823, the U.S. government persuaded the Seminole to move onto reservations in central and southern Florida to make way for white settlers. The tribe was promised equipment, livestock, and an annual payment of $5,000 for twenty years. The Seminole gave up 30 million acres of rich farmland for about 5 million acres of sandy, marshy land not well suited for farming. The Indians also agreed to stop protecting escaped slaves.

The move to the reservation took more than a year. Unable to hunt and farm while they waited, the people suffered widespread hunger and had to put up with illegal attacks by whites in search of runaway slaves. The Seminole were simply too exhausted to fight back and began to feel betrayed by the whites with whom they had made the treaty.

Tribe agrees to move to Indian Territory

Over the next ten years, whites in great numbers came and settled on former Seminole lands. Soon that land was filled and the whites were clamoring for more land. U.S. officials put pressure on some Seminole leaders and they signed the Treaty of Paynes Landing in 1832, agreeing to the relocation of the Seminole within three years to Indian Territory. (Indian Territory was the land that now forms most of the state of Oklahoma. During the 1800s, the U.S. government moved many tribes to Indian Territory as part of its plan to make the area into a state governed by those tribes.) In return for moving, the Seminole would receive annual payments of cash and goods for their former territory. However, this move would reunite them with the Creek, who by this time had become their bitter enemies.

The Second Seminole War

The move to Indian Territory was supposed to take place in 1835. Before it could begin, Seminole Chief Osceola started a rebellion that resulted in the Second Seminole War. Although the majority of the tribe moved to Indian Territory, nearly 500 hid in the Everglades with Osceola. For seven years the vastly outnumbered Seminole warriors put up a brave resistance, using hit-and-run tactics to resist 5,000 U.S. soldiers, striking at them and then disappearing back into the swamps. This conflict developed into the longest and costliest Indian War in the history of the United States. Federal officials became frustrated by the war costs and their inability to beat the Seminole. Federal troops captured Chief Osceola under a false flag of truce in 1837. He died in a prisoner-of-war camp not long after.

Osceola, leader of the Seminole in their resistance to being moved to Indian Territory in the 1830s.

Osceola's successor, Chief Coacoochee, carried on the fight but finally surrendered in 1841. By that time, most warriors had been killed or had submitted to moving west with the rest of their tribe. And so the Seminole became part of the movement of the "Five Civilized Tribes" to Indian Territory. The Five Civilized Tribes were the Chickasaw, Choctaw, Seminole, Creek, and Cherokee. They were given this name by their white neighbors and the U.S. government because they had adopted white customs in the late 1700s and early 1800s while trying to cope with whites taking over their homelands.

The Third Seminole War

Several hundred Seminole remained hidden deep in the swampy areas of the Florida Everglades. For about ten years they were largely left alone. Then in 1855 land surveyors for the federal government rudely trampled the cornfields and destroyed fruit trees at the

Everglades home of Seminole Chief Billy Bowlegs. An angry Seminole war party attacked the surveyors' camp and killed several members of the party, setting off the Third Seminole War (1855–58). In 1858 the U.S. government offered the Seminole money to leave Florida and relocate to Indian Territory. Although Chief Bowlegs and 123 men accepted the offer, a few hundred people did not. Their descendants now make up the Seminole people of Florida.

Seminole in Oklahoma

In Indian Territory the Seminole faced many hardships. Forced to live in harsh and unsanitary conditions with their former enemies, many Seminole died. In 1856, the surviving Seminole were given their own reservation.

White settlers soon set their sights on Indian Territory and began to move in, although it was illegal. They complained loudly that too much land was set aside for Indians. They also complained that living on isolated reservations, Indians were not assimilating (becoming like white Americans) quickly enough.

The U.S. government finally gave in to settlers' demands. To speed up the process of assimilation, allotment laws began to be passed in 1887. Allotment called for the division of reservations into small, individual parcels of land. Each Indian would be given an allotment to tend on his or her own, instead of large plots being tended by an entire tribe, as was their custom. Leftover land was to be opened up to white settlement.

In 1906 350,000 acres of Seminole land was divided into small parcels. Private ownership of land was a concept that went against Seminole beliefs. Because they could not live off the land as their relatives had done in the Everglades, many Oklahoma Seminoles had to sell off part or all of their land for money to buy food and clothing. By 1920, four-fifths of their allotted lands had either been sold off or they had been cheated out of it by whites. The now-landless people scattered, and their culture suffered. Tribal self-government was abolished with Oklahoma's statehood in 1906.

The people regrouped in the 1960s, adopted a constitution, and became the federally recognized Seminole Nation of Oklahoma. In 1990 they received $40 million for lands taken from them in Florida. Fourteen different groups of Seminole make up the Seminole Tribe of Oklahoma. Two of them are Freedman bands, descendants of slaves who found refuge with the tribe before their removal to Oklahoma.

Florida Seminole move from Everglades

Because their numbers were small and the settlers did not desire the land they inhabited, the Florida Seminole were left alone for nearly 75 years after the Seminole wars ended. More than once the federal government tried to bribe them to move west, but the offers were ignored. Finally, in 1932, the Seminole were convinced to move to land reserved for them in central and southern Florida. Some took up cattle herding, while others began to work for wages.

Today, the Seminole in Florida live on six reservations throughout the state. They are Brighton Reservation in central Florida; Big Cypress Reservation, north of the Everglades; Hollywood Reservation, southwest of Fort Lauderdale; Immokalee Reservation, southeast of Fort Myers; Tampa Reservation, on the eastern outskirts of Tampa, and the Ft. Pierce Reservation in St. Lucie County.

RELIGION

The religious beliefs of the Seminole were based upon those of the Creek, from whom they descended. They saw no separation between body, mind, and soul, and religion and medicine went hand in hand. They believed in the existence of spiritual beings that were fair and consistent in their dealings with humans. Some of their gods included the Preserver of Life, who gave life and took it away; the Corn Mother, who was the goddess of farming; and Thunder, the god of rain and war. In addition to good spirits, they also believed in water panthers and horned rattlesnakes that lived in the water and wrapped around swimmers and drowned them, and "little people" that lived in the forest, sometimes helping the Natives and sometimes tricking them.

Everyday rituals were practiced by everyone in the tribe to make sure the balance of nature was maintained. For example, people would ask forgiveness of an animal before killing it for food; before eating it, they tossed a piece of meat into the fire as a sacrifice to the slain animal. Medicine bundles were considered sacred. They were made up of 600 to 700 bits of stone, herbs, dried animal parts, feathers, and other objects and were used in ceremonies to insure the tribe's well being.

Most modern Seminole have adopted Christian religions, but there still remain those who favor the old religion and believe that the fate of the Seminole depends upon the balance of nature's forces.

The Seminole of Oklahoma call the "stomp dance" their traditional religion. The stomp dance is derived from the Green Corn

POPULATION OF SEMINOLE TRIBES: 1990

The Seminole mostly live in two major areas of the United States, Florida and Oklahoma. The Seminole of Florida occupy six reservations around that state, and the Oklahoma Seminole reside mostly in Seminole County. In the 1990 census, members of the various Seminole tribes identified themselves in this way:

Tribe	Population
Florida Seminole	518
Oklahoma Seminole	450
Seminole	14,596
Total	**15,564**

SOURCE: "1990 census of population and housing. subject summary tag file (SSTF) 13 (computer file): characteristics of American Indians by tribe and language." Washington, DC: U.S. Department of Commerce, Bureau of the Census, Data User Services Division, 1995.

Dance (see box on p. 323), a ceremony brought by the Seminole when they were removed from their Florida homelands.

LANGUAGE

The Seminole spoke two languages of similar origin, Muskogee and Mikasuki. The most common language was Muskogee, the Creek language. While Muskogee is still spoken by Seminole elders, it is not as common among young people.

GOVERNMENT

The people who made up the Seminole shared the governing system of most of the peoples of the southeast until their escape to the Everglades in the mid-nineteenth century, when the system broke down. Previously, each village and tribe had a government headed by a chief. The chief made decisions regarding such matters as food storage, celebrations, building projects, and agricultural planning. The chief's position was sometimes inherited but sometimes the chief was chosen by tribe members for his wisdom and experience. Advisers and council elders assisted the chief. Military strategy was the responsibility of the war chief. For major decisions, the opinions of all the citizens were sought.

In modern times, the six Seminole reservations in Florida are governed by elected tribal councils, whose members advise the federal government on matters that concern the tribe. In addition, the Seminole Tribe of Florida has a board of directors that is solely in charge of economic development.

The Florida Seminole adopted a constitution in 1957 and voted to officially become the Seminole Tribe of Florida. But one small group (who lived in camps along the Tamiami Trail highway) did not want to become part of the new organization. Instead, in 1962 they created the Miccosukee Tribe of Indians of Florida and gained federal recognition. Federally recognized tribes are those which the U.S. government maintains official relations and are entitled to financial and other help. The Miccosukee Reservation is located just south of the Everglades Agricultural Area.

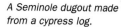
A Seminole dugout made from a cypress log.

The Seminole Nation of Oklahoma elects a chief and an assistant chief. All decisions about economic matters, social programs, and employment opportunities are the responsibility of a General Council, which is made up of two representatives from each of the tribe's fourteen groups.

ECONOMY

The men of the southern tribes that made up the Seminole hunted and fished, constructed buildings, and cleared land for farming. The women raised the children, cooked, and made pottery, baskets, and clothing. In Florida, before their retreat to the Everglades, the people took advantage of the abundant wild fowl and game.

Once in the Everglades, the Seminole people had to change their ways. The land was mostly unsuitable for farming, so women gathered wild plants while men spent their time fishing and hunting game. They were successful in raising pigs and chickens in the hot climate, but cattle did not fare well.

The Seminole used canoes carved from tree trunks to travel the shallow waters of the Everglades. During the 1800s, they hunted deer, otters, raccoons, rabbits, turtles, alligators, fish, and birds, which they used for food and pelts. At trading posts, they exchanged the pelts plus alligator hides, dried fish, beeswax, and honey for European supplies such as coffee, tobacco, cloth, metal pots, knives, and liquor.

Between 1870 and 1914, when much of the Everglades was drained by the state of Florida to stop the spread of diseases and aid land development, some Seminole in Florida began working for whites as hunters or fishermen. Today, Seminole people pilot airboats and serve as guides to white hunters. Although many still farm and raise cattle, they require other jobs as well to support their families. The people sell arts and crafts, plant grass, engage in logging, and wrestle alligators for tourists. They also work in tribal bingo facilities and gambling casinos that are their most profitable enterprises. The tribe also operates a hotel, citrus groves, smoke shops, hunting operations, a tribal museum, an aircraft company, and the Billie Swamp Safari.

Oil production, construction, agriculture, clothing shops, and small manufacturing provide most jobs for tribe members. The Oklahoma Seminole operate a bingo operation, a gaming center (a primary source of income), and two trading posts.

DAILY LIFE

Families

Several related families usually lived together in one camp. Groups of related families, called clans, were named after an animal such as the bird, otter, wolf, or snake. Children were born into the mother's clan. Families of the Seminole who escaped into the Everglades usually consisted of a husband and wife, their daughters and their husbands, children, and grandchildren.

In Seminole families, the men tilled the soil and the women planted and tended the garden. Although everyone worked together at harvest time, each family was responsible for harvesting its own share of food.

Buildings

Before the Seminole fled to the Everglades, they often lived in villages made up of about thirty families. Each family made use of two buildings. The first was for sleeping and cooking. The second building, which was two stories high, was used for storage and contained a special room where the head of the family would receive guests. To construct them, timber posts were sunk into the ground and cypress or pine boards were used to cover the framework to form walls. Bark shingles were used, and interior dividers separated the dwelling into rooms.

Life in the damp and hot climate of the Everglades made new types of buildings necessary. Called *chickees,* these were basically

A Seminole village in the Everglades.

open-sided huts with a raised floor and a roof covering made of palmetto leaves. They were developed during the early 1800s when the Seminole needed fast, disposable shelters while on the run from U.S. troops. To keep out mud and bugs, the plank floor was raised nearly three feet off the ground. The Seminole used these structures only for sleeping and the storage of personal items.

To keep the chickees as cool as possible, they were made without walls, and all cooking took place in a special cookhouse. The roof kept out rain and a fire that produced dense smoke was used to hold down the number of mosquitoes. There was no furniture, and possessions were hung from the rafters. People sat on the floor for eating, sewing, and other activities, and slept on mats on the floor. Children slept on animal skins in the hope that they would acquire the special qualities of that animal.

Clothing and adornment

Before their flight to Florida, Seminole people wore clothing typical of other southeastern tribes. In warm weather, men wore loincloths (flaps of material that cover the front and back and are suspended from the waist) and women wore knee-length skirts. Both were made from animal pelts or woven from plant fibers. In cooler weather, robes of fur or buckskin were draped over the shoulders. A light but warm cape was made by attaching bird feathers to a net woven from plant fibers. Children often went naked until puberty.

Although women wore nothing on their heads, men wore elaborate headpieces during ceremonial gatherings, sometimes shaped to resemble an open bird's wing. They painted their bodies and wore beads, wristbands, and arm bands.

The Seminole added their own creative touches to the woven cloth shirts they adapted from the whites. When they acquired sewing machines near the beginning of the twentieth century, they developed the distinctive patchwork designs for which they are famous (see "Stitchery"). Today, they are also known for the elaborate turban-like headdresses worn by men and the special way women sculpt their hair into a rounded, slightly flat peak or roll above the forehead. Women also wear many layers of brightly colored beaded necklaces on their necks, wrists, and ankles. These modes of dress are usually only worn for traditional ceremonies or tourist shows.

Food

When they lived in the northern part of Florida in the early eighteenth century, the Seminole planted corn, pumpkins, melons, squash, beans and other vegetables and tobacco. Crops were rotated in the fields each year to give the soil time to replenish. Men hunted and fished and the camps migrated about the Florida peninsula finding areas abundant in wild fowl and game as the seasons changed.

Once the Seminole moved to the Everglades, they relied more on fishing and hunting game for their food. The women gathered wild plants, and palmetto, cattail roots, and roots called *coontie* that were pounded and made into flour. The people also ate pineapples, oranges, and bananas, and palmetto berries were used to make molasses. In their very limited garden space they grew sweet potatoes, corn, pumpkins, sugar cane, and beans.

A favorite dish was hominy, made by mixing corn kernels with wood ashes and soaking the mixture overnight. Then the hulls were removed and the kernels were cooked for several hours and made into a thin soup. They were able to raise pigs and chickens in the hot climate, but not cattle. Even though snakes were abundant in the Everglades, the Seminole refused to eat their meat. They were afraid that doing so would anger the snake spirits.

Education

In traditional times, boys and girls were taught the roles considered appropriate to their gender. Mothers taught their daughters how to raise children, sew, and run a home. Boys learned by example and participation how to fish and hunt, and make and use canoes. The children all shared in the work of the village from an early age and learned to play quietly so as not to attract the attention of white men.

In the Everglades, children were taught to watch out for poisonous snakes, insects, and other dangerous creatures. They were shown how to play games. They were told never to try to outdo another person, and this trait of being non-competitive is retained in the culture even today. Children who misbehaved were sometimes subjected to dry scratching. For this, a wooden implement embedded with fish teeth or bone splinters was used to lightly scratch the wrongdoer, causing more shame than physical injury.

Formal education for Seminole children did not begin until the 1920s, when some elementary schools were started. During the 1930s and 1940s some children were sent to Indian boarding schools far away where they often felt lonely and were forced to adopt white ways.

Today, elementary age children attend school on or off the reservation, depending upon where they live. Although children are required to attend school until age sixteen, dropout rates are high. Since 1972 the tribe has worked with the Bureau of Indian Affairs to develop programs to teach pre-school children, to preserve the Seminole language and customs, and to provide vocational and financial assistance programs for students wanting to go to college. Increasing numbers of young people are attending college and taking professional jobs as doctors, lawyers, or engineers.

INDEPENDENT GROUP TRIES TO RETAIN TRADITIONAL WAYS

A group of Seminoles who call themselves the Independent Traditional Seminole reside about 30 miles northeast of Naples, Florida. They are not recognized as a tribe by the federal government and face opposition from many other Seminole people. The group, which numbers about 200, insists on living the traditional way. Their spokesperson, Danny Billie, has said they "represent the original Seminole nation that fought the U.S. government during the 1800s."

Some observers claim the Independent Traditional Seminole have indeed adapted some of the trappings of modern life, but in an unsafe way. One observer spoke of seeing electrical wires on the ground near the group's plywood chickees (houses) and voiced fears that their outhouses may be contaminating ground water. In the mid 1990s the Collier County, Florida, government backed down from its attempts to make the people move out of their chickees or bring them up to county building codes. In 1997 the Honor the Earth music tour, which raises money and awareness for ecological and Native issues, focused attention on the Independent Traditional Seminole group. They supported the people's efforts to have Florida pass a law that would protect the group from further legal actions for maintaining its way of life.

Healing practices

The Seminole used a variety of herbs to heal illnesses. The most important one was red root, the inner bark of a type of willow tree.

This root could be soaked in cold water and used as a remedy for nausea, fever, and swellings. It was also used for bathing. A potion made of the plant button snakeroot or bear's grass was pounded up and mixed with water. It was used for people with serious coughs and for snakebites and kidney troubles. Herbs and roots such as wormseed, horsemint, red cedar, and spicebush were also used to purify the body.

When the use of herbs did not result in a cure, shamans (pronounced *SHAY-mens*) who specialized in performing healing rituals were summoned. They rubbed the patient's body, sang or recited prayers, or used a comb-like instrument with tiny, sharp teeth to make scratches just deep enough to cause the patient to bleed slightly. The Seminole thought that a person's blood could become too abundant or too heavy, and this condition caused one to become ill, socially troublesome, or violent. The cause of illness was often thought to be the spirit of an animal that was angry or revengeful and the shaman was asked to calm the animal spirit. Some shamans underwent lengthy instruction in the healing arts while others were born with their talents. They could see and speak with supernatural powers and foresee the future. Today, health care is available at various clinics on or near the reservations.

ARTS

Stitchery

Seminole women are known for their artful stitchery, in which they piece together scraps of material in patchwork designs to produce colorful bands that are attached skirts, shirts, and other items made of a fabric called calico. Some of the designs are traditional while others are unique creations of the seamstress. The patterns are named for the items they resemble, such as arrows or spools. Complex designs, combining two or more simpler patterns, often are named for the woman who created them. Each Seminole reservation is known for its unique designs. Copying a design is looked upon as an honor by the originator of the design. Seminole women also create dolls from cloth-wrapped palmetto leaves stuffed with cotton that they dress in clothing and hairstyles that are historically accurate.

Oral literature

Seminole elders often told stories to children late at night, when they were safely tucked in under mosquito netting to protect them from insect bites. Seminole tales explain the origin of the world, why certain rituals are performed, and the origins of certain people. At the

Green Corn Dance (see box), people told long stories explaining how they came to have corn and why it was so important to them.

One of the Seminole origin stories tells how a turtle rose from the depths of the sea to rest. When his back started to crack, people emerged from out of the cracks. Then the cracks came together in squares and the people made their homes along the cracks that were streams in the earth.

CUSTOMS

Festivals

Most Seminole ceremonies had to do with fire or water, both considered very sacred. Of the many Seminole customs and rituals, the Green Corn Dance or ceremony was one of the most important and is still performed by some Natives (see box).

Today, most of the Seminole reservations have their own celebrations throughout the year. The Immokalee Reservation holds a powwow festival and rodeo in early February. A powwow is a celebration at which the main activity is traditional singing and dancing. In modern times, the singers and dancers at powwows come from many different tribes. The Hollywood Reservation holds a festival, powwow and rodeo in mid-February. The Brighton Reservation hosts an annual Seminole Arts and Crafts Festival and rodeo near the end of February.

In November, Fire on the Swamp is held at the Big Cypress Reservation, and the Tampa Reservation holds a Thanksgiving Indian Festival. Some activities at these festivals include Indian drumming, dancing, singing, sampling Native foods, alligator wrestling, airboat rides, and arts and crafts.

Birth and naming customs

Women gave birth at the baby house, a small structure used only for that purpose. The mother and newborn remained there until the

THE GREEN CORN DANCE OR CEREMONY

For the Seminole, corn planted in the early spring was ripe and ready to eat by early summer. The Green Corn Dance was held to celebrate the corn harvest. The ceremony also served as a time to visit with friends and family, give thanks, and make up to other people for past wrongs. Food, including dried corn, was prepared from the past year's harvest and shared by all. Men and boys fasted and drank *asi* ("the black drink") to make themselves pure and powerful. They consumed vast quantities of it until they vomited. They believed this gave them the energy to dance all night long.

While the men and boys were meeting, women closed out the year by clearing away all old and unusable items and putting out all the cooking and hearth fires. Spiritual leaders relit the fires as a symbol of the new year.

There were forty different Corn Dances and both men and women participated in them. The men sang while the women kept the beat with tortoise shell rattles. Villages also played each other in a fierce form of stickball. On the last day, the fires were put out and wood was laid out for a new fire. Four perfect ears of corn were placed on the fire, then prayers were offered and a sacred fire was lit to burn the corn. This fire was used to rekindle all the others in the village. Then the men ate the fresh, green corn that the women had prepared. After the fire had completely consumed the four perfect ears of corn, and the men had consumed four rounds of asi, the ceremony came to an end. The New Year had begun.

baby was four months old with the mother preparing all their food. During that time, the mother was thought to be "polluted" and men avoided her for fear of becoming ill. When the time had passed, the mother and new baby rejoined their household.

Seminole babies were immersed in a cold stream right after birth, the first of many purification ceremonies they would experience during their lives. Traditionally names were given to Seminole infants by a tribal elder on the fourth day after their birth. When they were twelve, young men were given new names at the Green Corn Ceremony (see box) to mark their maturity. They were then entitled to all the rights and privileges of any man in the village.

War rituals

The Seminoles were fierce warriors but fair to their enemies, whose lives they spared whenever possible. When men were preparing for war, they applied red paint to their faces, necks, and chests. Captured enemies were enslaved but permitted to marry women of the village. The children of these marriages became members of the tribe.

Courtship and marriage

Individuals had to choose as a marriage partner someone outside their clan (a large group of related families). When a young woman wished to marry, usually about age fourteen, she began to wear many beads and silver ornaments on her clothing. Sometimes a girl's family chose her marriage partner. Couples often courted one another by playing a gentle form of stickball. Usually, when two people wanted to marry, they merely consulted the leader of the woman's clan and went ahead, providing there were no objections. Afterward, they went to live with the bride's family for a few years, until they were able to start a new camp.

The woman was considered the head of the household. It was the husband's duty to provide cooking utensils, beads, blankets, and money, which were given to the bride's family. The Seminole rarely divorced.

Funerals

Seminole burial places were in remote spots in the swamp or woods. Often the body was placed in a wooden casket that was set above ground inside a small, thatched structure. All a person's belongings were buried with him or her, because it was believed that the tools would be needed in the afterlife. It was customary to break the items because only then could they accompany the dead on the journey to the afterlife.

CURRENT TRIBAL ISSUES

In the 1970s the modern world crept into the traditional ways of the Florida Seminole. It was fierce independence, courage, and pride that enabled these people to escape the attempted removal to Indian Territory. These same traits still run strong as they encourage their children to stay in school through graduation, work to improve health conditions on the reservations, and develop their businesses to provide jobs (see "Economy"). Television and radio, schools, and community centers, modern building construction and many other modern elements are now part of daily life on the reservation. The Seminole believe in a balance of old and new. They are also involved in environmental efforts to preserve the Everglades.

For the Seminole in Oklahoma, retaining their traditions, reviving their stomping grounds (where Native ceremonies take place), and raising educational and income levels are currently issues of concern.

NOTABLE PEOPLE

Chief Osceola (1804–1838) was a great hunter and fierce warrior. His people respected and valued him for his strong opposition to relocation to Indian Territory. He led Seminole warriors in a two-year campaign in the Florida Everglades that cost the U.S. government the death of 1,500 troops and $20 million. He continued to fight until his capture in 1842 and died mysteriously in prison.

Seminole Donald Fixico (1951–) is a professor of history and Native American studies. He has published many essays on Indian history, as well as a book on the effects on Native Americans of living in cities called *Urban Indian*.

Betty Mae Tiger Jumper (1927–) was the first Seminole to receive a high school diploma and went on in the 1960s to become the first woman elected as tribal chairperson. Active in political affairs, she has done much to improve the health, education, and social conditions among her people.

FURTHER READING

Brooks, Barbara. *The Seminole*. Vero Beach, FL: Rourke Publications, 1989.

Garbarino, Merwyn S. *The Seminole*. New York: Chelsea House, 1989.

Lee, Martin. *The Seminoles*. New York: Franklin Watts, 1989.

Official Homepage of the Seminole Nation of Oklahoma: [Online]
http://www.cowboy.net/native/seminole/index.html

Sneve, Virginia Driving Hawk. *The Seminoles*. New York: Holiday
House, 1994.

Bibliography

Books

Abrams, George H. J. *The Seneca People*. Phoenix, AZ: Indian Tribal Series, 1976.

The AFN Report on the Status of Alaska Natives: A Call for Action. Anchorage: Alaska Federation of Natives, 1989.

American Indian Reservations and Trust Areas. Washington, DC: U.S. Department of Commerce, 1996.

The American Indians: Algonquians of the East Coast. New York: Time-Life Books, 1995.

The American Indians: Hunters of the Northern Forest. New York: Time-Life Books, 1995.

Anderson, Gary Clayton. *Kinsmen of Another Kind: Dakota-White Relations in the Upper Mississippi Valley, 1650–1862*. Lincoln: University of Nebraska Press, 1984.

Anderson, Gary Clayton. *Little Crow: Spokesman for the Sioux*. St. Paul: Minnesota Historical Society Press, 1986.

Anderson, Gary Clayton. *Through Dakota Eyes: Narrative Accounts of the Minnesota Indian War of 1862*. St. Paul: Minnesota Historical Society Press, 1988.

Apess, William. *On Our Own Ground: The Complete Writings of William Apess, A Pequot*. Ed. Barry O'Connell. Amherst: University of Massachusetts Press, 1992.

Axtell, James. *The European and the Indian: Essays in the Ethnohistory of Colonial North America*. New York: Oxford University Press, 1981.

Ayer, Eleanor H. *The Anasazi*. New York: Walker Publishing, 1993.

Azelrod, Alan. *Chronicle of the Indian Wars*. New York: Prentice Hall, 1993.

Bahti, Tom. *Southwestern Indian Tribes*. Las Vegas: KC Publications, 1994.

Ballantine, Betty and Ian Ballantine, eds. *The Native Americans: An Illustrated History*. Atlanta: Turner Publishing, 1993.

Bamforth, Douglas B. *Ecology and Human Organization on the Great Plains*. New York: Plenum Press, 1988.

A Basic Call to Consciousness. Rooseveltown, NY: Akwesasne Notes, 1978.

Bataille, Gretchen M. *Native American Women: A Biographical Dictionary*. New York: Garland Publishing, 1993.

Beals, Ralph L. *Material Culture of the Pima, Papago, and Western Apache*. Berkeley, CA: Department of the Interior, National Park Service, 1934.

Bean, Lowell John. *Mukat's People: The Cahuilla Indians of Southern California*. Berkeley: University of California Press, 1972.

Beauchamp, William M. "Notes on Onondaga Dances." *An Iroquois Source Book*, Volume 2. Ed. Elisabeth Tooker. New York: Garland Publishing, 1985.

Beck, W. and Ynez Haas. *Historical Atlas of California*. Norman: University of Oklahoma Press, 1974.

Beckham, Stephen Dow. *Requiem for a People: The Rogue Indians and the Frontiersman*. Norman: University of Oklahoma Press, 1971.

Beckham, Stephen Dow, Kathryn Anne Toepel, and Rick Minor. *Native American Religious Practices and Uses in Western Oregon*. Eugene: University of Oregon Anthropological Papers, 1984.

Benson, Henry C. *Life Among the Choctaw Indians, and Sketches of the Southwest*. Cincinnati, OH: R. P. Thompson, 1860.

Berlainder, Jean Louis. *The Indians of Texas in 1830*. Washington, DC: Smithsonian Institution, 1969.

Berthrong, Donald J. *The Cheyenne and Arapaho Ordeal: Reservation and Agency Life in the Indian Territory*. Norman: University of Oklahoma Press, 1976.

Berthrong, Donald J. *The Southern Cheyennes*. Norman: University of Oklahoma Press, 1963.

Bieder, Robert E. *Native American Communities in Wisconsin, 1600–1960: A Study of Tradition and Change*. Madison: University of Wisconsin Press, 1995.

Biographical Dictionary of Indians of the Americas. Newport Beach, CA: American Indian Publishers, 1991.

Birket-Smith, Kaj and Frederica De Laguna. *The Eyak Indians of the Copper River Delta.* Copenhagen: Levin & Munksgaard, 1938.

Bischoff, William N. *The Indian War Diary of Plympton J. Kelly 1855–1856.* Tacoma: Washington State History Society, 1976.

Blaine, Martha Royce. *Pawnee Passage, 1870–1875.* Norman: University of Oklahoma Press, 1990.

Blaine, Martha Royce. *The Pawnees: A Critical Bibliography.* Bloomington: Indiana University Press for the Newberry Library, 1980.

Boas, Franz. *Chinook Texts.* Washington, DC: Bureau of American Ethnology Bulletin No. 20, 1894.

Boas, Franz. *Kwakiutl Ethnography.* Ed. Helen Codere. Chicago: University of Chicago Press, 1966.

Boas, Franz, ed. *Publications of the American Ethnological Society,* Vol. 1: *Fox Text,* by William Jones. Leyden: E. J. Brill, 1907.

Boas, Franz. *The Social Organization and the Secret Societies of the Kwakiutl Indians.* New York: Johnson Reprint Corporation, 1970.

Bolton, Herbert Eugene. *The Hasinais: Southern Caddoans As Seen by the Earliest Europeans.* Norman: University of Oklahoma Press, 1987.

Bourne, Russell. *Red King's Rebellion: Racial Politics in New England, 1675–1678.* New York: Atheneum Press, 1990.

Boyd, Maurice. *Kiowas Voices,* Vol. 1: *Ceremonial Dance, Ritual and Song.* Fort Worth: Texas Christian University Press, 1981.

Boyd, Maurice. *Kiowas Voices,* Vol. 2: *Myths, Legends, and Folktales.* Fort Worth: Texas Christian University Press, 1983.

Boyd, Robert. *People of the Dalles: The Indians of Wascopam Mission.* Lincoln: University of Nebraska Press, 1996.

Braund, Kathryn E. Holland. *Deerskins & Duffels: The Creek Indian Trade with Anglo-America, 1685–1815.* Lincoln: University of Nebraska Press, 1993.

Bray, Tamara L. and Thomas W. Killion. *Reckoning with the Dead: The Larsen Bay Repatriation and the Smithsonian Institution.* Washington, DC: Smithsonian Institution, 1994.

Brescia, William, Jr. "Choctaw Oral Tradition Relating to Tribal Origin." *The Choctaw Before Removal.* Ed. Carolyn Keller Reeves. Jackson: University Press of Mississippi, 1985.

Bringle, Mary. *Eskimos.* New York: Franklin Watts, 1973.

Brinton, Daniel G. *The Lenape and their Legends.* Philadelphia, 1884. Reprint. St. Clair Shores, MI: Scholarly Press, 1972.

Brown, Mark. *The Flight of the Nez Perce.* Lincoln: University of Nebraska Press, 1967.

Brown, Vinson. "Sioux, Eastern." *Dictionary of Indian Tribes of the Americas,* Vol. 3. Newport Beach, CA: American Indian Publishers, 1980.

Bruchac, Joseph. *New Voices from the Longhouse: An Anthology of Contemporary Iroquois Writing.* Greenfield Center, NY: Greenfield Review Press, 1989.

Bunte, Pamela A. and Robert J. Franklin. *From the Sands to the Mountain: Change and Persistence in a Southern Paiute Community.* Lincoln: University of Nebraska Press, 1987.

Burch, Ernest S. *The Eskimos.* Norman: University of Oklahoma Press, 1988.

Burnham, Dorothy K. *To Please the Caribou: Painted Caribou-skin Coats Worn by the Naskapi, Montagnais, and Cree Hunters of the Quebec Labrador Peninsula.* Toronto: Royal Ontario Museum, 1992.

Bushnell, David I., Jr. "The Choctaw of Bayou Lacomb, St. Tammany Parish, Louisiana (1909)." *A Choctaw Source Book.* New York: Garland Publishing, 1985: pp. 1–37.

Buskirk, Winfred. *The Western Apache.* Norman: University of Oklahoma Press, 1986.

Caduto, Michael J. *Keepers of the Earth.* Golden, CO: Fulcrum, 1988.

Cahokia. Lincoln: University of Nebraska Press, 1997.

Calloway, Colin G. *The Abenaki.* New York: Chelsea House Publishers, 1989.

Calloway, Colin G., ed. *Dawnland Encounters: Indians and Europeans in Northern New England.* Hanover, NH: University Press of New England, 1991.

Calloway, Colin G. *The World Turned Upside Down: Indian Voices from Early America.* Boston: St. Martin's Press, 1994.

Campisi, Jack. *The Mashpee Indians: Tribe on Trial.* Syracuse, NY: Syracuse University Press, 1991.

Carlisle, Richard. *The Illustrated Encyclopedia of Mankind.* New York: Marshall Cavendish, 1984.

Carlo, Poldine. *Nulato: An Indian Life on the Yukon.* Caldwell, ID: Caxton Printers, 1983.

Carlson, Richard G., ed. *Rooted Like the Ash Trees: New England Indians and the Land.* Naugatuck, CT: Eagle Wing Press, 1987.

Carter, Cecile Elkins. *Caddo Indians: Where We Come From.* Norman: University of Oklahoma Press, 1995.

Carter, Sarah. "Chapter 19—'We Must Farm to Enable Us to Live': The Plains Cree and Agriculture to 1900." *Native Peoples: The Canadian Experience.* Toronto: McClellan & Stewart, 1986.

Case, David S. *Alaska Natives and American Laws.* University of Alaska Press, 1984.

Cash, Joseph H. and Gerald W. Wolff. *The Comanche People.* Phoenix, AZ: Indian Tribal Series, 1974.

Castille, George Pierre, ed. *The Indians of Puget Sound.* Seattle: University of Washington Press, 1985.

Castillo, Edward D. and R. Jackson. *Indians, Franciscans, and Spanish Colonization: The Impact of the Mission System on California Indians.* Albuquerque: University of New Mexico Press, 1995.

Catlin, George. *Letters and Notes on the Manners, Customs, and Conditions of North American Indians.* Volume 2 (unabridged republication of the fourth [1844] edition). New York: Dover Publications, 1973.

Catlin, George. *North American Indians.* New York: Viking Press, 1989.

Chamberlain, Von Del. *When Stars Came Down to Earth: Cosmology of the Skidi Pawnee Indians of North America.* Los Altos, CA: Ballena Press and College Park: Center for Archaeoastronomy, University of Maryland, 1982.

Chalfant, William Y. *Without Quarter: The Wichita Expedition and the Fight on Crooked Creek.* Norman: University of Oklahoma Press, 1991.

Champagne, Duane, ed. *Chronology of Native North American History: From Pre-Columbian Times to the Present.* Detroit: Gale Research, 1994.

Champagne, Duane, ed. *Native America: Portrait of the Peoples.* Detroit: Visible Ink Press, 1994.

Champagne, Duane, ed. *The Native North American Almanac.* Detroit: Gale Research Inc., 1994.

Charlebois, Peter. *The Life of Louis Riel.* Toronto: New Canada Press, 1978.

Childers, Robert and Mary Kancewick. "The Gwich'in (Kutchin): Conservation and Cultural Protection in the Arctic Borderlands." Anchorage: Gwich'in Steering Committee, n.d.

Cleland, Charles E. *Rites of Conquest: The History and Culture of Michigan's Native Americans.* Ann Arbor: University of Michigan Press, 1992.

Clifton, James A. *The Prairie People: Continuity and Change in Potawatomi Indian Culture 1665–1965.* Lawrence: The Regents Press of Kansas, 1977.

Clifton, James A., *Star Woman and Other Shawnee Tales.* Lanham, MD: University Press of America, 1984.

Clifton, James A., George L. Cornell, and James M. McClurken. *People of the Three Fires: The Ottawa, Potawatomi and Ojibway of Michigan.* Grand Rapids, MI: Grand Rapids Inter-Tribal Council, 1986.

Cole, D. C. *The Chiricahua Apache 1846–1876: From War to Reservation.* Albuquerque: University of New Mexico Press, 1988.

Cole, Douglas. *Captured Heritage: The Scramble for Northwest Coast Artifacts.* Seattle: University of Washington Press, 1985.

Cook, Sherburne F. *The Conflict between the California Indian and White Civilization.* Berkeley: University of California Press, 1967.

Cordere, Helen, ed. *Kwakiutl Ethnography.* Chicago: University of Chicago Press, 1966.

Corkran, David H. *The Creek Frontier: 1540–1783.* Norman: University of Oklahoma Press, 1967.

Cotterill, R. S. *The Southern Indians: The Story of the Civilized Tribes Before Removal.* Norman: University of Oklahoma Press, 1954.

Covington, James W. *The Seminoles of Florida.* Gainsville: University of Florida Press, 1993.

Cox, Bruce Alden, ed. *Native People, Native Lands: Canadian Indians, Inuit and Métis.* Ottawa: Carleton University Press, 1987.

Crane, Verner W. *The Southern Frontier,* Greenwood, CT: Greenwood Press, 1969.

Crowder, David L. *Tendoy, Chief of the Lemhis.* Caldwell, ID: Caxton Publishers, 1969.

Crum, Steven J. *The Road On Which We Came.* Salt Lake City: University of Utah Press, 1994.

Curtis, Edward S. *The North American Indian.* Reprint. New York: Johnson Reprint Corporation, 1970.

Cushman, H. B. *History of the Choctaw, Chickasaw, and Natchez Indians.* New York: Russell & Russell, 1972.

Cvpvkke, Holátte (C. B. Clark). "'Drove Off Like Dogs'—Creek Removal." *Indians of the Lower South: Past and Present.* Ed. John K. Mahon. Pensacola, FL: Gulf Coast History and Humanities Conference, 1975.

D'Azevedo, Warren L., ed. *The Handbook of North American Indians,* Vol. 11: *Great Basin.* Washington, DC: Smithsonian Institution, 1986.

Dahl, Jens. *Indigenous Peoples of the Arctic.* Copenhagen: The Nordic Council, 1993.

Dauenhauer, Nora Marks and Richard Dauenhauer. *Haa Kusteeyí, Our Culture: Tlingit Life Stories.* Seattle: University of Washington Press; and Juneau, AK: Sealaska Heritage Foundation, 1994.

Dauenhauer, Nora Marks and Richard Dauenhauer. *Haa Tuwunáagu Yís, for Healing Our Spirit: Tlingit Oratory.* Seattle: University of Washington Press; and Juneau, AK: Sealaska Heritage Foundation, 1990.

Davis, Mary B., ed. *Native America in the Twentieth Century: An Encyclopedia.* New York: Garland Publishing, 1994.

Dawson, Dawn P. and Harvey Markowitz, eds. *Ready Reference: American Indians.* Pasadena, CA: Salem Press, 1995.

Deacon, Belle. *Engithidong Xugixudhoy: Their Stories of Long Ago: Told in Deg Hit'an Athabaskan by Belle Deacon.* Fairbanks: Alaska Native Language Center, 1987.

Deans, James. *Tales from the Totems of the Hidery,* Volume 2. Chicago: Archives of the International Folk-Lore Association, 1899.

Debo, Angie. *A History of the Indians of the United States.* Norman: University of Oklahoma Press, 1970.

Debo, Angie. *The Rise and Fall of the Choctaw Republic,* Second edition. Norman: University of Oklahoma Press, 1961.

Denig, Edwin Thompson. *Five Indian Tribes of the Upper Missouri: Sioux, Arikaras, Assiniboines, Crees, Crows.* Ed. John C. Ewers. Norman: University of Oklahoma Press, 1961.

Densmore, Frances. *Chippewa Customs.* St. Paul: Minnesota Historical Society Press, 1929; reprinted, 1979.

Densmore, Frances. *Choctaw Music* (Bulletin 136 of the Bureau of American Ethnology). DaCapo Press, 1936, reprint 1972.

Densmore, Francis. *Papago Music.* New York: Da Capo Press, 1972.

DeRosier, Arthur H. Jr. *The Removal of the Choctaw Indians.* Knoxville: University of Tennessee Press, 1970.

DeWald, Terry. *The Papago Indians and Their Basketry.* Tucson, AZ: DeWald, c. 1979.

Diedrich, Mark, *Dakota Oratory.* Rochester, MN: Coyote Books, 1989.

Dobyns, Henry F. *The Papago People.* Phoenix, Indian Tribal Series, c. 1972.

Dobyns, Henry F. *Papagos in the Cotton Fields, 1950.* Tucson, AZ: University of Arizona, Department of Anthropology, 1951.

Dockstader, Frederick J. *Great Native American Indians, Profiles in Life, and Leadership.* New York: Van Nostrand Runhold, Co., 1977.

Doherty, Robert. *Disputed Waters: Native Americans and the Great Lakes Fishery.* Lexington: University Press of Kentucky, 1990.

Doig, Ivan. *Winter Brothers.* New York: Harcourt Brace Jovanovich, 1980.

Driben, Paul. *We Are Métis.* New York: AMS Press, 1985.

Drucker, Philip and Robert F. Heizer. *To Make My Name Good: A Reexamination of the Southern Kwakiutl Potlatch.* Berkeley: University of California Press, 1967.

Duke, Philip. *Points in Time: Structure and Event in a Late Northern Plains Hunting Society.* Niwot: University Press of Colorado, 1991.

Dutton, Bertha P. *American Indians of the Southwest*. Albuquerque: University of New Mexico Press, 1983.

Dutton, Bertha P. *Indians of the American Southwest*. Englewood Cliffs, NJ: Prentice-Hall, 1975.

Eagle/Walking Turtle (Gary McLain). *Indian America: A Traveler's Companion,* Third edition. Santa Fe, NM: John Muir Publications, 1993.

Eastman, Charles A. *Old Indian Days*. Lincoln: University of Nebraska Press, 1991.

Eastman, Charles A. and Elaine Goodale Eastman. *Wigwam Evenings: Sioux Folk Tales Retold*. Lincoln: University of Nebraska Press, 1990.

Eckert, Allan W., *A Sorrow in Our Heart: The Life of Tecumseh*. New York: Bantam, 1992.

Edmunds, R. David. *The Potawatomi: Keepers of the Fire*. Norman: University of Oklahoma Press, 1978.

Edwards, R. David and Joseph L. Peyser. *The Fox Wars: The Mesquakie Challenge to New France*. Norman: University of Oklahoma Press, 1993.

Eells, Myron. *The Indians of Puget Sound: The Notebooks of Myron Eells*. Ed. George B. Castile. Seattle: University of Washington Press, 1985.

Eggan Fred. *The American Indian: Perspectives for the Study of Social Change*. New York: University of Cambridge Press, 1966.

Elliot, Michael L. *New Mexico State Monument: Jemez*. Santa Fe: Museum of New Mexico Press, 1993.

Elmendorf, W. W. *The Structure of Twana Culture*. Pullman: Washington State University, 1960.

Elmendorf, W. W. *Twana Narratives: Native Historical Accounts of a Coast Salish Culture*. Seattle: University of Washington Press, 1993.

Emmons, George Thornton. *The Tlingit Indians*. Seattle: University of Washington Press, 1991.

Erdoes, Richard. *The Rain Dance People*. New York: Alfred A. Knopf, 1976.

Ewers, John C. *Plains Indian History and Culture*. Norman: University of Oklahoma Press, 1997.

Fairbanks, Charles H. *The Florida Seminole People.* Phoenix: Intertribal Series, 1973.

Fehrenbach, T. R. *Comanches: Destruction of a People.* New York: Alfred A. Knopf, 1974.

Feit, Harvey A. "Chapter 8—Hunting and the Quest for Power: The James Bay Cree and Whitemen in the Twentieth Century." *Native Peoples: The Canadian Experience.* Toronto: McClellan & Stewart, 1986.

Fejes, Claire. *Villagers: Athabaskan Indian Life Along the Yukon.* New York: Random House, 1981.

The First Americans. Richmond, Virginia: Time-Life Books, 1992.

Fitting, James E. *The Archaeology of Michigan: A Guide to the Prehistory of the Great Lakes Region.* New York: Natural History Press for the American Museum of Natural History, 1969.

Fixico, Donald. "Tribal Leaders and the Demand for Natural Energy Resources on Reservation Lands." *The Plains Indians of the Twentieth Century. Ed. Peter Iverson. Norman: University of Oklahoma Press, 1985.*

Fontana, Bernard L. and John Paul Schaefer. *Of Earth and Little Rain: The Papago Indians.* Flagstaff, AZ: Northland Press, c. 1981.

Forbes, Jack D. *Apache, Navajo, and Spaniard.* Norman: University of Oklahoma Press, 1969, 1994.

Ford, Richard, R. *An Ecological Analysis Involving the Population of San Juan Pueblo, New Mexico.* New York: Garland Publishing, 1992.

Foreman, Grant. *The Five Civilized Tribes.* Norman: University of Oklahoma, 1934.

Fowler, Loretta. *Shared Symbols, Contested Meanings: Gros Ventre Culture and History, 1778–1984.* Ithaca, NY: Cornell University Press, 1987.

Franklin, Robert J. and Pamela A. Bunte. *The Paiute.* New York: Chelsea House, 1990.

Fredenberg, Ralph. "Indian Self-Determination." *Hearings before the Committee on Indian Affairs,* United States Senate. 73d Congress, 2d Session. On S. 2755 and S. 3645, Part 2: pp. 110–13, 1934.

Frey, Rodney. *The World of the Crow Indians: As Driftwood Lodges.* Norman: University of Oklahoma Press, 1987.

Fried, Jacob. "Aboriginal Population of Western Washington State." *Coast Salish and Western Washington Indians III*. Ed. David Agee Horr. New York: Garland Publishing, 1974.

Friesen, Gerald. *The Canadian Prairies: A History*. Lincoln: University of Nebraska Press, 1984.

Galens, Judy, Anna Sheets, and Robyn V. Young, editors. *Gale Encyclopedia of Multicultural America*. Detroit: Gale Research, 1995.

Gardener, Lion. "Lieft Lion Gardener: His Relation of the Pequot Warres (1660)." *Massachusetts Historical Society Collections*, third series, Vol. 3 (1833): pp. 131–60.

Garfield, Viola E. and Linn A. Forrest. *The Wolf and The Raven: Totem Poles of Southeastern Alaska*. Seattle: University of Washington Press, 1993.

Gibbs, George. *Indian Tribes of Washington Territory*. Fairfield, WA: Ye Galleon Press, 1972.

Gibson, Arrell M. *The Chickasaws*. Norman: University of Oklahoma, 1971.

Gifford, E. W. "Californian Kinship Terminologies." *University of California Publications in American Archaeology and Ethnology*. Vol. 18, No. 1. Reprint of Berkeley: University of California Press, 1922.

Gill, Sam D. and Irene F. Sullivan. *Dictionary of Native American Mythology*. London: Oxford University Press, 1992.

Giraud, Marcel. *The Métis in the Canadian West*. Translated by George Woodcock. Lincoln: University of Nebraska Press, 1986.

Goc, Michael J. *Land Rich Enough: An Illustrated History of Oshkosh and Winnebago County*. Northbridge, CA: Windsor Publications/Winnebago County Historical and Archaeological Society, 1988.

Goddard, Pliny Earle. "Life and Culture of the Hupa." *American Archaeology and Ethnology*, Vol. 3. Ed. Frederic Ward Putnam. Berkeley: University of California Publications, 1905. Reprint. New York: Kraus Reprint Corporation, 1964.

Goddard, Pliny Earle. "The Morphology of the Hupa Language." *American Archaeology and Ethnology*, Vol. 1. Ed. Frederic Ward Putnam. Berkeley: University of California Publications, 1903–1904. Reprint. New York: Kraus Reprint Corporation, 1964.

Goldman, Irving. *The Mouth of Heaven: An Introduction to Kwakiutl Religious Thought.* New York: John Wiley & Sons, 1975.

Goldschmidt, Walter R. and Harold E. Driver. "The Hupa White Deerskin Dance." *American Archaeology and Ethnology,* Vol. 35. Ed. A. L. Kroeber, et al. Berkeley: University of California Publications, 1943. Reprint. New York: Kraus Reprint Corporation, 1965.

Gonen, Amiram. *The Encyclopedia of the People of the World.* New York: Henry Holt and Company, 1993.

Goodwin, Glenville. *Myths and Tales of the White Mountain Apache.* New York: American Folk-lore Society, 1939.

Goodwin, Glenville. *The Social Organization of the Western Apache.* Chicago: University of Chicago Press, 1942.

Goodwin, Glenville. *Western Apache Raiding and Warfare.* Tucson: University of Arizona Press, 1971.

Grant, Bruce. *American Indians: Yesterday and Today.* New York: Dutton, 1960.

Green, Donald Edward. *The Creek People.* Phoenix: Indian Tribal Series, 1973.

Green, Michael D. *The Politics of Indian Removal.* Lincoln: University of Nebraska Press, 1982.

Gregory, H. F., ed. *The Southern Caddo: An Anthology.* New York: Garland Publishing, 1986.

Grinnell, George Bird. *Pawnee, Blackfoot and Cheyenne: History and Folklore of the Plains.* New York: Charles Scribner's Sons, 1961.

Grumet, Robert Steven. *Native Americans of the Northwest Coast: A Critical Bibliography.* Bloomington: Indiana University Press, 1979.

Haeberlin, Hermann and Erna Gunther. *The Indians of Puget Sound.* Seattle: University of Washington, 1967.

Hagan, Walter T. *The Sac and Fox Indians.* Norman: University of Oklahoma Press, 1958.

Hahn, Elizabeth. *The Creek.* Vero Beach, FL: Rourke Publications, 1992.

Hahn, Elizabeth. *The Pawnee.* Vero Beach, FL: Rourke Publications, 1992.

Haines, Francis. *The Nez Perces.* Norman: University of Oklahoma Press, 1955.

Haines, Francis. *The Plains Indians: Their Origins, Migrations, and Cultural Development.* New York: Thomas Y. Crowell Company, 1976.

Halbert, Henry S. "Courtship and Marriage Among the Choctaws of Mississippi (1882)." *A Choctaw Source Book.* New York: Garland Publishing, 1985.

Hale, Duane K. *Turtle Tales: Oral Traditions of the Delaware Tribe of Western Oklahoma.* Delaware Tribe of Oklahoma Press, 1984.

Harlow, Neal. *California Conquered: War and Peace on the Pacific, 1846–1850.* Berkeley: University of California Press, 1982.

Harrington, M. R. *Religion and Ceremonies of the Lenape.* New York: Museum of the American Indian Heye Foundation, 1921.

Harrison, Julia D. *Métis, People Between Two Worlds.* Vancouver: Glenbow-Alberta Institute, 1985.

Harrod, Howard L. *Becoming and Remaining a People: Native American Religions on the Northern Plains.* Tucson: University of Arizona Press, 1995.

Haugh, Solanus. *Papago, the Desert People.* Washington, DC: Bureau of Catholic Indian Missions, 1958.

Hauptman, Laurence M. *Tribes and Tribulations: Misconceptions About American Indians and Their Histories.* Albuquerque: University of New Mexico Press, 1995.

Hauptman, Laurence M. and James D. Wherry, eds. *The Pequots in Southern New England: The Fall and Rise of an American Indian Nation.* Norman: University of Oklahoma Press, 1990.

Haviland, William A. and Marjory W. Power. *The Original Vermonters: Native Inhabitants, Past and Present.* Hanover, NH: University Press of New England, 1981.

Heath, D. B., ed. *Mourt's Relation: A Journal of the Pilgrims at Plymouth (1622).* Reprint. Cambridge, MA: Applewood Books, 1986.

Heckewelder, John. *History, Manner, and Customs of the Indian Nations Who Once Inhabited Pennsylvania and the Neighbouring States.* Philadelphia: Historical Society of Pennsylvania, 1876.

Heizer, R. F. and M. A. Whipple, *The California Indians: A Source Book.* Berkeley: University of California Press, 1951.

Heizer, R. F. and T. Kroeber, eds. *Ishi the Last Yahi: A Documentary History.* Berkeley: University of California Press, 1979.

Heizer, Robert F., ed. *The Handbook of North American Indians,* Vol. 8: *California.* Washington, DC: Smithsonian Institution, 1978.

Helm, June, ed. *The Handbook of North American Indians,* Vol. 6: *Subarctic.* Washington, DC: Smithsonian Institution, 1981.

Hickerson, Harold. *The Chippewa and Their Neighbors: A Study in Ethnohistory.* New York: Holt, Rinehart and Winston, 1970.

Hines, Donald M. *Magic in the Mountains, the Yakima Shaman: Power & Practice.* Issaquah, WA: Great Eagle Publishing, 1993.

Hippler, Arthur E. and John R. Wood. *The Subarctic Athabascans.* Fairbanks: University of Alaska, 1974.

Hodge, Frederick Webb. *Handbook of American Indians North of Mexico.* New York: Pageant Books, 1959.

Hoig, Stan. *Tribal Wars of the Southern Plains.* Norman: University of Oklahoma Press, 1993.

Hoijer, Harry. *Apachean Culture History and Ethnology.* Eds. Keith H. Basso and Morris E. Opler. Tucson: University of Arizona Press, 1971.

Hoijer, Harry. *Chiricahua and Mescalero Apache Texts.* Chicago: University of Chicago Press, 1938.

Holt, Ronald L. *Beneath These Red Cliffs: An Ethnohistory of the Utah Paiutes.* Albuquerque: University of New Mexico Press, 1992.

Hoover, Herbert T. *The Yankton Sioux.* New York: Chelsea House, 1988.

Hornung, Rick. *One Nation Under the Gun: Inside the Mohawk Civil War.* New York: Pantheon Books, 1992.

Hothem, Lar. *Treasures of the Mound Builders: Adena and Hopewell Artifacts of Ohio.* Lancaster, Ohio: Hothem House Books, 1989.

Howard, James H., *Shawnee! The Ceremonialism of a Native American Tribe and Its Cultural Background.* Athens: Ohio University Press, 1981.

Hoxie, Frederick E. *The Crow.* New York: Chelsea House, 1989.

Hoxie, Frederick E., ed. *Encyclopedia of North American Indians.* Boston: Houghton Mifflin Company, 1996.

Hoyt, Anne Kelley. *The Bibliography of the Chickasaw.* Metuchen, New Jersey: The Scarecrow Press, 1987.

Hrdlicka, Ales. *Physical Anthropology of the Lenape or Delawares, and of the Eastern Indians in General.* Washington, DC: U.S. Government Printing Office, 1916.

Hudson, Charles. *The Southeastern Indians.* Knoxville: University of Tennessee Press, 1976.

Hudson, Peter J. "Choctaw Indian Dishes (1939)." *A Choctaw Source Book.* New York: Garland Publishing, 1985: pp. 333–35.

Hudson, Travis and Ernest Underhay. *Crystals in the Sky: An Intellectual Odyssey Involving Chumash Astronomy, Cosmology and Rock Art.* Socorro, NM: Ballena Press, 1978.

Hyde, George E. *Indians of the Woodlands: From Prehistoric Times to 1725.* Norman: University of Oklahoma Press, 1962.

Ignacio, Amera. "Her Remark Offended Me." *Native Heritage: Personal Accounts by American Indians, 1790 to the Present.* Ed. Arlene Hirschfelder. New York: Macmillan, 1995.

Indian America; A Traveler's Companion. Santa Fe: John Muir Publications, 1989.

Indian Reservations: A State and Federal Handbook. Jefferson, NC: McFarland & Co., 1974.

Iverson, Peter. *The Plains Indians of the Twentieth Century.* Norman: University of Oklahoma Press, 1986.

Ives, John, W. *A Theory of Northern Athapaskan Prehistory.* Boulder, CO: Westview Press, 1990.

Jennings, Francis. *The Invasion of America: Indians, Colonization, and the Cant of Conquest.* Chapel Hill: University of North Carolina Press, 1975.

Joe, Rita and Lynn Henry. *Song of Rita Joe: Autobiography of a Mi'kmaq Poet.* Lincoln: University of Nebraska Press, 1996.

Johansen, Bruce E. *Life and Death in Mohawk Country.* Golden, CO: North American Press, 1993.

Johnson, Elias. *Legends, Traditions and Laws of the Iroquois, or Six Nations, and History of the Tuscarora Indians* (1881). Reprint. New York: AMS Press, 1978.

Johnson, John F. C., ed. *Eyak Legends: Stories and Photographs.* Anchorage: Chugach Heritage Foundation, n.d.

Johnson, Michael G. *The Native Tribes of North America: A Concise Encyclopedia.* New York: Macmillan, 1994.

Johnston, Basil H. *Tales the Elders Told: Ojibway Legends.* Toronto: Royal Ontario Museum, 1981.

Jonaitis, Aldona. *Art of the Northern Tlingit.* Seattle, Washington: University of Washington Press, 1986.

Jonaitis, Aldona, ed. *Chiefly Feasts: The Enduring Kwakiutl Potlatch.* New York: American Museum of Natural History, 1991.

Jorgensen, Joseph G. *Salish Language and Culture.* Bloomington: Indiana University Publications, 1969.

Jorgensen, Joseph G. *The Sun Dance Religion: Power for the Powerless.* Chicago: University of Chicago Press, 1972.

Joseph, Alice, Jane Chesky, and Rosamond B. Spicer. *The Desert People: A Study of the Papago Indians.* Chicago, IL: University of Chicago Press, 1974.

Josephy, Alvin M. Jr. *500 Nations: An Illustrated History of North American Indians.* New York: Alfred A. Knopf, 1994.

Josephy, Alvin M. Jr. *The Indian Heritage of America.* New York: Alfred A. Knopf, 1968.

Josephy, Alvin M. Jr. *The Nez Perce Indians and the Opening of the Northwest.* New Haven, CT: Yale University Press, 1965.

Josephy, Alvin M. Jr. *Now That the Buffalo's Gone: A Study of Today's American Indians.* New York: Alfred A. Knopf, 1982.

Kalifornsky, Peter. *A Dena'ina Legacy: K'tl'egh'i Sukdu: The Collected Writings of Peter Kalifornsky.* Eds. James Kari and Alan Boraas. Fairbanks: Alaska Native Language Center, 1991.

Kappler, Charles J. *Indian Affairs, Laws, and Treaties,* four volumes. Washington, DC: U.S. Government Printing Office, 1929.

Kari, James, ed. *Athabaskan Stories from Anvik: Rev. John W. Chapman's "Ten'a Texts and Tales."* Fairbanks: Alaska Native Language Center, 1981.

Kari, James, translator and editor. "When They Were Killed at 'Lake That Has an Arm' (Kluane Lake)." *Tatl'ahwt'aenn Nenn': The Headwaters Peoples Country: Narratives of the Upper Ahtna Athabaskans.* Fairbanks: Alaska Native Language Center, 1985.

Kasner, Leone Leston. *Siletz: Survival for an Artifact.* Dallas OR: Itemizer-Observer, 1977.

Kennedy, Roger G. *Hidden Cities: The Discovery and Loss of Ancient American Civilization.* New York: Macmillan, 1994.

Kenner, Charles L. *A History of New Mexican-Plains Indian Relations.* Norman: University of Oklahoma Press, 1969, 1994.

Kent, Zachary, *Tecumseh.* Chicago, IL: Children's Press, 1992.

Kidwell, Clara Sue and Charles Roberts. *The Choctaws: A Critical Bibliography.* Bloomington: Indiana University Press for the Newberry Library, 1980.

Kirk, Ruth and Richard D. Daugherty. *Hunter of the Whale.* New York: William Morrow, 1974.

Klein, Barry T. *Reference Encyclopedia of the American Indian,* Seventh edition. West Nyack, NY: Todd Publications, 1995.

Klein, Laura F. and Lillian A. Ackerman. *Women and Power in Native North America.* Norman: University of Oklahoma, 1995.

Kluckhohn, Clyde and Dorothea Leighton. *The Navaho.* 1946. Revised edition. Cambridge, MA: Harvard University Press, 1974.

Korp, Maureen. *The Sacred Geography of the American Mound Builders.* New York: Edwin Mellen Press, 1990.

Kraft, Herbert C. *The Lenape: Archaeology, History, and Ethnography.* Newark: New Jersey Historical Society, 1986.

Kraft, Herbert C. *The Lenape Indians of New Jersey.* South Orange, NJ: Seton Hall University Museum, 1987.

Krech, Shepard III, ed. *Indians, Animals and the Fur Trade.* Athens: University of Georgia Press, 1981.

Kroeber, Alfred L. "The Achomawi and Atsugewi," "The Chilula.," "The Luiseño: Elements of Civilization," "The Luiseño: Organization of Civilization," "The Miwok," and "The Pomo." *Handbook of the Indians of California.* Washington, DC: U.S. Government Printing Office, 1925.

Krupp, E. C. *Beyond the Blue Horizon: Myths & Legends of the Sun, Moon, Stars, & Planets.* New York: Oxford University Press, 1991.

Lacey, Theresa Jensen. *The Pawnee.* New York: Chelsea House Publishers, 1996.

Ladd, Edmund J. "Zuñi Religion and Philosophy." *Zuñi & El Morro.* Santa Fe: SAR Press, 1983.

Langdon, Steve J. *The Native People of Alaska*. Anchorage: Greatland Graphics, 1993.

Laubin, Reginald and Gladys Laubin. *Indian Dances of North America: Their Importance to Indian Life*. Norman: University of Oklahoma Press, 1976.

Laughlin, William S. "The Aleut-Eskimo Community." *The North American Indians: A Sourcebook*. Ed. Roger C. Owen. New York: Macmillan, 1967.

Leach, Douglas E. *Flintlock and Tomahawk: New England in King Philip's War*. New York: Macmillan, 1959.

Leitch, Barbara A. *A Concise Dictionary of Indian Tribes of North America*. Algonac, MI: Reference Publications, 1979.

Lewis, Anna. *Chief Pushmataha, American Patriot: The Story of the Choctaws' Struggle for Survival*. New York: Exposition Press, 1959.

Lewis, David Rich. *Neither Wolf Nor Dog: American Indians, Environment, and Agrarian Change*. Oxford: Oxford University Press, 1994.

Liptak, Karen. *North American Indian Ceremonies*. New York: Franklin Watts, 1992.

Lowie, Robert H. *The Crow Indians*. Lincoln: University of Nebraska Press, 1983.

Lowie, Robert H. *Indians of the Plains*. Garden City, NY: Natural History Press, 1963.

Lucius, William A. and David A. Breternitz. *Northern Anasazi Ceramic Styles: A Fieldguide for Identification*. Center for Indigenous Studies in the Americas Publications in Anthropology, 1992.

Lund, Annabel. *Heartbeat: World Eskimo Indian Olympics: Alaska Native Sport and Dance Traditions*. Juneau: Fairweather Press, 1986.

Lurie, Nancy Oestreich. "Weetamoo, 1638–1676." *North American Indian Lives*. Milwaukee: Milwaukee Public Library, 1985.

MacEwan, Grant. *Métis Makers of History*. Saskatoon: Western Producer Prairie Books, 1981.

Madsen, Brigham D. *The Shoshoni Frontier and the Bear River Massacre*. Salt Lake City: University of Utah Press, 1985.

Mahon, John K. *History of the Second Seminole War 1835–1842.* Gainsville: University of Florida Press, 1967.

Maillard, Antoine Simon and Joseph M. Bellenger. *Grammaire de la Langue Mikmaque.* English translation published as *Grammar of the Mikmaque Language.* New York: AMS Press, 1970.

Mails, Thomas E. *The Cherokee People: The Story of the Cherokees from Earliest Origins to Contemporary Times.* Tulsa, OK: Council Oak Books, 1992.

Mails, Thomas E. *The Mystic Warriors of the Plains: The Culture, Arts, Crafts and Religion of the Plains Indians.* Tulsa: Council Oaks Books, 1991.

Mails, Thomas E. *Peoples of the Plains.* Tulsa, OK: Council Oak Books, 1997.

Mails, Thomas E. *The Pueblo Children of the Earth Mother.* Vol. 2. Garden City, NY: Doubleday, 1983.

Malinowksi, Sharon, ed. *Notable Native Americans.* Detroit: Gale Research, 1995.

Malinowski, Sharon and Simon Glickman, eds. *Native North American Biography.* Detroit: U•X•L, 1996.

Malone, Patrick M. *The Skulking Way of War: Technology and Tactics Among the New England Indians.* Lanham, MA: Madison Books, 1991.

Mandelbaum, David G. *The Plains Cree: An Ethnographic, Historical, and Comparative Study.* Regina, Saskatchewan: Canadian Plains Research Center, 1979.

Markowitz, Harvey, ed. *American Indians,* Pasadena, CA: Salem Press, 1995.

Marquis, Arnold. *A Guide to America's Indians: Ceremonials, Reservations, and Museums.* Norman: University of Oklahoma Press, 1974.

Marriott, Alice L. *The Ten Grandmothers.* Norman: University of Oklahoma Press, 1945.

Marriott, Alice and Carol K. Rachlin. *Plains Indian Mythology.* New York: Thomas Y. Crowell, 1975.

Martin, Calvin. *Keepers of the Game: Indian-Animal Relationships and the Fur Trade.* Berkeley: University of California Press, 1978.

Matthiessen, Peter. *In the Spirit of Crazy Horse.* New York: Viking Penguin, 1980.

Maxwell, James A., ed. *America's Fascinating Indian Heritage.* New York: The Reader's Digest Association, 1978.

Mayhall, Mildred P. *The Kiowas.* Norman: University of Oklahoma Press, 1962.

Mays, Buddy. *Indian Villages of the Southwest.* San Francisco: Chronicle Books, 1985.

McBride, Bunny. *Molly Spotted Elk: A Penobscot in Paris.* Norman and London: University of Oklahoma Press, 1995.

McFadden, Steven. *Profiles in Wisdom: Native Elders Speak About the Earth.* Sante Fe: Bear & Co., 1991.

McFee, Malcolm. *Modern Blackfeet: Montanans on a Reservation.* New York: Holt, Rinehart and Winston, 1972.

McGinnis, Anthony. *Counting Coup and Cutting Horses: Intertribal Warfare on the Northern Plains 1738–1889.* Evergreen, CO: Cordillera Press, 1990.

McKee, Jesse O. and Jon A. Schlenker. *The Choctaws: Cultural Evolution of a Native American Tribe.* Jackson: University Press of Mississippi, 1980.

McKennan, Robert, A. "The Upper Tanana Indians." *Yale University Publications in Anthropology: 55.* New Haven, CT: Yale University, 1959.

Melody, Michael E. *The Apaches: A Critical Bibliography.* Bloomington: Indiana University Press, 1977.

Merriam, C. Hart. "The Luiseño: Observations on Mission Indians." *Studies of California Indians.* Edited by the Staff of the Department of Anthropology of the University of California. Berkeley: University of California Press, 1962.

Meyer, Roy W. *History of the Santee Sioux: United States Indian Policy on Trial.* Lincoln: University of Nebraska Press, 1993.

Miller, Bruce W. *Chumash: A Picture of Their World.* Los Osos, CA: Sand River Press, 1988.

Miller, Jay. *The Delaware.* Chicago: Childrens Press, 1994.

Milliken, Randall. *A Time of Little Choice: The Disintegration of Tribal Culture in the San Francisco Bay Area, 1769–1810.* Menlo Park, CA: Ballena Press, 1995.

Milloy, John S. *The Plains Cree: Trade, Diplomacy and War, 1790 to 1870.* Winnipeg: University of Manitoba Press, 1988.

Minge, Ward Alan. *Acoma: Pueblo in the Sky.* Albuquerque: University of New Mexico Press, 1976.

Minority Rights Group. *Polar Peoples: Self Determination and Development.* London: Minority Rights Publications, 1994.

Mississippian Communities and Households. Tuscaloosa: University of Alabama Press, 1995.

Momaday, N. Scott. *The Way to Rainy Mountain.* Albuquerque: University of New Mexico Press, 1969.

Moore, John H. *The Cheyenne Nation: A Social and Demographic History.* Lincoln: University of Nebraska Press, 1987.

Moorhead, Max L. *The Apache Frontier: Jacobo Ugarte and Spanish-Indian Relations in Northern New Spain, 1769–1791.* Norman: University of Oklahoma Press, 1968.

Moquin, Wayne, ed. *Great Documents in American Indian History.* New York: Da Capo Press, 1973.

Morgan, Lewis H. *League of the Ho-de-no-sau-nee or Iroquois.* New Haven, CT: Human Relations Area Files, 1954: p. 243.

Morrison, R. Bruce and C. Roderick Wilson, eds. *Native Peoples: The Canadian Experience.* Toronto: McClellan & Stewart, 1986.

Murie, James R. *Ceremonies of the Pawnee.* Smithsonian Contributions to Anthropology, No. 27. Washington, DC: Smithsonian Institution, 1981. Reprint. Lincoln: University of Nebraska Press for the American Indian Studies Research Institute, 1989.

Murphy, Robert F. and Yolanda Murphy. "Shoshone-Bannock Subsistence and Society." *Anthropological Records.* 16:7. Berkeley: University of California Press, 1960.

Myers, Arthur. *The Pawnee.* New York: F. Watts, 1993.

Myers, William Starr, ed. *The Story of New Jersey,* Volume 1. Ed. New York: Lewis Historical Publishing Company, 1945.

Mysteries of the Ancient Americas: The New World Before Columbus. Pleasantville, NY: The Reader's Digest Association, 1986.

Nabakov, Peter and Robert Easton. *Native American Architecture.* New York: Oxford University Press, 1989.

Nairne, Thomas. *Nairne's Mushogean Journals: The 1708 Expedition to the Mississippi River.* Jackson: University Press of Mississippi, 1988.

Native Cultures in Alaska. Anchorage: Alaska Geographic Society, 1996.

Newcomb, W. W. Jr. *The Indians of Texas: From Prehistoric to Modern Times.* Austin: University of Texas Press, 1961.

Newkumet, Vynola Beaver and Howard L. Meredith. *Hasinai: A Traditional History of the Caddo Confederacy.* College Station: Texas A & M University Press, 1988.

Noble, David Grant. *Pueblos, Villages, Forts & Trails: A Guide to New Mexico's Past.* Albuquerque: University of New Mexico Press, 1994.

Northway, Walter. *Walter Northway.* Fairbanks: Alaska Native Language Center, 1987.

Norton, Jack. *Genocide in Northwestern California: When Our Worlds Cried.* San Francisco: Indian Historian Press, 1979.

O'Brien, Sharon. *American Indian Tribal Governments.* Norman: University of Oklahoma Press, 1989.

Olmsted, D. L. *Achumawi Dictionary.* Berkeley: University of California Press, 1966.

Olson, Ronald L. *The Quinault Indians.* Seattle: University of Washington Press, 1967.

O'Neill, Laurie A. *The Shawnees: People of the Eastern Woodlands.* Brookfield, CT: The Millbrook Press, 1995.

Opler, Morris Edward. *An Apache Life-Way.* New York: Cooper Square Publishers, 1965.

Orr, Charles, ed. *History of the Pequot War.* Cleveland: Helman-Taylor, 1897.

Ortiz, Alfonso, ed. *The Handbook of North American Indians,* Vol. 10: *Southwest.* Washington, DC: Smithsonian Institution, 1983.

Ortiz, Alfonso. *The Pueblo.* New York: Chelsea House Publishers, 1992.

Osgood, Cornelius. "Ingalik Mental Culture." *Yale University Publications in Anthropology: 56.* New Haven, CT: Yale University, 1959.

Oswalt, Wendell H. "The Crow: Plains Warriors and Bison Hunters." *This Land Was Theirs: A Study of North American Indians.* Mountain View, CA: Mayfield Publishing, 1988.

Owen, Roger C., James J. F. Deetz, and Anthony D. Fisher, eds. *A Guide to Indian Tribes of the Pacific Northwest.* Norman: University of Oklahoma Press, 1986.

Owen, Roger C., James J. F. Deetz, and Anthony D. Fisher, eds. *Indians of the Pacific Northwest: A History.* Norman: University of Oklahoma Press, 1981.

Owen, Roger C., James J. F. Deetz, and Anthony D. Fisher, eds. *The North American Indians: A Sourcebook.* New York: MacMillan, 1967.

Parsons, Elsie Clews. "Notes on the Caddo." *Memoirs of the American Anthropological Association,* No. 57. Menasha, WI: American Anthropological Association, 1941.

Parsons, Elsie Clews. *Pueblo Mothers and Children.* Ed. Barbara A. Babcock. Santa Fe: Ancient City Press, 1991.

Parsons, Elsie Clews. *The Social Organization of the Tewa of New Mexico.* American Anthropological Association Memoirs, Nos. 36–39. Reprint. New York: Kraus, 1964.

Patencio, Francisco. *Stories and Legends of the Palm Springs Indians As Told to Margaret Boynton.* Los Angeles: Times-Mirror Press, 1943.

Paterek, Josephine. *Encyclopedia of American Indian Costume.* Santa Barbara: ABC-CLIO, 1994.

Pauketat, Timothy R. *Temples for Cahokia Lords.* Ann Arbor: University of Michigan, Museum of Anthropology, 1993.

Peat, F. David. *Lighting the Seventh Fire: The Spiritual Ways, Healing, and Science of the Native American.* NY: Carol Publishing Group, 1994.

Penney, David W. *Art of the American Indian Frontier: The Chandler-Pohrt Collection.* Seattle: University of Washington Press, 1992.

Perdue, Theda. *The Cherokee.* New York: Chelsea House Publishers, 1989.

Peroff, N. C. *Menominee Drums: Tribal Termination and Restoration, 1954–1974.* Norman: University of Oklahoma Press, 1982.

Perry, Richard J. *Apache Reservation: Indigenous Peoples and the American State*. Austin: University of Texas Press, 1993.

Perry, Richard J. *Western Apache Heritage: People of the Mountain Corridor.* Austin: University of Texas Press, 1991.

Perttula, Timothy K. "The Caddo Nation." *Archeological and Ethnohistoric Perspectives*. Austin: University of Texas Press, 1992.

Phillips, G.H. *Indians and Indian Agents: The Origins of the Reservation System in California, 1849–1852*. Norman: University of Oklahoma Press, 1997.

Place, Ann Marie. "Putting a Face on Colonization: Factionalism and Gender Politics in the Life History of Awashunkes, the 'Squaw Sachem' of Saconet." *Northeastern Indians Lives*. Ed. Robert S. Grumet. Amherst: University of Massachusetts Press, 1996.

Pond, Samuel. *The Dakota People or Sioux in Minnesota as They Were in 1834*. St. Paul: Minnesota Historical Society Press, 1986.

Pope, Saxton T. "The Medical History of Ishi." *University of California Publications in American Archaeology and Ethnology*. Vol. 13, No. 5. Berkeley: University of California Press, 1920.

Pope, Saxton T. "Yahi Archery." *University of California Publications in American Archaeology and Ethnology,* Vol. 13, No. 3. Berkeley: University of California Press, 1923.

Porter, Frank W. III. *The Coast Salish Peoples*. New York: Chelsea House Publishers, 1989.

Powers, Stephen. "The Achomawi." *Tribes of California*. Berkeley: University of California Press, 1976. Reprinted from *Contributions to North American Ethnology*, Vol. 3. Washington, DC: U.S. Government Printing Office, 1877.

Preacher, Stephen. *Anasazi Sunrise: The Mystery of Sacrifice Rock*. El Cajon, CA: The Rugged Individualist, 1992.

Press, Margaret L. "Chemehuevi: A Grammar and Lexicon." *Linguistics,* Vol. 92. Berkeley: University of California Press, 1979.

Rand, Silas Tertius. *Dictionary of the Language of the Micmac Indians, Who Reside in Nova Scotia, New Brunswick, Prince Edward Island, Cape Breton, and Newfoundland*. Halifax, Nova Scotia: Nova Scotia Print Co., 1888. Reprint. New York, Johnson Reprint Corp., 1972.

Ray, Arthur J. *Indians in the Fur Trade: Their Role as Trappers, Hunters & Middle Man in the Lands Southwest of Hudson Bay, 1660–1860.* Toronto: University of Toronto Press, 1974.

Reddy, Marlita A. *Statistical Record of Native North Americans.* Detroit: Gale Research, 1996.

Rice, Julian, ed. *Deer Women and Elk Men: The Lakota Narratives of Ella Deloria.* Albuquerque: University of New Mexico Press, 1992.

Richardson, Rupert Norval. *The Comanche Barrier to the South Plains Settlement.* Glendale, CA: Arthur H. Clarke, 1955.

Roberts, David. *In Search of the Old Ones.* New York: Simon & Schuster, 1996.

Rockwell, Wilson. *The Utes: A Forgotten People.* Denver, CO: Alan Swallow, 1956.

Rohner, Ronald P. and Evelyn C. Rohner. *The Kwakiutl: Indians of British Columbia.* New York: Holt, Rinehart and Winston, 1970.

Rollings, Willard H. *The Osage: An Ethnohistorical Study of Hegemony on the Prairie-Plains.* Columbia: University of Missouri Press, 1992.

Rountree, Helen C., ed. *Pocahontas's People: The Powhatan Indians of Virginia through Four Centuries.* Norman: University of Oklahoma Press, 1990.

Rountree, Helen C., ed. *Powhatan Foreign Relations, 1500–1722.* Charlottesville: University Press of Virginia, 1993.

Rountree, Helen C., ed. *The Powhatan Indians of Virginia: Their Native Culture.* Norman: University of Oklahoma Press, 1989.

Ruby, Robert H. *The Chinook Indians: Traders of the Lower Columbia River.* Norman: University of Oklahoma Press, 1976.

Ruby, Robert H. and John A. Brown. *A Guide to Indian Tribes of the Pacific Northwest.* Norman: University of Oklahoma Press, 1986.

Russell, Frank. *The Pima Indians.* Tucson: University of Arizona Press, 1975.

Salisbury, Richard F. *A Homeland for the Cree: Regional Development in James Bay 1971–1981.* Kingston & Montreal: McGill-Queen's University Press, 1986.

Salzmann, Zdenek. *The Arapaho Indians: A Research Guide and Bibliography.* New York: Greenwood Press, 1988.

Samuel, Cheryl. *The Chilkat Dancing Blanket*. Seattle: Pacific Search Press, 1982.

Sando, Joe S. *Pueblo Nations: Eight Centuries of Pueblo Indian History*. Santa Fe: Clear Light Publishers, 1992.

Sauter, John and Bruce Johnson. *Tillamook Indians of the Oregon Coast*. Portland OR: Binfords and Mort, 1974.

Sawchuck, Joe. *The Métis of Manitoba: Reformulation of an Ethnic Identity*. Toronto: Peter Martin Associates, 1978.

Schlesier, Karl H. "Introduction," and "Commentary: A History of Ethnic Groups in the Great Plains A.D. 500–1550." *Plains Indians, A.D. 500–1500: The Archaeological Past of Historic Groups*. Ed. Karl H. Schlesier. Norman: University of Oklahoma Press, 1994.

Schultz, Willard James. *Blackfeet and Buffalo: Memories of Life among the Indians*. Norman: University of Oklahoma Press, 1962.

Schuster, Helen. *The Yakimas: A Critical Bibliography*. Bloomington: Indiana University Press, 1982.

Segal, Charles M. and David C. Stineback, eds. *Puritans, Indians and Manifest Destiny*. New York: Putnam, 1977.

Seger, John H. *Early Days among the Cheyenne and Arapaho Indians*. Ed. Stanley Vestal. Norman: University of Oklahoma Press, 1956.

Seiler, Hansjakob. *Cahuilla Texts with an Introduction*. Bloomington: Indiana University, 1970.

Shaffer, Lynda Norene. *Native Americans Before 1492: The Moundbuilding Centers of the Eastern Woodlands*. New York: M. E. Sharpe, 1992.

Shames, Deborah, ed. *Freedom with Reservation: The Menominee Struggle to Save Their Land and People*. Madison: National Committee to Save the Menominee People and Forests/Wisconsin Indian Legal Services, 1972.

Shawano, Marlene Miller. *Native Dress of the Stockbridge Munsee Band Mohican Indians*. Stockbridge Munsee Reservation Library, n.d.

Shipek, Florence. *Pushed into the Rocks: Southern California Indian Land Tenure, 1769–1986*. Lincoln: University of Nebraska Press, 1990.

Silverberg, Robert. *The Mound Builders*. Greenwich, CT: New York Graphic Society, Ltd., 1970.

Siy, Alexandra, *The Eeyou: People of Eastern James Bay.* New York: Dillon Press, 1993.

Slickpoo, Allen P. and Deward E. Walker Jr. *Noon Nee-Me-Poo: We, the Nez Perces.* Lapwai: Nez Perce Tribe of Idaho, 1973.

Smelcer, John. "Dotson'Sa, Great Raven Makes the World." *The Raven and the Totem: Traditional Alaska Native Myths and Tales.* Anchorage: Salmon Run, 1992: pp. 124–25.

Smith, Anne M., ed. *Shoshone Tales.* Salt Lake City: University of Utah Press, 1993.

Smith, F. Todd. *The Caddo Indians: Tribes at the Convergence of Empires, 1542–1854.* College Station: University of Texas A&M Press, 1995.

Smith, Marian W. *Indians of the Urban Northwest.* New York: AMS Press, 1949.

Smith, Marian W. *The Puyallup-Nisqually.* New York: Columbia University Press, 1940.

Snow, Dean R. *The Iroquois.* Cambridge, MA: Blackwell Publishers, 1994.

Speck, Frank G. *Penobscot Man: The Life History of a Forest Tribe in Maine.* Philadelphia: University of Pennsylvania Press, 1940.

Speck, Frank G. *A Study of the Indian Big House Ceremony.* Harrisburg: Pennsylvania Historical Commission, 1931.

Spector, Janet D. *What This Awl Means: Feminist Archaeology at a Wahpeton Dakota Village.* St. Paul: Minnesota Historical Society Press, 1993.

Spicer, Edward H. *Cycles of Conquest: The Impact of Spain, Mexico, and the United States on the Indians of the Southwest, 1533–1960.* Tucson, AZ: University of Arizona Press, 1962.

Spindler, George and Louise Spindler. *Dreamers With Power: The Menomini Indians.* New York: Holt, Rinehart & Winston, 1971.

Spittal, W. G., ed. *Iroquois Women: An Anthology.* Ohsweken, Ontario: Iroqrafts Ltd., 1990.

Spradley, James P. *Guests Never Leave Hungry: The Autobiography of James Sewid, A Kwakiutl Indian.* New Haven: Yale University Press, 1969.

Statistical Data for Planning Stockbridge Munsee Reservation. Billings, MT: U.S. Department of the Interior, Bureau of Indian Affairs, 1975.

Steele, Ian K. *Warpaths: Invasions of North America.* New York: Oxford University Press, 1994.

Steward, Julian H. *Basin-Plateau Aboriginal Sociopolitical Groups.* Washington, DC: Smithsonian Institution. *The Bureau of American Ethnology Bulletin,* No. 120. Washington, DC: U.S. Government Printing Office, 1938.

Stewart, Omer C. *Peyote Religion: A History.* Norman: University of Oklahoma, 1987.

Stevens, Susan McCullough. "Passamaquoddy Economic Development in Cultural and Historical Perspective." *World Anthropology: American Indian Economic Development.* Ed. Sam Stanley. The Hague: Mouton Publishers, 1978.

Stockel, H. Henrietta. "Ceremonies and Celebrations." *Women Of the Apache Nation: Voices of Truth.* Reno: University of Nevada Press, 1991.

Subarctic. Ed. June Helm. Washington, DC: Smithsonian Institution, 1981.

Suttles, Wayne, ed. *The Handbook of North American Indians,* Vol. 7: *Northwest Coast.* Washington, DC: Smithsonian Institution, 1990.

Swanson, Earl H, ed. *Languages and Culture of Western North America.* Pocatello: Idaho State University Press, 1970.

Swanton, John Reed. *Indian Tribes of the Lower Mississippi Valley and Adjacent Coast of the Gulf of Mexico.* Washington, DC: U.S. Government Printing Office, 1911.

Swanton, John Reed. *The Indian Tribes of North America,* Vol. 1: *Northeast.* Washington, DC: Smithsonian Institution. Reprinted from: *The Bureau of American Ethnology Bulletin,* No. 145. Washington, DC: U.S. Government Printing Office, 1953.

Swanton, John Reed. *Source Material for the Social and Ceremonial Life of the Choctaw Indians.* Bulletin No. 103. Washington, DC: U.S. Government Printing Office, 1931.

Symington, Fraser. *The Canadian Indian: The Illustrated History of the Great Tribes of Canada.* Toronto: McClelland & Stewart, 1969.

Tanner, Helen H., ed. *Atlas of Great Lakes Indian History.* Norman: University of Oklahoma Press, 1987.

Tantaquidgeon, Gladys. *Folk Medicine of the Delaware and Related Algonkian Indians.* Harrisburg: Pennsylvania Historical and Museum Commission, Anthropological Series 3, 1972.

Tantaquidgeon, Gladys. *A Study of Delaware Indian Medicine Practice and Folk Beliefs.* Harrisburg: Pennsylvania Historical Commission, 1942.

Teit, James A. "The Salishan Tribes of the Western Plateaus." *Bureau of American Ethnology Annual Report.* No. 45. Ed. Franz Boas. 1927–1928.

Tennberg, Monica, ed. *Unity and Diversity in Arctic Societies.* Rovaniemi, Finland: International Arctic Social Sciences Association, 1996.

Terrell, John Upton. *American Indian Almanac.* New York: World Publishing, 1971.

Thomas, Cyrus. *Report on the Mound Explorations of the Bureau of Ethnology.* Washington, DC: Smithsonian Institution, 1894.

Thomas, David Hurst, ed. *A Great Basin Shoshonean Source Book.* New York: Garland Publishing, 1986.

Thompson, Chad. *Athabaskan Languages and the Schools: A Handbook for Teachers.* Juneau: Alaska Department of Education, 1984.

Thompson, Judy. *From the Land: Two Hundred Years of Dene Clothing.* Hull, Quebec: Canadian Museum of Civilization, 1994.

Through Indian Eyes: The Untold Story of Native American Peoples. Pleasantville, NY: Reader's Digest Association, 1995.

Tilton, Robert S. *Pocahontas: The Evolution of an American Narrative.* New York: Cambridge University Press, 1994.

Tohono O'Odham: History of the Desert People. Arizona: Papago Tribe, c1985.

Tooker, Elisabeth, ed. *An Iroquois Source Book,* Volumes 1 and 2. New York: Garland Publishing, 1985.

"Traditional and Contemporary Ceremonies, Rituals, Festivals, Music, and Dance." *Native America: Portrait of the Peoples.* Ed. Duane Champagne. Detroit: Gale Research, 1994.

Trafzer, Clifford E. *The Chinook.* New York: Chelsea House, 1990.

Trafzer, Clifford E. *Yakima, Palouse, Cayuse, Umatilla, Walla Walla, and Wanapum Indians.* Metuchen, New Jersey: Scarecrow Press, 1992.

Trigger, Bruce G., ed. *The Handbook of North American Indians,* Vol. 15: *Northeast.* Washington, DC: Smithsonian Institution, 1978.

Trigger, Bruce G. *Natives and Newcomers: Canada's "Heroic Age" Reconsidered.* Manchester: McGill-Queen's University Press, 1985.

Trimble, Stephen. *The People: Indians of the American Southwest.* Santa Fe: NM: Sar Press, 1993.

Tyson, Carl N. *The Pawnee People.* Phoenix: Indian Tribal Series, 1976.

Underhill, Ruth. *The Autobiography of a Papago Woman.* Menasha, WI: American Anthropological Memoirs #48, 1936.

Underhill, Ruth. *Life in the Pueblos.* Santa Fe: Ancient City Press, 1991.

Underhill, Ruth. *Singing for Power.* Tucson: University of Arizona Press, 1979.

United American Indians of New England. "National Day of Mourning." *Literature of the American Indian.* Ed. Thomas E. Sanders and Walter W. Peek. Abridged edition. Beverly Hills, CA: Glencoe Press, 1976.

The Vinland Sagas: The Norse Discovery of America. Translated by Magnus Magnusson and Hermann Palsson. Baltimore: Penguin, 1965.

Vogel, Virgil J. *American Indian Medicine.* Norman: University of Oklahoma Press, 1970.

The Wabanakis of Maine and the Maritimes: A Resource Book About Penobscot, Passamaquoddy, Maliseet, Micmac, and Abenaki Indians. Philadelphia: American Friends Service Committee (AFSC), 1989.

Waldman, Carl. *Atlas of the North American Indian.* New York: Facts On File, 1985.

Waldman, Carl. *Encyclopedia of Native American Tribes.* New York: Facts on File, 1988.

Waldman, Carl. *Who Was Who in Native American History: Indians and NonIndians From Early Contacts Through 1900.* New York: Facts on File, 1990.

Waldman, Harry, ed. "Caddo." *Encyclopedia of Indians of the Americas.* St. Clair Shores, MI: Scholarly Press, 1974.

Walens, Stanley. *Feasting with Cannibals: An Essay on Kwakiutl Cosmology.* Princeton, NJ: Princeton University Press, 1981.

Wallace, Anthony F. C. *The Death and Rebirth of the Seneca: The History and Culture of the Great Iroquois Nation, Their Destruction and Demoralization, and Their Cultural Revival at the Hands of the Indian Visionary, Handsome Lake.* New York: Knopf, 1969.

Wallace, Anthony F. C. *King of the Delawares: Teedyuscung 1700–1763.* Philadelphia: University of Pennsylvania Press, 1949.

Walthall, John A. *Moundville: An Introduction to the Archaeology of a Mississippian Chiefdom.* Tuscaloosa: University of Alabama, Alabama Museum of Natural History, 1977.

Warren, William W. *History of the Ojibway People.* St. Paul: Minnesota Historical Society Press, 1885, reprint 1984.

Waterman, Thomas T. "The Yana Indians." *University of California Publications in American Archaeology and Ethnology,* Vol. 13, No. 2. Berkeley: University of California Press, 1918.

Weatherford, Jack. *Native Roots, How the Indians Enriched America.* New York: Ballantine Books, 1991.

Wedel, Waldo R. *An Introduction to Pawnee Archeology.* Bulletin of the Smithsonian Institution, Bureau of American Ethnology, No. 112. Washington, DC: U.S. Government Printing Office, 1936. Reprint. Lincoln, NE: J & L Reprint, 1977.

Wedel, Waldo R. *Prehistoric Man on the Great Plains.* Norman: University of Oklahoma Press, 1961.

Wells, Samuel J. and Roseanna Tubby, eds. *After Removal: The Choctaw in Mississippi.* Jackson: University Press of Mississippi, 1986.

Weltfish, Gene. *The Lost Universe: Pawnee Life and Culture.* Lincoln: University of Nebraska Press, 1977.

Weslager, Clinton A. *The Delaware Indian Westward Migration.* Wallingford, PA: Middle Atlantic Press, 1978.

Weslager, Clinton A. *The Delaware Indians: A History.* New Brunswick, NJ: Rutgers University Press, 1972.

White, Leslie A. *The Acoma Indians, People of the Sky City.* Originally published in *47th Annual Report of the Bureau of American Ethnology.* Washington, DC: Smithsonian Institution, 1932; Glorieta, NM: The Rio Grande Press, 1973.

White, Raymond. "Religion and Its Role Among the Luiseño." *Native Californians: A Theoretical Retrospective.* Eds. Lowell J. Bean and Thomas C. Blackburn. Socorro, NM: Ballena Press, 1976.

White, Richard. *Land Use, Environment, and Social Change.* Seattle: University of Washington Press, 1992.

Wilbur, C. Keith. *The New England Indians.* Old Saybrook, CT: Globe Pequot Press, 1978.

Wilker, Josh. *The Lenape.* New York: Chelsea House Publishers, 1994.

Wilson, Terry P. *The Underground Reservation: Osage Oil.* Lincoln: University of Nebraska Press, 1985.

Wissler, Clark. *Indians of the United States.* New York: Doubleday, 1940.

Witherspoon, Gary. *Language and Art in the Navajo Universe.* Ann Arbor: University of Michigan Press, 1977.

Wolcott, Harry F. *A Kwakiutl Village and School.* Prospect Heights, IL: Waveland Press, 1984.

Wood, Peter H., Gregory A. Waselkov, and M. Thomas Hatley, eds. *Powhatan's Mantle: Indians in the Colonial Southeast.* Lincoln: University of Nebraska Press, 1989.

Wood, W. Raymond. "Plains Trade in Prehistoric and Protohistoric Intertribal Relations." *Anthropology on the Great Plains.* Eds. Raymond Wood and Margot Liberty. Lincoln: University of Nebraska Press, 1980.

Woodward, Grace Steele. *Pocahontas.* Norman: University of Oklahoma Press, 1969.

Woodward, Susan L. and Jerry N. McDonald. *Indian Mounds of the Middle Ohio Valley: A Guide to Adena and Ohio Hopewell Sites.* Newark, OH: McDonald & Woodward Publishing Co., 1986.

Worcester, Donald E. *The Apache.* Norman: University of Oklahoma Press, 1979.

The World of the American Indians. Washington, DC: National Geographic Society, 1974.

Wright, Muriel H. *A Guide to the Indian Tribes of Oklahoma.* Norman: University of Oklahoma Press, 1951, 1986.

Yenne, Bill. *The Encyclopedia of North American Indian Tribes.* New York: Crescent Books, 1986.

Yenne, Bill and Susan Garratt. *North American Indians.* Secaucus, NJ: Chartwell Books, 1984.

Young, Mary Elizabeth. *Redskins, Ruffleshirts, and Rednecks.* Norman: University of Oklahoma Press, 1961.

Periodicals

Alexander, Don. "A First Nation Elder's Perspective on the Environment" (interview with Haida Nation activist Lavina White). *Alternatives* (March/April 1994): p. 12.

Angulo, Jaime de. "The Achumawi Life Force" (Extract, "La psychologie religieuse des Achumawi." *Anthropos* 23, 1928). *Journal of California Anthropology* 2, No. 1 (1974): pp. 60–63.

Arden, Harvey. "Living Iroquois Confederacy." *National Geographic,* Vol. 172, No. 3 (September 1987): pp. 370–403.

Barrett, Samuel A. "The Ethnogeography of the Pomo and Neighboring Indians." *University of California Publications in American Archaeology and Ethnology* 6:1 (1908): pp. 1–332.

Barrett, Samuel A., and Edward W. Gifford. "Miwok Material Culture." *Public Museum of the City of Milwaukee Bulletin* 2:4 (1933): pp. 117–376.

Capron, Lewis. "Florida's Emerging Seminoles." *National Geographic,* Vol. 136, No. 5 (November 1969): pp. 716–34.

Carlson, Paul H. "Indian Agriculture, Changing Subsistence Patterns, and the Environment on the Southern Great Plains." *Agricultural History* 66, No. 2 (1992): pp. 52–60.

Carney, Jim. "Drinking Cut Short Sockalexis' Pro Career." *Beacon Journal* (October 13, 1995).

Crisp, David. "Tribes Make Manufacturing Push: Advocates Use Network to Expand Reach." *Billings Gazette* (February 11, 1996).

Dixon, Roland B. "Achomawi and Atsugewi Tales." *Journal of American Folk-Lore* 21, No. 80 (1908): pp. 159–77.

Dixon, Roland B. "Notes on the Achomawi and Atsugewi Indians of Northern California." *American Anthropologist* 10, No. 2 (1908): pp. 208–20.

DuBois, Constance Goddard. "The Religion of the Luiseño Indians of Southern California." *University of California Publications in American Archaeology and Ethnology* 8, No. 3 (1908): pp. 69–186.

Durham, Michael S. "Mound Country." *American Heritage,* Vol. 46, No. 2 (April 1995): p. 118.

Egan, Timothy. "Tribe Stops Study of Bones That Challenges Its History." *New York Times* (September 30, 1996): A1, A10.

Euler, Robert C. "Southern Paiute Ethnohistory." *Anthropological Papers.* 78:28. University of Utah (April 1966).

Fagan, Brian. "Bison Hunters of the Northern Plains." *Archaeology* 47, No. 3 (1994): pp. 37–41.

Farrell, John Aloysius. "Cheyenne Know Cost, Perils Tied to Energy Development." *Denver Post* (November 21, 1983).

Fischman, Joshua. "California Social Climbers: Low Water Prompts High Status." *Science,* Vol. 272 (May 10, 1996): pp. 811–12.

Fontana, Bernard L. "Restoring San Xavier del Bac, 'Our Church': Tohono O'odham Work to Restore the 200-Year-Old Church Built by Their Ancestors." *Native Peoples* (Summer 1995): pp. 28–35.

French, Bob. "Seminoles: A Collision of Cultures, Independent Indians' Lifestyle Faces Scrutiny," *Sun-Sentinel* (December 24 , 1995).

Garth, Thomas R. "Atsugewi Ethnography." *Anthropological Records* 14, No. 2 (1953): pp. 129–212.

Garth, Thomas R. "Emphasis on Industriousness among the Atsugewi." *American Anthropologist* 47, No. 4 (1945): pp. 554–66.

Gifford, E. W. "Notes on Central Pomo and Northern Yana Society." *American Anthropologist* 30, No. 4 (1928): pp. 675–84.

Gifford, E. W. and A. L. Kroeber. "Culture Element Distributions, IV: Pomo." *University of California Publications in American Archaeology and Ethnology* 37(4): pp. 117–254.

Gildart, Bert. "The Mississippi Band of Choctaw: in the Shadow of Naniw Waiya." *Native Peoples* (Summer 1996): pp. 44–50.

Goddard, Pliny Earle. "Chilula Texts." *University of California Publications in American Archaeology and Ethnology* 10, No. 7 (1914): pp. 289–379.

Halbert, Henry S. "The Choctaw Creation Legend," *Publications of the Mississippi Historical Society* 2 (1901): pp. 223–34.

Halbert, Henry S. "A Choctaw Migration Legend." *American Antiquarian and Oriental Journal,* 16 (1894): pp. 215–26.

Halbert, Henry S. "Nanih Waiya, the Sacred Mound of the Choctaws," *Publications of the Mississippi Historical Society* 2 (1899): pp. 223–34.

Hanks, Christopher C. and David Pokotylo. "The Mackenzie Basin: An Alternative Approach to Dene and Metis Archaeology." *Arctic,* Vol. 42, No. 2 (1989): pp. 139–47.

Heizer, R. F. "Impact of Colonization on Native California Societies." *Journal of San Diego History,* 24:1 (1978): pp. 121–39.

Heizer, R. F. and T. Kroeber, eds. "Indians Myths of South Central California." *University of California Publications in American Archaeology and Ethnology* 4, No. 4 (1907): pp. 167–250.

Hooper, Lucile. "The Cahuilla Indians." *University of California Publications in Archaeology and Ethnology,* 16, No. 6 (April 10, 1920): pp. 315–80.

Horn, Patricia. "Polluting Sacred Ground." *Dollars and Sense* (October 1992): pp. 15–18.

"Incinerator Planned Near Pipe Spring." *National Parks* (July/August 1990).

"Indian Roots of American Democracy." *Northeast Indian Quarterly* (Winter/Spring 1987/1988).

Johnson, Kirk. "An Indian Tribe's Wealth Leads to the Expansion of Tribal Law." *New York Times* (May 22, 1994): p. 1.

Keegan, John. "Warfare on the Plains." *Yale Review 84,* No. 1 (1996): pp. 1–48.

Kelly, Isabel T. "Southern Paiute Ethnography." *Anthropological Papers.* 69:21. University of Utah (May 1964). Reprint. New York: Johnson Reprint Corporation, 1971.

Kniffen, Fred B. "Achomawi Geography." *University of California Publications in American Archaeology and Ethnology* 23, No. 5 (1928): pp. 297–332.

Koppel, Tom. "The Spirit of Haida Gwai." *Canadian Geographic* (March/April 1996): p. 2.

LaDuke, Winona. "Like Tributaries to a River," *Sierra* 81, No. 6 (November/December 1996): pp. 38–45.

LaFrance, Joan. "Essay Review." *Harvard Educational Review* (Fall 1992): pp. 388–95.

Lekson, Stephen H. "Pueblos of the Mesa Verde." *Archaeology,* Vol. 48, No. 5 (September/October 1995): pp. 56–57.

Lepper, Bradley T. "Tracking Ohio's Great Hopewell Road." *Archaeology,* Vol. 48, No. 6 (November–December 1995): p. 52.

Lincecum, Gideon. "Life of Apushimataha." *Publications of the Mississippi Historical Society* 9 (1905–06): pp. 415–85.

Linden, Eugene. "Bury My Heart at James Bay: the World's Most Extensive Hydropower Project Has Disrupted Rivers, Wildlife, and the Traditions of the Quebec Indians. Is It Really Needed?" *Time* Vol. 138, No. 2 (July 15, 1991): p. 60.

Lindgren, Kristy. "Sgt. David H. Mace Shot Wampanoag David Hendricks Eleven Times and Is Still a Free Man." *News From Indian Country,* 7, No. 4 (1993): pp. 1–2.

"Makah Tribe's Net Snares Gray Whale." *Oregonian* (July 18, 1995).

"The Makah's Case for Whale Hunting." *Seattle-Post Intelligencer* (June 8, 1995).

"Menominee Honored at UN Ceremony for Forest Practices." *News From Indian Country,* IX, No. 9 (Mid-May 1995): p. 3.

Menominee Indian Tribe of Wisconsin. "Land of the Menominee" (brochure), c. 1994.

"The Menominee Nation and Its Treaty Rights." *News From Indian Country,* IX, No. 11 (Mid-June 1995): p. 2.

Menominee Nation Treaty Rights, Mining Impact, and Communications Offices. "Protect Menominee Nation Treaty Rights." *News From Indian Country,* X, No. 10 (Late-May 1996): p. 14A.

Millin, Peggy Tabor. "Passing the Torch: Technology Saves a Culture." *Native Peoples,* 9, No. 3 (1996): pp. 48–54.

Momatiuk, Yva and John Eastcott. "*Nunavut* Means Our Land." *Native Peoples* 9, No. 1 (Fall/Winter 1995): p. 42.

Mooney, James. "Calendar History of the Kiowa Indians." *Seventeenth Annual Report of the Bureau of American Ethnology.* Washington, DC: U.S. Government Printing Office, 1898.

Morrison, Joan. "Protect the Earth Gathering Focuses Mining Opposition." *News From Indian Country,* X, No. 5 (Mid-March 1996): p. 2.

Newman, Peter C. "The Beaching of a Great Whale." *Maclean's*. (Vol. 104, No. 37): p. 38.

Norman, Geoffrey. "The Cherokee: Two Nations, One People." *National Geographic* (May 1995): pp. 72–97.

"1,000 Gather to Oppose Exxon." *News From Indian Country*, X, No. 10 (Late-May 1996): pp. 1A, 5A.

Peterson, Lindsay. "Living History: Ruby Tiger Osceola, a 100-Year-Old Seminole Indian, Is Both a Link to the Past and a Leader for the Future." *The Tampa Tribune* (March 12, 1996).

Petit, Charles. "Ishi May Not Have Been the Last Yahi Indian." *San Francisco Chronicle* (February 6, 1996).

Plungis, Jeff. "Administering Environmental Justice." *Empire State Report* (January 1995): pp. 61+.

Roberts, Chris. "Schemitzun: The Pequot People's Feast of Green Corn and Dance." *Native Peoples*, Vol. 7, No. 4 (Summer 1994): pp. 66–70.

Rossiter, William. "CSI Opposes Whaling by the Makah." *Cetacean Society International*. Vol. 5, No. 1 (January, 1996).

Sapir, Edward. "Yana Texts." *University of California Publications in American Archaeology and Ethnology* 9, No. 1 (1910): pp. 1–235.

Sapir, Edward. "The Position of Yana in the Hokan Stock." *University of California Publications in American Archaeology and Ethnology* 13, No. 1 (1917): pp. 1–34.

Sapir, Edward and Leslie Spier. "Notes on the Culture of the Yana." *Anthropological Records* 3, No. 3 (1943): pp. 239–98.

Shaw, Christopher. "A Theft of Spirit?" *New Age Journal* (July/August 1995): pp. 84+.

Sparkman, Philip Stedman. "The Culture of the Luiseño Indians." *University of California Publications in American Archaeology and Ethnology* 8, No. 4 (1908): pp. 187–234.

Spier, Leslie. "The Sun Dance of the Plains Indians: Its Development and Diffusion." *Anthropological Papers of the American Museum of Natural History* 16, No. VII (1921): pp. 459–525.

Stirling, Matthew W. "Indians of the Far West." *National Geographic* (February 1948): pp. 175–200.

Strong, W. D. "The Plains Culture in the Light of Archaeology." *American Anthropologist* 35, No. 2 (1933): pp. 271–87.

Stuart, George E, "Etowah: A Southeast Village in 1491." *National Geographic,* 180, No. 4 (October 1991): pp. 54–67.

Theimer, Sharon. "Menominee Nation Lawsuit Wins Over Motion to Dismiss." *News From Indian Country,* X, No. 5 (Mid-March 1996): p. 3A.

Thompson, Ian. "The Search for Settlements on the Great Sage Plain." *Archaeology,* Vol. 48, No. 5 (September/October 1995): pp. 57–63.

Thurston, Harry and Stephen Homer. "Power in a Land of Remembrance: Their Rivers, Lands." *Audubon.* (Vol. 93, No. 6): p. 52.

Tobias, John L. "Canada's Subjugation of the Plains Cree, 1879–1885." *Canadian Historical Review,* Vol. 64 (December 1983): p. 519.

Todhunter, Andrew. "Digging Into History." *Washington Post Book World* (May 26, 1996): pp. 9, 13.

Turner, Steve and Todd Nachowitz. "The Damming of Native Lands." *Nation,* Vol. 253, No. 13 (October 21, 1991): p. 6.

Van Natta, Don Jr. "Tribe Saw a Promise, but Party Saw a Pledge." *New York Times* (August 12, 1997): A1, C20.

"The Water Famine." *Indigenous Peoples' Literature* (January 7, 1996).

Wedel, Waldo R. "Some Aspects of Human Ecology in the Central Plains." *American Anthropologist* 55, No. 4 (1953): pp. 499–514.

"Welcome to the Land of the Menominee-Forest." *News From Indian Country,* IX, No. 14 (Late-July 1995): p. 6.

White, Raymond. "Luiseño Social Organization." *University of California Publications in American Archaeology and Ethnology* 48, No. 2 (1963): pp. 91–194.

White, Raymond. "The Luiseño Theory of 'Knowledge.'" *American Anthropologist* 59, No. 2 (1957): pp. 1–19.

White, Raymond. "Two Surviving Luiseño Indian Ceremonies." *American Anthropologist* 55, No. 4 (1953): pp. 569–78.

Williams, Lee. "Medicine Man." *New Mexico Magazine* 62 (May 1984): pp. 62–71.

Web Sites

Beckman, Tad. "The Yurok and Hupa of the Northern Coast." [Online] http://www4.hmc.edu:8001/humanities/indian/ca/ch10.htm (accessed on April 22, 1999).

The Cheyenne Indians. [Online] http://www.uwgb.edu/~galta/mrr/cheyenne (accessed on April 21, 1999).

Lawrence, Elizabeth Atwood, "The Symbolic Role of Animals in the Plains Indian Sun Dance." [Online] http://envirolink.org/arrs/psyeta/sa/sa.1/lawrence.html (accessed on April 21, 1999).

Magagnini, Stephen. "Indians find 'new buffalo' in casinos." *The Modesto Bee Online.* [Online] http://www.modbee.com/metro/story/0,1113,4447,00.html (accessed on April 22, 1999).

Powersource Consultants. *Important Dates in Cherokee History.* [Online] http://www.powersource.com:80/nation/dates.html (accessed on April 21, 1999).

Stockbridge-Munsee Home Page. [Online] http://www.pressenter.com/org/tribes/munsee.htm (accessed on April 21, 1999).

CD-ROMs

"Cherokee Language." *Microsoft Encarta 96 Encyclopedia.* Redmond, WA: Microsoft, 1993–95.

Kappler, Charles, ed. *Treaties of American Indians and the United States. Treaties with the Menominees, 1817, 1831 (February 8 and February 17), 1832, 1836, 1848, 1854, 1856. Treaty with the Chippewa, 1833. Treaty with the Stockbridge and Munsee, 1839,* version 1.00. Indianapolis: Objective Computing, 1994.

Schoolcraft, Henry R. "Archives of Aboriginal Knowledge" and "Thirty Years with the Indian Tribes," on *The Indian Question,* version 1.00. Indianapolis: Objective Computing, 1994.

Other Sources

Klasky, Philip M. "An Extreme and Solemn Relationship: Native American Perspectives: Ward Valley Nuclear Dump." A thesis submitted to the faculty of San Francisco State University in partial fulfillment of the requirements of the degree Master of Arts in Geography, May 1997.

Low, Sam. *The Ancient World* (television documentary). QED Communications, Inc./Pennsylvania State University, 1992.

Mashantucket Pequot Nation. "The Fox People." (Leaflet), c. 1994.

Mashantucket Pequot Nation. "The Mashantucket Pequots: A Proud Tradition" and "Foxwoods Resort Casino." (brochures), n.d.

Acknowledgments

Grateful acknowledgment is made to the following sources whose works appear in this volume. Every effort has been made to trace copyright, but if omissions have been made, please contact the publisher.

"Blueberry Pudding." Marx, Pamela. From *Travel-the-World Cookbook* by Pamela A. Marx. Copyright © 1996 by Pamela A. Marx. Reproduced by permission of Addison-Wesley Educational Publishers, Inc.

"The Bluebird and Coyote." *American Indian Myths and Legends* edited by Richard Erdoes and Alfonso Ortiz. Copyright © 1984 by Richard Erdoes and Alfonso Ortiz. Reproduced by permission of Pantheon Books, a division of Random House, Inc.

"Ceremony and Song." Ruoff, A. LaVonne Brown, ed. *Literatures of the American Indian.* Chelsea House Publishers, 1991. Copyright © by Chelsea House Publishers, a division of Main Line Book Co. All rights reserved. Reproduced by permission.

"Cheyenne Bread." Cox, Beverly, and Martin Jacobs. From *Spirit of the Harvest.*" Copyright © 1991 Stewart, Tabori & Chang. Reproduced by permission.

"Chippewa Wild Rice." Copyright © 1965 by Yeffe Kimball and Jean Anderson. From *The Art of American Indian Cooking* published by Doubleday. Reproduced by permission of McIntosh & Otis, Inc.

"Choctaw Acorn Biscuits." Cox, Beverly, and Martin Jacobs. From *Spirit of the Harvest.* Copyright © 1991 Stewart, Tabori & Chang. Reproduced by permission.

"Comanche Chickasaw Plum Bars." Kavasch, E. Barrie. From *Enduring Harvests: Native American Foods and Festivals for Every Season.* Copyright © 1995 Globe Pequot Press. Reproduced by permission.

"Coyote in the Cedar Tree." Ramsey, Jarold. From *Coyote Was Going There: Indian Literature in the Oregon Country.* Copyright © 1977 University of Washington Press. Reproduced by permission.

"Coyote Wants To Be Chief." Premo, Anna. From *Shoshone Tales*. Edited by Anne M. Smith. University of Utah Press, 1993. © 1993 by the University of Utah Press. All rights reserved. Reproduced by permission.

"The Death of Wiyót, the Creator." Curtis, Edward S. From *The North American Indian." Edited by Frederick Webb Hodge. Copyright © 1970 Johnson Reprint Corporation.*

"The Emergence." Tithla, Bane. From *Myths and Tales of the White Mountain Apache*. Copyright © 1939 American Folklore Society. Reproduced by permission.

"An Encounter with the Tamciye." Garth, Thomas R. From *Atsugewi Ethnography*. Copyright © 1953 Anthropological Records.

"The Girl and the Devil." Bushnell, David I. From *Choctaw Myths and Legends*. Copyright © 1985 Garland Publishing. Reproduced by permission.

"Glacial Mists Cooler." Kavasch, E. Barrie. From *Enduring Harvests: Native American Foods and Festivals for Every Season*. Copyright © 1995 Globe Pequot Press. Reproduced by permission.

"Of Glooskap and the Sinful Serpent." Leland, Charles G. From *The Alogonquin Legends of New England: or Myths and Folklore of the Micmac, Passamaquoddy, and Penobscot Tribes*. Copyright © 1884 Houghton, Mifflen. Reproduced by permission.

"High Plains Pemmican." Kavasch, E. Barrie. From *Enduring Harvests: Native American Foods and Festivals for Every Season*. Copyright © 1995 Globe Pequot Press. Reproduced by permission.

"The Horrible Bear." Jewell, Donald P. From *Indians of the Feather River: Tales and Legends of Concow Maidu of California*. Copyright © 1987 Ballena Press. Reproduced by permission.

"How the Chumash Came To Be." Blackburn, Thomas C. From *December's Child: A Book of Chumash Oral Narratives*. Copyright © 1975 Berkeley: University of California Press. Reproduced by permission.

"How the Clans Came To Be." From *Creek Lifestyles, Customs and Legends*. Ryal Public School. Reproduced by permission. [Online] http://www.edumaster.net/schools/ryal/creek.html (18 September 1998).

"How the Moon Was Made." Clay, Charles. From *Swampy Cree Legends*. The Macmillan Company of Canada Limited, 1938. Copyright, Canada 1938 by The Macmillan Company of Canada Limited. All rights reserved.

"How Youth Are Instructed by Tribal Elders." Spindler, George, and Louise Spindler. From *Dreamers with Power: The Menomini Indians.* Copyright © 1971 Holt, Rinehart & Winston. Reproduced by permission.

"Jerky." Frank, Lois Ellen. From *Native American Cooking: Foods of the Southwest Indian Nations* by Lois Ellen Frank. Copyright © 1991 by Lois Ellen Frank. Reproduced by permission of Clarkson N. Potter, a division of Crown Publishers, Inc.

"King Philip's Prophecy." William Apess. Reprinted from Barry O'Connell, ed., *On Our Own Ground: The Complete Writings of William Apess, a Pequot.* (Amherst: University of Massachusetts Press, 1992). Copyright © 1992 by the University of Massachusetts Press.

"Mary O'Brien's Apricot Blueberry Cookies." Kavasch, E. Barrie. From *Enduring Harvests: Native American Foods and Festivals for Every Season.* Copyright © 1995 Globe Pequot Press. Reproduced by permission.

"Mohawk Baked Squash." Wolfson, Evelyn. From *The Iroquois: People of the Northeast.* Copyright © 1992 The Millbrook Press. Reproduced by permission.

"The Morning Star." Lacey, Theresa Jensen. From *The Pawnee.* Chelsea House Publishers, 1995. Copyright © 1996 by Chelsea House Publishers, a division of Main Line Book Co. All rights reserved. Reproduced by permission.

"Nanabozho and Winter-Maker." Coleman, Sister Bernard, Ellen Frogner, and Estelle Eich. From *Ojibwa Myths and Legends.* Copyright © 1962 Ross and Haines.

"Navajo Peach Pudding." Frank, Lois Ellen. From *Native American Cooking: Foods of the Southwest Indian Nations* by Lois Ellen Frank. Copyright © 1991 by Lois Ellen Frank. Reproduced by permission of Clarkson N. Potter, a division of Crown Publishers, Inc.

"Pawnee Ground Roast Pound Meat with Pecans." Kavasch, E. Barrie. From *Enduring Harvests: Native American Foods and Festivals for Every Season.* Copyright © 1995 Globe Pequot Press. Reproduced by permission.

"Powhatan Hazelnut Soup" Copyright © 1965 by Yeffe Kimball and Jean Anderson. From *The Art of American Indian Cooking* published by Doubleday. Reproduced by permission of McIntosh & Otis, Inc.

"Puffballs with Wild Rice and Hazelnuts." Kavasch, E. Barrie. From *Enduring Harvests: Native American Foods and Festivals for Every Season.* Copyright © 1995 Globe Pequot Press. Reproduced by permission.

"The Rabbit Dance." Bruchac, Joseph. From *Native American Animal Stories.* Copyright © 1992 Fulcrum Publishing. Reproduced by permission.

"The Race." Grinnell, George Bird. From *Cheyenne Campfires* Copyright © 1926 Yale University Press. Reproduced by permission.

"Simi Chumbo." Kavasch, E. Barrie. From *Enduring Harvests: Native American Foods and Festivals for Every Season.* Copyright © 1995 Globe Pequot Press. Reproduced by permission.

"Sioux Plum Raisin Cakes." Kavasch, E. Barrie. From *Enduring Harvests: Native American Foods and Festivals for Every Season.* Copyright © 1995 Globe Pequot Press. Reproduced by permission.

"Southeast Native American Pecan Soup." Cox, Beverly, and Martin Jacobs. From *Spirit of the Harvest.* Copyright © 1991 Stewart, Tabori & Chang. Reproduced by permission.

"The Stolen Squashes." Reed, Evelyn Dahl. From *Coyote Tales from the Indian Pueblos.* Sunstone Press, 1988. Copyright © 1988 by Evelyn Dahl Reed. Reproduced by permission.

"Succotash." McCullough, Frances, and Barbara Witt. From *Classic American Food Without Fuss* by Barbara Witt and Frances McCullough. Copyright © 1996 by Barbara Witt and Frances McCullough. Reproduced by permission of Random House, Inc.

"The Sun Dance Wheel." Monroe, Jean Guard, and Ray A. Williamson. From *They Dance in the Sky: Native American Star Myths.* Copyright © 1987 Houghton Mifflin. Reproduced by permission.

"Wampanoag Cape Cod Cranberry Pie." Kavasch, E. Barrie. From *Enduring Harvests: Native American Foods and Festivals for Every Season.* Copyright © 1995 Globe Pequot Press. Reproduced by permission.

"Why the Bear Waddles When He Walks." Marriott, Alice, and Carol K. Rachlin. From *American Indian Mythology.* Copyright © 1968 Cromwell. Reproduced by permission.

"Windwalker Pine Nut Cookies." Kavasch, E. Barrie. From *Enduring Harvests: Native American Foods and Festivals for Every Season.* Copyright © 1995 Globe Pequot Press. Reproduced by permission.

The photographs and illustrations appearing in U•X•L Encyclopedia of Native American Tribes were received from the following sources:

Covers Volume 1: tepee, **Library of Congress;** Seminole thatched houses, **P & F Communications. David Phillips, photographer;** Volume 2: Rocky Mountains from Ute Reservation, **North Wind Picture Archives. Reproduced by permission;** Taos Pueblo scene, **Library of Congress;** Volume 3: Inuit mother and child, **National Archives and Records Administration;** Young man at Sioux powwow, **Sygma Photo News. Photograph by F. Paolini. Reproduced by permission;** Volume 4: Ramona Lugu, Cahuilla in front of home, **Los Angeles Central Library. Reproduced by permission;** Tlingit longhouse with totem poles, **Corbis. Photograph by Tom Bean. Reproduced by permission.**

© 1998 North Wind Picture Archives. Reproduced by permission: pp. 3, 133, 405; **National Anthropological Archives. Reproduced by permission:** pp. 15, 1066, 1071; **Print by M. J. Burns. North Wind Picture Archives. Reproduced by permission:** p. 21; University of Pennsylvania Museum. Reproduced by permission: pp. 23, 1040, 1192; **Photograph by Frank C. Wotm. Library of Congress:** pp. 24, 25; **North Wind Picture Archives. Reproduced by permission:** pp. 32, 42, 51, 90, 109, 121, 141, 160, 172, 246, 247, 290, 317, 319, 329, 346, 373, 379, 381, 400, 418, 419, 443, 463, 468, 476, 498, 527, 534, 599, 637, 687, 693, 722, 756, 766, 785, 792, 796, 814, 827, 884, 897, 975, 1140; **Library of Congress:** pp. 36, 91, 146, 166, 219, 313, 416, 582, 615, 676, 732, 769, 778, 824, 848, 856, 908, 963, 965, 1087, 1117, 1162, 1173; **Bettmann. Reproduced by permission:** pp. 39, 45, 874; **AP/Wide World Photos, Inc. Reproduced by permission:** pp. 53, 84, 118, 138, 271, 305, 424, 458, 503, 750, 841, 1009, 1246; © **1997 N. Carter/North Wind Picture Archives. Reproduced by permission:** pp. 62, 92, 497, 499; Photograph by Bruce M. Fritz. *The Capital Times.* Reproduced by permission: p. 63; CORBIS/Bettmann. Reproduced by permission: pp. 67, 108, 188, 356, 533, 828, 832, 877, 925; **Photograph by W. H. Wessa. Library of Congress:** p. 68; **Archive Photos. Reproduced by permission:** pp. 148, 153, 192, 358, 482, 485, 526, 578, 1048; **National Archives and Records Administration:** pp. 152, 178, 296, 348, 436, 464, 538, 546, 592, 635, 641, 643, 645, 748, 793, 810, 960, 1165, 1217, 1235; **Photograph by C. M. Bell. National Archives:** p. 176; © **1977 North Wind Picture Archives. Reproduced by permission:** p. 202; © **1994 North Wind Picture Archives. Reproduced by permission:** p. 209; **National Archives:**

pp. 234, 807, 935; Granger Collection. New York. Reproduced by permission: p. 249; © 1995. North Wind Picture Archives. Reproduced by permission: pp. 388, 465, 492, 553, 601, 892; © 1993 North Wind Pictures Archives: p. 391; Mesa Verde National Park/National Park Service. Reproduced by permission: p. 402; Painting by Waldo Mootzka. Photograph by Seth Rothman. Dick Howard Collection. Reproduced by permission: p. 460; Southwest Museum. Reproduced by permission: pp. 477, 479, 480, 979, 991, 1050; Photograph by Edward S. Curtis. The Library of Congress: pp. 512, 567, 694, 1116, 1256, 1259; Photograph by Edward S. Curtis. CORBIS. Reproduced by permission: pp. 517, 547; CORBIS/Arne Hodalic. Reproduced by permission: p. 519; © 1991 N. Carter/North Wind Picture Archives. Reproduced by permission: p. 535; CORBIS/E. O. Hoppe. Reproduced by permission: p. 550; Photograph by T. Harmon Parkhurst. Courtesy Museum of New Mexico, negative number 7454: p. 559; Photograph by Bluford W. Muir. CORBIS. Reproduced by permission: p. 579; Photograph by Orville L. Snider. CORBIS. Reproduced by permission: p. 581; CORBIS/Adam Woolfit. Reproduced by permission: p. 585; CORBIS/David G. Houser. Reproduced by permission: pp. 606, 950; CORBIS/Tom Bean. Reproduced by permission: p. 610, 1269; CORBIS. Reproduced by permission: pp. 670, 672, 768, 922; CORBIS/Joel Bennett. Reproduced by permission: p. 675; Provincial Archives of Manitoba. Reproduced by permission: p. 714; Photograph by Wiliam S. Soule. National Archives and Records Administration: p. 736; CORBIS/ Brian Vikander. Reproduced by permission: p. 773; Photgraph by Alexander Gardner. CORBIS. Reproduced by permission: pp. 782, 784; Photograph by William S. Soule. The Library of Congress: p. 783; Photograph by William H. Jackson. National Archives and Records Administration: p. 840; Buffalo Bill Historical Center, Cody, WY. Gift of Mrs. Cornelius Vanderbilt Whitney. Reproduced by permission: p. 883; Photograph by Eadweard Muybridge. National Archives and Records Administration: p. 934; Photograph by Larry Philllips. Institute of American Indian Arts Museum, Santa Fe: p. 952; Los Angeles Public Library. Reproduced by permission: p. 992; California History Section, California State Library. Reproduced by permission: p. 1018; CORBIS/David Muench. Reproduced by permission: p. 1021; Smithsonian Insititution, Bureau of American Ethnology. Reproduced by permission: pp. 105, 1036; CORBIS/Ed Young. Reproduced by permission: p. 1081; American Museum of Natural History. Reproduced by permission: p. 1126; CORBIS/

Natalie Fobes. Reproduced by permission: pp. 1142, 1221, 1224; Photograph by Blankenburg Photo. CORBIS/PEMCO—Webster Stevens Collection; Museum of History & Industry, Seattle. Reproduced by permission: p. 1144; Photograph © Thomas Hoepker. Reproduced by permission of Joe Manfredini: p. 1177; Photograph by William McLennan. University of British Columbia Museum of Anthropology. Reproduced by permission: p. 1179; KWA-Gulth Arts Ltd. Reproduced by permission of Richard Hunt: p. 1194; Photograph by Edward S. Curtis. Univerversity of Pennsylvania Museum. Reproduced by permission: p. 1198; Photograph by Anthony Bolante. Reuters/Archive Photos. Reproduced by permission: p. 1207; CORBIS/Museum of History and Industry, Seattle. Reproduced by permission: p. 1210; CORBIS/Seattle Post–Intelligencer Collection. Museum of History and Industry, Seattle. Reproduced by permission: p. 1254; Courtesy Dept. of Library Services American Museum of Natural History, Neg. No. 41184. Reproduced by permission: p. 1268; Reproduced by permission of Preston Singletary: p. 1271; Photograph by Jeff Greenberg. Archive Photos. Reproduced by permission: p. 1272; Photograph by Winter and Pont. CORBIS. Reproduced by permission: p. 1274.

Index

Italic type indicates volume numbers; boldface type indicates entries and their page numbers; (ill.) indicates illustration.

Maidu *4:* **1061-1076,** 1062 (map), 1066 (ill.), 1071 (ill.), 1121, 1126

Maidu Indian World Maker Route *4:* 1066

Main Poche *1:* 156

Maine *1:* 11

Makah *4:* 1136, **1201-1214,** 1202 (map), 1207 (ill.), 1210 (ill.)

Makah Cultural and Research Center *4:* 1205, 1209

Makah Reservation *4:* 1201, 1205, 1209

Maliseet *1:* 17, 19, 22

Malki Museum, Morongo Reservation *4:* 995

Mandan *3:* 722, 723, 727, 731

Mangas Coloradas *2:* 430

Manhattan Island (ill.) *1:* 32

Manhattan Purchase *4:* 1133

Manifest Destiny *4:* 1161, 1203, 1229

Manissean *1:* 101

Manitoba *3:* 683

Manitoba Act of 1870 *3:* 708, 711

Manitoba Métis Federation *3:* 711

Manitou 1: 204

Manittoo *1:* 104

Mankiller, Wilma *1:* 220, 263

Manuelito *2:* 506

Maricopa *2:* 476, 509, 512, 514

Marin *4:* 1090

Marine Mammal Protection Act of 1972 *3:* 625

Martha's Vineyard *1:* 199, 206

Martin, Mungo *4:* 1198

Martin, Philip *1:* 292

Mary O'Brien's Apricot Blueberry Cookies (recipe) *1:* 258

Masaw *2:* 466

Mashantucket (Western Pequot) *1:* 129-130, 134-136, 138, 140-141

Mashantucket Pequot Indian Land Claims Settlement Act (1983) *1:* 135

Mashantucket Pequot Museum and Research Center *1:* 138

Mashapaug *1:* 101

Mashpee *1:* 205

Mashpee Manufacturing Company *1:* 206

Mashpee Wampanoag Indians *1:* 200, 206

Masked Dancers (Pueblo) *2:* 530

Masks (ills.) *1:* 42; *4:* 1179, 1194

Maskwas, John (ill.) *1:* 148

Mason, Charlie *2:* 401

Mason-Dixon line *1:* 216

Massachusett *1:* 101, 105

Massachusett language *1:* 205

Massachusetts *1:* 11, 19, 258

Massachusetts Bay Colony *1:* 103

Massacre at Wounded Knee *3:* 868, 875

Massasoit *1:* 201-203, 212

Masset Indian Reserve *4:* 1169, 1175

Mastahmo *2:* 477, 486

Mathews, Alex , Pawnee chief (ill.) *3:* 841

Mathews, John Joseph *3:* 835

Matrilineal kinship system *1:* 2194: 1136

Mattaponi *1:* 157, 167

Mayan *1:* 295; *2:* 404

McCartys, New Mexico *2:* 549

McGillivray, Alexander *1:* 223

McKay, Mabel *4:* 1120

McKinley Country Fair *2:* 598

Means, Russell *3:* 876, 887

Meares, John *4:* 1202

Measles and mumps *1:* 4

Medicine bundle *1:* 148; *3:* 724, 740, 786, 799

Medicine Creek Treaty *4:* 1229

Medicine Lodge Religion (Midewiwin) *1:* 64

Medicine Lodge Society *1:* 116

Medicine Lodge Treaty of 1867 *3:* 765

Medicine Man School *2:* 502

Medicine Rocks *4:* 1245

Medicine Society *1:* 148

Meeker massacre *2:* 374

Meeker, Nathan *2:* 373

Mekoche *1:* 194

Membertou, Henri *1:* 77, 85

Memphis, Tennessee *1:* 221

Mendocino Reservation *4:* 1111

Mennonites *3:* 767

Menominee *1:* **59-74,** 60 (map), 62 (ill.), 67 (ill.), 265

Menominee Indian Tribe of Wisconsin *1:* 59-60

Menominee Restoration Act *1:* 64, 66

Mesas *2:* 397, 571

Mesa Verde, Colorado *2:* 381, 397, 399, 409

Mescalero Apache *2:* 417, 420 (ill.), 433-435, 427, 529

Mesquakie (Fox) Indian Settlement *1:* 169, 170, 173, 179

Metacomet (King Philip) *1:* 202-203, 210, 212

Methodists *1:* 35, 226, 272; *4:* 1178

Métis *3:* 654, 656, 660, 662, 683, 685, 687, **703-719,** 704 (map), 714 (ill.)

Métis Association of Saskatchewan *3:* 711

Métis National Council *3:* 711

Métis provisional government *3:* 707

Metoac *1:* 129, 134

Metoaka *1:* 168

Mexican American War *2:* 330, 389, 392, 393, 413, 511, 528, 547, 558, 567; *4:* 977, 1080